THE BRINK

President Reagan and the
Nuclear War Scare of 1983

Marc Ambinder

Simon & Schuster Paperbacks

New York · London · Toronto · Sydney · New Delhi

Simon & Schuster Paperbacks
An Imprint of Simon & Schuster, Inc.
1230 Avenue of the Americas
New York, NY 10020

First Simon & Schuster trade paperback edition July 2019

SIMON & SCHUSTER PAPERBACKS and colophon are registered trademarks
of Simon & Schuster, Inc.

For information about special discounts for bulk purchases,
please contact Simon & Schuster Special Sales at 1-866-506-1949
or business@simonandschuster.com.

The Simon & Schuster Speakers Bureau can bring authors to your
live event. For more information or to book an event, contact the
Simon & Schuster Speakers Bureau at 1-866-248-3049
or visit our website at www.simonspeakers.com.

Manufactured in the United States of America

1   3   5   7   9   10   8   6   4   2

Library of Congress Card Number: 2018285888

ISBN 978-1-4767-6037-7
ISBN 978-1-4767-6038-4 (pbk)
ISBN 978-1-4767-6039-1 (ebook)

For Michael

Contents

"I turn back to your ancient prophets in the Old Testament and the signs foretelling Armageddon, and I find myself wondering if, if we're the generation that's going to see that come about."

—RONALD REAGAN, OCTOBER 28, 1983[1]

"If word ever came, that they had pushed the button, yes, we would have had to set all of ours in motion."

—RONALD REAGAN, 1989[2]

"God almighty, [Reagan] can bring the world damn near to an end."

—ADMIRAL WILLIAM CROWE, CHAIRMAN, JOINT CHIEFS OF STAFF[3]

"We listened to the hourly circuit verification signal and believed we could recognize a release order. Under these conditions when we detected NATO actually preparing to launch, we would want to pre-empt your launch with our own nuclear strikes."

—GENERAL-LIEUTENANT GELII VIKTOROVICH BATENIN, FIRST DEPUTY CHIEF OF THE SOVIET GENERAL STAFF[4]

Author's Note on Sources and Quotations

All words in quotations come directly from a source's mouth, or from a source's direct and contemporaneous recounting of what he or she said, or from an unchallenged or verified document or secondary source attributing those words to someone. I have italicized quotations when I could not independently verify the wording or when sources told me they could not recall exactly what was said.

I interviewed more than one hundred people for this book, including eight direct participants in Able Archer 83 and a dozen former intelligence officials with direct knowledge of secret programs and spy craft during this period. Many agreed to share their experiences on the record.

Cast of Characters

UNITED STATES

President Ronald Reagan

Vice President George H. W. Bush

General Alexander Haig: Secretary of State, 1981–1982

George Shultz, Secretary of State, 1982–1988

Caspar Weinberger, Secretary of Defense, 1981–1988

William Casey, Director of the Central Intelligence Agency, 1981–1987

General Richard Ellis, Commander in Chief, Strategic Air Command, 1977–1981

General Bernard Rogers, Supreme Commander Allied Forces, Europe, 1979–1987

General Bennie Davis, Commander in Chief, Strategic Air Command, 1981–1985

General John "Jack" Vessey, Chairman of the Joint Chiefs of Staff, 1982–1985

Judge William P. Clark, National Security Advisor, 1982–1983

Robert "Bud" McFarlane, National Security Advisor, 1983–1985

Richard Perle, Assistant Secretary of Defense for International Security Policy, 1981–1987

Jack Matlock, Senior Director for European and Soviet Affairs, National Security Council, 1983–1987

Admiral John Poindexter, Deputy National Security Advisor, 1983–1985

Oliver North, Special Assistant to the President, National Security Council, 1981–1986

Thomas Reed, Special Assistant to the President, former director of the National Reconnaissance Office and father of Project Pegasus, 1982–1987

Colonel William Odom, Military Assistant to the National Security Advisor, 1978–1981

Robert Gates, Deputy Director of Intelligence, CIA, 1981–1986

Fritz M. Ermarth, senior CIA analyst selected to write a Special National Intelligence Estimate (SNIE) on the Soviet war threat in 1984

David McManis, the CIA's national intelligence officer for warning

Brigadier General Leonard Perroots, senior air force intelligence officer, US Army Europe, 1983–1984

THE SOVIETS (AND FRIENDS)

Leonid Brezhnev, General Secretary, 1966–1982

Yuri Andropov, General Secretary, 1982–1984

Konstantin Chernenko, General Secretary, 1984–1985

Mikhail Gorbachev, General Secretary, 1985–1991

Viktor Chebrikov, KGB Chairman

Vladimir Kryuchkov, KGB Deputy Chairman

Erich Mielke, director of the East German Intelligence Service (Stasi)

Markus Wolf, chief of foreign intelligence, Stasi

Horst Männchen, Stasi SIGINT chief

Nikolai Ogarkov, Marshal of the Soviet Union, Chief of the General Staff

Dmitriy Ustinov, Minister of Defense (died 1984)

Andrei Gromyko, Minister of Foreign Affairs

Anatoly Dobrynin, Soviet Ambassador to the United States

V. K. Bondarenko, captain of the Soviet *Victory II* attack submarine

Gennadi Osipovich, Soviet air defense fighter pilot

Stanislaw Petrov, deputy director for combat algorithms at the Russian Ground Command and Control Center

THE SPIES

Oleg Gordievsky, a KGB officer based at Soviet embassy in London (spied for the SIS)

Arkady Guk, the KGB *rezident* (chief officer) in London

John Scarlett, Oleg Gordievsky's SIS case officer

Rainer Rupp, a senior NATO intelligence officer (spied for the Stasi)

Jeffrey Carney, a US Air Force intelligence officer who worked with the National Security Agency (spied for the Stasi)

Ryszard Kukliński, Colonel Polish People's Army (spied for the CIA)

SOLDIERS, SAILORS, CITIZENS

Captain Lee Trolan, commander of the 501st Army Artillery Detachment

Captain Gary Donato, Assistant Weapons Officer, USS *Kamehameha*

Gail Nelson, senior intelligence analyst, US Army Europe

Al Buckles, senior noncommissioned officer, US Strategic Air Command

Steven Schwalbe, analyst of Soviet forces, Defense Intelligence Agency

Jim Vink, CIA officer detailed to DMSPA

Suzanne Massie, author and Soviet culture analyst

Nina Tumarkin, academic and Soviet culture expert

Major Acronyms and Programs

C3 (command, control, and communications): the circulatory system for the transmission and execution of nuclear war orders.

CINC: Commander in Chief.

Defense Mobilization Systems Planning Activity (DMSPA): the cover office for the National Programs Office, which ran the mobile presidential successor command post program during the Reagan administration. Its creation was spelled out in the still-classified National Security Decision Directive 55, signed by President Reagan in 1982.

EAMs (Emergency Action Messages): EAMs often contain nuclear-weapons-related instructions generated by the National Military Command Center, its alternate sites, the Strategic Air Command, and Commanders in Chief of nuclear commands, including NATO. Lee Trolan's EAMs were received through a system called Emergency Management Authentication System (EMAS).

Intelligence Agencies

In the United States: the Central Intelligence Agency (CIA), responsible for foreign intelligence collection and covert action; the National Security Agency (NSA), responsible for signals intelligence collection and electronic warfare; the Defense Intelligence Agency (DIA), responsible for providing intelligence to military commanders; the National Reconnaissance Office (NRO), which builds and runs spy satellites.

In Britain: the Secret Intelligence Service (SIS), popularly known as MI6.

In the Soviet Union: the Komitet Gosudarstvennoy Bezopasnosti (KGB), responsible for foreign intelligence and SIGINT; the Glavnoye

Razvedyvatel'noye Upravleniye (GRU), responsible for military intelligence SIGINT. In East Germany: the Stasi, the intelligence service, and its HVA, the Main Directorate for Reconnaissance.

Missiles

Intermediate-Range Ballistic Missile (IRBM): a supersonic missile with an effective range of more than 1,000 kilometers (620 miles) but less than 5,500 kilometers (3,540 miles). Missiles capable of traveling these distances could threaten Europe when launched from the Soviet Union and vice versa.

Intercontinental Ballistic Missile (ICBM): a missile designed to travel more than 3,400 miles and capable of striking a target on a different continent with one or more warheads.

NATO

GLCM: a mobile, ground-launched cruise missile with a maximum range of 1,600 miles.

Pershing II: developed in the late 1970s and fielded in the 1980s by NATO; a direct-to-target missile with a maximum range of up to 1,100 miles and bearing a warhead with a yield up to 50 kilotons.

Soviet Union

SS-20: an intermediate range mobile missile capable of striking NATO.

SS-25 (the Sickle): the missile that kept the CIA up at night; destined to become the mainstay of the Soviet ICBM fleet.

United States

National Command Authority (NCA): The president, functioning in his role as Commander in Chief of all US forces, with an emphasis on his prerogative to initiate a nuclear weapons release.

National Military Command Center (NMCC): the Pentagon's war room, the beating heart of the American worldwide military machine.

National Security Decision Directive 12 (October 1, 1981): President Reagan's strategic forces modernization program.

National Security Decision Directive 13 (October 19, 1981): President Reagan's nuclear war doctrine.

National Security Decision Directive 55: Enduring National Leadership (September 14, 1982): The secret plan to bolster the US defensive deterrent by giving the presidency—not the current president—a chance to survive a first nuclear strike. NSDD-55 borrowed heavily from President Carter's Presidential Directive 58 in endorsing the use of randomly situated mobile command posts and the rapid (and random) identification of a presidential successor in the wake of a nuclear attack.

National Security Decision Directive 75 (January 3, 1983): The blueprint for Reagan's fight to end the Cold War.

NIESO: National Intelligence Emergency Support Office. Created by Presidential Directive 58, it existed outside the CIA as a separate organization designed to "shadow" the intelligence community and provide the president and potential successors with critical information in the aftermath of a nuclear attack. Also called the National Intelligence Emergency Support Staff.

NORAD: North American Aerospace Defense Command, the nexus of US early-warning satellites and sensors.

Presidential Directive 58 (June 30, 1980): President Jimmy Carter's plan for continuity of government after a nuclear strike. It authorized the creation of five Presidential Successor Support Staff units (called TREETOP teams by the Pentagon) and the predesignation of individuals to serve and train for those roles. It also directed the White House Military Office to identify new, secret locations to shelter the president during nuclear emergencies, it upgraded the president's emergency shelter under the West Wing, and it called upon Congress and the Supreme Court to coordinate their contingency plans with the executive branch. It distributed new, electronically tagged cards to presidential successors and appropriated funds to modernize the Emergency Broadcast System and prioritize the president's ability to communicate with nuclear force commanders.

Presidential Directive 59 (August 26, 1980): President Carter's nuclear war policy guidance, released shortly before he left office.

RYAN (or VRyan, or Rian): the English initialization of the Cyrillic acronym for "Surprise Nuclear Attack," Project RYAN was the top collection priority of the Soviet GRU and KGB during President Reagan's first term.

SAC: The Strategic Air Command, headquartered in Omaha, Nebraska, with thousands of weapons in its arsenal.

SACEUR: The Supreme Allied Commander Europe: the commander of all NATO forces; when authorized by NATO's political committee, he could direct the nuclear custodial brigades to transfer custody of warheads to field artillery, fighter, and missile units in Europe for use. The SACEUR was also "dual-hatted" as the CINCEUR—the Commander in Chief for US forces in Europe—who could authorize the employment of nuclear weapons when directed by the president of the United States.

SIOP: Single Integrated Operational Plan, otherwise known as the United States's base nuclear war plan. At least seven hundred pages long, with annexes, it was revised twice during the period covered by the book.[1]

SOSUS: Sound Surveillance System. A network of ocean-based sensors that served as the main US underwater early-warning network to detect Soviet nuclear submarines.

WHEP: White House Emergency Plan/White House Emergency Procedures. Classified procedures governing the evacuation of the president from the White House and the identification of potential successors. Jointly administered by the US Secret Service and White House Military Office's Office of Presidential Contingency Programs.

Prologue

Before the order to release the nukes came in, the sun had set over the dry pines of the patch of land called the Fulda Gap in West Germany, the autumn cold was hard, and Captain Lee Trolan, commander of the 501st Army Artillery Detachment, a nuclear weapons custodial brigade, tried to keep warm and focus on the intricate set of procedures he was shortly to execute.

Three hours had elapsed since the start of the "special weapons" portion of a major North Atlantic Treaty Organization military exercise called Able Archer 83, an annual dry run, practicing for what would happen during a real war: when NATO's nuclear warheads would be transferred, upon orders from higher authorities, from their American custodians to their foreign counterparts across Europe.

With only about thirty American infantrymen and weapons technicians, and a smaller, rotating crew of nineteen- and twenty-year-old German conscripts, Trolan controlled enough nuclear firepower to destroy the advancing armies of the Warsaw Pact (named after a treaty of friendship between the Soviets and her allies in 1955) as well as cities, the countryside, and who knows what else. He was often kept in the dark about his targets.

Trolan's base jutted out from the eastern edge of a tiny town called Killianstädten. The missile launch and radar site were situated a half a kilometer south, straddling a rural road that led to a smaller town named Mittelbuchen. The Germans often placed the missiles in the middle of working farmers' cornfields at least a half a kilometer down the way from any township. They had become prominent features of West Germany's Cold War landscape. You couldn't get from there to here without seeing one.

Trolan and a lieutenant were locked inside the 501st's crypto shack, tucked inside of a metal barn, its exterior patrolled by military policemen with automatic weapons. Two sets of cyclone fences guarded its perimeter. The Germans who manned them also ran the kitchen.

The boss of these Western forces, NATO's Supreme Allied Commander of Allied Forces in Europe, General Bernard Rogers, hated having to "mortgage" the defense of Europe to a nuclear response.[1] This meant that the numbers of conventional forces his armies were destined to face were just too overwhelming for nuclear weapons not to be contemplated as a first response. The placement of those weapons on German (and Polish and Italian and Dutch) soil was Europe's existential burden.

During war, the Warsaw Pact armies would attack with 90 divisions of troops and tanks; NATO would have 40, at most, because they had spent the past decade focusing on better technology and doctrine, while Eastern Europe, led by the Soviets, churned out war machines, fueled by a conviction that *might* would force NATO to submit early. For NATO, then, nuclear weapons were the gap fillers. Americans back home, conditioned to assume that only the adversary or the devil on his shoulder would usher in Armageddon,[2] probably did not know that, by the reckoning of both West and East, the first nation to break the nuclear taboo would be their own, using warheads, very likely, held by the unit that Trolan commanded. For the past forty years, the war plans of *both* NATO and the Warsaw Pact predicted the first volley of nuclear weapons would come from the NATO forces to ward off a crushing Warsaw Pact air and ground invasion—an "assumed penetration into the corps area" was the official term.

As the military gears churned, a parallel political process would begin in NATO, because you couldn't do anything with a nuclear weapon unless a lot of really important non-military people agreed. These procedures were complicated, and they had to be rehearsed, in the open, and regularly. In 1975, with an eye toward demonstrating resolve, NATO's defense committee decided to unify its separate fall exercises by merging them under an umbrella called Autumn Force. Each year, the final exercise in the series would rehearse the nuclear weapons release procedures themselves. It was given the name Able Archer. *Able* was a random adjective allocated by a Pentagon computer to Allied Command Europe's forces for exercises and special projects; *Archer* was picked off a list of nouns.[3]

At the start of the Able Archer exercise, some of those warheads, W-31s, cylinders with the diameter of a bicycle wheel and the length of a peacock feather, had been mated to the bodies of their delivery units, the aging but potent, wing-shaped Nike Hercules missiles. Others rested in a below ground vault about 60 feet from the crypto shack.

If Trolan ever received a type of message known as an Emergency War Order, he and his crew would unlock the Permissive Action Link (PAL) that disabled the nuclear triggering mechanism, plug in an arming pin, and then transfer a live missile down range, to the custody of a German anti-aircraft unit, the 2nd Battery/23 FLARAK battalion. The Luftwaffe controlled the launch complex and their radars and had a commanding, unobstructed view of the surrounding countryside, into the city of Hanau, with its huge army base, over Frankfurt, Germany's transport hub, and to the east, with the Fulda plains merging into the border with East Germany.

A Nike-Hercules missile would shoot skyward at a rate of more than 1,400 miles per hour, dropping its booster after just 5 seconds; it could travel as high as 9 miles, if need be. The warheads would home in on radio frequency pulses to find their targets, and then angular momentum, gravity, and drift would take over. The Nike Hercs had an effective range that allowed them to target huge chunks of massed armored cavalry inside East Germany. Mainly, they were designed to immolate the incoming enemy air force, like the hulking Russian T-95 Bears, or their sleek Tu-22 Backfire bombers.

A speaker box chirped. The red light on a green phone flashed. "Message incoming," his communications sergeant called out.

So it begins, Trolan thought. Everyone in the small command post tensed. The base was on alert; all the soldiers sweated in their full wartime kit, trucks were fueled, burping exhaust, and idling as the Nike Hercules missiles stood erect in their launchers.

Trolan's 501st Army Artillery Detachment had to rehearse for war; these exercises were their only real chance to simulate at least some of the conditions they might face. The chain of command could scrutinize the speed and accuracy with which they carried out their assigned tasks.

A Telex next to the phone spit out a piece of paper. Trolan tore it off, sat down, pushed it next to his codebook, and began the elaborate fifteen-minute process of decryption. The preamble he decoded flagged it as an Emergency Action Message from the Commander in Chief of US forces in Europe, the CINCEUR. The CINCEUR, known in his NATO role as SACEUR, could authorize him to release the weapons. The CINC wore several hats, depending upon which part of the military he happened to be commanding or which country he happened to be from; the hats all endowed him with different powers, the product of forty years of compromises between the fragile democracies of Europe, who craved the protection afforded by NATO as much as they chafed at its martial prerogatives and argued about its priorities.

As Trolan began to decipher the instructions, he grimaced, then stopped, dropping his grease pencil. The message was too short, by half. In the lingo nuclear weapons officers used, it *broke*, meaning that someone who had the up-to-date codes had encoded it, and Trolan, after decoding, could read it. But the format was not right. By rule, if the format was off, he had to disregard the message.

The system of nuclear command and control was barely translucent even to Trolan, who was a cleared, trained, certified end user. Messages had to get from a dozen places to a thousand more, some of them deep underwater, some of them in the air, both realms where physics and logistics made it impossible for a commander to just pick up a phone and bark out an order. Nuclear messages were at once uncannily simple to understand even as they were frustratingly hard to compose. Every nuclear user around the world had to be on the same page, literally, so that they could decode the messages offline; that is, after they'd received it over whatever radio or telegraphic source they were using. The messages, therefore, had to be short; they had to be encrypted; they had to include some authentication so that Trolan and his colleagues would know that the instruction was legit, and above all, they had to be intelligible. A properly formatted message was essential. An incorrectly formatted message during real war could mean the difference between thousands of lives saved and millions of lives lost.

So, it was a big, big deal to Lee Trolan that some idiot had just sent him a message that was formatted incorrectly; it used an old format, actually, not the new one he had just spent three days at NATO school learning.

Maybe, he thought, someone at HQ had screwed up—one hell of a mistake, right in the middle of the biggest exercise of the year.

Trolan pulled a phone to his ear and pushed a button that connected him with the duty officer in Heidelberg. He gave the colonel on the other end of the line the date and time of the message and the preamble that flagged it.

"Captain, I didn't send out that message," the colonel insisted.

Trolan held his composure. Maybe there had been a shift change, and maybe the colonel hadn't been briefed on all the traffic.

"No, sir, I'm pretty sure you did."

No, the colonel insisted. He was looking through the logbooks. "I don't know what to tell you, Captain, but we didn't send that message."

When Trolan hung up, his mind began to cycle through the possibilities. How could a message like that, an EAM, be sent to his unit without coming from headquarters? Was it possible? The sender would need to have access to the microwave towers that shot beams of energy into his crypto shack. And he'd have to have stolen the updated NATO cipher book. Aside from the Emergency Action technicians who manually encrypted the messages in their secure command bunkers, no one was even supposed to see such highly classified cryptologic material. When those codebooks left their safes, two people had to have their eyes on them at all times.

So, this message was more than just an anomaly; it was an impossibility.

At this moment, as he began to lead his team through the most critical phase of the most sensitive and demanding nuclear release exercise of the year, something or someone certainly foreign and probably dangerous was pushing into the regimented and secure world that Lee Trolan controlled.

———

At around the same time that Lee Trolan huddled in his shack awaiting his release, General Colonel Ivan Yesin, the commander of the SS-20 Pioneer regiments for the Soviet Strategic Rocket Forces, spent the night in a special bunker somewhere in the hills outside Moscow.

If the order came, Yesin's men could have launched the missiles, their warheads aimed at the NATO bases like Lee Trolan's, in 2 minutes and 30 seconds.

Yesin had served in the Soviet military since the 1960s, through the Cuban Missile Crisis and numerous other scares.

He had never felt closer to war.

Introduction

A nuclear priesthood gave order to the earth after World War II. It derived its authority from a truth: not since Nagasaki had one country ever used a nuclear weapon against another. This understanding may well have been a contingent fact, the product of historical accidents, not political intentions, but it instantiated a sacred aura to the product of forty years of secret knowledge, game theory, and technological determinism. In America, the doctrine of the elect was a military document colloquially referred to as the SIOP, which stood for Single Integrated Operational Plan. It was written and revised by a small set of colonels and civilians attached to the Strategic Air Command. Few others ever got to read it, even as it controlled the daily lives of millions and as its execution could destroy a world of billions.

Everything nuclear was subordinated to the SIOP; it had the right of the crown to every piece of nuclear anything the United States had ever built. Forces, fleets, missiles, reconnaissance planes, and hundreds of thousands of troops were all said to be SIOP-committed, which meant that no one else could use them. And of course, the SIOP was designed not just to fight a war but to posture against one. Its size and ambit would deter the Soviet Union from nuclear aggression, but nuclear aggression instigated by Moscow was unlikely because the Soviet Union felt itself under siege and surrounded since its incipient revolution in 1917 and had lost far more in war than any other nation on earth. The SIOP, therefore, was designed to fight an *improbable* war, and its immense power constrained the choices of American presidents. ("Forget the SIOP and all that crap" is what Richard Nixon said, without irony, and with considerable frustration, when his generals would tell him they were having trouble filling his orders to bomb North Vietnam because they'd have to divert SIOP resources.)

If John F. Kennedy had succumbed to the pressures of his military and decided to launch a nuclear strike against Cuba, or decided to take a Soviet nuclear submarine that been trawling American surface ships off the Atlantic coast, about twenty minutes would elapse between the moment he began to authenticate his order and the moment an ICBM nose cone left its silo, or a bomber with its nuclear arsenal enabled flew itself into position.

Our basic model for decision making in nuclear emergencies is still quite incomplete. There are hundreds of books written about the Cuban crisis. New documentaries seize on scraps of new evidence and fragments of audio to re-create in real time the decisions made by the Excom in the White House. For the sake of official history and American lore, it's an ideal crisis in many ways. Both the Soviets and the United States were aware of what was happening while it was happening, and that maximized the chances that politicians would be able to step in and resolve it. We can live with the Cuban Missile Crisis because, in our mythology, the United States came out of it with a win, and the world did not combust. We learned lessons about how not to escalate crises, and these lessons took, so much so that it created an expectation that any future nuclear crisis could not be as bad as the Cuban Missile Crisis ever became. It seemed like the theory of mutually assured destruction, the belief that nuclear war was so inherently destructive, absurd even, that no side would ever win if both sides had an equally sized deterrent and could signal properly.

But we forget that Cuban Missile Crisis is far from the only time when nuclear forces went on worldwide alert; it happened in October 1969, when Richard Nixon decided to try to scare the Russians by pretending he was a madman and, willy-nilly, authorized the Strategic Air Command to increase its readiness—in our metaphor, the safety was removed from its gun deliberately—to confuse and frighten the North Vietnamese and their Soviet masters.[1] This was his protest against the confining strictures of the Single Integrated Operation Plan, or SIOP, which he believed limited his options as commander-in-chief.[2]

The propensity for personality and politics to intrude into the sacred realm of nuclear decision-making outside of the narrow lane provided for by the law is one reason why the system was engineered to be guns-ready.

The truth, as revealed by a number of enterprising historians and authors, including Bruce Blair, a former nuclear missile launch officer who has spent more than thirty years studying the subject, is that nuclear command and control was built from the bottom up and exhibits at its core a fundamental tension that in crisis will only practically be resolved by choosing the course that biases the president toward a launch before a nuclear detonation on US soil.[3]

Watery motivations attend to the concept of a "side," in any discussion of nuclear war. Countries are elaborate constructs, full of people with genetic, familial, and cultural ties to one another, the type of ties that throw up biological obstacles to empathy or compassion. Leaders are elected or anointed to, first, protect their own tribes. A nuclear weapon is real, a fact of nature, caring nothing about anything, and certainly not respectful of human political contraptions or responsibilities. Since the dawn of the nuclear age, politicians have bought into the necessary fallacy that this invention can be controlled. Do you blame them? I don't. What other choices were there? An arms race was the logical extension of the way humans organized themselves in the twentieth century.

As soon as the Soviet Union developed an intercontinental ballistic missile capable of reaching the United States, the R-7 Semyorka, which boosted Sputnik into orbit in 1957, nuclear war plans, strategies, and deterrence theories became educated hedges at best. The first country to fire weapons would likely be the first country to destroy the others' nuclear arsenal.[4] So a president would be forced to decide quickly, almost always in the absence of reliable information, whether to retaliate, if only to ensure that the physical stuff of deterrence itself—the nuclear-tipped missiles and weapons—were available to him after the adversary's first strike.[5] Decent intelligence, as much as good sense, was the nuclear priesthood's binding force. Its clergy liked to tell itself that "under attack," or "warning," meant that there would be unambiguous evidence that missiles were on their way: there was a glimpse of the moral high ground in knowing that, at least, the other side actually fired first.

If the Soviets convinced themselves that the West was on the precipice of a surprise decapitation attack, the Soviets would move first. Or it would move further toward the brink. That was doctrine. That was *logic*. The Soviets called it "retaliatory meeting;" the Americans called it "launch under attack."[6] The cutting-off-the-head part was key. In the Soviet Union, the Politburo made decisions about war and peace. If the US could wipe out the leadership at the beginning of a war, it could dictate the terms for its termination; the US could really win, the Soviets could really lose. The reverse was true, too. If the Soviets could easily knock out the president and his successors, there would be no real reason for either side to bargain in good faith, aside from good faith itself, which neither side had. A survivable presidency was essential for peace.

It was clear to Ronald Reagan from very early in his presidency that he could not actually fight a war against the Soviet Union and win it unless he was prepared to strike first. At the same time, he had inherited the heavy saddle of the SIOP, a document that the nuclear theorist Herman Kahn once bitingly referred to as a war orgasm.[7] Kahn was a heterodox thinker. He disdained nuclear orthodoxies, but he worried that even the smartest among his fellow scientists would not be able to transcend herd instincts. He thought that nuclear war was a possibility and, with the right preparations, actually manageable. He did not know Ronald Reagan. Most Americans did not know what Ronald Reagan would really do when thrown into the unpredictable stew of a crisis. Would he think and reason as a leader, cultivating a more critical faculty that granted him the imagination to think beyond the reciprocal interests that bind flocks to their clergy and clergy to their flocks?

From the fall of 1983 to the spring of 1984, the tail end of Reagan's first term, the relationship between the United States and the Soviet Union, already flying low, spiraled into the sea. Misunderstandings, the consequence of trying to control the uncontrollable, hurtled the world toward a conflict that not one single thinking person on either side ever wanted.

The vast intelligence-gathering sensors of the Soviet Union had turned up their gain to indications that the West was planning a nuclear attack. They found what they were looking for. Soviet fears about the exercise of which Lee Trolan was a major participant, Able Archer 83, were as genuine as they turned out to be mistaken, very real but not, in the end, true. And so, the Soviets prepared to strike first.

They moved nuclear weapons from secret storage locations to vaults near alert aircraft. They confined their troops to their garrisons. They dispersed mobile nuclear missile launchers. They gave front-line infantry troops real ammunition and food that would last for two weeks.

If the Soviets *truly* went on secret combat alert because the Americans were holding a nuclear exercise, the elaborate system of physical constraints, procedural safeguards, and geopolitical understandings that held the nuclear arsenals of both countries in check had somehow hollowed out.

This book explains the origins of this brittle brinksmanship. It recounts the scary series of close encounters that tested the limits of the ordinary men and powerful leaders alike. And it shows how supple, flexible, and compassionate political leadership ultimately triumphed over the strife of interests, helping the two countries sue for a fragile peace.

PART I

DECAPITATION

CHAPTER 1

Détente's Rise and Fall

IN THE EARLY 1970S, COLONEL GENERAL ANDREI DANILE-
vich, then in the research of the Soviet General Staff (the equivalent to the
US Joint Chiefs of Staff), had overseen the Soviets' first large-scale quan-
titative and computer assessment of a nuclear war. In cold, hard numbers,
in the best of circumstances:

- The Soviet military would be virtually powerless after a first strike.
- At least 80 million Soviet citizens would be dead.
- It would be virtually impossible to quickly rebuild and reconstitute
  critical infrastructure because more than 80 percent of the country's
  heavy industry would be destroyed.
- Europe would be a nuclear wasteland for years.

Leonid Ilyich Brezhnev, the General Secretary of the Communist
Party of the Soviet Union, watched this happen. He was "visibly terrified,"
Danilevich remembered.

During the exercise, three launches of ICBMs with dummy warheads
were scheduled.

To enhance realism, Brezhnev was given an actual button to push.

Three years before this exercise, in June 1973, Brezhnev had visited
the White House. The enduring image from the summit was that of a Russian premiere playfully whispering into Richard Nixon's ear. Brezhnev was
ebullient that day. Nixon was his *equal*. The American president's secret
friendly gestures to China had given the Kremlin a chance to counter

with open overtures to the United States, and so, Nixon and Brezhnev had agreed in May 1972 to the first treaty that limited the use of strategic weapons in the nuclear age: the Strategic Arms Limitation Treaty (SALT). They had also signed a measure to limit the development of defenses against nuclear missile attacks, reasoning that if mutual vulnerability were ratified into the framework for further reductions, the actual advent of war would be a remote possibility at best.[1]

Just a few months after Brezhnev returned to Russia, détente was tested by reality.

Israel had armed its Jericho missiles with nuclear weapons, desperate to force a reluctant Nixon to reprovision their military after a preemptive attack by Syria and Egypt. The blackmail worked, and the United States provided guns, ammunition, and intelligence that allowed Israel to save itself. Nixon and Secretary of State Henry Kissinger had worried that US involvement in this conflict would give cause for oil-producing countries to withhold supplies as a bargaining chip, which would push the US to menace those countries, which would spark a heated response from the Soviet Union.

And that, they believed, would threaten the vitality of détente. After Israeli forces started to tighten the noose around Egypt's Third Army, despite the US having promised the Soviets Israel would not do so, Egypt asked for, and obtained, direct assistance from Moscow. But the Soviets decided to go further. They readied their bomber squadrons in Moscow and made sure that the US knew about it. A heavily fortified column of Soviet ships carrying armaments moved into the narrow slit of water between Black Sea and the Mediterranean.[2] On October 24, a telegram from Brezhnev announced his intention to intervene unless a ceasefire was brokered immediately. Nixon had fallen asleep, possibly drunk.[3] (Watergate was in its end game. He had just fired the special prosecutor he had earlier appointed to absolve himself.)

In the Situation Room, the National Security Council deliberated *in Nixon's absence*; after a discussion that included the possibility that this cascading crisis could lead to global war, the council decided to raise the Defense Condition (DEFCON) level to 3, around midnight. ICBM missileers in their silos across the Midwestern United States strapped themselves into chairs to brace for incoming nuclear explosions.[4] The Soviets noticed immediately, because the message (the length of a tweet, as is the launch order) was transmitted over an unsecured telephone network called the PAS (Primary Alerting System) that used commercial landlines, which they could easily monitor.[5] Victor Israelyan, a senior minister at the time, recalls that Yuri Andropov, then the chairman of the KGB, recommended raising the Soviet alert status. The Defense Minister, Andrei Grechko, wanted to move 70,000 troops toward the battlefield. "The participants realized that the central issue was whether the Soviet Union was prepared to confront the US and engage in a large-scale war." Fortunately, the Soviets decided not to respond at all, assuming that it was Nixon's jitters and penchant for provocative action that had generated the American change in nuclear status.[6]

It later emerged that the Soviets could not muster the same type of public display that accompanied the DEFCON changes. They were, as Israelyan said, "unprepared." The crisis abated because one side chose not to act (or simply could not).

But the president of the United States was barely involved in these decisions. As his Watergate crisis grew, Nixon's new Secretary of Defense James Schlesinger, worried that Nixon was increasingly paranoid and self-protective, almost childlike at times, and not in the right frame of mind to make military decisions. He secretly investigated what would need to happen if a president wanted to order US troops to fortify Washington so that he could keep himself in office. Schlesinger kept a gimlet eye on the Commandant of the Marine Corps, General Robert D. Cushman Jr., a Nixon loyalist who had helped the CIA meddle in domestic politics. He ordered the chairman of the Joint Chiefs of Staff to notify him if Nixon or anyone else at the White House ordered any major military action; Schlesinger had no confidence that he would be informed beforehand.[7] In essence, Schlesinger prepared an unconstitutional counter-coup against a possible hypothetical unconstitutional coup from the duly elected president. This nuclear crisis had little to do with direct geopolitical conflict escalation and everything to do with messy domestic politics and human psychology. Brezhnev was in the middle of it. It scared him.

Danilevich stood beside the Soviet leader and watched him contemplate the decision to push the button.

Visibly shaking, and pale, Brezhnev turned toward the head of his general staff, and asked, for clarification: would there be any real-world consequences?

"Andrei Antonovich, are you sure this is just an exercise?"

His hands, Danilevich remembered, trembled.[8]

That was the first and last time that Brezhnev would participate in a nuclear exercise. His health was in decline. He had recurring bouts with amnesia and forgetfulness after a massive heart attack in 1976. The Politburo barely functioned then, consisting of a cadre of central committee members who were, in the words of one Defense Intelligence Agency (DIA) analyst, "doting, ineffectual sycophants." Many were old; some were senile. But they did not force Brezhnev to relinquish power after he ceased to function as an effective president because his pliability was seen as much less threatening to the ruling oligarchy than new blood would be.[9]

Into this leadership vacuum stepped four ambitious, canny men. Together, they ruled the country's military, intelligence, and nuclear institutions during the next ten years.

Andrei Gromyko was the acerbic, hard-headed minister of state, in office since 1957. Dmitry Ustinov was the chief of the central committee's military and defense policy committee and the patron of the Soviet defense industry. Yuri Andropov was the chairman of the KGB, responsible for intelligence gathering at home and abroad. But most interesting, for our purposes, was Nikolai Vasilyevich Ogarkov, by 1977 the chief of the General Staff, the Soviet equivalent of the chairman of the US Joint Chiefs.

Though the massive Soviet state drifted for years, plodding with ponderous but powerful momentum in whatever direction compromises among powerful organizational and bureaucratic interests might take it, it had a nuclear vector. Gromyko and others in the Politburo believed that the future of the Soviet Union lay in the application of détente across all parts of its empire. The outspoken Ogarkov chafed under the political constraints imposed upon him by both the tone and substance of Brezhnev's negotiations with the Americans.[10] He believed that the 1972 Strategic Arms Limitation Treaty (SALT) had consigned the Soviet nuclear deterrent to history because it so severely limited the Soviet ability to catch up with American missile technology. He accused the US and NATO, and (remarkably) "NATO apologists" within the Politburo of seeking to undermine the principles of détente by changing the rules midstream: the

US and NATO would not consider cruise missiles based in Europe to be "strategic" weapons but had insisted that the new generation of supersonic Soviet fighter bombers be so designated, regardless of what kind of armament they carried or how long they could stay airborne without refueling.[11]

In 1974, at Vladivostok, the United States and the Soviet Union had essentially agreed to table those issues, capping the number of strategic bomb delivery vehicles—subs, missiles, bombers—at 2,400 each, with 1,320 weapons allowed to contain multiple warheads. Because the size and reach of the Soviet ICBM force was the foundation of its deterrent, the Soviets would reject proposals that would chop the numbers of deployed ICBMs in any form without extracting qualitatively equivalent concessions from the United States. The 1979 SALT II treaty proposals, which Gromyko, Ustinov, and Brezhnev supported, would have allowed the Soviets to retain their numerical edge in the ICBM forces, but would, in just about every other arena, kneecap the development of nuclear technology. It would cap the number of "delivery vehicles" at 2,250. But SALT II never went into effect; the Soviet invasion of Afghanistan convinced President Carter to pull the treaty from its probable ratification by the US Senate. The US would adhere to its limits, grudgingly; it meant, for certain, that the future of nuclear warheads would be to pack more on one missile—to MIRV them up. (MIRV stood for Multiple Independently Targetable Reentry Vehicle.) "A lot of people looked at arms control as a way to get more nuclear weapons, rather than fewer nuclear weapons," an American defense analyst said.[12]

Ogarkov understood well that he was fighting a rear-guard battle to modernize the Soviet military. His solution, which had won the backing of the General Staff by the time Reagan was inaugurated, was to shift the entire focus of the Soviet defense posture away from nuclear conflict and toward the development of a massive, effective, technologically agile conventional force. Ogarkov, too, had concluded that a nuclear war might be survivable. He believed that the doctrine of mutually assured destruction—MAD—had an expiration date, particularly as both empires developed the capacity to carry out swift, surgical, surprise decapitation strikes against the other. Ogarkov believed that both the US and the Soviet Union had interlocking interests that might lock them into a confrontation in a theatre, or region, without letting it spill over onto the rest of the globe—and the European continent would be ground zero.[13]

The Soviets believed that the US Department of Defense was always on the prowl for ways to get ahead of the politicians who ran it, in much the same way as the Soviet military had developed a momentum of its own within the tighter confines of its own political system. For all intents and purposes, the Soviets had determined that both sides had real and visible vulnerabilities, intractable weaknesses that made the prospect of losing a nuclear exchange more viable. The Soviets worried, for example, that their own political system of central control made it easier for the US to plan a decapitation strike.[14]

As the arms race accelerated, Soviet war plans evolved. No longer did they anticipate responding to a first strike from the US. Instead, all plans for major wars assumed that the Soviets would find a way to attack first, because, quite simply, the side that did attack first would have the best chance to win.[15] The Soviets would pound their chests and bluff, when they had to, to prevent the US from assuming that it had achieved strategic superiority. Priority would be given toward *sabotage* of the nuclear command and control system and then toward aggressive espionage, not only to steal US secrets but to find ways of discrediting US strategic doctrine as well. Soviets would stress their advantages: silo hardness, throw weight (heavy weapons), mobility, leadership continuity and survivability.[16] Skepticism about limited nuclear strikes—for the US, limited meant "in Europe" and to the Soviets, Europe was home—advances in silo hardening and of multiple warheads on missiles—had persuaded the general staff to conclude that the enemy would have enough nuclear weapons left after a first strike to retaliate.[17] Like the US, the General Staff also began to develop plans to launch nuclear weapons on *warning*—a "retaliatory meeting strike" is what they called it. But the technology to accurately detect missiles and their trajectories didn't exist for the Soviets in the 1970s.[18] The system was glitchy. Only human spies and signals could determine whether the US was about to strike. This was one reason why more emphasis was placed on human intelligence until Soviet satellite and technical intelligence technology caught up with the rest.

Marshal Ogarkov and his budding revolution found resistance in several corners. Ustinov was responsible to the politicians, who were overwhelmingly concerned with nuclear politics and had short-term imaginations.[19] The politicians, even in the Soviet Union, were accountable to some degree to the Soviet populace, whose support was essential. The Soviets had their guns versus butter debate, too. Revolutionizing the Soviet military would take a lot of money away from economic development.[20] The Russian military engineer Viktor Kalashnikov had foreseen early in the Cold War that the United States would try to force the Soviet Union to commit the maximum resources to nuclear and other weapons in order to squeeze its economy. When Ogarkov became the chief of the general staff, the Soviet Union was committing *60 percent to 70 percent* of its industry to defense needs, and its economy was fragile. Real GDP declined yearly.

By the late 1970s, the Soviets determined that the effective power of the US nuclear arsenal increased by a factor of 3 over the Soviet nuclear arsenal, primarily due to better accuracy and targeting technology.[21] The Soviets knew that their brand-new SS-18 Satan and SS-19 Stiletto intercontinental ballistic missiles were good, but they weren't great. They certainly did not perform as well as the US intelligence community assumed they would. The Soviets had a good bead on what the US intelligence community believed, thanks to ubiquitous leaks, its own network of spies, and the ever-helpful congressional hearings that forced defense officials to testify on the record.

They knew that the earliest CIA projections about these weapons—the projects that put these missiles' accuracy at within a radius of quarter of a mile or so—were more correct than the ones than American defense hawks adopted as fact by the end of the 1970s. Those false estimates—the ones Ronald Reagan came to believe as gospel—projected that existing Soviet warheads could probably strike within a circular radius of just 400 feet of their exact target.[22]

The difference between a quarter of a mile and 400 feet is the difference between a missile silo surviving a nuclear strike or being destroyed by it. The Soviets knew that if their own warheads were used to strike first, the US ICBM force would *not* be obliterated; at least several hundred ICBMs could be launched in retaliation.[23]

Like the Americans, the Soviets strove for strategic superiority, paying lip service to MAD and privately looking for ways to one-up what they

saw as the cutting edge in American technology. While the American mis-
estimates had deterrent value, they also fed the beast that would rise up to
slay the (nonexistent) dragon. To the Americans, a window of vulnerability to their own decapitation was opening.[24] To the Soviets, their growing
weakness begot increased pressure for the Soviets to consider preemptive
strikes, which would be equivalent of a first-strike plan.[25]

When it became clear, early on, that their invasion of Afghanistan
would be a disaster to the Soviets and expose a gap in their defenses because they had committed so many troops to the cause, the Politburo ex-
pedited plans to field the multi-warhead, 5,000-kilometer-range SS-20
missiles in silos across the Soviet Union. The SS-20s, which the Soviets
called Pioneers, were mobile. Their launch convoys could move anywhere; the missiles could hit targets all across Western Europe, Asia, the
Middle East, and Africa. Their effect was destabilizing. Europe was terrified of them.

And so, NATO decided to respond, in kind. The US would field to
five countries in Europe cruise missiles, both stationary—the Pershing
IIs—and mobile—the Ground-Launched Cruise Missiles, or GLCMs
(pronounced "Glick-ums"). The West's missiles would not actually touch
European soil until later in the decade, but their projected capabilities
were far more menacing. The Soviets believed that the Pershing IIs could
reach Moscow. That meant the Soviet leadership could be five minutes
away from decapitation at any moment once they were deployed. Brezhnev, among others, understood this in his gut.

Brezhnev's meeting, back in 1973, with a second American
president—a future American president, to be sure—only added to
the anxieties he carried with him as the 1980s dawned. Ronald Wilson
Reagan's life was not ordinary. He had saved seventy-seven lives in the
course of one summer as a lifeguard. He starred in more than fifty movies. He was an effective, popular president of the Screen Actors Guild
from 1947 to 1954, taking on strikers led by artists with (assumed) ties
to Communism. To the public, he insisted that Hollywood could rid itself of communists without government intervention. At the same time,
to the FBI, he was confidential informant T-10, helping the authorities
compile a blacklist. He consumed Soviet dissident literature, re-reading
Arthur Koestler's *Darkness at Noon* and Whitaker Chambers's *Witness*. He

divorced his first wife, married Nancy Davis, and found his second career on the mashed-potatoes circuit as a corporate ambassador for General Electric. He consumed GE's culture and adopted its beliefs. He spoke to more than several hundred audiences, met tens of thousands of American workers face-to-face, and made millions of dollars.[26] He once gave more than a dozen speeches in a single day. He would later describe his "self-conversion," his adoption of an unfettered belief in free markets and free minds, even as he retained an affection for Franklin Delano Roosevelt. He watched the Democratic Party move left toward John F. Kennedy, and, under the tutelage of his GE job, he grew skeptical of trade unions.[27] GE endowed him with the skills of a politician. His speech at the 1964 Republican convention turned him into a household name among conservatives, speaking of his journey out of the Democratic Party and telling the delegates that he and they had a "rendezvous with destiny."[28] He blasted socialism, and what he called the "enslavement" of millions in Soviet satellite countries. "There's no argument over the choice between peace and war, but there's only one guaranteed way you can have peace—and you can have it in the next second—surrender," he said.[29] It was the best speech Republicans had heard all week, and his profile rose higher than that of their nominee, Barry Goldwater. The party recruited him to run for governor of California. He won the election.

It was in 1973 in this formal capacity that Reagan met Brezhnev one morning in San Clemente, California. Brezhnev knew that Reagan was a movie actor, charismatic, and the leader of a wing of his party. But he was ill prepared by his aides, who had assumed that their breakfast meeting would be a courtesy call. Nixon had taken care not to lecture Brezhnev in their informal gatherings, but Reagan, by his own account, had no such strictures.

Are you aware, Reagan asked, that the hopes and dreams of millions depend on the agreements you're reaching?

I am dedicated, Brezhnev had replied, *to fulfilling those hopes and dreams.*[30] Brezhnev would later say he found Reagan insulting—and "obscurantist."

Reagan finished his second term in California and ran for president in 1976. He almost stole the Republican nomination from the moderate wing of the party. Four years later, he stood behind a podium to accept

it, blasting Carter's weakness, indecision, mediocrity, and incompetence."
He spoke, too, of his "first and foremost" objective: "the establishment of
lasting world peace.[31]

It would not come from détente. Reagan did not believe the Soviets
were equals. Instead, he believed, as near gospel, that the Soviet Union had
spent the 1970s pouring money into their capacity to deliver and survive
a first nuclear strike.

CHAPTER 2

Toward Protracted Nuclear War

AS THE SOVIET NUCLEAR DOCTRINE EVOLVED TO PRE-empt an American nuclear surprise, the Americans realized in the late 1970s that their plans for continuity of government were far too vulnerable to a Soviet attack. The leader of the Free World could not endure or survive a nuclear first strike.

On July 7, 1977, at 7:34 a.m., a simulated alert pulsed along secure White House Communications Agency circuits to the Anacostia alert facility for the Marine One helicopter, and to other locations. Seven minutes later, the designated "gold" squadron pilot landed on the South Lawn. Nine minutes later, at 7:50 a.m., the helo, having scooped up the president, a few key staff members, and military aides, rendezvoused at Andrews Air Force Base with the National Emergency Airborne Command Post jet, (known as NEACP, pronounced "Kneecap"). The airplane then sluiced down the runway and took off. Time was called. In just 22 minutes, the president could be evacuated, in the air, and safe from attack.[1] President Jimmy Carter knew that the exercises did not realistically simulate the threat that existed. Even before the Soviets developed ICBMs capable of avoiding the eyes of American imagery and measure-and-signature satellites, the USSR's deep-water navy was capable of launching a submarine-based ballistic missile at Washington, DC, that could cruise undetected entirely until conventional air defense radar along the coasts of the United States picked it up. Since these missiles didn't arc into the atmosphere, and since their launch did not give off much of a flash, this strategic capability of the USSR became one basis for stealth attack rehearsals that almost never succeeded in evacuating key leaders in time. The second: a submarine-launched ballistic missile (SLBM) fired anywhere off the coasts would explode during the upward portion of its trajectory—about 3 minutes after launch—and generate an electromagnetic pulse that shorted every electrical circuit on the East Coast.

The nuclear war plan Carter was given and the defense budget he inherited had been revised to reflect these new fears. The updated nuclear war menu had four major attack options:

1. destroy all threatening military targets in the Soviet Union and Eastern Europe,
2. destroy Soviet Union and Eastern European military targets plus all economic and industrial targets that would allow the Soviets to reconstitute a nuclear capacity,
3. destroy Chinese military and leadership threats, and
4. destroy Chinese military and leadership threats and their reconstitution capability.

In addition, it included eleven selective attack options and six categories of withholds—the "destroy *these* but not *those*" options to preserve the appearance of an ability to terminate a war.[2] The strikes he could launch were smaller in mega tonnage. The communication networks he would use to launch them would be resilient, according to the Pentagon. Their idea was that the president could limit the spreading contagion of nuclear war by devastating the world a bit less, or by controlling its escalation in the aftermath of an attack. Carter's National Security Advisor, Zbigniew Brzezinski, didn't buy it. But no one had a better idea.

The Pentagon's guestimate was that the president would have, at best, three minutes between notification and detonation.[3] One reason was that Soviet SSBNs often parked themselves just outside of US territorial waters, perhaps 12 miles off the coast. They didn't yet carry the more accurate nukes, but one day soon they would. Evacuating the president was a necessary, albeit wholly insufficient, part of preserving continuity. If the attack seemed limited, the White House Emergency Plan called on the

Secret Service and White House Military Office to fly or drive the president to one of eight underground bunkers within 100 miles of Washington, DC. Each offered line-of-sight microwave communications with the Pentagon and the Alternate National Military Command Center, located beneath granite rock on the border of Pennsylvania and Maryland.[4] The Soviets knew where these failsafe locations were, though; this safety net was very loose. Even if the president were to find his way to a plane in the air, or to a safe house, he would be a figurehead without a way to talk to the country unless several hundred others, including a thirty-two-person emergency operations team, had successfully made it to their own pre-prepared sites. The president could speak to the nation only if the Emergency Broadcast System was operational; this required the activation of the circuit within the enormous bunker at Mount Weather, in Virginia, a circuit that had no reliable backup until the end of the Reagan presidency.[5] And if, in the air, the president needed to transmit emergency war orders, it was not certain that he could so on a secure voice circuit, particularly if he was overseas.

Carter "wanted to be able to be awakened at three o'clock in the morning and not be confused, and understand what he was going to see, what the voice would sound like on the other end of the line, and that sort of thing," an aide said.[6] After the drill, Brzezinski directed Colonel William Odom, his military assistant, to conduct a soup-to-nuts review of the entire system. He would first examine presidential continuity programs; he would also, upon Brzezinski's orders, be given full access to the Pentagon's command and control procedures. Were they sufficient? And if so, what were they sufficient for? Odom found a few positives. One was that there were a number of redundant communication systems that linked the place which would first pick up signs of a nuclear launch—NORAD—with the person who would made the call to retaliate—the president—and the nuclear commands that would execute the orders, primarily, the Strategic Air Command in Omaha, Nebraska.[7] This satisfied one basic requirement: "to recognize that we are under attack, to characterize that attack, to get a decision from the president, and to disseminate that decision prior to the first weapon impacting upon the United States," according to SAC's commander in chief, Richard Ellis.[8] Odom looked at ongoing tests of the emergency conference network that would connect the president to his nuclear commanders.[9] The calls could be convened quickly. But the network itself was not secure. The Soviets could easily tap in.

Although AT&T had figured out a way to give these presidential communication systems priority routing on their public telephone exchanges, rerouting the traffic after nuclear blasts would be akin to moving every passenger to a back of an airplane in free-fall.[10]

Odom found that a system called SACCS (the Strategic Automated Command and Control System) was highly vulnerable and often blinked out in bad weather. SACCS was critical to communication in any nuclear war because it allowed ICBM wing commanders to receive targeting instructions and distribute them to launch silos.

What disturbed Odom, as he learned more about the system, was what he heard from the nuclear commanders. They did not believe that civilians on the White House staff paid any attention to the war plans. The Pentagon had no way to reconstitute nuclear forces after an attack, or to reestablish presidential command and control after it was lost. The military had spent billions since the days where they were clearly superior to the Soviet Union on communications networks (eight of them in tandem operating worldwide), its command centers (more than one hundred), its computer networks (about sixty-five), and its regional communication nodes (eighty-five), all part of a contraption called the Worldwide Military Command and Control System (WWMCCS).

The Cuban Missile Crisis accelerated the fielding of command post aircraft for theatre commanders, a limited Post Attack Command and Control System 135 aircraft that would allow a general on board to transmit launch codes to ICBM silos from the air, and failing that, a purse full of communications rockets designed to transmit nuclear "go" codes without human interventions to the poor souls in surviving ICBM bases.[11]

The Strategic Air Command had planes that could receive information about damage and detonations and then report it back to whoever was in charge, and they could transmit a limited number of emergency war orders from the air—all improvements. But "things would just cease in their world about 6 to 10 hours after they received the order to execute the SIOP," Odom later wrote.[12] The military relied on studies that assumed that the five primary command centers that the president might use— the White House, the NMCC at the Pentagon, the Alternate National

Military Command Center, the secure communications facility under Camp David (codename Orange One), and the underground bunker at Mount Weather (codename Site B)—would be incapacitated by as few as nine ballistic missiles within 30 minutes of any attack.[13]

Another 35 ICBMs would obliterate the fixed primary and alternate command posts that all SAC bases relied on.[14] As one study concluded, "the national political and joint military command structure . . . is highly vulnerable and could not be counted upon to complete its minimum essential retaliatory functions if attacked."[15] The American nuclear war plan was supposed to be used only as a deterrent, for defense. But increasingly, its writers realized it could never be used if the other side struck first.

Getting word, too, was a problem. The commander of NORAD had one job: to provide the president with tactical warning and attack assessment. The Pentagon had tried for years to update the early-warning sensors that NORAD used to detect incoming missiles and planes. The sensors were sophisticated, but the computers were not. Slight changes in atmospheric density could perturb the entire system. Everything ran on the same set of computers, and software updates to, for example, the air defense algorithms could, and did, migrate to cause glitches in other systems, like those that translated raw data about ballistic missiles into pixels that humans could see on a screen.[16]

On November 9, 1979, engineers uploaded a computer tape containing a hypothetical version of the Soviet nuclear war plan onto an auxiliary computer. For reasons that remain unknown to this day, that exercise data leaked into the processing systems that fed the main display terminals at NORAD's command center. Then, the information relayed itself instantaneously to the National Military Command Center in the Pentagon, to the White House Situation Room, to the Strategic Air Command, to the Alternate National Military Command Center. Immediately, the NMCC convened an air threat conference call with watch officers. The alert ended within six minutes when none of the independent sensors used to confirm missile attacks registered any anomalies, but not before the duty officer at the White House had called Brzezinski and informed that 220—check that, 2,400—missiles were on the way.[17] NORAD wisely decided to move all its testing outside of Cheyenne Mountain after that.[18]

Five months later, a data processor at an early-warning radar site at

Mount Hebo in California computed an erroneous trajectory for two submarine-launched ballistic missiles that had taken off from the waters off the Kuril Islands in the Pacific. The US had been informed about the tests beforehand, but, as the battle staff watched at NORAD, the projected ground zero for one of them suddenly appeared in the shape of a fan over the Western United States.

Three months after that, an inexpensive transistor malfunctioned three times in three different systems over the course of nine days, and started injecting bits of data into the stream of ones and zeros that NORAD's central processors were receiving from its sensors. Each time, the Pentagon had to convene an emergency conference call. It happened again a few months after that.[19] The Soviets naturally saw these alerts for what they were: a demonstration of incredible vulnerability and a source of danger. During each one, the Strategic Air Command automatically generated some of its alert assets, including, at various points, the emergency presidential backup plane and even nuclear-armed fighter bombers.[20] Malfunctions had loosened the safety catch on the nuclear trigger without human intervention or intention.

That was one reason why Brezhnev, in a telegram to President Carter, said that error should cause the leader of any country "extreme anxiety." "What kind of mechanism is it that allows a possibility of such incidents?" A defensive Pentagon gave the White House fighting language to use in reply. Instead of acknowledging the error, they said that Brezhnev's information was based on false Soviet propaganda.[21]

The snotty response by the United States covered for the truth: the early-warning system was not reliable. Forget decision time: how could the president know that the information getting to him was real? Odom at the time worried that the Russians could just as easily have spoofed the system. He might have known that the air force and the National Security Agency were developing elaborate plans to spoof the Soviet's own sensors, too.

In April 1978, NORAD generated an air sovereignty alert, and the NMCC convened a threat assessment call. The US was testing its new Poseidon missiles that week, and the Soviets were conducting provocative drills with their bombers, some of them flying close to US territory. For unknown reasons, the White House Situation Room duty officer thought the call was a test and did nothing. The National Security Council was out of the loop.[22] Human error was rife throughout the supposedly fail-safe nuclear command and control system.

For political leaders, this was scary ₤tuff. The system could not keep pace with the demands placed on it. As Brezhnev said in his first missive to Carter, "It turns out that the world can find itself on the brink of a precipice without the knowledge of its president or of other US leaders." The Soviets took a hard look at the American false alarms and learned from them, speeding up the fielding of their own systems and emphasizing the idea that warning had to be independent. The KGB directed *rezidenturas* to interpret them as false-flag efforts to suggest that American nuclear command and control systems weren't very advanced, and therefore the Soviets had nothing to worry about—"thus providing a cover for possible surprise attack" by the Americans.[23] It would turn out that the Soviets had a lot to be worried about, too. Warning was an illusion.

Alfred E. Buckles enlisted in the air force a few days after finishing high school. It was 1957. From the Bay of Pigs invasion through the beginning of the Reagan administration, Buckles climbed the ranks of "the command and control business," as he put it. He was a SAC communications officer. He pulled duty as an emergency actions controller at the National Military Command Center at the Pentagon. He operated the consoles that transmitted emergency action messages from commanders to deployed forces in the field. He flew on SAC's airborne command post. He wrote nuclear war plans—the SIOPs—as part of the Joint Strategic Planning and Targeting Staff, eventually serving as its executive director. His institutional knowledge of strategic command and control convinced his superiors to create special jobs for him, and when he retired from active service, they converted his position to a civilian one, a supremely uncommon vote of confidence in his abilities. Very few members of the US military knew more about the nuclear decision chain than Alfred Buckles. "If the Soviets wanted to know all of our nuclear secrets, all they would have had to do was kidnap Al Buckles and figure out how to make him talk," a former colleague said of him.[24]

In 1977, President Carter had nominated General Richard Ellis to be the commander in chief of the Strategic Air Command. Ellis was the youngest pilot to be given command in World War II, a brilliant lawyer with an exacting and discerning mind, and a former head of US Air Forces in Europe. It fell to Buckles, by then the chief master sergeant at SAC, to brief him on nuclear decision making. Ellis had been privy to most of the US Air Force's most sensitive projects, but nuclear procedures and the SIOP were so heavily compartmented that he came in knowing very little about the relationship between his command, its authorities, and the president.

"We went down and put together the end-to-end story," Buckles recalls of the briefing. "He could ensure that the forces were equipped and trained and postured, but he was kind of surprised at what he couldn't do—he couldn't do anything with the nuclear forces after they were committed." SAC regularly assessed the hardiness of the US system as it would respond to two scenarios: codenamed SIERRA, a Russian attack when "both countries were fully alert," and a surprise, spasm attack, or INDIA. It turned out that the level of system arousal and preparation did not matter. "Most fixed, land-based primary and alternate command centers were destroyed within thirty minutes," which forced all follow-on emergency action messages designed to tell the force how to retaliate to the Minimum Essential Emergency Communications Net, the system of last resort, which used relatively jam-resistant airborne command posts, very-low-frequency antennas, and commandeered satellites. But this system's performance, too, was "severely hindered," and connectivity with the president was not assured, according to a top-secret study conducted at the time.[25]

General Ellis's top worry, though, was a sea-based threat. By the late 1970s, the US could track Soviet nuclear submarines leaving ports using imagery satellites, direction-finding sonar, and secretly implanted seabed arrays. They'd watch the Soviet subs transit the narrow gap between Greenland, Iceland, and the United Kingdom. But then they'd disappear. The United States was blind to the locations of the Soviet subs as they crossed the Atlantic. The US Navy had spent billions to develop its Sound Ocean Surveillance System (SOSUS). SOSUS arrays measured the sound reflecting and refracting against huge tectonically created trenches under the Atlantic and the Pacific. They could passively detect the noise made by Soviet submarines as they traversed these sound channels, because sound, especially at low frequencies, could travel for hundreds of miles without losing much of its strength.[26] Beginning in 1952, the navy began to lay strung-together hydrophones at key chokepoints in the Atlantic. Within three years, SOSUS arrays protected both coasts and Alaska. Within five years, the navy had processing centers devoted to analyzing the frequency chunks, called tonals, that Soviet subs created when they crossed a SOSUS "beam." With triangulation and some trigonometry, the navy could pinpoint the location of subs in near real time.[27] SOSUS worked wonders for the US for more than fifteen years. Soviet subs were always louder than US subs, often by as much as 25 to 30 decibels. Navy intelligence catalogued Soviet efforts to quiet them, but the US, realizing its advantage, continued to refine the SOSUS arrays and their processing, and stayed one step ahead.

This gap disappeared, suddenly, in the late 1970s. The Soviets began to deploy their naturally quieter attack submarines to deeper waters away from the US Atlantic coast, part of a tactical shift to protect their nuclear submarines, which had to be there to maintain the Soviet Navy's strategic deterrent. The Soviets, thanks to the efforts of their spies and engineers, could now launch missiles from protected "Bastions" near their territory. This, in turn, complicated SOSUS detection, because sound travels less well in shallower waters.[28] By investing so heavily in passive acoustical quieting technology, the US had forced the Soviet submarine force to cluster its faster, quiet attack subs—those that didn't have the capability to launch ballistic nuclear missiles—around its noisier, slower SSBNs—the B stands for "ballistic"—because the SSBNs would inevitably be priority targets for the US during war. At the same time, advances in acoustical detection of submarines ran up against the limits of physics.

In 1978, the Soviets deployed their first Victor III-class submarine from the Komsomolsk shipyards. The 350-foot ship bore an impressive array of anti-submarine warfare and intelligence-gathering features, but what worried US intelligence the most was that it was significantly quieter than any Soviet sub that had come before it.[29] SOSUS arrays were primed to pick up the *tonals*, the frequency spasms that were created by the popping generated by the bubbles from a sub's propellers. The Soviets had somehow figured out how to reduce the noise signatures from these cavitations. Soviet engineers also managed to mask the sounds that emanated from the cooling system in their nuclear reactors, another source of sound for SOSUS microphones. That they did so quickly suggested to the navy that espionage had been involved, because the Victor III seemed to adopt some of the US's technological advantages in quieting while simultaneously exploiting SOSUS's inherent vulnerabilities. (Indeed, it would later turn out that an American working for the National Security Agency, John Edward Walker, had been passing top-secret codeword documents on these precise capabilities to the Soviets for years.)[30]

By 1979, though, the Soviet Navy advances had frustrated SOSUS collectors to the point where the subs would disappear off the coast of the Soviet Union and then reappear, near the coast of Washington, giving the president and his advisors a mere six minutes to decide what to do if a nuclear cruise missile were launched from one of them. The SSNs still possessed enough conventional and nuclear firepower to decapitate the US government. Given this reality, virtually everything that SAC had assumed about nuclear decision planning was rendered moot.

Odom's attention, though, had turned to larger questions. He focused on the presidential nuclear decision handbook and found its language mind-bogglingly obtuse. The military didn't really know what sort of language would be useful and comprehensible to civilians executing the decisions. Then he discovered that the new LNOs (limited nuclear options)—which had been added to the SIOP at the direction President Nixon, through his Secretary of Defense James Schlesinger—bore no resemblance to any policy option the real president would actually consider.[31] There was no allowance in these war plans for real-world, real-time changes to the situation.[32]

He wondered, *Why couldn't a policy be developed that figured out how to use nuclear weapons in a way that would advance US national and strategic goals?*[33]

Figuring out how to answer that question, and then to turn it into a war plan revision, became Odom's holy grail. First, he had to convince everyone that although nuclear war might mean the end of the sitting government, it might not mean that the world had to end. This violated a taboo, and, of course, the tenets of assured destruction. And if the government could be fortified along with civil defense, then *survivability* automatically implied that the president would have more options.[34]

Intelligence satellites could fairly accurately assess damage to a degree of granularity that would allow for retargeting, but the SIOP assumed that that process would rely upon satellites in existence, not the satellites that were planned. The big difference: the intelligence agency in charge of satellites, the National Reconnaissance Office, was slowly but surely moving its systems to near-real-time radar and electro-optical imagery platforms and moving away from its legacy Hexagon satellites with film canisters that had to be recovered at sea and processed.

Why couldn't those satellites be used to give the president maximum flexibility as commander in chief? If the questions Odom and his colleagues asked were provocative, the solutions he proposed did not seem radical. Boost civil defense. Fix defense communications. Redraw the SIOP and its associated systems to give the president maximum flexibility before, during, and after a nuclear attack, and establish a federal requirement for enduring constitutional government.[35]

The changes to the SIOP were added late—in May 1980. A draft of the final presidential directive was sent to Carter days later, but the National Security Council didn't discuss it in full until months later, owing (or so the NSC claimed), to the particularities of the president's schedule.[36] Presidential Directive 59, signed on July 25, 1980, committed the US to endure a nuclear war that lasted beyond an exchange of first strikes:

> so as to preserve the possibility of bargaining effectively to terminate the war on acceptable terms that are as favorable as practical, if deterrence fails initially, we must be capable of fighting successfully so that the adversary would not achieve his war aims and would suffer costs that are unacceptable, or in any event greater than his gains, from having initiated an attack.

The directive enshrined what Odom had long argued: the president should be able to choose to use nuclear weapons and conventional weapons in pursuit of "specific policy objectives," and not just the preprogrammed SIOP options. Intelligence would help the nuclear forces instantly retarget after first strikes to "control escalation."[37] The US would not "rely on launching nuclear weapons on warning that an attack has begun," but it would institute "pre-planning" to make sure that the nuclear force was survivable, so as "to provide the president the option of so launching."[38] Such "pre-planned options, capable of relatively prolonged withhold or of prompt execution, should be provided for attacks on the political control system and on general industrial capacity," according to the directive. Of the 50,000 or so targets in the National Strategic Targeting Database, only 2,500 were designated as "strategic" or nuclear.[39]

And exercises would be emphasized to practice: at least two per year had to involve the "National Command Authorities"—the president or his duly designated successor.[40]

The substance of Presidential Directive 59 leaked almost immediately, and its major tenets were splashed across front pages around the country. This was deliberate. In public, Harold "Hap" Brown, Jimmy Carter's secretary of defense, was grilled, over and over: wouldn't the capacity to limit attacks actually make both sides more likely to engage in them?[41] The Joint Chiefs leaked, too: they warned that their own studies suggested that, as currently constituted, the US ICBM force would be largely annihilated if absolutely nothing was done before the first missiles arrived.[42]

The Soviet Union's Marshal Ogarkov found PD-59 illogical. It was a feint, he believed at first, to justify the expense of a new, more accurate ICBM missile, the MX.[43] Then a more grim interpretation set in. The new doctrine was an attempt at psychological conditioning, designed to instill fear in the public and the US Congress about Soviet capabilities and their intention to strike first. In turn, that would raise a clamor for the US to strike preventatively.[44]

The ambiguous language made for grim interpretations, exactly what the Soviets had feared: the US had committed to a policy of actually fighting a nuclear war and of absorbing a first strike.[45] The Soviets understood the US nuclear doctrine in the context of the new missiles that were due to be placed in Europe by 1983. The US could, therefore, fight a war that would be limited to the European continent.[46] The Soviets felt confined.[47] The sharp bull's-eye was now on their leadership and rendered them more vulnerable to a first decapitating strike by the United States.

Squishing a new nuclear doctrine in to the end of an administration was bad governing. Not anticipating it would leak—and that the leaked interpretation would come to dominate political discussions—was malpractice, a "case study in how not to make national security policy," noted Marshall Shulman, a State Department advisor and graybeard on Soviet thinking.[48] In a memo, he pointed out a logical fallacy that became glaring later on: if you want to somehow limit war and increase the chances that both sides can communicate after an exchange of first strikes, why on earth would your preferred targets be the very mechanisms that would allow Russian leaders to contact you and then agree to stop the war—and then see that the military carries out orders to stop it?[49]

As Carter's presidency drew to a close, nuclear commander Ellis requested an urgent meeting with the president. It was a difficult time. Fifty-two American hostages were still being held in Tehran. The incoming and outgoing administrations were openly sniping at each other. Ellis and Buckles traveled to Washington in early December 1980, hoping that President Carter would not want to leave too much broken glass on the table. The president could make some immediate decisions that would increase the decision time. They did not want to wait for a new administration, focused on myriad other things, to come in and face more delays. Buckles recalls the essence of Ellis's message to Carter. At best, given the current technology, the president might have only a few minutes to make decisions, and he might have very little information to go on. He might not know how any weapons were en route—just the fact that a bunch were. He might know what the targets would be—just broad geographic area estimates. He might not even be told whether the missiles came from Russia, or China, or somewhere else—it was 50/50 that the satellites could see enough to determine that, if they saw the missile launches at all.

"Mr. President," Ellis told Carter, "we are spending a lot of money and time to train and equip this force, and actually, we're killing ourselves to make sure that the nuclear force is ready to go to defend this nation, but until we fix the presidential decision-making and presidential support component and until we assure connectivity, we are kind of wasting our money."

Carter simply responded: "I understand this, General. I understand it very well." He drafted a message to Brown, ordering him to create the architecture of a program that would focus solely on strategic connectivity. Carter did not want to leave any more glass on the table for his successor.

Brown tasked Ellis to come up with a series of recommendations—near term and long term—on the decision problem. Buckles became the point person on the project. He worked through Christmas that year, and four days before Ronald Reagan's inauguration, he had his first meeting with the president-elect.

CHAPTER 3

Decapitation

THE MEETING WITH GENERAL ELLIS AND AL BUCKLES would be Ronald Reagan's first exposure to the secrets of the SIOP, and to the rather large problems he would inherit in commanding it.[1] He came with a few preconceptions. Many of the incoming president's advisors had participated in a now-infamous exercise by hardened Cold Warriors to try to "correct" a bias in the CIA's estimates of Soviet capabilities and intentions in the late 1970s. "The Soviets have not built up their forces, as we have, to mainly deter a nuclear war. They have built their forces to fight a nuclear war, [and] they see enormous persuasive power accruing to a nation which can face the prospect of a nuclear war with confidence in its survival."[2] That's how Daniel O. Graham, a former DIA director, would favorably summarize their conclusion. World domination remained the Soviet's paramount goal. Reagan believed it.

General Ellis began the meeting by noting that the US would probably never attack first, so he would restrict his remarks to a second-strike scenario, which was policy. He told Reagan about the attack detection network, overwhelming him with an array of acronyms denoting specific radars, satellites, and sensors. He described to Reagan the centralized process to get him information and the decentralized process to distribute his war orders to the forces. Then he ticked off the different communications systems that the military used to execute his decisions. He mentioned the program of post-attack reconnaissance to see what damage the first attacks had done. Then he described the plans to reconstitute the forces, if any were left.[3] Buckles said that Ellis did not elide over the gaps that SAC had discovered during the past several years. Getting any information back to the president after nuclear execution would be highly difficult, if not possible. "This business of extended hostilities or enduring nuclear strategy is so foolish, if there was anything to it to begin with," Ellis would say later.[4]

Reagan asked Ellis about strategic defense. What could the US do if a single, errant ICBM managed to be fired accidentally? Ellis told Reagan about a few pilot projects involving ballistic missile intercepts. But the technology was very raw. For now, there was no defense.

Reagan took all this in. In 1966, he had bonded with the father of the hydrogen bomb, Edward Teller, over their shared dislike of the liberal establishment. The Hungarian-born Teller felt that the scientific community had been co-opted by the peace movement and didn't take the threat from the Soviet Union seriously. Vocal, consistent protests outside his home and office angered him further. Beset by bouts of depression, Teller found in Reagan his savior, and Reagan found the nub of an intriguing idea.[5] The Soviets were openly discussing missile defense, Teller told Reagan over lunch at the Lawrence Livermore National Laboratory. The United States seemed to have abandoned the idea. The scientist sketched out how a system might work: a laser fired from the ground, or from space, could home in on and destroy a missile before it began its descent into the atmosphere. To Teller, if computers could calculate a missile's arc, they could direct concentrated energy to any point along that arc.[6]

When candidate Reagan toured NORAD for the first time in 1979, he asked about missile defense, was told that Russians had tried and failed to design a good system, and left unsatisfied. One exchange stuck in his mind, and he would repeat it over and over in later years. He asked what sort of defense the US had if the Soviets decided to launch even a single intercontinental ballistic missile. The battle staff general on duty had told him, "We have none."[7]

Toward the end of the briefing, Ellis turned to Buckles, who showed Reagan several slides, each with a hypothetical nuclear war scenario. The slides listed the choices the president would have to make given the scenario's input, and noted in red the short amount of time he'd have to make it. If the Soviets launch a ballistic missile, "This is a very fragile part of the system," he told Reagan. "We aren't certain we can get a decision from you in time. And if that decision is made to absorb an attack before we retaliated, then we'd have a huge problem."

Reagan didn't say much else during the briefing, Buckles later recalled, but the questions he did ask suggested that he quickly understood the message: he had this great war plan to run, but under many scenarios, it just wasn't possible. Fixing this would take years,[8] Ellis told Reagan, but SAC and the Pentagon had come up with a few steps in the interim. One of them: move the president's emergency escape and command airplane—which was on 10-minute standby at Andrews Air Force Base—to the middle of the country. That way, the plane might survive a first strike, even if the president didn't. Reagan endorsed the idea. "Well, Dick," he told Ellis, "Whenever we see this coming, I want to come live in your house in Omaha, and you can come live in my house here."[9]

———

Reagan took the presidential oath of office on January 20, 1981. He was sixty-nine years old. Three months later, on March 30, the president lay on a trauma bed inside the emergency room entrance of George Washington University Hospital. His body was nearly in shock. Doctors could see blood bubbling up in his now-deformed chest cavity, spurting out of the tube they had forced through the muscle and fat below his collarbone. His blood pressure had dropped to 70/0, which meant that, in between the heart's feeble beats, his arteries could not circulate what little blood his ventricles were able to pump out.[10]

None of John Hinckley's six bullets directly hit the president. His wound was an accident, a consequence of how quickly the agent in charge of his security detail that day, Jerry Parr, had reacted. Less than a second after the first loud *pock* rang out outside the Washington Hilton hotel, Parr's right forearm forced Reagan's body forward, just as Reagan hunched up his shoulders and instinctively lowered his head.

Hinckley's fourth bullet hit the hard, armored frame around the open door of the presidential limousine, which deflected some of its energy, but not enough to prevent the casing from ricocheting upward, where it traveled a few inches in the span of microseconds, entering Reagan's body just under his left armpit. The bullet crunched a rib, blew open a hole in his left lung, and landed an inch from the artery that supplies the body with blood from the heart.[11] His voice weak and hoarse, Reagan could only focus on the pain. "I feel so bad," he said to a nurse, over and over. "I really feel awful. I can't breathe."[12] To another, he asked: "Am I dying?"

On television, ABC News anchor Frank Reynolds told viewers that Reagan was not injured; that he went to George Washington University Hospital to check on the status of his aides and law enforcement officers who were. A producer handed Reynolds a bulletin. "He wasn't shot—wait. Oh my God. He was shot. The president has been shot." Reynolds gripped his ears, enraged that he had spent fifteen minutes telling the world that the president was all right. He then read the rest. Reagan was stable.

But the president was not stable. He was dying.

At the White House, his staff had never rehearsed what would happen if the president were shot, or hospitalized, or even in a benign way, diverted from his schedule off campus. Ed Meese, his counselor and de facto chief of staff, found James Baker, his de jure chief of staff, on a conference call with Mike Deaver, the third member of Reagan's "troika" of top aides. Deaver had rushed to the hospital within moments of the shooting. The president was shot through the back, Deaver was saying.[13] It had been nearly 20 minutes since the president was shot, and Baker realized that none of the cabinet had been officially informed. Most had probably learned about the shooting from their own aides, who had interrupted meetings with news from television accounts. Even the Secret Service didn't know what had happened. The Secretary of the Treasury, Don Regan, was told by a member of his security detail that Reagan was not shot. Al Haig, the former general who was Secretary of State, called Baker to say that he was on his way to the White House. Baker ordered an aide to notify Vice President George H. W. Bush, who was in the air somewhere, returning from Texas.

The first call to Bush's plane came not from the military assistants manning the secure consoles in the Situation Room, or from the National Military Command Center, at the Pentagon, but from Bush's press secretary, Peter Teeley, who happened to be the ranking staff member in the Office of the Vice President when Baker's secretary called. Teeley told an aide to the vice president that there had been an incident. He did not mention that Reagan had been shot.[14] Baker decided to go to the hospital. That was, after all, where the president was.[15] At the Pentagon, the Defense

Secretary, Caspar Weinberger, did not know about the shooting until 30 minutes after it had happened. He decided to go to the White House, but he was delayed because his staff could not find his official driver.[16]

Haig was the lone member of the cabinet who had real-time experience with presidential emergencies. As a former joint staff officer who had been indoctrinated into the realm of secret programs that are supposed to kick in to preserve lines of authority during times of crisis, Haig was appalled by what he found when he arrived at the White House. No one could say for sure whether the vice president had been notified. Connections with Air Force Two were spotty. No one knew exactly where the Secretary of Defense was at that point—he was in traffic, somewhere, en route to the White House, out of contact.[17] Later that afternoon, Haig would become a laughingstock for his clumsy attempt to establish order, but at that moment, within an hour after the assassination attempt, he was the only member of Reagan's team to think about the presidency and not, in a fashion, the health of the president itself.

This wasn't arrogance or an attempt to seize power; it was training and experience. He had been present when Richard Nixon was sleeping as the DEFCON was raised during the 1973 Yom Kippur War. He knew how Nixon's aides reacted during the final months of Nixon's presidency. He remembered how stubborn Nixon had been when he was diagnosed with viral pneumonia. Haig knew that human beings would react viscerally during crises, and that they would draw on direct experience to create a zone of safe thoughts within their own heads. That may have well been fine for people like Michael Deaver and for Nancy Reagan, but it would be catastrophic for the nation if the president's men were focused only on the president, he thought.[18]

Remarkably, it fell to Haig to make sure that the vice president had been told what he needed to know about the emergency. No one in the White House could say for sure. There was even a delay in determining how to patch through the emergency high-frequency voice circuit aboard Air Force Two. When Haig reached Bush, he thought he heard Bush say that he was returning to Washington, but he could not be sure. He had arranged through the Pentagon for a companion message to be enciphered and sent to a Teletype machine on board the aircraft, but he never knew whether Bush received it.[19]

"No plan existed," Haig would later recall. "We possessed no list of guidelines, no chart that established rank or function. Our work was a matter of calling on experience and exercising judgment."[20] In fact, White House counsel Fred Fielding had begun to put together a binder full of checklists, documents, and authority charts in case emergency actions were required. But that package of information wasn't ready by March 30. Just six days earlier, Haig had been informed that Vice President Bush would be in charge of crisis management, a decision that had been made to keep Haig in his own box. Haig felt disrespected and wanted to resign. Bush hadn't the foggiest idea of what he'd actually do if a crisis occurred; he hadn't had time to think about it yet.

But an hour later, Haig marched up to the press briefing room and told the nation, "As of now, I am in control here, at the White House." In doing so, he made the situation much worse. It wasn't so much because he had bungled the Constitution's order of succession. It was because he conflated lines of authority. Someone had to be in charge of crisis management at the White House; that person didn't even have to be a constitutional officer. National Security Advisor Richard Allen did not want Haig in charge and had convinced Reagan to formally assign that responsibility to Bush. But what would happen if Bush wasn't present? No one knew.

Someone, obviously, had to be president, in charge of the nation. Someone had to be acting in that capacity if the president himself could not. And someone had to be the designated command authority for the release of nuclear weapons. During the first hours—if not days—following the shooting of Ronald Reagan, it became unclear, not only to Haig but to many in the government, what these different spheres of authority entailed, who occupied them and under what laws and procedures, and how power was legitimately transferred—and indeed, whether it could be legitimately transferred at all.

When Haig returned to the Situation Room, he found his colleagues angry. They were concerned that he had inadvertently misled the country about the alert status of nuclear forces. Weinberger, acting as the Secretary of Defense, had received word that the US Navy had reported four Soviet submarines inside the box—the millions of square miles' perimeter that the Soviets patrolled near the East Coast of the United States. Most days, there were two. For two days a month, there were four; submarines were rotated out. March 30 was one of those rotational occasions. When Weinberger was reminded of this, some hours after the assassination attempt, he decided it would be prudent to be prudent. One of the subs rotating out had begun to make a long northerly arc. In doing so, it passed closer to the East Coast than it normally would have. The navy always included EFT—estimated fly times—with its daily classified Soviet naval briefing. Weinberger wanted to know how long it would take for a Soviet missile to reach Washington. He sent an aide to collect the last report of the data.[21] Weinberger did not want to raise the nuclear alert status because he knew that the Soviet Union would detect that change, and a cascade of reciprocal alert-raisings could escalate. But he found the circumstances too unusual to do nothing. He wanted to be "ready to go on alert."[22]

To Weinberger, and to Allen, that made sense. There was precedent. After John F. Kennedy was shot, SAC had raised its alert status. But when Haig heard this explanation, his frustration boiled over. To the military, "being ready to go on alert" meant nothing. Either forces were in a heightened state of alert, or they weren't. This was a consequence of the logic of nuclear decision-making and its associated rules—hierarchical, explicit, and categorical—designed to wage and win nuclear wars, and not, as Weinberger might have assumed, to give the political authorities more time to decide what to do.

Before Haig had assured the country about not being in an increased state of vigilance, he wanted to clarify with Weinberger—who kept using the term *alert*. Haig raised his voice. "What kind of alert, Cap?" Weinberger was on the phone with the chairman of the Joint Chiefs of Staff, who was translating the civilian secretary's wishes into the vocabulary of strategic readiness that the military machine could understand and execute.

Weinberger looked up. "It's just a standby alert. Just a standby alert."

"You're not raising readiness?" Haig asked.

"No," he said. He wasn't doing anything about *actual, official, formal* readiness. He just thought it would be a good idea for the JCS chairman to stay in the National Military Command Center. Weinberger's mind went back to the question of alerts. The SAC, the Secretary of Defense assumed, "until we know more about what happened, will probably put themselves on alert."[23]

Haig then asked a question that clarified the matter for everyone in the room. "Do we have a football?" A football was the leather satchel containing the president's nuclear decision handbook and several other classified items that would be used only when catastrophe struck.

Treasury Secretary Regan, who had been listening to the argument, had had enough. "Al, don't elevate it! Be careful."

But there was a second football in the room. It was by Allen's side. The White House Military Office kept a spare football in their secure vault in the Executive Office Building, and Allen had asked a staff member to bring it to him. He had also asked for an extra nuclear authenticator, a credit-card-sized wafer with an alphanumeric code on it, known as the biscuit. Allen would later recall that he found nothing remarkable about the question. "Why not have all of that stuff there, just in case?"[24]

The card that Allen now had was identical to the one next to the driver's license in President Reagan's wallet, which was in a bloody plastic bag, somewhere in George Washington University Hospital, its existence, because the object itself was classified, a secret to almost everyone there. Weinberger's own military aide had a football, too. His authentication code was different. Had the question about whether to employ nuclear weapons suddenly been asked of Weinberger, and had Weinberger read his own code to the emergency actions controller in the National Military Command Center, it would be him—Weinberger—whose identity was confirmed.

But if, in the heat of the arguments inside the Situation Room, the controlling authorities decided that a nuclear strike was necessary, and if they had authenticated the decision using the spare biscuit kept at the White House, the military would have registered the action as coming from the president of the United States, a man, who, at that moment, was undergoing emergency surgery.

It would get worse. When Haig returned from the briefing room, Weinberger reported that the military decided that the best course of action would be to move pilots on alert status from their ready rooms to the cockpits of their planes. It would save a few minutes' time. One of the Soviet submarines—Weinberger now had the exact data—was 2 minutes closer to the coast than normal.

How was this not *a defense condition increase,* Haig wondered.

It was, Weinberger temporized, an increase of readiness "within" DEFCON 5. Neither Haig nor Weinberger seem to have realized that SAC bombers were the only element of the US military outside of US forces in Korea who were permanently operating at DEFCON 4.[25]

Vice President Bush said that he did not assume any special powers at any time during the thirteen days President Reagan was in the hospital. But presidential spokesman Larry Speakes said several times on the day of the shooting that Bush had "automatically inherited national command authority." Numerous officials are now on the record as saying that they doubted the president's cognitive capacity to make decisions during the first (at least) seven days.[26]

Fred Fielding's binder wasn't finished when Hinckley took his shots at Reagan.[27] There was no real nuclear alert that day, so the lessons learned were more limited: the White House did not manage the crisis well.

———

On the day Reagan returned to the White House, he wrote in his diary: "Whatever happens now I owe my life to God and I will serve him every way I can."[28] A few weeks later, Cardinal Terence Cooke, archbishop of the Diocese of New York, came by to give his blessings. "The hand of God was upon you," Cooke said. "I know," the president replied. "I have decided whatever time I have left is for Him."

The content of Reagan's faith has played a conspicuous role in the historical arguments between his most ardent fans and his fiercest critics. One side says that Reagan's religious convictions hastened the end of Communism. The other says it convinced him of the futility of making deals with the devil, thus prolonging the agony of the Cold War.[29] To nonbelievers, it was plain scary that Reagan doted throughout his adult life on the Bible's end-time prophecies—cryptic phrases written thousands of years ago acquired a mystical power and held sway over the man who controlled the release of nuclear weapons. His sincere belief in the reality of evil shaped his view of the conflict between East and West.[30] His anger at the Soviets was real, too. They not only promoted atheism, but they persecuted believers and poisoned the minds of children against believers.[31] Reagan thought often, and wrote often, about the impressionable minds of young, insecure children in the Soviet Union.

Reagan would later trace the birth pangs of his personal faith to a book he read when he was just eleven or twelve:[32] *That Printer of Udell's: A Story of the Middle West.* The titular printer's journey is classically redemptive. As a boy, his perfect, noble Christian mother dies, leaving him to be raised by his faith-questioning alcoholic father. Young Dick Walker is saved for Christ by a printer named Udell, and then pastors himself to a fallen city. He redeems a prostitute, who becomes his wife, and gets elected to Congress. (Walker's good words include a "workfare" program to help the poor men of the town. Self-reliance is emphasized over "sentimental" welfare.) The book's author, Harold Bell Wright, chastised "Sunday Christians" who would whisper a few words in private and then get on with their modern lives outside the church. He wrote to instruct Christians about how they could practice their faith in a world that seemed to be off its moorings.

When Reagan finished the book, he told his mother he wanted to be baptized and base his life around the "traveling printer whom Harold Bell Wright had brought to life." The book, he later wrote, had a profound effect on his conception of the "triumph of good over evil," and it would, by his own admission, set him on a course that he tried to follow even into his presidency. A few days later, along with two dozen other boys, Reagan was baptized, again, this time on his own choosing. His faith journey had begun.[33]

The Disciples of Christ fell well within the mainstream of American Christianity when Ronald Reagan was baptized into the faith. Most of Reagan's biographers pass over the degree to which fundamentalism was yoked to a set of beliefs that included not simply the providential position of America in the world but also to the darker and more relevant energizing force for evangelical efforts: the belief that the End of the World was imminent.[34]

When Reagan wrote often of God's Plan (he capitalized the words himself),[35] he was speaking of a template that was knowable only after it was experienced, and not of a general blueprint God created for the world, one that Christians could figure out about in advance. Reagan was certainly more assured that God existed, than He had a plan, and that his goal was to live as God would have him live, than he was about the correspondence of any world event with a verse from the Book of Revelation.

Reagan's deep faith in God was often mocked. So was his morality: there was a right and a wrong, and almost no in between, not ever. His critical biographer, Edmund Morris called it "childlike,"[36] but since it happened to be the way that most American adults said they viewed morality, it was not extraordinary. At the same time, Reagan's lifelong flirtation with prophecy was unassailably part of his makeup. Advisors such as Bud Mc-Farlane would warn him from bringing the subject up in public.

Reagan talked often of the End Times with Reverend Billy Graham. In 1971, as governor of California, he was musing out loud that all the signs were "in place for the battle of Armageddon and the Second Coming of Christ."[37] During his presidential campaign, he agreed with Reverend Jim Bakker that the world might indeed be on the brink of the rapture. He had read Hal Lindsey's *Late Great Planet Earth*.[38]

Reagan saw himself at the juncture of an antimony: if we were in the last generation, and Christ was coming, and history was about to end, it was nevertheless his biblical responsibility to be a peacekeeper as he understood the term.

––––––

As soon as Reagan decided to devote his presidency to the calling he felt from God, he took action. He told Haig he wanted to write a personal note to Brezhnev, proposing a relationship that would treat the Soviet leader as "a human being." Reagan believed that private words would have a much greater effect on the Soviet leader than a formal letter.

As the historian Paul Vorbeck Lettow discovered, the State Department took Reagan's letter, edited it heavily, ridding it of those antinuclear sentiments that Reagan advisors such as Richard Pipes, the Harvard academic who had served as Reagan's leading Sovietologist, found dismaying, and sent it back to the president.

On April 24, two letters went out. One was a five-page-long missive, drafted by the State Department, that responded, charge by charge, to Brezhnev's starchy and emotionless letter to Reagan a month earlier. Reagan's handwritten letter, which recalled the time that the two men had first met, way back in 1976, was appended to the end.[39] It said little about nuclear abolition. The nuclear establishment had shoved the president away from his own instincts. This pattern would repeat itself, over and over, as the locus of the superpower conflict shifted to Europe, where the threat to hundreds of millions of people from intermediate-range nuclear missiles and nuclear artillery shells was a fact of ordinary life.

CHAPTER 4

Man in the Gap

Killianstädten, West Germany

WILLIAM LEE TROLAN BELIEVED HIS DNA COMPELLED
him to serve his country.

A great-great-grandfather was one of the first company commanders
in the States, leading the 15th of Virginia during the Revolutionary War.
Relatives fought each other at the Battle of Murfreesboro during the Civil
War. Family lore held that both died while holding their respective flanks
while battling for the same small piece of terrain. Trolan, who went by his
middle name, graduated near the top of his class at West Point in 1979 and
had his choice of assignments. He wanted to be part of the action. That
meant cavalry or artillery.

In 1981, he was promoted to second lieutenant and joined a nuclear
artillery unit: the Bravo Team of the 501st US Army Artillery Detachment, 5th Group, 59th Ordinance Brigade. The teams of the 501st had
custody of dozens of nuclear warheads called W31s, each packing up to 30
kilotons of explosive power.[1]

Trolan had wondered why, as an air defender, he had to guard nukes.
Why wouldn't an ordinance officer with an explosives team be in charge?

"The answer I got was that it was to make the point to our allies in
Germany that this unit was important enough to assign combat soldiers
to," he recalled.

The 501st held about four acres near Killianstädten; it was the southernmost nuclear custodial unit of 5th group and the closest to the East German border.

It lay smack dab in the middle of the Fulda Gap, the navigable expanse of land that stretched from the German border to Frankfurt-am Main.[2] The Fulda corridor furnished Napoleon with his escape route after Leipzig; it was the treeless plain along which American armies marched to secure Germany late in World War II, and the focus of NATO strategy since the mid-1950s. Creighton Abrams, the commander of the 7th Armored Cavalry in Europe during the Cuban Missile Crisis, called it a "playground for tanks." It was the smallest geographical container of earth that could reasonably claim bragging rights for having convinced weapons designers to titrate nuclear yields precisely to destroy tanks that rumbled across it. If the Warsaw Pact, led by the 8th Soviet Guards Army, took the Fulda from the US Army V Corps, North would be cut off from South, supply lines would be snipped off in the middle, and NATO would have to retrench in or behind France.[3] Keeping the Fulda was essential to maintaining the integrity of nearly 700 miles of NATO's main lines. It was ground zero for World War III.

———

The military tends to describe the estimates damage incurred by an enemy as an "effect." If Warsaw Pact aircraft and tanks begin to cross down the Fulda, the effect called for in NATO's General Defense Plan was a dose of 8,000 rads across 30 percent to 40 percent of the target area, enough atom-splitting power to cause "immediate permanent incapacitation," according to an army field manual.[4] But corps commanders couldn't simply call for nuclear artillery shells or air-burst weapons. A "package" had to be requested in advance. Commanders were taught to "backtime" their desired employment of nuclear weapons by at least 14 hours, because it would take at least that for the request to be considered and authorized from higher headquarters—and from the president of the United States. The decision chain worked like this: the commander of the field artillery unit that Trolan supported, or one of the army corps commanders that the field artillery unit was chopped to, would send a request to employ nuclear weapons to the Central Army Group (CENTAG) headquarters

in Heidelberg or perhaps its secret wartime bunker. There, nuclear planners would vet the request against the needs of the V Corps Artillery commanders and the 4th Tactical Air Force, charged with patrolling the area
of Northern Germany from the ground and air, respectively. From there,
the request would move to the two-star general at Camp Hendrick in
the Netherlands, home to AFCENT—the Allied Forces Central Europe
headquarters—which would noodle, validate, and send it up to Supreme
Commander of Allied Command Europe, the SACEUR, in Casteau, Belgium. The SACEUR's nuclear operations cell would approve the request
and throw it across the Atlantic to the chairman of the Joint Chiefs of Staff,
whose nuclear operational cell would then prepare a "selective release"
package for the president of the United States.[5] The president and his advisors would look at this request and then decide whether to consult with
allies; the National Command Authority was allotted three hours to make
the decision whether to approve the nuclear package.

And then the decision had to be communicated back down, through
the SACEUR, to the custodial commanders of about ninety-five sites,
each of which would release its armed nuclear weapons to the field forces
of eight allies: West Germany, Greece, Turkey, Italy, the Netherlands, Belgium, Canada, and the United Kingdom.[6]

"It was played at varying lengths in exercises, but in reality you couldn't
expect that the minute the command group at SHAPE decided they want
to go they would get an instant response to sort of go ahead and go," Captain William Bliss, a NATO nuclear planner, said. "And I would certainly
never expect an instant reply to come back; if it did, it meant that it was
being played in a response cell and due regard was not being given to it.
But I mean this would have been the most massive end to Europe as we
knew it."[7]

As the military gears churned, a parallel political process would begin
in NATO. In 1975, with an eye toward demonstrating resolve, NATO's
defense committee decided to unify its separate fall exercises by merging
them; the political preconditions would be common among them. And
this made sense: in real life, deteriorating conditions on the Continent
would indeed trigger the plans that major troop reinforcement exercises like Crested Cap, aimed at clearing a path for American warplanes
to fly across the Atlantic, and Reforger, which brought actual troops to

Germany, were meant to practice. Each year, the final exercise in the series would rehearse the nuclear weapons release procedures. It was called Able Archer.

———

NATO was a collection of member states, each with its own political and military concerns. Diplomats looked at the world differently. Political and military interests occasionally overlapped, but they often undercut each other. And no country wanted to centralize too much power in NATO as an institution. The member countries argued whether exercises took up too much time, but also, as the price of oil rose, whether they consumed too much fuel. Generals would complain when major field exercises were reduced to command post rehearsals. NATO ambassadors would get pressure from their own defense departments, who were concerned about individual readiness requirements. These exercises might sap them of supplies they'd need in a real war. On the other hand, the generals had a point: how the *hell* were the forces going to exercise their war plans?

But NATO *countries* had a much easier contingency plan: if NATO itself was wiped out, diplomats in the country's capitals would simply take over NATO's planning functions. No backup headquarters was needed.

There was no way to tell whether NATO would act as one unit during a crisis. The member nations shared a doctrine—flexible response—that few understood until Alexander Haig, during his tenure as SACEUR, led a Europe-wide effort to standardize training and make sure that words that meant something in one language were associated with proper words in the others.

Broadly, the war games exercised two contingencies: how to hold the line in a conventional war against a Soviet force with superior numbers and just what events would convince NATO to employ its nuclear weapons. For NATO exercises, the NATO Council Operations and Exercise Committee (COEC), which was comprised of senior war planners from NATO member states, would sketch a series of movements, maneuvers, and inciting incidents. They'd then submit the draft to all of the NATO countries for approval. Each country, in turn, would show the draft exercise to their defense ministries and their chief diplomats. Feedback would then flow back to the NATO cell, which would rewrite the script. The

NATO military committee, made up of its defense representatives, would have final approval.

The scenarios often stretched the imagination. During one war game, NATO exercise planners proposed to rile its players by suggesting that Poland and Czechoslovakia would persecute German minorities in their own countries, a move that would almost certainly have triggered a vicious response by other Warsaw Pact countries, notably East Germany.

The game writers could get too glib. Would a Soviet leader, even after a hardline coup, style himself as "Generalissimo," like Stalin did? Or would he continue to call himself "General Secretary"? The State Department thought the latter.

And occasionally, they scripted events that had already happened in the real world. The HiLEX exercise in 1977 initially called for Norway to establish a larger fishing zone around its territory, leading to immediate Soviet protests and aggressive naval exercises. But Norway had done that in real life, a year earlier, and the Soviets had simply moved their exercises farther away.[8]

The exercises were prime target for rival spies. Targeting the communication networks across which the military and nuclear consultations would flow was probably the highest tactical priority of Soviet and Warsaw Pact officers in the field. Most of these networks were secure, protected by scramblers or code machines. The members of NATO's political committee would confer over a high-frequency system called NATO Secure Voice if they were not in the same room,[9] which they never were.[10]

The nuclear execution messages themselves—the last line of communication—were protected by a theoretically unbreakable cipher; not only would the transmissions themselves be encrypted, but the alphanumerics within them would have been *pre-enciphered* before transmission. You could only decrypt them if you had the exact same codebooks provided by the National Security Agency, and getting those codebooks was next to impossible. They were protected like the nuclear material themselves, individually numbered, and required two-person control at all times.

But possessing the codebooks was not required to get a sense of what was going on. The length of messages was a clue to their content, as was their "loudness"—a receiver could figure out where it was sent from by analyzing the hills and valleys of voice or electronic prints. Voice operators themselves had ticks that could be used to discriminate among them. By November of 1983, the Soviet Union had thousands of analysts working solely on these patterns.

"In an emergency situation and when military exercises are taking place, operation of lines of communication may be switched to the 'minimize' system, in which the volume of ordinary telephone calls and telegraphic messages is sharply curtailed, and channels of communication cleared for transmitting urgent messages," a secret Soviet spy cable noted.

"If this system is institution in countries which have nuclear weapons, especially if it [is] on a global scale, this may provide a serious warning signal that the adversary is preparing for R"—Ryan—preemptive attack. Only intercept stations could provide this warning. "In addition, changes in the method of operating communications systems and the level of manning may in themselves indicate the start of preparation for [sudden nuclear war]."[11]

The Emergency Message Authentication System (EMAS) console that spit out the nuclear control orders in Lee Trolan's security shack was connected to a network of microwave towers called the Central European Line of Sight system, itself of a larger network called the European Command and Control Console System. It relied on patches in the German public telephone backbone to connect field sites with headquarters, so although transmissions could be rerouted in emergencies, the lines could be tapped. A backup system on the high-frequency band, Cemetery Net, would retransmit all nuclear release orders. NATO had one communications satellite in operation in 1983, although it wasn't clear whether it was reliable enough to transmit nuclear orders. The European Command could use some of the frequencies controlled by the US Air Force's main satellite communication constellation, but during a real war, those might not be available.[12] If all worked perfectly, and it never did, commanders could choose one (or all) of six different ways to get Trolan the release order. If his unit had been dispersed to its secret field site, he would have the orders with him—perhaps a "time on target" authorization that instructed him to release the weapons at a certain point—or he would wait for the HF radios to squawk.

Getting the "release" order did not mean that Trolan's nukes would be launched. It simply meant that the permission to launch them had been given to the tactical commander. The German Luftwaffe unit would receive the actual order to fire—or not fire—over entirely separate communication lines.[13]

The nuclear warhead itself was pretty safe; you could drop it on its nose and it wouldn't go off. You could try to destroy it with explosives, or with a bullet, but the worst that would happen is that the explosives inside the warhead would detonate, killing everyone within 50 yards or so and leaking plutonium. No one ever managed to steal a warhead, but the arming and fusing mechanism were so precisely engineered by 1982 that a thief who didn't belong to a nation-state wouldn't know what to do with it and might well have used it as a giant doorstop.

The psychological pressure of nuclear custodial duties was hard enough for Trolan, but evaluators from SACEUR would press the limits of the system he had developed on base—and then push past it. You were expected to be perfect as you went through your wartime paces. Trolan dealt with the avalanche of expectations by rationalizing. If he could open up the safe just a second faster, punch the warheads to the Germans more quickly, then maybe, just maybe, he could forestall something.

The unit held Tac Evals—Tactical Evaluations—weekly. As a commander, he could shed his chem-bio-nuke gear and walk around with the evaluators. To bring home the realities of war, his team would practice the nuclear release procedures under unusual conditions. "Okay, the team commander is dead," the evaluator might say. Or "communications with higher headquarters have been cut off." How his guys responded to those deviations, within the confines of procedures, tested their tensile strength.

Pulling the nuke duty did not set up Trolan for a good army career, as his wife reminded him constantly. But his lack of professional ambition freed him to focus on the mission. The warheads themselves were fairly secure. But the site itself was a hellhole. He found it dilapidated. Fence fabric designed to keep nosy neighbors from watching the drills was easily torn off. Watchtowers that reminded him of *Stalag 13* were in different states of disrepair. The German conscripts who manned the outer perimeter were not well trained and were unreliable. He was down staff, too. As captain, he was authorized to have two second lieutenants; during his tenure at the base, he only had one. That meant he had to work weekends, often. His salary was $1,000 a month.[14]

Trolan saw his first East German MiG fighter jet after just a few weeks at the base.

On a cloudless day, one flew across his field of view without any warning, leaving a loud guttural wake. The Group of Soviet Forces in Germany regularly tested NATO air defense readiness with these "accidental" flights; they used these flights to collect intelligence on the state of readiness at Trolan's camp. The Soviets knew that their MiGs were pretty safe if they stayed within 30 kilometers of the border; standard NATO operating procedures called for an air defense stand-down when they first detected a stray. The US Air Force would scramble a combat air patrol to chase them away if they stayed too long. If the Soviet pilots ever did take fire during one of these "accidents," they'd automatically know that NATO had enhanced its combat posture.[15] The saber rattling jangled his nerves and reinforced Trolan's belief that, at some point during his stay in Germany, he was going to see something big go down. He would often wonder if the stray MiG he saw was the one that would be carrying a missile aimed at his nuclear vault.

By 1983, Bernard Rogers, the SACEUR, had 7,000 individual nuclear warheads—most of them artillery shells—under his command.[16] At the higher DEFCONs, the Defence Planning Committee of NATO had to sign off on any changes he wanted to make. At DEFCON 3, he could authorize the custodial brigades to "generate" them for wartime conditions, a process that took about two hours. (Once "generated," the warheads were ready for immediate use.)

At DEFCON 2, he had the authority to order their dispersal to secret wartime sites;

At DEFCON 1, he alone could order the transmission of the nuclear release order, wearing his NATO hat, for non-US forces, or as commander of US forces in Europe, for US forces.

During the first stages of a war, or at the first register of an alert or a real change in the DEFCON status, the custodial units of these nukes would almost certainly be targeted for sabotage by the Soviet military special forces teams that had burrowed into West Germany. By intercepting these orders, they could "ignite the Soviets' avowed doctrine of preemption."

During the volatile period where DEFCON 2 had been declared the command and control system would be at its most fragile, paradoxically, so—once again—NATO relied on what had to be exceptional intelligence in order to give these units the chance to prepare. Its General Defense Plan assumed as much.[17]

But Lee Trolan's 501st AAD was told they'd get a few hours of warning *at most*. His team would practice emergency self-destruction, under the illusion that his ragtag mix of infantry and German conscripts could hold off an assault for two hours—that was how long it took to disable the nuclear warheads for good and destroy the codebooks. "We were taught to expect war every day," Trolan said. They had *secret*-secret emergency self-destruct plans that weren't even shared with the Germans: they could call in air strike from friendly A-10 Thunderbolt aircraft, or they could mate the warhead to the missile and deliberately create a fault in the firing circuit. If the short was created at precisely the right point, the missile would launch about 10,000 feet into the air, and then its C-4 would explode. So long as Trolan and his team hadn't completed the procedure to enable the nuclear control module to fire, the explosion would rain down nuclear particles, but there would be live human beings below it.[18]

CHAPTER 5

Project RYAN

IN ROME, ON MAY 13, 1981, A LITTLE OVER A MONTH after the attempt on Ronald Reagan's life, a young Turk named Mehmet Ali Ağca opened fire and nearly killed Pope John Paul II in Saint Peter's Square. At the CIA, some saw the hand of the Soviet Union, wondering whether the KGB would authorize the political assassination of a man who threatened Communism. The intelligence community threw resources into a campaign to blame the Soviets. Reagan, still recovering from his own brush with death, felt a strong kinship with the new pope, whom he had not met.[1]

The KGB leadership did not appear to know how eager the CIA was to see a grand design in these recent events. They had something else on their minds that month. Section chiefs from around the world had flown to Moscow for a series of meetings about the future. The first chief directorate, in charge of foreign intelligence gathering, was alarmed by political and military changes in NATO and the United States and had decided to reorient its priorities. In Poland, labor strikes had crippled the economy, and Moscow worried about a revolution that could not be contained by the Polish government.

Marxism in Poland was imposed by force, and Soviet dominion was sustained by the threat of an invasion directed by Moscow. The Soviet military was stretched thin. During the previous five years, a half million troops had moved eastward to contain the threat of China. More than 60,000 Soviet combat troops, and much of its war materiel preordained for use in Europe, were tied up in Afghanistan. In 1979, the Soviets had reluctantly invaded Afghanistan to prevent the takeover of the Afghan government by Islamists; the war became a magnet for Soviet enemies to do whatever they could to enlarge the conflict, sucking in so many resources that war plans for conflicts elsewhere had to be revised. On May 16, 1981, in an auditorium at the Lubyanka, General Secretary of the Politburo Leonid Brezhnev, who was seventy-five and frail, and Yuri Andropov, his bespectacled, pragmatic, and feared intelligence chief, took turns addressing KGB *rezidents*.[2] As a senior KGB officer later recalled: "The new American administration, he declared, was actively preparing for nuclear war. To the astonishment of most of his audience, Andropov then announced that, by a decision of the Politburo, the KGB and GRU were for the first time to cooperate in a worldwide intelligence operation codenamed RYAN."[3]

RYAN—Raketno Yadernoye Napadenie (Ракетно ядерное нападение), RYaN, or "nuclear missile attack"—would coordinate the flow of warning intelligence through a small analysis office in the First Chief Directorate called the Institute for Intelligence Problems. This new bureau would use computer analysis and create a matrix based on unambiguous signs of nuclear war preparation. The minutiae of communication patterns received special priority. From the start of Project RYAN, the opponent's nuclear exercises would be watched more closely by the Soviet and Warsaw Pact intelligence services, and the Soviet Union would ratchet up its own nuclear alert status, just in case.

What was expected from KGB *rezidents* around the world would change: the enemy's counterintelligence was crafty, and the Soviets envisioned that the US and NATO would create fog machines designed to throw the KGB off the scent of any surprise attack. A senior KGB officer later explained: "[i]n practical terms: When we draft the list of indicators, we have to try to include only those who are indispensable for a surprise nuclear missile attack." The implication: a de-emphasis on regular foreign intelligence work.[4]

A month later, Andropov signed his name to a coded message to all Russian embassies worldwide. RYAN was to be their top priority. "Not since the end of World War II has the international situation been as explosive as it is now," he wrote.[5]

That was the theory, anyway. In practice, it would take more than a year before RYAN got off the ground. The KGB *rezidenturas* in Western countries did not believe that imminent nuclear war was a threat worth paying attention to.[6] Andropov, in particular, although not given to delusions about the domestic situation, saw conspiracies everywhere. And his directives were often met by the bureaucratic equivalent of eye rolling. In 1978, he believed that the CIA had decided to foment internal instability inside the Soviet Union and that the American intelligence establishment created a single secret unit to conduct deep cover sabotage operations. (The CIA had no such intentions, nor the capabilities.)

One reason why Andropov could speculate so freely about Western intentions was that the KGB had few sources of political intelligence.[7] He refused to believe what he read in the sources that were available to him, especially the Western press, which often captured US political intentions as accurately as any intelligence could.

When Erich Mielke, the head of the East German intelligence service, the Stasi, visited Andropov in July, he found the KGB chairman in a dour mood. Mielke tried flattery. Muscovites seemed happy, he said. The beautiful stadiums built for the 1980 Olympics were a triumph of socialism, he said. No wonder the Americans would not send their athletes to participate. The notes of the meeting suggest that Andropov had no response, launching instead into a statistics-laden summary of the Soviet domestic economy. Growth was lower than projected. So was consumer goods production. Brezhnev wanted to make the economy more efficient, Andropov said.

Internationally, his principal worry was a campaign of ideological subversion and psychological warfare promulgated by the new Reagan administration, which intended to spend $220 billion to upgrade its military. The correlation of forces, which Andropov found more or less balanced at the time, would shift in the future unless the Soviets responded in kind. "Reagan's vulgar speeches show the true face of the military-industrial complex," Andropov said. "They have long sought such a figure. Now, they have finally found it in the form of Reagan."[8] Toward the end of their meeting, Andropov asked Mielke if there was anything the East Germans needed from the KGB. An accurate war plan for NATO, Mielke replied, would be helpful. Andropov did not tell him that the Bulgarians had been passing along those plans for years.

Andropov did not mention the imminent threat of nuclear war, nor did he mention RYAN. His assessment of Soviet prospects reflected his personal ambitions. Brezhnev would die, sooner rather than later. Andropov intended to succeed him. He needed allies from within the Politburo, and, in reluctantly supporting the decision to intervene in Afghanistan two years earlier, he had cast his lot with the Soviet military-industrial complex and its titular leader, Dmitriy Ustinov, the Defense Minister.[9] Andropov angled to be the face Soviet military-industrial complex. He had reason to hype the American threat. It was in the interest of his political coalition to do so.[10] Andropov might also have been trying to motivate his troops. Soviet officials who had long interacted with the West believed that the invasion of Afghanistan had gutted the Soviet's last chance to revive détente with Carter. The aging Politburo was saying, in essence, that détente had been killed by Reagan's election.[11] And the inability to collect good political intelligence on American leaders was particularly dangerous for the Soviets: their theory of nuclear deterrence required an accurate assessment of political intentions as much as it did the ability to know whether American ICBM silos could be destroyed by three or five weapons.[12]

———

In Moscow, Oleg Gordievsky, another young Andropov protégé, heard nothing about RYAN, even though he was posted to KGB headquarters. Gordievsky looked the part of a KGB operative—square jaw, pursed lips, narrow eyes—except his hair was so blond as to be conspicuous. He looked Nordic. It helped his cover at previous postings, in places like Copenhagen. At one time a rising star in the First Chief Directorate, his career floundered when, while posted to Denmark, he fell in love with a woman who was not his wife.

Oleg Gordievsky's first pangs of political sentiment came at age fourteen. The police had just arrested fourteen Jewish doctors and charged them with an improbable plot to kill communist leaders. Gordievsky lived across the hall from a Jewish family; they were his friends, levelheaded, patriotic, and rational. He could not reconcile the anti-Semitism he heard from the party with his own experience. He began to question everything. He would eavesdrop on his father's conversations with friends late at night and left with the impression that the labor camps he read about were full of ordinary people, not traitors. His mother would tell him of the fear she lived with when he was a baby: neighbors would disappear; she could remember the heavy boots tramping upstairs to arrest one, seemingly at random.[13]

By sixteen, he had no knowledge of the West but knew the Communist system was "neither sincere nor honest."[14] He joined the KGB through his father's connections. It offered him an escape. He could live abroad and see the world. In August 1962, at twenty-four years of age, he took his oath: "I, entering into the ranks of the Armed Forces of the USSR, commit myself to defend my country to the last drop of blood, and to keep State Secrets."[15] He married his first wife, a Russian-born teacher of German named Yelena, and accepted his first field assignment in Copenhagen, in 1966.

Two years later, when Soviet tanks advanced on Prague, intending to crush the student rebellion that bolstered the reform government of Alexander Dubček, Gordievsky snapped. His loyalty to the Soviet system was dead. He decided to change sides. He called Yelena on an open line, one he knew was monitored by the Danes, and expressed his indignation.[16]

It would be another five years before he had his first meeting with a Western agent. And then another year of testing his bona fides. The British were skittish. The KGB often ran so-called dangle operations, where they'd send a false defector with damaging information designed to confuse the rival secret service and protect other, more sensitive operations.

Even real defectors often provided fluffed-up information to increase their value. The accusations of one, a particularly knowledgeable and equally paranoid KGB major named Anatoliy Golitsyn, almost single-handedly destroyed the Soviet operations of the Secret Intelligence Service, MI-6, and the domestic Secret Service, MI-5. The more important Golitsyn became, the grander his stories became, including an allegation that a British prime minister and a deputy head of the SIS were KGB agents. Gordievsky thought Golitsyn was a paranoid fantasist—there were many in the intelligence service.[17]

Gordievsky grew frustrated with the delays and almost cut contact.

But beginning in 1975, trust was established, and secret documents began to flow. He knew his first handler, a gentle but deceptive Scot, by a pseudonym—Michael. His second was an ambitious and clearheaded officer who spoke five languages and impressed upon Gordievsky how valuable he was. Espionage against the USSR became Gordievsky's passion. His day job became a hobby. In 1977, Gordievsky fell in love with a woman who was not his wife. She was Leila Aliyeva, a typist at the World Health Organization. Divorce was not an immediate option, so an uneasy truce between his first love, Yelena, and his new love, Leila, existed. In the cloistered world of the Soviet embassy, Gordievsky's colleagues soon learned of the affair.[18]

He could not be fired for it, but he learned that he would not be promoted because of it.

Gordievsky was assigned to a staff position Moscow; he would be grand errand boy for the puritanical personnel department at KGB headquarters. For two years, he watched the world revolve from inside the Lubyanka, a former insurance company building that had become the headquarters of the secret service in 1918. He spent his days cultivating relationships with party officials, attending lectures on counterintelligence by the likes of Kim Philby, a high-ranking British spy who had long ago defected to Russia, and picking up intelligence gossip but generally keeping to himself. He was biding his time. He had to get to London.

To do so, he had to ingratiate himself—those were his words—with the head of the First Chief Directorate's British section, Igor Titov, a man whose concept of the West boiled down to its warrant for licentious behavior. Titov would use the special diplomatic pouch from London to amass his own supply of Western pornography, using it for his own gratification as well as to ply subordinates with rewards for favors.[19]

With Titov's blessing, Gordievsky learned English and began to consume its literature and history. Having access to the KGB's library, he could read Winston Churchill's biographies and Somerset Maugham's fiction; he became a dilettante. He would later recall raising suspicion by praising Churchill's gentlemanly manners to a train full of KGB colleagues. His divorce came through, and he and Leila became the parents of two sons. By April 1981, his superiors felt he had done enough penance.

At the time, Moscow could send seventeen KGB officers to its embassy in London. Each visa had to be approved by the host government, no small task because each was slated for an official job, one that would give them diplomatic status and cover. The British knew that around half the embassy's staff were trained intelligence operatives, but they tended to be young, inexperienced, and junior—on purpose. Veteran KGB officers who had run spies in another European capital would be known to the Western intelligence establishment, and the British Foreign Office, which was in charge of approving all applicants from the Soviet government, would not issue a known KGB spy a work visa. British spy fiction would have the world think that Her Majesty's secret services would be eager to accept already identified KGB officers to Britain—all the easier to surveil them and perhaps turn them. But in practice, the intelligence services did not have the time, the budget, or the resources to plan such elaborate counterintelligence operations.

So it was somewhat of a surprise to Gordievsky's KGB superiors, then, that the British accepted Moscow's appointment of him as counselor, a senior position in the political affairs section of the embassy. *A stroke of good fortune*, Gordievsky thought. His bosses assumed that Gordievsky would be rejected, but they knew that the British wanted to expand by one position the number of official posts in *their* embassy in Moscow. This exchange was as friendly as Soviet and Western tit-for-tat got.[20]

It took more than eight months for the British to vet Gordievsky, a delay the KGB First Chief Directorate attributed more to bureaucratic brinksmanship than anything else. Gordievsky polished his English and prepared his family for the move.

CHAPTER 6

Warning

AT THE HEADQUARTERS FOR US ARMY EUROPE'S IN-
telligence division in Heidelberg, Germany, Gail Nelson was looking for
serious warning signals that the Soviets were about to move on Poland. He
was the senior analyst, responsible for interpreting the signs and signals of
crises, providing warning of war and political intentions, and deciphering
the complex code of relationships between the Politburo in Moscow and
the Polish leadership in Warsaw, between the KGB and the Polish Internal
Front.

In an era of satellite reconnaissance and signals intercepts, Nelson
kept his most valuable insights on notebooks he stashed in safes. From
European newspapers, Nelson had a good understanding of what was happening. But that wasn't enough. Seeing a crack in the Warsaw Pact was one
thing. But, as General Frederick Kroesen, his superior, had reprimanded
his intel analysts the year before, his job was more pressing. "God damn it,
Major," he told one. "I know what the Soviets are capable of doing! What
I want to know is what they are going to do!"

An internal conflagration in Poland raised the possibility of war in
Europe. The Soviets had used military exercises as cover for pressure and
eventual attacks before, most notably in Czechoslovakia in 1968. NATO
had missed that one; its member states were irate and demanded better
intelligence.

More generally, NATO's conception of Soviet war doctrine assumed
that the Warsaw Pact would use legerdemain to catch the West off guard.
The disposition of forces arrayed on both sides of the border gave an edge

to the pact if they managed to surprise NATO intelligence. So, NATO was always looking for surprises. There were a warning center at Ramstein Air Base with up-to-date information on the Soviet order of battle, an air defense intelligence center at Börfink, and a third 24/7 watch in Stuttgart, the headquarters of the European Command.[1]

Kroesen was responsible for the 7th Army, which needed seventy-two hours to prepare for a contingency. Nelson's job was to give Kroesen advance warning of anything. The worst-case scenario would be an all-out Soviet invasion to break the counterrevolution. Ten thousand Soviet troops were already in Poland, integrated with Polish troops.[2] The most likely scenario, according to Nelson's estimates at the time: the Internal Front would impose some sort of martial law, responding to the dual pressures of Moscow to fix the situation and to the internal instigation from Solidarity. He believed that the threat from Solidarity was acute. Its success could embolden dissident and labor movements in other Soviet satellites, smash the lock that the Polish communist party held on power and mobility in the country, undermine confidence in the capacity of the Soviets to interact effectively with Warsaw Pact militaries. But the big catch: Unlike previous Warsaw Pact insurrections, the problem in Poland did not originate within the Communist Party. Any Soviet response that undermined the Polish Communist Party could empower Solidarity even as it threatened it militarily.[3]

Many of Nelson's contemporaries in the intelligence community thought the Polish crisis would resolve itself. The Soviets would do anything to prevent the contagion from spreading, and the Northern Group of Soviet Forces was its most reliable bulwark; ergo, the Soviets would have to invade at some point. But Nelson's analysis suggested the opposite. The Polish government could handle labor strikes, just as it had at least four times since 1956.

In Washington, the National Security Council was sorting through the aftermath of several crises. On June 10, Israeli warplanes destroyed an Iraqi nuclear reactor at Osirak, and Reagan struggled to respond. Haig was about to depart for a crucial trip to China. But the Polish situation was "very dicey," Richard Allen told Reagan. "You should know that there are deep splits within the intelligence community on what we think they are going to do. Some believe the Soviets will, and some believe the Soviets won't."

Still, with only two divisions in Poland—the Soviets would need thirty
to prosecute an invasion—dramatic action seemed far off.[4] Reagan asked
Allen to draw up a list of ways that the US could help Solidarity, quietly.

To outsiders, Andropov did not betray any panic about Poland. "For
the most part," he told an East German colleague in July, "the Polish events
have had no impact on our country. In general, people hold negative opinions of those events. However, in the western regions of the USSR, there
has been some influence. There was a small group of workers who went on
strike. The situation was clarified with party methods. Still, other occur-
rences are possible. We must be prepared." But the Politburo was obsessed
with little else. Andropov wanted action. He felt the Poles had acted too
rashly when they recognized Lech Walesa's labor unions to ratchet down
the crisis of 1980, and he thought his colleagues were dithering. There
were military imperatives. Strategic communication lines and satellite
ground stations in Poland were vulnerable to sabotage and terrorism, and
if a revolution proceeded unchecked, East Germany would be cut off,
physically, from the Soviet Union. Brezhnev was attending regular meetings again. His health had improved. But his anxiety about intervention
was significant. He endorsed aggressive military exercises, a not-so-subtle
attempt to "intimidate Polish authorities by implying that they would use
both their own forces in addition to other Warsaw Pact forces if necessary
to restore order," Colonel Ryszard Kukliński, a senior martial law planner,
later recalled. The exercises had an edge to them: field hospitals staged
along the Polish border.[5]

As the Polish crisis burned hotter, Reagan's advisors saw a transfor-
mational opportunity. Poland's economy was a "basket case," and it owed
$17 billion to Western countries.[6] "The potential ripple effect through-
out eastern Europe is of major strategic importance," Deputy Secretary
of State William Clark put it. Allen argued for a stronger response. "The
Polish people and the West would lose if Solidarity were crushed." Secretary of Defense Weinberger favored the bare minimum for now, which
was $50 million in food aid. Reagan worried that economic problems of
an essentially communist nation couldn't be cured by Western aid, and he
did not want to prop up the Polish government only to see it strengthened
after Solidarity was crushed.[7] "I question whether there is any benefit to
the United States in bailing out the government of Poland, a government

which may be as hostile to us as the Soviets," he said. Allen suggested that the US wait to see whether the Soviets would invade. Reagan wondered whether an invasion would be met with any actual resistance. "Surely, the Poles would resist," CIA Director Bill Casey said.[8]

As fall gave way to winter, Gail Nelson noticed that Wojciech Jaruzelski, the powerful Polish Defense Minister who was allied with Moscow, was using language in his speeches reminiscent of how the Polish government had responded to previous labor crises. His main source was the accurate Reuters news bulletins from its bureau chief in Warsaw. "I culled from the news and those innuendoes enough information, as well as my own readings, to see that they were going to repeat the same crackdowns as they had done five times before. The pattern was already there."[9]

The Defense Intelligence Agency saw a different pattern. As data came in, its analysts looked for signs of rhetoric that matched the sequence of events before the external invasions of Hungary and Czechoslovakia. Three times during the fall of 1981, the DIA issued warning notices to the Joint Chiefs of Staff predicting an imminent Soviet invasion. Three times, the Soviets did not invade. The intelligence community lost confidence in the DIA director, Lieutenant General Eugene F. Tighe. In September, James A. Williams, an army veteran who had overseen intelligence operations in Heidelberg, replaced Tighe. Williams sent an all-hands memo to military intelligence analysts everywhere. Warning would be his priority. But it took a long time before the DIA was free of political influence. Nelson had signed his name to a memo predicting that the Poles would impose martial law. His job was on the line. Army analysts who failed to warn the government ahead of the 1968 Czech invasion had been fired. "I was not going to be played by guys in DIA who saw this crisis independent of historical precedent," he said later.

Nelson had come to these conclusions without knowing that the CIA had a highly placed human source inside the Polish army: Colonel Ryszard Kukliński, the officer in charge of drawing up the martial law plans. Even the Polish crisis was not important enough for them to sacrifice their asset. Over nine years, he delivered more than 40,000 pages of top-secret Warsaw Pact military planning documents. The CIA did not allow any information he provided to be distributed to the hundreds of senior American policy makers who consumed the National Intelligence Daily.[10] Only a select few, including Allen, knew of his existence.[11] Even Weinberger was kept in the dark.

The CIA's granular-level knowledge of Polish martial law planning helped prevent the Reagan administration from making rash decisions or overplaying its hand. Kukliński, who signed his reports "Jack Strong," told the CIA in mid-September that when marital law came, "it will be introduced at night, either between Friday and a work-free Saturday or between Saturday and Sunday, when industrial plants will be closed. Arrests will begin around midnight, six hours before an announcement of martial law is broadcast over the radio and television. Roughly 600 people will be arrested in Warsaw, which will require the use of around 1,000 police in unmarked cars."[12] If the Soviets did invade Poland, the threat of nuclear war in Europe would rise, and overnight.

CHAPTER 7

Zero-Zero

AS THE NSC STRUGGLED TO BRIDGE REAGAN'S INSTINCTS
on Poland with the practical realities of what America and the West could
do, the Department of Defense was about to hand the president another
set of unappealing policy options on a separate but related issue: the missiles slated for NATO. The Pentagon had grave doubts about the efficacy
of the American intermediate-range nuclear weapons that would soon
deploy to Europe to counter the Soviet SS-20s. Top-secret assessments
sent to Reagan at the beginning of his presidency and not shared with
NATO suggested that the Pershings and the GLCMs would be useless in
a real war.[1]

The Soviets responded with a massive, semi-covert crusade to whip
up antimissile sentiment in Europe. Through the KGB, they funded
Christian protest movements, and then became silent, sometimes clandestine partners to legitimate nuclear-freeze campaigns, catalyzing and
capitalizing on genuine fears that existed in Europe. NATO allies who
had been in favor of the missile deployment now demanded that the
US simultaneously negotiate a way out of having to deploy them in the
first place. Some countries wanted the US to stop the deployments. That
would be a no-go, but by 1981, US arms control diplomats worked on
two separate tracks: one for NATO, which was arguing with itself about
how, where, and when to deploy the US missiles, and a second track with
the Soviets, debating whether they'd be needed at all. Reagan would not
accept anything less than the promise of full peace; neither would he put
his weight behind a proposal that made America look like it was weak or

lacked the will to stand up to Soviet belligerence, which, for him, was a historical given.

A bit of nifty bureaucratic maneuvering by Richard Perle, the Assistant Secretary of Defense for International Arms Control, concentrated Reagan's mind around a tantalizing option: what if he proposed getting rid of all of the new NATO deployments—going to zero—if the Soviets were to withdraw everything they'd already fielded?

Perle thought his idea was elegant and brilliant. Reagan found it consistent with his long-term desire to see nuclear weapons eliminated. The proposal was a substantive expression of that aim, the first time anyone in his administration had proposed eliminating an entire category of nuclear arms.[2] The State Department hated it. The Soviets, they believed, would reject it out of hand.[3]

Reagan had come to conclude that the policy would give him the most sway over how the US conducted the negotiations. The preferred State Department's proposal, which proposed reductions to the lowest mutually acceptable level, was different from zero. The politics were different. The likelihood of success was different. Zero was the *toughest* proposition that could be put in front of the Soviets. But Reagan was not bent on getting an agreement. He wanted an agreement consistent with his objectives.

It did not escape notice, however, that the fielding of weapons the US didn't really think it needed in NATO would give them something to give up during future negotiations.[4] The basic US arms control strategy, then, was premised on deploying missiles—and then removing them.[5]

Haig would not let it go, insisting on modifying or qualifying zero-zero long after Reagan made clear that he had taken the other option. Haig's tenacity got on Reagan's nerves.[6] He felt that his hard-won diplomacy was for naught. He fought the administration, which backhanded him as the spokesman for Europe. He fought against naysayers who felt he was in league with the arms control establishment. And he lacked clear guidance from Reagan.[7] In cabinet meetings, he would beg Reagan, saying it was "vitally important" that he receive clear negotiating instructions that tracked with the old SALT II language—only then would the Soviets reciprocate. Anything new would be a disaster, he thought. "We cannot afford to send a message to our allies that we are now imposing new conditions on the beginnings of the TNF negotiations," he told Reagan.[8]

In Haig's view, the European allies did not need a pistol pointed at their heads. Haig felt zero-zero was contradictory and unattainable. It would never happen in current conditions, and since it could never happen, its unattainability engendered even more suspicions among the Europeans, especially Germany's Helmut Kohl. Reagan did not believe that an agreement was essential to foreign policy. This was his long-held view, an epiphenomenon of his instinctive distrust of anything associated with détente, where agreements were pursued simply because the establishment thought agreements were good.[9]

A classified Defense Intelligence Agency white paper, "Warsaw Pact coverage of NATO Targets," had given Perle, a sub-cabinet-level political appointee who rarely briefed Reagan, the chance to introduce the idea to Reagan in person. The DIA analysis suggested that the maximum number of warheads needed to destroy NATO's command and control facilities was 150. The DIA arrived at this (relatively) small number because NATO countries were open, democratic, and compact. It was hard to hide anything. The Soviets knew this. So, if the US accepted a proposal where the Soviets would wind up having fewer than 150 warheads, the European continent would be safer.

Anything more than that—even down to the level of 200, which was seen at the time by the arms control cognoscenti as a low number for the Soviets—and the opposing army had basically everything it needed to destroy Europe. From the Defense Department's perspective, the new missiles were silly afterthoughts. Though said to be highly mobile, they were not. The logistics train required to move them was large, and so the Soviets would notice any movement. In DOD parlance, these missiles gave NATO no strategic advantage because they could be destroyed before they were launched. Besides, the last thing that the German and British governments would do during a time of heightened tension would be to start moving nuclear missiles around their countryside. The GLCMs in particular had a logistics trail that numbered more than 100 vehicles. They would be based at a handful of known locations and would be under constant surveillance by the Soviets. If, for some reason, the Soviets wished to disable them, it would take nothing more than a hunting rifle, its ammo easily piercing the fuel tank.

What the US and NATO would be giving up if they reduced the

Pershing and GLCMs "wasn't worth a damn," Richard Perle would later say, so long as the Soviets had sufficient numbers of SS-20s for a decapitating strike. The Pershings and GLCMs probably weren't worth deploying in the first place. And pressing for the elimination of SS-20s was verifiable, something that could be counted and seen. Zero-zero was, for a while, not worth more than the stock paper it was typed on. Weinberger managed to sell the concept to Reagan, assuming that his approval was all they needed. They were wrong. Zero-zero's critics inside the administration thought it a profoundly bad idea, and knew that it would sew dissension inside NATO. Such a pie-in-the-sky idea was bound to be interpreted by Moscow as an aggressive acceleration away from détente; and détente, although unfavorable in sheer power-balance metrics to the United States, was popular in Europe because it reduced the real likelihood of nuclear conflict.

Perle and others shared a hardline view of European defense. Even as NATO's political leaders fretted about provocation and the loss of their own influence, what they needed, from a baseline, was a guarantee that the US would defend them if war ever came. A "date certain" for TNF negotiations, rather than endless studies, for which Haig argued. Perle would later concede that it was arrogant to assume that he knew NATO's needs better than NATO knew their own, but his logic squares with the policy later adopted by the Reagan administration: it would take firm and public measures to reassure NATO that the Soviets could not, ever, assume that the United States would sit out an armed conflict on the continent. Paradoxically, this made NATO even more nervous.

————

Reagan's mind was still on Poland. On December 10, 1981, the president approved $100 million in grain subsidies to the Polish government.

On December 13, the Polish government declared martial law.

Two days later, Reagan had lunch with Cardinal Agostini Casaroli, the wise Vatican Cardinal Secretary of State and chief foreign affairs counselor to Pope John Paul II. Reagan had read through a report from the Pontifical Academy of Sciences warning of the horrors of nuclear winter. Brezhnev was getting the same briefing that day.[10] "The conditions of life following a nuclear attack would be so severe that the only hope for humanity is prevention of any form of nuclear war," the report concluded. The Pope had endorsed the study after visiting Hiroshima in February and later getting briefed on how countries could not prepare in advance for the enormous displacement and suffering that would result from even a limited nuclear change.[11]

That struck Reagan: in the event of a war, no number of doctors could care for the wounded, he said. "It is easy to understand the horror of nuclear war," Casaroli replied. "It is less easy to figure out how to keep it from occurring." Reagan explained his arms control strategy to Casaroli, noting in candor that it was inadequate. "Currently, the only way to deter nuclear war is to arm as strongly as the potential opponent," Reagan said. "However, this is not good enough. There could be miscalculations and accidents." And that was the paradox of the nuclear age, the cardinal said. "A credible military deterrent depended on a resolve to incur the horrors of that war if necessary."

The Pope had taken to calling the prevention of nuclear war the compelling moral challenge of his time—more so than Communism. There had to be some way to "break out of the arms spiral" that spurred each side to escalate. Implicitly, the Vatican was challenging Reagan to put statecraft before nuclear policy.

Casaroli had a carrot. The US was the "sanctuary" for the future of the world, he said. The Vatican had informal but regular communication with the Soviet leadership, and it had proved useful. To induce Reagan to think more positively about negotiations with the Soviets, he offered Reagan a private channel to the Pope. The Vatican had little political power, but "it was morally strong and might be helpful." The pontiff could not, he warned, take sides.[12]

Although some historians have seen in this meeting the seeds of Reagan's secret alliance with the Pope to bring rapid change to Europe, Casaroli seemed to have a different agenda. On Poland, the news of the day, he counseled caution. "The Poland situation is unique: completely surrounded by Warsaw Pact countries, cut off from any direct contact with the West. It is the Pope's belief that change in Eastern Europe would come only gradually and at the same rate in all Eastern European countries. The Pope is convinced that over time such liberalization will occur, but no one could know how long the process would take," he told Reagan.

"Is there anything we should be doing now?" Reagan asked.

"The United States and other Western observers should not act until they know what the real situation is in Poland. It is too bad there is a great lack of good information," the Vatican secretary replied. Soviet spies might even have compromised Solidarity, he warned.

Reagan took a different tack. "The Vatican and the Pope have a key role to play in events in Poland and elsewhere in Eastern Europe. The Pope's visit to Poland showed the terrible hunger for God in Eastern Europe."[13]

In Poland and elsewhere, the president wanted action. He was impatient with the progress of his foreign policy agenda. By early 1982, his vigor was back. His energy reflected the architecture that a new National Security Advisor, William P. Clark, had set up. The domestic situation was grim; Reagan would be pressed to raise taxes and cut defense spending to deal with a growing deficit, demands that preoccupied him every night as he wrote in his diary. Reagan became openly frustrated with the Soviet Union's opacity and stubborn refusal to see the world as it was.

In his diary and in his public and private comments, Reagan cast their leaders as monolithic and unyielding in their opposition to capitalism, religious freedom, and mutual coexistence. Not for nothing: Soviet leaders, too, had just about the same belief about Reagan. They ignored his statements about peace and focused on his increasingly militant rhetoric about war and its consequences. They also detected the real implications of his economic agenda and began to wrestle with the fact that he was mobilizing the United States to move to a position of advantage over the USSR.

Clark, an attorney and cattle rancher from Ventura County, California, had been Reagan's troubleshooter, turning around Reagan's governor's office after a sex scandal forced the departure of senior aides in 1967. Reagan upped him to chief of staff. No one knew Reagan's leadership style more closely. Other aides would roll their eyes when Reagan would start to ramble, off-topic, but Clark would listen. He divined messages in these frequent discursions. Reagan appreciated how Clark let him be him. They began to "share a brain," Clark's aide Roger W. Robinson later wrote. Cap Weinberger called him simply Reagan's "best friend."[14]

But Clark knew little about national security. As president-elect Reagan filled out his cabinet, his counselor, Edwin Meese, worried that Haig, a creature of Washington who was chosen as Secretary of State to signal continuity to the capitol city, would use his chest full of medals to bully the White House. Meese told Reagan that the State Department's number two, its chief operating officer, had to be someone loyal to the president and someone who could fix the department's legendary institutional dysfunction.[15] That was where Clark would go. Haig had told him: "You are going to run the building; I am going to run the world."[16]

Clark knew he could see Reagan whenever he wanted, and that there would be no intermediary when he wanted to talk with the director of the CIA or the secretaries of State and Defense.[17] When Reagan made the announcement, the press approved. In a short time, Clark had become fairly well respected by Washington's standards. It was assumed that his views on the Soviet Union mirrored Reagan's and that his experience as a judge and a manager would balance out his open ideological disdain for the Soviets.[18]

Clark first changed the staff. He brought in Robert G. "Bud" McFarlane, a Marine who had briefed Reagan on foreign policy during the campaign, and elevated the profiles of others, including Paula Dobriansky, a scholar of Eastern Europe who was the daughter of an anticommunist dissident, and Ken deGraffenreid, the senior Republican staffer on the Senate Select Committee on Intelligence. He stocked the NSC with men and women he believed would have the gumption to execute the policy that he and Reagan devised, including his deputy, John Poindexter, a highly regarded admiral who knew the Pentagon inside and out. To keep the secretaries of Defense and State in the loop, he talked with them a dozen times a day.

He would trade on his closeness with the Reagan family, his personal affability to manage, and the sharpness of his mind. He had no reason to worry about Reagan's loyalty, and this allowed him to feel comfortable bringing in advisors to brief Reagan.[19] The biggest source of stress for Clark would not be heavy-handed cabinet secretaries, the press, or even the Soviets. It would be other members of Reagan's inner staff, particularly Michael Deaver and James Baker, the chief of staff, both of whom had wanted to bring Clark in to the White House to marginalize Meese, Reagan's archconservative counselor, who had grown into an influential whisperer of ideas that Reagan would easily, and sometimes to the chagrin of the rest of his staff, repeat in public. But Clark reported to one person.

When Reagan, fed up with leaks by insiders (a few by Baker, and others by liberals in the State Department) that undercut national security

announcements, suggested that his inner staff take a polygraph, this suggestion, too, leaked, as did Baker's outrage about it. Baker's leaking was
an open secret. He saw the move as an "administrative Bill of Attainder"
directed at him and his authority.[20]

When he became National Security Advisor, Clark was determined
to win the Cold War through sound management of policy.[21] He would
use presidential directives to translate Reagan's policy wishes into directives that the CIA, the Defense Department, and other executive agencies
would then execute.[22] He was a prisoner of paper. He had spent his professional life authoring judicial opinions that laid down the law. He assumed
that Reagan would not be able to negotiate meaningfully with the Soviets
until the US had completed its defense buildup, and not until its policy
reflected the iron will of Ronald Reagan. Diplomacy was on the shelf for
now. Priority one was: have something new to say.[23]

––––––

A few weeks before negotiations with the Soviets began, Haig tried one
final time to get a more realistic proposal from Reagan. He'd present zero-
zero, and then "within twenty-four hours of announcing this, the real
question you will be asked in Europe is whether that's your only position?
Would the US accept significant reductions?"

Reagan was silent, but Weinberger was not. "We'd lose any negotiations by answering such questions." Haig grew frustrated. "Cap, we're
talking around each other. We both agree we want zero—"

"Then we should say so," Weinberger interjected. Reagan said he
would bridge the gap. If the Soviets accepted zero-zero, he, the president,
would negotiate in good faith elsewhere. "There will be no end to the questions," said Haig. The European consensus would fracture if the US offered
a position that Europe knew the Soviets would find untenable. Reagan was
unmoved. "We will say we intend to negotiate in good faith, but we will
start at the outset with our offer."

Haig: "Skepticism in Europe is great. This is clear from my discussions
with foreign ministers."

Reagan: "They may be expecting slogans. But, properly worded, our
position can be convincing and can persuade."

Haig: "The Germans want the zero option under ideal circumstances.

They want a package that is manageable. But if we say, 'zero only,' the Soviets will say, 'Fine, let's define the "zero option."' And then the Soviets will include aircraft and forward-based systems, et cetera, and we will have to say, 'No.' We all want enough air in our opening position to be able to fall off it to keep our allies with us and the Soviets at bay."

Weinberger: "The likelihood of the Soviets offering zero is remote. Our proposal . . . will set them on their heels. Our position has the support of our allies, people around the world can understand it, and the president can communicate it."[24]

As a candidate, Reagan promised to negotiate with the Soviets on strategic weapons from day one.[25] But he hadn't done any negotiating yet. Weinberger wanted to wait for the new defense program to be introduced. His chief arms control negotiator, Eugene Rostow, proposed to delay talks until at least March of 1982. In public, the Soviets accused the United States of delaying negotiations to gain a strategic advantage—namely, to rearm. They were correct.

In private, Rostow was saying the same thing. Before the US should negotiate at all, he told Reagan, it had to have developed a second-strike capability—a requirement of the SIOP—without which, he said, "it would be impossible to use our conventional forces anywhere in the world."

Close the window of opportunity for the Soviets, he said. Don't let them take advantage of the US before it can effectively counter the SS-20s (by deploying cruise missiles to Europe) or the large Soviet ICBM force (by building new missiles, hardening old ones, and modernizing strategic command and control).

Negotiations would be tantamount to a retreat—"and the effects of such a perception of an American retreat were incalculable—and all bad," he said.

The Soviets were nearing a first-strike capacity, and if the US started to talk before it could counter that, the "pressures of the nuclear equation would make the doctrines of launch on warning more plausible and more possible," he warned.[26]

Reagan reluctantly yielded, again. Direct, face-to-face bargaining on all the larger issues would wait.

CHAPTER 8

Ivy League '82

FREDERICK LAW OLMSTEAD'S GRAND MAGNOLIAS WERE lightly speckled in melting snow when Ronald Reagan sat down to work in the Oval Office on March 1, 1982.[1] It would be a mundane work day, according to the schedule given to the press and to the entry he added to his diary that night. He had no public meetings. He was supposed to finish some speeches. It had been nearly a year since John Hinckley's bullet tore through his lungs. Reagan's energy was not up to full strength, and his focus on any given day could wax or wane.

During the middle of the afternoon, Reagan snuck down to the Situation Room. Something unusual was going on. William C. Rogers, a former Secretary of State and Chief of Staff of the Army, was in *his* chair. A secret war game was in progress. Rogers was concentrating on the black-and-white pages of a top-secret binder—a version of the football—the president's nuclear decision handbook. With a few phrases, he could activate the SIOP—the central organizing principle of the Cold War—a document that called for, within two minutes, as much as 95 percent of available ICBMs, 20 percent of bombers, and 66 percent of nuclear submarines to be available to the president.

The fictional world in Rogers's book was two days into a major crisis. A sudden North Korean invasion forced South Korea into submission, resulting in high alert among US forces in the Pacific. Rogers asked for a briefing on Soviet forces. Where were their nuclear submarines? Were any of their wartime communications nodes active? Had any Warsaw Pact countries gone to a heightened state of alert?[2]

Over the course of that day, answers came in. Yes—the air force intelligence cell was tracking Soviet fuel tankers inbound to East Germany. In the afternoon, the navy reported that one of its patrol frigates had been buzzed, rather aggressively, by a Soviet MiG.[3] Then the frigate was *gone*.

A military assistant rushed in. As Reagan watched from the side, the aide uttered the words that a president never wanted to hear in real life: "We've got an OPREP 3 Pinnacle"—that's a high-priority message denoting an event of major significance. The flag word was NUCFLASH. The frigate had just been nuked by the USSR.[4]

In the war game scenario, the commander of US forces in the Pacific had ordered his ships dispersed, hoping to provide survivable communication links to nuclear forces destroyed in the Pacific. Why destroy the backups first? The savvy nuclear planners knew that destroying the backups would be the smartest way to force an opponent to give up quickly—because the moment they detected an anomaly, they'd assume that their primary links would be destroyed, and then they'd switch over. The first missile—fired from just off the West Coast, went undetected by US warning systems, and fell somewhere near Denver. And suddenly, the US was blind to its West. The Soviets had used a submarine-launched ballistic missile to take out the ground station for the Defense Satellite Program space-based infrared sensor, which orbited over Panama and covered the Pacific Ocean.[5]

Moments later, other nuclear submarine launches were detected by older radar systems. Next, the underground command post at the Strategic Air Command headquarters in Omaha was obliterated. Then, the thick granite slabs that protected the North American Aerospace Command under Cheyenne Mountain in Colorado dissolved like tissue. A map of the United States, projected on a screen hanging from one side of the Situation Room, began to change color, from white to red.

Over the wire, aides called out rapid-fire updates: Early-warning satellites spotted what the Pentagon assumed were Soviet SS-19 missiles, the most accurate in the Soviet arsenal, but they didn't seem to be on their way to major American cities. The first targets became clear: the US command and control system itself. Missiles zapped backup and backup-backup communication links for the president and his staff. A flight of them wiped out Washington, DC, almost as an afterthought. A hundred or so, launched over the Arctic, aimed at the six US Minuteman/MX ICBM clusters in the American West. Then came the conventional version of the nuclear apocalypse. It took just a couple of missiles to pulverize major American cities, starting with Chicago.

As Rogers, the stand-in president, consulted with his aides to devise a response, the real president, Ronald Reagan stared at the screen. "Before the president could sip his coffee," a participant would later write, "all the urban centers and military installations in the US were gone."

By the end of the hour—roughly 3:00 p.m. EST—the entire country was covered in red. This was just an exercise—officially termed Ivy League '82—but Reagan sat for a while in "stunned disbelief."[6]

Ivy League '82 was the biggest nuclear exercise the Pentagon had ever coordinated. It took months for the exercise staff inside the Joint Chiefs of Staff to write it. The inputs and outputs reflected the evolving nuclear strategy. Could the survivability of the presidency be ensured from STAR-TEX to ENDEX? Would there be enough ICBMs left after the first Soviet strike to respond with a show of force large enough to prevent a follow-on attack? Could the army mobilize within the US to support a long, costly war?[7]

There were two sides: Blue versus Orange. Blue was the good guys; Orange was adversaries. The Pentagon tried to get the best (and most hawkish) Soviet experts inside the military planning directorates to play as Orange during these games. Convention dictated that in exercises the enemy never be named, an emolument for public relations purposes. Of course, not calling the Soviet Union the Soviet Union only added to the sense of artificiality that inevitably attaches to a virtual nuclear war in peacetime. You could use a stopwatch to measure how long it would take for a ballistic missile launched from an Orange submarine loitering off the East Coast, but you could never replicate the fear and panic that would push a human limbic system to its breaking point if one believed that a real nuclear weapon was on its way.

The air force had long appreciated the human element of panic, which was one reason why missileers in ICBM silos were deliberately cut off from television news broadcasts during their shifts. How could the Strategic Air Command ensure that the keys would be turned when the orders were given? Repetition. Make the process of releasing nuclear weapons so routine that, even if they were aware of real-world scenarios, their training would kick in.[8]

In theory, the president stood at the top of the decision chain, so if the logic held, commanders in chief would only achieve a level of detachment required to make decisions in nuclear crises only if they ran through the procedures regularly. President Eisenhower, and later, President Carter, excepted, they almost never did. Aside from rudimentary information about the war plans and how they'd be executed, presidents of the United States were generally ignorant about the actual mechanics of waging a nuclear war.

Major Oliver North, deputy director of politico-military affairs at the National Security Council, had suggested to Clark that the presidential decision-making portion of Ivy League be held at the White House that year, and not at the Pentagon. North worried about what he saw as a tremendous perception gap between the war plans as written and their capacity to be carried out. He believed that Reagan's inner circle, his political staff, sheltered the president from the realities of strategic decision making. As North told one associate during the planning stages of Ivy League, "The president needs to know what he's going to get himself into."[9]

Traditionally, the Pentagon held Ivy League in conjunction with two others: Nine Lives, which tested the secret continuity of the presidency programs, and Readiness Exercise (Rex), Alpha, which the new Federal Emergency Management Agency (FEMA) used to rehearse the rest of the government's emergency preparedness plans.

For Ivy League, at least three alternate command posts would be tied telephonically into the White House Situation Room. Successor support teams would ride in buses to their contingency locations, and the bus drivers would record the time it took on their stopwatches. Stand-in cabinet members would be relocated to bunkers. Bombers at SAC bases would cycle through their alert phases. The communication links that tied NORAD to the White House, the White House to the Pentagon, the Pentagon to SAC, SAC to NATO, SAC to its airborne command posts, the airborne command posts to nuclear submarines, missile control centers to individual launch modules—all would be involved, tested, stressed.

In late January, George M. Houser, the chief of nuclear exercises in the operations directorate of the Joint Chiefs of Staff, sent North an official six-page summary of Ivy League, a "Notice of a Significant Military Exercise." Houser's intention was to spell out the risks and benefits. Twenty-two command posts across the US, Canada, Europe, and the Pacific would be active participants. In West Germany alone, five separate cells would send inputs to the Pentagon. Ivy League would test every major nuclear and conventional communications network, and all of the backups, too.

"The test of the command structure for a nuclear war will show America's iron resolve readiness," Houser wrote. But secrecy was paramount: the scenario might give hints about how the US would respond in the real world, and their aggressive use in Ivy League would "undermine our stated position, namely, that these would be used solely as a deterrent." Not only might the Soviets glean information about American war plans, but they could also misinterpret the activation of command centers as the pretext for something else.

So too, he added, might the European countries that were part of NATO. At the time, although NATO had secret war plans of its own, they were kept separate from the SIOP, which focused on US strategic assets, such as intercontinental ballistic missiles and nuclear fighter jets primed to fight inside the borders of the Soviet Union.[10] Throughout NATO's history, this disjuncture gnawed at Europe. The Europeans did not know, or could not know, whether the SIOP actually conflicted with the US plan to defend NATO countries in the event of a Soviet or Warsaw Pact invasion. Nuclear submarines, for example, had to designate a certain number of missiles as "SIOP-committed" depending on where they were located at any moment.[11] Missiles already programmed for use in a conflict with the Warsaw Pact would be reprogrammed—and then, depending upon the assignment, given back to NATO. In theory, US war plan writers would make sure that the two did not conflict, but the bifurcation—the product of geography as much as history—fueled perpetual suspicions that the US Air Force in particular saw West Germany as America's nuclear playground. That was why, Houser was implying, the exercise scenario couldn't leak to the public. Within a day of Ivy League's fictional Warsaw Pact invasion, the war game projected the first use of nuclear weapons by the Soviets—the game's pretext for the nuclear decision given to the game's president.[12]

By early February 1982, Ivy League had grown so large, committing more than 1,000 men and women to a top-secret game that would last over the course of several days, that the military started to push back. Planners in the Joint Staff operations directorate didn't want to spare the staff. Ivy League conflicted with an important NATO nuclear release procedures exercise, Crested Cap, and the US Army in Europe couldn't staff both.[13] Privately, some officers applied pressure to colonels who ran the Joint Exercise Staff to create artificialities that would water down the exercise.

The inputs J3 developed for the exercise were so sensitive that Rogers, whom Reagan had personally chosen to be the stand-in president, required a new set of security clearances from the Pentagon.[14]

Within a few days, though, Houser's memo got out. Columnist Jack Anderson obtained it, ostensibly by a DoD official who found it to be warmonger-ish.[15] Within a few days, newspapers across Europe printed maps of the NATO command posts that would be active for the exercise. The Pentagon reacted to the leak with silence.[16]

When Thomas Reed, a former Secretary of the Air Force and director of the National Reconnaissance Office, first reported to the White House for a special assignment in February, North briefed him on the status of Ivy League. Reed asked Clark when the president had last been briefed on the SIOP, the continuity of the presidency plans, the whole nuclear shebang. Clark said he could not remember. More than a few of Reagan's closest aides wondered if he'd ever be able to "push the button."

Clark encountered resistance from image-conscious deputy chief of staff Michael Deaver and other members of the staff when he proposed that Reagan observe the exercise. He had surmised that Reagan, who had no aptitude for settling disputes among the staff, would be impressed if he were invited to take part. He knew Reagan's mind. The president interpreted the world by reaching back to fables, archetypes, old stories; he would remember nothing if you merely discussed it with him. But if you showed him something, especially something with a resonance, "something that had a *thwack* to it," a friend said, he would never forget it.[17]

Clark asked Deputy Secretary of Defense Frank Carlucci to write a letter to the president. Reagan read it on February 8. "Exercise Ivy League provides an excellent opportunity for you to observe SIOP execution," Carlucci wrote. "The exercise provides a basis for understanding situations which impact upon the SIOP decision-making process and follow-on continuity of government problems. I therefore invite you to observe the SIOP decision process from 1845 to 1915 hours on Thursday, March 4th. I am inviting the Vice President to take part in the same portion of exercise by flying in the NEACP."[18]

There was a problem. Reagan would be out of town that week, campaigning for Republican congressional candidates and then taking a few half-days to recuperate in Los Angeles. That trip would not be canceled. Nancy Reagan would not allow it. Since the exercise was spread out over four days, the scenario couldn't be upended at the last minute and the SIOP execution phase be transferred to the beginning. Doing so would undercut the value of Ivy League for everyone except for the president.[19]

So, Clark, Reed, North, and the JCS exercise staff hit upon a compromise. They would do it twice. Once—for fake—with the real president. And then, two days later, for real—with the fake president. The NSC also nixed one element: having the vice president participate from the National Emergency Airborne Command Post itself would be noticed by Soviet intelligence, if not by the US media, and be far too provocative to Europe, and certainly to the Soviet Union.

Right before dinner on March 1, 1982, as the exercising continued elsewhere, Reed, Reagan, his National Security Advisor, William Clark, and several officials from the Pentagon convened again in the Situation Room.[20]

"This is a SIOP briefing," Reed began.[21]

"What does that stand for?" Reagan asked.

Reed looked at Secretary of Defense Caspar Weinberger, who said that he, too, did not know what the initials stood for. Surely they knew what it was—but was it worrisome that they did not know its name?

Weinberger's military assistant chimed in: "SIOP—Single Integrated Operational Plan."

The SIOP was a war plan, but it was more than a war plan: it was *the* war plan; the instructions for directing the US military to fire its nuclear weapons "in one orgasmic thump," a military aide to the president later put it.[22] The commander of the Strategic Air Command (SAC) and the chairman of the Joint Chiefs of Staff had given Reagan the SIOP briefings twice before. He had also instructed on how he would go about choosing the various options the SIOP presented to the president. But to Reed, Reagan's command of the knowledge seemed vulnerable, and neither he nor Clark could recall whether Reagan had ever taken the time to see the SIOP used in the context of decision making during a crisis. That was the main reason why Reed and Clark wanted him to observe the Ivy League exercise earlier in the day. Those first briefings for whatever reasons had not stuck.

"So, we opened the football and said, here's the manual, here are your options, given the stuff that's happening—you can hit Moscow, you can hit the Soviet Union and China, maybe something else," Reed said.

They went over the terminology—still opaque to Reagan—of the SIOP. There were the MAOs (Major Attack Options), the RNOs (Regional Nuclear Options), the LNOs (Limited Attack Options, also called the Selective Nuclear Options), and the withholds—attack these targets but not these targets. The actual targets were supposed to flow from guidance from the president himself, but which, in reality, connected only vaguely to the nuclear policy that the civilians who ran the government had laid out.[23] Depending upon the conditions that an incipient war would be fought within, the SIOP Reagan was working off of was supposedly flexible. It could direct more than four thousand potential permutations of thermonuclear war.[24]

Each MAO, RNO, and LNO had two digits and one letter associated with it. If Reagan wanted to attack Soviet military depots only—this might be a LNO—the handbook would instruct him to transmit this combination—say, "34 Frank"—to his military aide, who would have an open line to the National Military Command Center.

"So, what would happen now?" the president asked.

Reed slid the binder over to Reagan.

"Well, you'd need your authenticator. Do you have your authenticator?"

Reagan reached into his back pocket and pulled out a black wallet. He fished out a thin wedge of plastic, a little thicker than a credit card. It had been in his wallet when he was shot. He flashed a wan smile. "Right next to my driver's license."

———

The card, a "biscuit," in nuclear terminology, was white and laminated. On its face were several eight-digit alphanumeric combinations. So far as the world knew, without these numbers, the entire nuclear establishment could brick.[25] To "authenticate" a nuclear order, an Emergency Actions officer in the National Military Command Center would break open a sealed package containing the same set of codes. Over the phone, he would read the "challenge" code—a code printed on the left of the card—and Reagan would have to read the corresponding "authenticate" code on the right of the card. And that was it. That was how a war would start, or a war would end. This "positive control" was intended to ensure that only the president, or his authorized successors, could direct the start of nuclear war. If the US was under attack, the Emergency Action Plan of the Joint Chiefs of Staff (JCS-EAP) spelled out how the NMCC, if not destroyed, or a surviving command post would find a person who had the proper nuclear authentication codes. The officer in charge would try to contact every name on a list of authorized successors until he found one. That could well have been the vice president or the Secretary of Defense, the two cabinet members most likely to be able to connect rapidly with the NMCC; each had a military aide with a briefcase containing a satellite phone; each had their own biscuits.

The biscuits, however, were merely identifying tools. If the Secretary of Defense directed the nuclear war from the NMCC itself, his identity was not in question and his nuclear authorization would be accepted if no one else above him in the chain—the president, namely—answered the rapidly dialed call with a correct biscuit authentication. The NMCC would assume that the president had instructed the secretary to initiate a nuclear war, but, well into the Reagan administration, the president was not necessary to the chain of command. If he couldn't be contacted in an emergency, he was presumed to be dead.[26]

There was another layer of nuclear subterfuge. The JCS-EAPs spelled out, in vague terms, what would happen *if* a nuclear attack was confirmed and *neither* the president nor any successor could be reached.

For just this very circumstance, the commanders in chief of the Strategic Air Command, of the Pacific Command, and of the European Command were designated as "pre-positioned NCAs." They could fight nuclear wars without any direction, or extra codes, from higher authorities.

Their job was to carry out the nuclear order, but absent one, they were instructed to confirm that an attack was under way, hopefully with complete confidence, and then transmit the war orders they carried. In practical terms, the CINCs were instructed not to assume NCA authority until a nuclear bomb had exploded on US soil.[27]

In real life, would they wait?

General Ellis at SAC had even advocated that the full SIOP be placed aboard the alert Airborne Command Post so that its brigadier general would have maximum flexibility to redirect an ongoing war, if he so chose.[28]

Figuring out what the Soviets would actually do during a war was an exercise in mirror imaging. The Soviet/Orange cell had a few options. The first was a limited counter-force volley: they would launch SLBMs, and then ICBMS, at strategic military targets only,[29] and spare Washington, and its bunkers, and major population centers. It would be the least bad option; it would mean that the US government would be alive and ready to concede, but they would not be able to respond, if the counter-force attacks destroyed all of the "second strike" weapons. Colonel Bill Odom's thinking had found its way into the SIOP. There was no way, unless the Soviets used every single one of their weapons, that they could destroy the entire US ICBM arsenal. The US SLBM force would be intact, and enough ICBMs would be left to allow for a response of some sort. And that, in turn, made the whole exercise of counterforce untenable, because the next targets—cities—would be more visible, and certainly more likely to result in retaliation.[30]

In the Ivy League scenario, an SLBM made it from ship to shore, detonating inside the United States within six minutes. The Orange Cell chose a much larger, more immediate, throw-everything-at-the-enemy "spasm" attack, the contours of which were not immediately known to the game's players. That meant that the NMCC's search for a president or successor could not last longer than a few minutes. Since the players happened to be pre-positioned in the Situation Room, the NMCC could focus on the execution of war orders. But what would have happened if it took *more than* six minutes to find someone a president?

The Pentagon knew that secret pre-delegation rules would have kicked in. First, the CINCSAC (Commander in Chief, Strategic Air Command),

General Ellis, would become the National Command Authority. "That, in my opinion was the most likely scenario in the event of a Soviet nuclear strike, since the US command system was so vulnerable at the time," an air force officer who participated in nuclear planning said later.

If the CINCSAC were able to move to his own alternate command post before SAC headquarters was destroyed, *he* would be acting president. The classified pre-delegated chain of command would devolve from the CINCSAC to whichever general officer was aboard the Looking Glass aircraft, one of which was always in the air. The Soviets could not have directly taken out this command post even if they knew where it was.

If CINCSAC or the Looking Glass airplane did not survive long enough to issue nuclear orders after the first nuclear detonation, which could have been a high-altitude electromagnetic pulse that fried the plane's avionics and knocked them out of the sky,[31] then the other nuclear CINCs would have succeeded, starting with the Commander in Chief of US forces in the Atlantic, then the Commander in Chief of US forces in the Pacific, and then the Commander in Chief of all US forces in Europe.[32] Each would be in his own airplane, with any luck. They'd be in communication with one another, with a bit of additional luck, before the start of hostilities.

How would they communicate among themselves in a post–nuclear war environment? How would they know who was in charge? "The likelihood was high that all of them would have independently acted with the result that any number of possibly contradictory nuclear orders could be floating out in the radio ether," the air force officer said.

After first notification of an incoming missile, "Where would I be?" Reagan then asked Reed. The answer was complicated, Reed knew. The Pentagon would have convened a significant-event conference call before they'd recommend an evacuation; at DEFCON 3, the White House Emergency Plan required the president to leave the White House anyway.[33]

"If you're at the White House, they'd have you scamper into a helicopter, flying to Mount Weather," Reed told him.

Reagan paused.

"Absolutely not," Reagan said. "That's George's job." The vice president,

Reagan said, should go off wherever. Reed told him that, with enough warning, or if there was a sense of impending crises, with any luck, Bush would already be in the air, in an airborne command post.

"No," Reagan continued, shaking his head. "If this ever happens," he told the rest of the people in the Situation Room, "I'm going to be right here."

Which meant, in essence, that Reagan would die in the first wave of attacks. He and Bush would be killed if the attacks came by surprise. Reagan was astonished that the system lacked redundancy and seemed so weak. How could a president make confident decisions about nuclear war, even in advance, if the provisions for his survival were so thin?

So, you wouldn't want to try to escape? Reed and Clark asked Reagan this several times.

No, the president, said. "My job is to stay here to try to solve the problem," Reed recalls him saying.

"I've looked at these systems," Reed told Reagan, referring to the continuity of government arrangements. He knew them from his days as the top civilian in charge at the air force, but also as the senior defense executive in charge of telecommunications. "They're Wizard-of-Oz-like. They won't work."

(In months to come, exercise participants would note the lack of reliable communications as one of the government's most pressing problems.)

Jimmy Carter had recognized the deficiency and had issued a series of executive orders trying to rectify it. The bad news, Reed told Reagan, is that "We aren't moving fast enough. And we're way behind the Soviets."

Reagan had few, if any real friends, but instead, he had a stable of people he trusted, and Reed was one of them. He ran Reagan's campaign for governor in 1976 and had been an advisor ever since. He was also a former director of a big spy agency, the National Reconnaissance Office, and had trained as a nuclear engineer. He knew more about the weapons and their command and control than anyone in Reagan's near orbit.

"Those briefings left a clear impression in [Reagan's] mind," Reed said later. "No one could survive a nuclear war, not the presidency, certainly, and this really bothered him, because he had assumed, as I guess all other presidents did, that he'd have time to think and make a decision about nuclear conflicts, but he realized that not only was the system weak, but that it was set up as if it were going to fail."[34]

Before President Carter's attempt to revise them, the basic plans to ensure the continuity of the presidency could be described in a paragraph: those in the chain of succession were given laminated cards, with a code name and telephone number. In the event of an emergency, it was their responsibility to call the number, tell the White House Communications Agency operator where they were, use their code phrase to identify themselves, and wait for instructions. If they planned to leave the Washington, DC, area, they had to call something named the Central Locator Service and provide a full itinerary.

When Colonel William Odom began his bow to stern review of the SIOP and nuclear procedures, he discovered the desiccated state of the continuity programs, and encountered resistance from the Joint Chiefs of Staff when he tried to change them. A 37-page document, the WHEP—the White House Emergency Plan—spelled out the procedures for safeguarding the first family and presidential successors, identifying surviving successors and for communicating with the surviving military command authorities. Before a foreseeable emergency or after a bolt from the red, federal agencies with critical functions would dispatch three cadres of officials. Cadre A would staff an emergency operations center located at or near the headquarters of the agency. Cadre B would be whisked to the Mount Weather bunker or to an alternate near Olney, Maryland. Cadre C would make their way to one of ten FEMA regional centers. From there, they'd direct local efforts to reconstitute basic government functions. The President would be taken to one of seven hardened relocation facilities in the Washington area, or he'd be raced to NEACP plane, or, if he were traveling out of state, he'd be taken to the nearest military base with secure communications and protection from the effects of a nuclear blast. The WHEP gathered dust for decades. It did not evolve to account for either the new nature of the nuclear threat from the Soviets or the new technology that convinced the nuclear priesthood that a war might not be Armageddon.

Carter's Presidential Directive 58 set up a presidential successor dispersal system, designating key officials in advance for a special 50-person cadre that would form in place around the surviving successor, preserve two-way communication between surviving successors and others in the line of succession and two-way authentication between the surviving successors and the military.[35] Smaller teams, nicknamed TREETOP cadres by the Pentagon, would be transported to other surviving cabinet officers. PD-58 created a new secret intelligence agency called NIESO—the National Intelligence Emergency Support Office—that would allow the CIA to provide the president with critical information if their headquarters in Langley were destroyed. It called upon the Pentagon to study the feasibility of establishing an "anywhere" presidency: what would it take to allow wherever the president was to be exactly where he needed to be? There, he'd be able to manage "the full spectrum of modern warfare, from crisis operations through execution of an initial nuclear exchange and conduct of prolonged nuclear war to conflict termination,"[36] a top Pentagon official told Congress in early 1982. It also changed the system for tracking presidential successors. Before, each successor had to manually notify the Federal Preparedness Agency with their schedules by telephone or mail. After, they were given cards, embedded with chips, that could be tracked from microwave towers. Later, they'd be tracked by Pentagon satellites.

During the Ivy League exercise, Reagan discovered that if the Soviets wanted to decapitate the government, they could. And "we knew that the Soviet Union had made plans for its leadership to survive nuclear war by having them whisked off to a network of secret underground tunnels under Moscow," Oliver North recalled. "But what would our leadership do?"[37]

The classified answer, he knew: the president would not survive. So, the president would pre-delegate nuclear retaliation decisions to the military. Until the presidential successor problem was fixed, the pre-designated NCAs, including the officer in charge of the Looking Glass airborne command post, now had access to the entire war plan, and all the codes needed to execute it.

"I remember Oliver North coming into my office, throwing down some papers, and saying, "We can't have a brigadier general executing the SIOP. That's the president's job." Reed said.

Reed knew that the Pentagon was conducting tests to determine the effects of electromagnetic pulses on electronics and planning a new Ground Wave Emergency Network as a failsafe for contingency communications, but it hadn't made any progress on the most important part of the whole contraption—ensuring there was someone to run it all. He found that the Army's Joint Crisis Management Capability, a quasi-secret agency, had tested building a command post inside a hardened truck, loading it inside a C-130 cargo jet, and dropping it off at a random airfield. The Pentagon set up a Studies Analysis and Gaming Agency to model war games, plan continuity exercises, and provide decision books for presidential successors.[38] The air force's CONSTANT BLUE plan to evacuate presidential successors had half the required resources needed to operate, according to its charter.

There were more practical problems. "Suppose, for example, that the president does not survive the attack, the Vice President has been killed in his helicopter, and the Speaker of the House has collapsed and died of a heart attack. Suppose further that the highest-ranking member of the cabinet who is alive is the Secretary of the Treasury, who had gone out to Wisconsin to give a speech. The rest of our government, the American people, and particularly the military, must be informed that the secretary is now the constitutional President, but it's still too dangerous to announce his exact location. In the absence of normal channels of communication, how does the president assert his authority? How does he stop the war?"[39] Oliver North ran through these scenarios and had no answer for them.

The enormously complicated physics of containing and then sustaining a nuclear explosion had proven far easier to understand and replicate than the technological and human-factor leviathans that arose in the United States and the Soviet Union to harness it. The soundness and reliability of nuclear command and control was largely a myth, a just-so story, designed to give everyone from American voters to their presidents a sense of comfort that the requirements on this side of the globe for mutually assured destruction to work in favor of peace—specifically—an elected president, with accurate knowledge of the world situation, good advice from subordinates, the technical means to transmit a launch order, the mechanisms to carry it out, and the ability to ride out a crisis—exist, pre-packaged in a break-glass alcove somewhere in the White House Situation Room.

The SIOP organized the choices that the president could make at the beginning of a nuclear conflict. Either fire all the missiles, or sit there and take the hit. It was all there, in black and white. This wasn't deterrence *in theory*. It was the real blueprint for Cold War policy.[40] And here's what it told Reagan: It probably wouldn't matter if he memorized the numbers on his authenticator card to save a few seconds worth of decision-making time. It wouldn't even matter if he wanted to surrender. A nuclear war *could not* be won. And not only could a nuclear war not be won, he, the president, would not be there to *lose* it. Pentagon planners could not conceive of a scenario where a United States President would survive the initial salvo of a nuclear war.[41] But the US itself might survive, or enough of it would. What would happen then?

Reagan was reminded of one of the first briefings he had gotten as President. He asked General Ellis of the SAC how many Americans would die under the assumptions of current war plans. One hundred and fifty million, he was told. "For Americans who survived such a war, I couldn't imagine what life would be like. The planet would be so poisoned that the survivors would have no place to live," he later wrote. "Even if nuclear war did not mean the extinction of mankind, it would certainly mean the end of civilization as we knew it."[42]

Yet that day, Reagan was learning that he had no other choices. If nuclear war was inevitable, then so was, he believed, Armageddon. Waging one would be unthinkable. Reagan's aversion to nuclear weapons was no stronger than anyone else's, but as president, nuclear policy was his own. The two choices—kill and then die or simply die—were revoltingly insufficient to him. They fed his religious fears about the imminence of the apocalypse as foreseen in the Bible. Several of his closest aides, including National Security Advisor Bud McFarlane, would conclude that Reagan adopted an urgency about nuclear abolition because he imputed to history a direction that was guided by unseen forces. One of them was Satan; the devil's chosen vessel was the Soviet Union; his chosen instruments: nuclear weapons.[43]

———

By the time of the Ivy League exercise, Reagan had asked for the moon on defense, according to critics. He would get more than the moon. Congress bought into the reality of an invigorated deterrent. Money flowed to hundreds of congressional districts across the country as defense contractors parceled out their production plants to account for optimum American political geography. The MX missile, ostensibly designed to neuter—and therefore provide a measure of deterrent to—the Soviet ICBM threat, got a third of the new money. Nearly $5 billion would reinvigorate the B-1B bomber program, whose jets and missiles were supposed to evade Soviet radar used to detect the older fleet of US fighters. The budget poured billions into research on laser weapons, into stealth technology, into exotic jamming weapons that could blind Soviet sensors, into hardened tanks, precision guidance, and more lethal ammunition.

None of this technology mattered—not the bomber, the missiles, the tech—if the commander in chief had no faith in the system designed to employ them during war. Although President Carter drew attention to this major strategic gap and proposed a framework for thinking about modernization in the context of enduring constitutional government and survivability, the Pentagon generally focused on the part of the problem it knew how to answer: match the Soviets, warhead for warhead, targeting scheme for targeting scheme.

Thomas Reed, the special assistant to the president, had already spent a career in black programs: he had directed the National Reconnaissance Office when even its name could not said be in public; he had designed two thermonuclear warheads; he had run the worldwide defense communications apparatus in the mid-1990s. His challenge for the next several months would take him to parts of the government that even he had never been able to access. But he had a mandate from the president, and doors generally locked tight to civilians were opened.

Reed emerged a few months later with an audacious plan to ensure the survival of the presidency. It fit in with a series of other strategic modernization directives coalescing at this time. The president "had to be secure in the knowledge that the United States would never be decapitated," Oliver North, Reed's project chief, later wrote.[44]

At the very least, Reagan could not negotiate arms control agreements if he believed that any concession would cause his own house of cards to collapse. The less tenable and viable that command and control of nuclear weapons became, the more the president had to rely on brute strength to deter the adversary. There was a direct correlation between the survivability of the presidency and the visibility, the *thickness*, of the deterrent.

There was no way to ensure the survival of the president. "We were not longer going to go with a plan that said, if something happens, go to X. Yes, X is Top Secret, but as soon as the Soviets figure out where X is, they'll put one hundred kilotons there."

Reed's idea borrowed from a concept used by General Curtis LeMay to confuse the Germans who tried to figure out where Americans would bomb next based on where they had bombed before. LeMay decided to assign bombing lines at random, often rolling the dice to choose between one of two courses. Reed had figured out how to apply the principle of randomness to continuity of government. His plan, as he saw it, was the only way, short of nuclear abolition, that the United States government could be expected to survive a protracted nuclear conflict.

By September 1982, Reagan would enshrine Reed's work in National Security Decision Directive 55 (NSDD-55). The document was so sensitive that its title, "Enduring National Leadership," was classified Top Secret. The code name assigned to the project was "Pegasus." NSDD-55 authorized the creation of a "National Programs" office to coordinate continuity of the presidency programs with the White House Military Office.[45] It ordered the Secretary of Defense to appoint a director of the program and seed funding for its projects. A cover office, called the Defense Mobilization Systems Planning Activity (DMSPA) would write and exercise the Pegasus plans, and procure the hardware. A small subcomponent, run out of the White House Military Office would liaise with FEMA and coordinate the execution.

CHAPTER 9

Bogging Down

SECRETARY OF STATE HAIG HAD PLAYED IN PLENTY OF war games, and given the publicity associated with his intervention after Reagan's assassination, he tended to stay away from the rest of them. His plate was quite full, besides. No dove, he found himself fighting a president eager to authorize all sorts of covert actions, sanctions, and economic warfare measures to somehow bring the Soviet system down. At the time, Haig was too far in the weeds to see it, but he had become a fly in the ointment. Reagan wanted things done. He wanted to move against the Soviets. He wanted to reduce NATO and its allied countries' interdependence on the Soviet Union. Clark, for example, had said US policy was to "force our principal adversary, to bear the brunt of its economic shortcomings."[1] Haig got in the way.

Haig smarted from a decision early in the administration to put the vice president in charge of crisis management, which Haig saw as his responsibility. Reagan wanted Bush to manage crises like earthquakes.[2] He was frustrated that Casey, Clark, and Reagan were preoccupied with third-world adventuring, which required lending implied and actual moral and financial support to authoritarian regimes in South America to prevent the contagion of communism. He sparred with the whip-smart, hard-headed US ambassador to the UN, Jeane Kirkpatrick, when Britain decided to fight off an Argentinean invasion of a disputed territory, the Falkland Islands. To Prime Minister Margaret Thatcher, the principle of free choice for the Falklanders was a sine qua non; she was duty bound to defend the integrity of the union.

Thatcher pushed Reagan to provide significant assistance, such as intelligence assets, and even political cover. Kirkpatrick warned that interfering with Argentina's adventurism would set relations back. Haig preferred neutrality, the most difficult of all positions to sustain. His efforts at public diplomacy were messy and failed.

The principle seemed solid: why challenge the Soviets militarily while subsidizing their economy? It fell at odds with the essential interdependence of Europe and Russia, something that Reagan did not like but had no reasonable hope of breaking.

For a month, the allies had been working out a compromise. Haig was its arbiter, and he arguably was about to hand Reagan a major victory. Europe would not help the Soviets with trade credits, thereby reducing cash flows to the USSR; the pipeline sanctions would be eased a bit to allow previously existing contracts to continue. Reagan hated this arrangement. He initially felt "like a mule who is ready to kick." He didn't want to go overseas just to give up its principles "for a harmonious meeting." "What is it worth to go to Versailles? All you get in some jet lag."[3]

In Versailles, Reagan did not press the compromise. It was ignored a week later, too, at a follow-up meeting in Bonn. And when Reagan returned to the United States, he announced he would extend the sanctions. The mule kicked hard.[4]

Britain and France were on a tear about the new sanctions. The White House staff did nothing to implement Haig's compromise. Reagan seemed to ignore his Secretary of State. At the same time, Haig was trying to contain a long-simmering crisis in Lebanon, which threatened to throw the Middle East into a many-sided war.

In late June, Reagan, urged on by Meese and Clark, fired Haig.

"The only disagreement was whether I made policy or the Secretary of State did," Reagan said in his diary.[5]

––––––

In June 1982, the nuclear freeze movement attracted more than a million people to a rally in Central Park. By the end of the year, more than 2 million Americans had signed a version of antinuclear activist Randall Forsberg's original petition. Cities and towns held referendums on the freeze. Polls showed that Americans supported its ideas—a halt to further nuclear weapon development and a pledge not to intervene in spheres outside the country's proper arena—by a vote of four to one.[6] The freeze movement had unified the Catholic Church with every mainline denomination. Fundamentalists who saw the Soviet Union as evil were the only holdouts, and they were outnumbered.[7] Battle lines were drawn. "Peace Toy Fairs" vied with the new GoBots for the attention of children.[8]

At first, the freeze movement annoyed the Reagan administration. But they came to see it as an existential threat to their defense buildup. It presented an alternate version of the world. At the nexus of public opinion and congressional politics, peace was a no-brainer, at least as rhetoric.[9] Congress had approved billions for Reagan's buildup. With the economy on the decline and nuclear brinksmanship on the rise, it became easier to support.[10] Reagan warned that a freeze would render the US "vulnerable to nuclear blackmail." His aides hinted that Soviet communists out of Moscow controlled the movement. Americans did not seem to believe that. They began to support it more strongly.[11] A student at Columbia University, Barack Obama, spoke for many when he hoped that the movement would mature into a campaign against militarism in all its forms.[12]

An ill-timed leak from the Pentagon gave the freeze movement an iron core. In May, a Pentagon official slipped the *New York Times* a copy of a top-secret 125-page draft of Weinberger's five-year defense strategy. Where Jimmy Carter's nuclear directive focused on destroying Soviet command and control nodes as a means of deterring a first attack or controlling escalation, the US warfighting strategy under Reagan was premised on actually fighting—and then winning—a war. The US had to be able to smash the Soviets into submission, repeatedly, through all phases of a conflict, preserving the ability to scorch the earth if necessary.[13]

Correspondingly, the army, navy and air force were called upon to redraft war plans with the aim of decapitating the Soviet leadership in the first stages of a conflict. When the document was made public, Weinberger tried to argue that critics were using semantic games to portray the document as more sinister than it was. But he also had to argue that the US had committed hundreds of billions of dollars to winning a war that, at least in public, the US still insisted could not be winnable and had to be avoided, a war that would "deny the Soviets a victory which we say cannot be obtained by either side."[14]

Reagan had signed off on a top-level umbrella strategy for national security a few weeks earlier.[15] Its premise was: deterrence first, and if that fails, winning a war. Obviously, the US would try to win the wars it was forced to fight. "You show me a Secretary of Defense who's planning not to prevail, and I'll show you a Secretary of Defense who ought to be impeached."[16] Fair enough. "War plans are created for all contingencies. But strategy is more than a woo-woo word, and it encompasses more than just war plans. The reality was that by this time, we had the capacity to fight and win a nuclear war. In the past we hadn't, and now we did. So, we had to make sure all the services built, trained, and equipped their forces to reflect this new reality, and that changed everything," says Thomas Reed.[17] In the past, fighting wars was just a threat.

CHAPTER 10

The View from London

"THE MARCH OF FREEDOM AND DEMOCRACY ... WILL leave Marxist-Leninism on the ash heap of history." With those words, addressed to the parliament of the United Kingdom, Ronald Reagan pivoted toward a radical new approach to deal with the challenges posed by the Soviet Union. He had decided on this approach six months earlier, in the middle of his frustrations over the Siberian pipeline sanctions. There could never be a return to détente. The free world was good, it had the better ideas, and it would take the offense against the forces of evil when it needed to. If the language seemed awkward and moralistic to observers, it was natural to Reagan.

President Reagan and the KGB spy Oleg Gordievsky both set foot in London for the first time that month. Their first memories of the city were probably similar: a tangy concatenation of fumes from unfiltered jet fuel, at Heathrow, and then from the tailpipes of cars that clogged the motorways on the way, for Gordievsky, to Kensington High Street, where he and his family were to live.

For security reasons, Air Force One taxied to a deserted series of hangars at Heathrow where the smell was so overwhelming that security agents covered their faces as they waited for the president to disembark. London was a friendly city, but the Secret Service was nervous. Scotland Yard insisted that they carry no weapons. The Secret Service advance teams ignored them, and brought rifles, grenade launchers, and pistols. These were confiscated. Eventually, an agreement was sketched out. Two members of the Service could be armed, but their guns could only carry six bullets each. The US got around this prohibition by smuggling heavy weapons in the trunk of the presidential limo.[1]

Reagan was impatient with Europe's dithering on economic sanctions, and Prime Minister Thatcher, though not amused by the enormous, royal-like entourage that Reagan brought, found his speech at Westminster Abbey magnanimous.[2] Thatcher might have wished that Reagan had given more attention to her own political problems, and she was not favorably disposed to the United States at the moment, given its floundering approach to the Falklands. Like many, she wondered what policies would give life to Reagan's grand ideas.[3] His speech, widely covered in Europe, received little attention back home.

––––––––

Gordievsky went to work in the KGB *rezidentura*, which occupied its own floor of the Soviet embassy in Kensington. A locked, guarded door opened up to a wide expanse, where junior officers had their desks. The head of the *rezidentura*, Arkady Guk, had his own office, as did a few of the senior officers. The cipher room, which contained communications equipment and safes for highly classified documents, was protected by another lock. There were no windows; the *rezidentura* was encased in steel to protect it from eavesdropping.[4]

He first noticed the paranoia. Gordievsky's superior, Guk, a corpulent vodka drinker given to conspiracies, was an inveterate gossip and saw himself as a rival to the Soviet ambassador, Viktor Popov, whom he accused of being a British agent.[5] To keep Moscow placated, Guk insisted that his officers send a stream of reports back, even if they had nothing to say. Gordievsky watched his colleagues send to Moscow rewritten versions of political gossip items they'd find in specialty British newspapers. Guk bragged to Gordievsky about a CND antinuclear march that had shut down central London a few days earlier, taking credit for organizing it. Gordievsky knew it was nonsense.[6]

The night after his second full day of work, Gordievsky slipped out of the embassy and walked a short while, wondering if anyone was watching him. He dialed a phone number that his handler had given him years ago, in Copenhagen. To his relief and delight, the handler answered. Or—wait—no—it was a voice recording. "Hello Oleg! Welcome to London.

Thank you so very much for calling. We look forward to seeing you. Meanwhile, take a few days to relax and settle in. Let's be in touch at the beginning of July."[7]

A week later, Gordievsky followed instructions, and met his new handler, Jack, for the first time. Jack's real name, Gordievsky later learned, was John Scarlett. The two men bonded. They walked to a safe house nearby, in Bayswater, where the Russian was given the keys to a home that would be his to hideout in if he ever decided that his life was in danger. The initial plan was to meet once a month.[8]

————

On Friday, June 26, 1982, George Shultz, an executive at the Bechtel energy company, was in the middle of an important presentation, in London, a few miles away from the KGB residency. His secretary slipped him a note: George Clark from the White House was on the line. Shultz ignored it; he did not know a George Clark. After the meeting, his secretary corrected herself: it was *Bill* Clark, Reagan's National Security Advisor. The president wanted to speak confidentially with Shultz.

Shultz surmised it might have something to do with Haig's resignation, but he was not sure. When, at the American embassy, he got the president on the line, it took all of five minutes for him to accept Reagan's request.[9] Shultz would of course serve his president as Secretary of State. The next day, he and his wife O'Bie flew the Concorde to Washington, where his Diplomatic Security Service detail and official motorcade waited.

Where Clark was aloof to concerns that the economic policy directives were hurting US businesses, Shultz felt them paramount. Since he had done business overseas with Bechtel, he knew how allies felt about being led around by the nose, and wondered why the US had decided to take direct action without cooperating with Europe. Unless these impulses, fed by hardliners on the NSC and elsewhere, were harnessed, negotiations with the Soviets on everything would be hindered. He did not know what Reagan believed about all of this. But 1983 would be critical for NATO; so long as the pipeline dispute remained front of mind, NATO would be "impossible to manage."[10] As Shultz briefed himself by calling world leaders, he learned how desiccated the state of negotiations between the USSR and the US really were. "The Soviets can't read you," West German Chancellor Helmut Schmidt had said to him. "The superpowers are not in touch with each other's reality."

Shultz found a White House preoccupied by who reported to whom, less engaged on core policy questions and more engaged on how they would be carried out and how they would be seen domestically.

Shultz thought back to a speech Reagan had given at Stanford as a candidate; the best way forward would require "time and will to hold off the Soviet military threat long enough for America to regain its resolve . . . to demonstrate how to use freedom and open markets as the organizing principles for political development, and to do so long enough to allow communism's failures to be fully recognized and play themselves out."[11] Shultz was on board with these principles. He did not think they were sufficient.

———

In July, the Democrats decided that they would run on the nuclear freeze. In August, a nonbinding resolution urging a nuclear freeze failed by one vote in Congress. The Speaker of the House, Tip O'Neill, had warned about the "50,000" nuclear weapons in the world, and instead of decelerating the arms race, "the foot is on the accelerator, and it is getting heavier, and heavier."[12] In November, voters in eight states from Oregon to Michigan gave the freeze a thumbs-up in referenda. The economy was the top issue in the election, but supporters of the freeze picked up more than a dozen votes.[13] The *New York Times* called it the "largest single referendum on a single issue in the nation's history."[14]

A few weeks later, a freeze resolution passed the house. Reagan seethed. But the resolution had no teeth to it. Democrats mustered little in the way of opposition to Reagan's actual defense policies. They gave him almost everything he asked for that year. It was an impressive display of symbolic protest, but ultimately, it was a paper tiger. Plenty in Congress, such as Senator Ted Kennedy from Massachusetts and Senator Mark Hatfield from Oregon, were true believers. They saw parity between the superpowers and a chance to make progress toward peace. Reagan saw a strategic imbalance, the prospect of revenge from frustrated American liberals, and the hidden hand of Brezhnev, and then, when he died, Andropov.[15]

Officially, the president had a vision that went beyond the freeze movement.[16] But if there was to be a peace movement, Reagan wanted to lead it his own way. In Europe, where the Soviet Union had influence (and agents in place), the freeze movement threatened to derail the deployment of the GLCMs and the Pershings. His advisors, looking ahead to the reelection in 1984, worried that it had crystalized concern among some voters about his apocalyptic rhetoric. Fifty-one million American Catholics had gotten a pro-freeze pastoral letter from Catholic bishops before the midterm elections.[17] The largest congregations of American Jews and mainline Protestants favored a freeze.

Reagan was frustrated that negotiations with the Soviets had not borne fruit. But he was still trapped by his obligations to the Single Integrated Operational Plan and the pressure to adjust his policy to fit its constraints. One example: if the Soviets knew that the US would have the ability to degrade its first-strike capacity significantly, "we would greatly reduce the nightmare paralyzing our people," said Arms Control Disarmament Agency chief Eugene Rostow.[18] Rostow knew his audience. Reagan himself was paralyzed by fear of a first strike. He was arguing that the best way to reduce the threat to the US would be to increase the threat to the Soviet Union—the old zero-sum logic that Reagan wrestled with. Reagan felt SALT II was flawed because it allowed the Soviets to build up their ICBM force very quickly.

Reagan's advisors were talking him into endorsing an agreement that would "restore the balance" before agreeing to reductions. By the middle of 1982, Reagan was on track to *increase* the number of nuclear weapons the United States produced. And Leonid Brezhnev was on his deathbed. The Soviets were nervous and provocative. They held aggressive military exercises in June that included live missile launches. The exercises lasted seven days. The DIA's conclusion: the Soviets wanted to send the message that they, too, could ride out a nuclear war.[19]

PART II

TO THE BRINK

CHAPTER 11

1983

IT WAS CRISP AND COMFORTABLE ON JANUARY 1, 1983, and for once, the president could afford to sleep a little late. He was in Rancho Mirage, California, about as far away as he could get from the White House, which suited him just fine. Three years earlier, in Palos Verdes, just a few days before military movers would arrive to take his belongings to Washington, Nancy Reagan noticed that the boxes she gave him were empty. Reagan would not pack. *Why, Ronnie?* The president-elect teared up and told her: "I don't want to go."[1] He would spend as much time away from the White House as possible. California was his island away from the world.

The annual New Year's trip west brought the Reagan presidency to the 200-acre estate in Rancho Mirage, California, that Leonore and Walter Annenberg turned into an amalgam of Shangri-La and Camp David. For twenty years it had been a magnet for men of power and influence, a retreat close to everywhere but in the middle of nowhere. When the Reagans were not in residence, queens, prime ministers, actors, and singers might be. But Annenberg prized the White House visits, even as they transformed his oasis into an armed camp.[2]

So regularly did the Reagans visit that the White House Communications Agency (WHCA) had set up a permanent node, a secure switch that connected the mansion and one of its outbuildings to a microwave site at March Air Force Base, and by buried wire to a satellite transmission facility in Northern California. It was a wise but expensive precaution: when Richard Nixon first stayed at Sunnyvale more than a decade earlier, the phone company was not able to install a temporary circuit in time. For several hours, Nixon's WHCA team waited, with crypto gear and coding materials and no lines to connect them to. Had a war broken out, Nixon would have been useless. In 1983, the WHCA setup was more modern. Digital bits generated from wherever the president happened to be would zip up to an orbiting military satellite, and then from there, pulse down to ground facilities about a dozen miles south of the Pentagon. A hardened cable formed the last leg of the link to the National Military Command Center, where an Emergency Actions controller waited at all times to transmit an emergency war order. The military aides who traveled with Reagan had at least two other means to reach the Pentagon in the event that Reagan needed to start, end, or modify a war, although the communications pathways they had set up were more convoluted, involving contingency microwave towers, airborne command posts, and high-frequency networks that the Soviets always monitored. A satellite phone was never more than twenty feet from Reagan. Even when he rode horseback, his military aide would tuck the nuclear decision handbook into a saddlebag.[3]

On New Year's Eve, Reagan, wearing a festive red sweater vest, had been entertained along with a hundred other guests by a Rancho Mirage neighbor, Bob Hope. Before a lavish meal, the Reagans danced on a floor made of imported Italian marble and posed for a picture with guests in front of one of the Annenberg's paintings, a Picasso or a Van Gogh.[4] He managed an off-the-record stop at the nearby Marriott, where the White House press corps was camping out. They asked about his golf game. "Three pars that day," Reagan told them.

The Secret Service was on alert. The CIA had sent along warnings that Libyans might try to kill Reagan in California. (This threat was perennial, if unrealized.) The budget was coming up, and House Democrats had momentum. Someone had leaked an internal analysis forecasting slower growth in 1983, something Reagan felt obligated to deflect with humor.

"We are always trying to be more conservative," he joked.[5] His own staff was prodding him to make decisions against his own wishes on the economy, and to give in to Democratic desires to cut back on defense, but Reagan resisted, growing more impatient as he read about leaks emanating, he was certain, from liberals burrowed in the Treasury Department and budget office. Unemployment rates had begun to fall, and Reagan's poll numbers had begun to rise again.

"Are you optimistic about a return to arms negotiations?" a reporter had asked him.

"A little," Reagan had said.

———

Leonid Brezhnev had died two months earlier. Some in Reagan's inner circle believed he had been helped to the grave by the KGB, which was eager to install Yuri Andropov into power. At Brezhnev's funeral, Vice President George H. W. Bush found Andropov, who was shorter in person than he looked on television, willing to talk. As an icebreaker, the former CIA director joked to the former KGB chairman that they shared a background in common.[6] (They had both been their respective country's top spy.) Bush did not pick up on the Soviet paranoia about nuclear decapitation. He did note that Andropov seemed to be in less than optimal health. The CIA reported that Andropov had a heart condition, and perhaps, kidney troubles. But the agency predicted that Andropov "would prove to be a formidable adversary."[7] At his predecessor's funeral, Andropov had pulled aside Muhammad Zia-ul-Haq, the president of Pakistan, and threatened to crush him unless he cut off support to the Afghan mujahedeen.[8]

Any public optimism ended on New Year's Day, when the Soviet news agency, Tass, published a broadside against the White House, saying that Reagan alone was responsible for the deadlock in arms negotiations, having adopted a policy that "by hook or by crook" would result in a "unilateral weakening" of Soviet defenses.[9]

On January 17, 1983, Reagan approved a formal strategy for dealing with the Soviet Union. National Security Decision Directive 75 was the product of nearly two years of work by Richard Pipes. Pipes's initial draft called for economic warfare against the Soviet Union. Reagan stripped those provisions out, wary that the document could leak and confirm Soviet perceptions of US imperialism.[10]

Pipes found working with Reagan frustrating. He believed the president shared his basic views of the Soviet system, but he found Reagan often unwilling to endorse them in public or follow through on policies that would put them into place. Reagan would always say that he would not reward Soviet intransigence, but he was given to gestural politics that seemed always to give the Soviets a way to save face.

Pipes blamed Nancy Reagan and the more liberal Michael Deaver for keeping Reagan away from his national security counselors. Pipes had little face time with the president. It did not occur to Pipes that a policy of pushing the Soviet Union to the brink of its own self-destruction was not Reagan's aim. Pipes believed that the mercurial Secretary of State George Shultz was pulling the president too far in the direction of compromise, and that the strong differences of opinion Reagan was subjected to in National Security Council meetings had worn the president out.

Shultz also found Reagan exasperating at times. He had come to see Reagan as a chameleon, often reflecting back the views of the person he had just heard or spent time with. To Shultz, it meant that the process for getting information to the president had a direct effect on what policies the president would endorse.[11] At the same time, Shultz appreciated that Reagan had never told him to stop and had never turned down a chance to make an explicit overture to the Soviets. The end game was the same: direct, face-to-face talks. Sometimes, Reagan seemed too impulsive, even too confident in his own abilities just to talk the Soviets down; at other points, he wondered whether there was anyone over there who would listen. Shultz understood the outcome Reagan wanted and pledged to make sure that when Reagan did talk, the atmosphere would reflect the strengths that Reagan brought to them.

At the end of the month, Reagan made a dramatic proposal to sit down with Andropov, wherever and whenever, to sign an agreement to get rid of all intermediate-range nuclear missiles. That meant the Soviet SS-20s and all the Pershings and GLCMs. Zero-zero was still the policy, so in inviting Andropov "to sign something he rejected," the *Washington Post* noted, Reagan was making a play for public opinion in Europe.[12]

Andropov refused the invitation. The US, he grumbled, barely concealed that its weapons were no longer used for deterrence but were in fact "realistically designed for a future war."[13] From the East German's spies in NATO, he was swimming in assessments showing how, even without the Pershings and GLCMs, even with the Warsaw Pact's bigger army, the West, through technology and gamesmanship, had altered the balance of forces there. He was worried about news from Britain, which had decided to upgrade its four Polaris submarines with new Trident II missiles. France's eighteen land-based missiles were in the middle of getting MIRVed—their destructive power would quadruple.[14] Furthermore, Andropov was developing a style of leadership that alienated the military, which had been used to coercing Brezhnev into making decisions. Andropov liked to be left alone. He did not spend New Year's with Gromyko or Ustinov, as was his custom before he became the head of state. The old spymaster wanted to see every paper, every intelligence report. He delegated nothing.[15]

After Shultz returned to a snowy Washington from a well-received trip to China in early February, Reagan tried again to open a line of communication with the Soviet Union. He wanted to talk. He wanted to know if he, too, could make a trip like that, but to Moscow. Shultz thought for a moment and then told Reagan that, while plausible, even the possibility of a summit would have to be explored gingerly.

Every time he had brought it up before, Reagan replied, somewhat piqued, his own national security cabinet would shut down the idea. (He allowed that he had not helped matters by allowing himself to indulge in rhetoric that was so archly anti-Soviet.)[16]

Shultz said he would shop the idea around and promised to bring Reagan back a plan. He took a few days and then circulated a memo through the National Security Council listing four ideas for direct engagement. The feedback was entirely negative.[17] He found that Reagan "was much more willing to move forward . . . than I had earlier believed." And Reagan was the boss.

Shultz had plans to meet a few days later with the long-serving Soviet ambassador to Washington, Anatoly Dobrynin. Reagan should drop by the meeting, Shultz suggested, and open a personal connection with a man who had Andropov's ear. Knowing that Reagan's aides would go ballistic if they found out, he kept the meeting secret until hours beforehand, when he informed Clark, who was angry, and Deaver, who was ecstatic.[18] Shultz knew well that back channels that went around cabinet agencies were out of fashion, but here, the ends justified the means.

Sneaking the Soviet ambassador into the East Wing would not produce anything like a breakthrough, and was likely to confuse Reagan, Clark thought.[19] Shultz was aware that a number of Reagan's staff forthrightly believed that their boss would be steamrolled in any discussions with the Soviet Union and wanted to keep him at a remove from actual discourse solely for his own protection, a notion Shultz found offensive.

He knew that Reagan had special requirements, just like other political principals, but if he was well-briefed and well-stewarded, he was confident that Reagan could function quite well in the room.[20]

Even Dobrynin did not know of Reagan's plans in advance. He and Shultz had been meeting, in private, in a conference room off Shultz's offices in the State Department, for several months. Reagan was lightly aware of these contacts. Judge Clark was initially kept out of the loop, until Weinberger had mentioned them in a late December cabinet meeting. The Defense Department read into the meetings the intrigue that Shultz and Dobrynin were conspiring against *them*, working to bring an approach for enhanced diplomacy to Reagan. Clark again saw the hands of Deaver and Nancy Reagan, both of whom were getting worried about the 1984 election and knew that Reagan had to be seen to at least try to settle down the world.[21]

Dobrynin had met Shultz less than a year earlier. Initially, the discussions were light and feathery. The two men felt each other out. The Soviet ambassador was not impressed with the former Marine, who did not have a firm grasp on his own administration's arms control policies and did not seem equipped with the nerve to fight against the heavyweights who were always pushing Reagan further away from the table. By early 1983, Dobrynin had come to respect Shultz more, but the American was still a "functionary," a technocrat, who was too "deliberate" and unwilling to push his boss. If America was going to engage with the Soviets on a deeper level, the impetus would not come from Shultz or anyone else; it would have to come from the president.[22]

———

On February 15, over coffee in a private study on the second floor of the White House residence, Reagan took Dobrynin's measure. Dobrynin, then sixty-three, was a large man, with a prominent, shiny forehead that made his facial features seem smaller. His hair was white, betraying the decades of labor that his ambassadorial charm covered well. He listened with widened eyes, betraying nothing. New acquaintances mistook his meditative calm and slow head nods for agreement.

Reagan was direct. He wanted to establish a confidential channel to convey important messages to Andropov, a channel that would function as a valve to release built-up tension. The president said he was mystified that the Soviets assumed that he was a "crazy warmonger."

"But I don't want war between us. That would bring countless disasters," he said. *Do you*—meaning Soviet leaders—*really believe this about me?* Twice Reagan asked this question of Dobrynin.

When the US had a monopoly on nuclear weapons and a much more prosperous economy after World War II, nuclear war with the Soviet Union was unthinkable; so why would the Soviets believe that the US would want to strike now?[23]

Surely, the American people don't want war, and neither do the Soviets, Dobrynin replied. How would Reagan feel if *he* were a Soviet leader and had to contend with a huge rearmament, the expansion of the opposing country's military across the globe, defense spending, and nuclear modernization? "Let me put it bluntly," he said. "We regard the rearmament program now in the United States under way amidst political tension between the two countries as a real threat to our country's security."

Reagan replied that the United States believed that communist ideology was the main threat. He described to Dobrynin the way he saw the Russian system: "It was self-justifying and saw itself as the only viable way. Countries that adopted it would survive; others wouldn't. The US didn't have a legitimate future because it would never embrace the inexorable march toward Marxist-Leninism. The Soviets, meanwhile, could legitimate any military action in any country they wanted, because their view of history was linear and deterministic," he wrote.

The Americans, Reagan said, "believe in our future, and we will fight for it."

To the Russian, the American president seemed well briefed, but not well informed. When Dobrynin took his opportunity to lay out in detail the Soviet position on intermediate nuclear forces, Reagan responded with a sound-bite answer about the threat to NATO countries from Soviet missiles in Europe.

"So, let the delegations keep working," Reagan said.

Dobrynin recalls quoting Yuri Andropov in response: "More deeds, less words." He told Reagan that it would be easier for him as a "newcomer, one who is not burdened with the load of the past, to make a first step, even if it is a symbolic one."

Reagan had just such a gesture in mind.

————

A number of American Pentecostal Christians had been holed up in the basement of the American embassy in Moscow for six years, unable to leave because of Soviet exit restrictions. For years, Reagan had followed their plight, five members of one family, two members of another. In March 1979, when the eighth member of their group found that his own visa was denied, he threatened to detonate a bomb. Soviet security forces killed him. Reagan found inspiration in his story. The Pentecostals, who belonged to the largest religious group in the Soviet Union, had braved a freezing winter to make their way from Siberia to Moscow to plead for their exit visas to the United States. "Détente is supposed to be a two-way street," he said. "Our wheat and technology can get into Russia, so why can't the Vashchenko and Chernogorsk families get out?"[24]

Even though their situation was trivial in the grand scheme of nuclear diplomacy, its resolution would be meaningful to the American public, if not merely to Reagan, the second consecutive evangelical American president. "If you can do something about the Pentecostals or another human rights issue," the president told Dobrynin, "we will simply be delighted and will not embarrass you by undue publicity, by claims of credit for ourselves, or by crowing."[25] Make this accommodation in the name of decency, Reagan was saying, and we'll give you the credit. Dobrynin promised to take the proposal to Moscow.

At the time, though, it was not clear whether anyone was around to receive the message. Less than six months into his tenure as General Secretary, Yuri Andropov had fallen ill. His absence at two Politburo meetings in March was noticed worldwide. The CIA started another Soviet leader deathwatch.[26] The agency had one good source—a friend of a nurse who worked in the clinic that treated Soviet leaders. His kidneys were failing.[27] Kremlinologists kept busy. While Andropov was recuperating, Gromyko, the Foreign Minister, got promoted to a new political post. His main rival, Konstantin Chernenko, a favorite of Brezhnev, was maneuvering for power. But then he disappeared, too, apparently suffering from pneumonia. To the intelligence community, the domestic instability and secrecy left basic questions unanswered: who made decisions about war and peace? Who controlled the nuclear weapons? Was the military orchestrating it all from behind the curtain?[28]

———

On February 27, Margaret Thatcher traveled the short distance from 10 Downing Street to give a talk to her party's youth leadership—the Young Conservatives. Entering the ballroom at the Highcliff Hotel, she was introduced to a number of visitors from the diplomatic core. One of the first hands she grasped belonged to a man with close cropped blond hair and a thin smile—Oleg Gordievsky.[29]

Thatcher knew that Gordievsky was a KGB officer serving under official cover. She did not know, for certain, that he was her most valuable source of intelligence on the Soviet Union. She had been kept in the dark by choice, even though she was an avid consumer of spy novels and curious about the techniques used by Her Majesty's secret services.[30] There might have been a glint of recognition in her eye, perhaps an inchoate sense that Gordievsky was the one; after all, she had read hundreds of pages of transcripts taken from his tape-recorded sessions. She was one of the few to see his reporting in the raw. It would come to her in the form of transcripts slid into red-jacketed folders. Her red box was for regular secret intelligence. The red jackets full of Gordievsky's information were kept in a special blue briefcase.

Gordievsky's reporting instilled in Thatcher a confidence in her dealings with the United States and the Soviet Union. She knew the Soviet leadership trigger points, because Gordievsky had provided a detailed map of them. Her advisors, who read tear-lined reporting that took out the clues identifying Gordievsky as a member of the KGB *rezidentura*, were skeptical, but Thatcher, from the beginning, had faith that the essence of Gordievsky's take was true: Moscow was afraid of a decapitation attack. It truly was a caged bear.[31]

The day Thatcher met Gordievsky, though, she held nothing in reserve. Domestic political pressures trumped, for the moment, concerns about a gathering storm.

Thatcher's relationship with Reagan at that point was ambiguous and occasionally tense. She needed the US to keep a low profile. Like the American public, the British people seemed to be of two minds: they would vote for leaders who promised to take the fight to the Soviet Union, but they would send messages insisting that their leaders support a peace movement, supporting disarmament in the polls, protesting by the hundreds of thousands, reviving the nascent Campaign for Nuclear Disarmament. Half the public feared nuclear war. Seventy percent of Brits blamed US policies for bringing it closer.[32]

The Campaign for Nuclear Disarmament was a formidable political enemy. Its public narrative portrayed Thatcher as a sycophant of Reagan's; one CND poster had them "embracing like Rhett and Scarlett" in *Gone with the Wind*.[33]

Thatcher's government had agreed to buy new Trident II D-5 missiles from the United States in 1982 and fit them aboard the Polaris submarines that served as the UK's nuclear deterrent. That arrangement was not popular. But her leadership in the Falklands War gave her political cover. The upcoming deployments of the GLCMs threatened to upset this favorable balance, especially if the Labour Party's strong antinuclear stance served as an acceptable outlet for their fears.[34]

So, her speech that day tried to buck up Young Conservatives in terms that the British people would find acceptable and did so by using historical analogies that shocked liberal sensibilities. She compared the threat posed by the Soviet Union to the existential destruction that Hitler's Germany had wrought about the UK. "If, in the nineteen-thirties, the Allies had been faced by Nazi SS-20s and Backfire bombers, would it then have been morally right to have handed to Hitler total control of the most terrible weapons which man has ever made?"[35]

"The so-called balance of terror keeps the peace," Thatcher said. "The deterrent has worked—it would be madness to throw it away."[36]

"Many of the one-sided disarmers, don't face up to the logic of their case," she thundered. "They don't suggest that America should give up its bomb. They don't think that's realistic. They suggest instead that Britain should make an individual moral gesture. They want us to disengage from what they call the confrontation of the superpowers and set a moral example."

"Mind you, it's an odd kind of morality which allows you to renounce your own nuclear weapons, secure in the belief that you are protected by someone else's. Evidently the nuclear bomb is too horrific for the British to own, but not too horrific for the Americans to protect us with. So long as they do it from their soil and not from ours. We are to be protected by our allies, but contribute nothing toward that protection. That, a moral gesture? 'Some morality—some gesture.' Some alliance—some friendship."

A Reagan aide thought it was the toughest speech against the Soviets that Thatcher ever made. Shultz, for one, believed it was the strongest argument against a nuclear freeze that he ever heard.[37]

Gordievsky might have appreciated the moral case, but he no doubt felt discomfort. Comparing the Soviets to Hitler was not the way to reduce the tensions he knew were real.

Gordievsky was spending long hours at the residency. The KGB had just updated its list of intelligence requirements to detect NATO preparations for a first nuclear strike, sending a long list of wants and asking the resident, Arkady Guk, to respond by the end of March with a detailed plan to collect them.[38] The deliverables were due in November, before NATO went ahead with the Pershing deployments. The warheads on those missiles could reach Moscow within five minutes, or so the Soviets believed, and the KGB had to have a plan in place to detect the secret preparations that might go into a bolt-from-the-blue attack.

The USSR knew that every American ICBM could be launched within ten minutes of a presidential decision; 70 percent of all US Navy nuclear missiles were on permanent war footing, as were 30 percent of American bombers. These forces did not need to prepare for war. But NATO was different. NATO had to reach a consensus before deciding to use nuclear weapons. Countries would have to agree on an attack. That meant that dozens, if not hundreds, of potential agents would know at least a week in advance about the hour of execution.[39]

According to the new RYAN project's dictates, Guk's thirteen officers had to:

- collect data on where government officials would be taken during a nuclear emergency;

- identify the location of major fallout shelters;
- monitor blood banks to see whether prices paid per pint were rising—a sign (to the KGB) that the UK might be preparing for mass burn casualties;
- keep key government officials under constant surveillance;
- recruit new agents in NATO who would steal war plans for them;
- map the pre-crisis communication system that the British leadership would use in the days leading up to a sudden war;
- identify and target technical personnel who would have to be read in to secret nuclear war plans;
- determine whether churches and banks would be notified in advance, too.

Gordievsky found these micro-assignments absurd. Guk assigned most junior officers in the residency the task of monitoring the movements of every senior British official and had to borrow a colleague's car to begin the assignment.[40]

Every bit of information, no matter how trivial, would be passed on to Moscow, feeding the RYAN computer. "We would report that a new motorway was about to be built, leading from such a place in Bristol to some other place, connecting two ports, places in the sea. And obviously it has a very high strategic significance. To Moscow, it could be one of many first signs for the preparation of a sudden nuclear attack," Gordievsky would recall.

He passed the RYAN requirements memo to SIS's John Scarlett. The SIS updated the CIA in their weekly meeting, though they refused to give the Americans a copy of the document. Protecting Gordievsky was paramount, even if it meant the intelligence the CIA would see was watered down.

At Langley, the CIA's Robert Gates remembers, the early reports given to them by the British about this perfidious Soviet project called RYAN, were anodyne. They were just the lists of war warning requirements. The US had similar lists, too.[41] "No one really paid much attention," he said.

CHAPTER 12

The Evil Empire

THATCHER SPENT THAT SPRING OF 1983 DRAWING
daggers on the Campaign for Nuclear Disarmament. Reagan was similarly
focused like a laser on the United States's potent nuclear freeze movement. It had to be stopped. It could jeopardize Europe's support for the
Pershing and GLCM deployments. Its momentum might even cost him
his re-election.[1]

Richard Cizik watched it all with dismay. He was a young associate at
the National Association of Evangelicals, the largest group of unaligned
churches in the United States, but still a small fish in the sea of hardline
Christian political groups. A graduate of Denver Seminary, he had voted
for Jimmy Carter in 1976 and fell behind Reagan in 1980 after the Soviets invaded Afghanistan and Cizik found Carter's response to be lacking.
He thought Soviet expansionism needed a response, a moral response. He
had watched the massive peace marches and worried that his fellow Christians had lost their compass. But he did not think the president was making the right case. "There was too much of a vacuum," he said. He drafted
a letter to the White House inviting Reagan to speak at the NAE's next
convention, the first week of March. It went out under the name of Cizik's
boss, Robert P. Dugan.

A month later, he received a call from Anthony Dolan, a Reagan
speechwriter and his team's in-house conservative whisperer. Cizik flew
to Washington and met with Dolan over coffee. Cizik hoped the speech
would address the fundamental differences between the two political
systems in a way that helped opponents of a nuclear freeze keep the

faith. The speech should frame the debate as a response to evil, Cizik told Dolan.

Politically, the White House thought the timing was right. When Reagan had addressed Parliament in June 1982, the State Department had cut out words calling the Soviets evil and stripped out sections equating the freeze movement with appeasement. What was left of that speech was well-received but laundered too much, and bleached, and failed to attract much attention domestically. Dolan flipped back through his files and found those phrases.[2] Many went in word for word to the NAE address. Communism "is another sad, bizarre chapter in human history whose last pages even now are being written." Appeasement—a word that was especially sensitive in Britain—was easier on the ears at the NAE convention in Orlando.

Dolan and Cizik would joke that the drafting of the speech went unnoticed by the White House. "The State Department ignored it. They assumed it was just a speech to a bunch of Christians," Cizik said. Dolan, who was Catholic, joked that as "house conservative," he was given the speech, like a dog given some red meat to chew on.

The first draft that Reagan saw had the word *evil* in it seven times.[3] Dolan's boss, Aram Bakshian Jr., loved it. He knew it would make news. One line jumped out:

"So, in your discussions of the nuclear freeze proposals I urge you to beware the temptation of pride—the temptation to blithely declare yourselves above it all and label both sides equally at fault, to ignore the facts of history and the aggressive impulses of an evil empire, to simply call the arms race a giant misunderstanding and thereby remove yourself from the struggle between right and wrong and good and evil."

At once, Reagan was beating back on moral equivalence, calling Communism what it was, signaling to Christians that they had a moral duty to work against the evil of the Soviet Union. He raised the twin specters of appeasement and weakness. Dolan had crafted a gem.

"Senior foreign policy people were not paying attention," Bakshian said later.[4] "I recall reading the speech draft before I sent it on and getting to the 'Evil Empire' reference and thinking, *Now, if I flag this in any way, it's going to get pulled*. But first of all, it *is* an evil empire, what the hell, and if someone up there disagrees or is nervous about it, it's up to them to notice it." As soon as Reagan saw the passage, he approved it. It proved impossible to excise after that.[5] Reagan shaved the edges off of some of Dolan's conservative dog whistles and trimmed some of the allegory. He added a passage about birth control and deleted one about organized crime.[6]

On March 8, Cizik wasn't allowed in the room at the Sheraton Hotel and Conference Center in Orlando. He was too junior, even though the speech was his idea. He found a seat in the press room, next to ABC News's Sam Donaldson. Cizik counted the applause lines—sixteen of them, "thunderous, just thunderous." When Reagan called the Soviet Union the "focus of evil in the modern world," he saw Donaldson's eyebrow shoot up. "That's not in here," the ABC newsman said. Reagan had added the line two days before. That was Cizik's first clue that the president had modified the speech.[7] Reagan had added another line that struck Cizik. Calling the Soviets *evil* "does not mean we ought to isolate ourselves and refuse to seek an understanding with them. I intend to do everything I can to persuade them of our peaceful intent," Reagan said.[8]

Cizik cringed when the Marine Band struck up "Onward, Christian Soldiers" as soon as the speech ended. He wondered if reporters would interpret it as a subtle call for a religious crusade, which was not at all his intention.

It was "the worst presidential speech in American history," thundered historian Henry Steele Commager. The *New York Times'* Anthony Lewis, a guardian of Washington's liberal consensus, termed it "outrageous" and even "primitive." The official Soviet response came through Tass. The speech suggested Reagan "can think only in terms of confrontation and bellicose, lunatic anti-Communism."[9]

In unexpected quarters it was received with joy. Gary L. Mathews, a senior analyst on the State Department's Soviet desk, had long been accustomed to presidents cowering in the face of the banal sins of the USSR: its detention of religious minorities, its harassment of dissidents, its invasion of Afghanistan. The perception that the Soviets were an evil empire was not foreign to the national security bureaucracy, and predated Reagan's coining of the phrase. But even Zbig Brzezinski, Carter's Polish-born Secretary of State, could not bring himself to call the Soviets evil, even as the Soviets persecuted his direct relatives. Thomas Hutson, the consul general in Moscow during Carter's presidency, had seen "so many people adversely affected by this system and said he agreed with Reagan. Arthur

Hartman, the ambassador to Moscow in 1983, accepted the premise, but "what I could not accept was that this would be the sort of language of our discourse with the Soviet Union, I just didn't think as a practical matter that it was going to get us anywhere." Robert E. McCarthy, the press officer at the US embassy, said of the phrase: "It was true, though, one might have picked other words. I don't recall it as a big issue; let me put it that way."[10]

Geoffrey Chapman, a political officer in Moscow, would come across Russians in the provinces who would mention the phrase. "People would ask me about this or that Reagan administration policy and challenge me to justify it. But it was not unusual to come across people who had a certain admiration for the United States. There was a dichotomy in many ordinary Soviets' minds between the American people and the American government: an admiration of and respect for Americans, for our way of life, for our entertainment industry, for the resilience and output of our economy, but a lack of understanding of—indeed outright opposition to—what the Reagan administration was up to."[11]

At dinner shortly after the speech, Nancy Reagan complained to her husband that she thought he had gone too far. "They *are* an evil empire," Reagan replied. "It's time to shut it down."[12]

CHAPTER 13

SDI and Sabotage

THE BALLISTIC MISSILE DEFENSE TEST SCHEDULED for this early February morning was seven years in the making, and the stakes were high. For years, the army had been trying to develop a basic defense against incoming missiles, but the program lacked momentum and the right mix of technology and enthusiasm to move forward. Few scientists thought that a missile could destroy another missile by running into it. The math was too difficult. The technology was not there yet. After six years, though, the army thought it had something decent. And since Congress had appropriated money for the tests, the tests would happen regardless.

An old Minuteman ICBM would be retrofitted with pods that gave out the electronic signature emitted by a Soviet missile. Missileers would launch it into the atmosphere from Vandenberg Air Force Base in Northern California.[1] A short while later, an interceptor missile would launch from the Kwajalein missile range near Hawaii.

When the rigged Minuteman began to track downward on its parabola, having reentered the atmosphere, the interceptor would lock on to the electronic emissions from the target missile, hone in on it, and then explode, diverting or destroying the incoming warhead before it reached a critical altitude or vector.

The US could not, of course, precisely mimic the characteristics of an existing Soviet warhead. And, of course, the test itself could determine only whether a team that had a reliable guess about the trajectory of one warhead—a team that would know exactly when that warhead would launch, too—would be able to aim its interceptor well enough to hit within the immediate vicinity.[2]

The test was not rigged. But it *was* deceptive. If the intercept hit the missile, then, great—the accurate results, when made public by the Pentagon, would demonstrate to the Soviets that the US had advanced its counter-missile program. However, if the missile and interceptor did not meet in the air, a special pod on the missile would initiate a self-destruct sequence if the *miss* was near enough to fool Soviet satellites. Because the Soviets were watching the test from orbits above the Pacific and listening to the unsecured high-frequency radio nets used by the US Army to communicate, they might see the test as a success even if it wasn't. That was the goal.

When the missiles fired that day, the intercept didn't come close to hitting the target. Its infrared sensor failed. Such was the reality of ballistic missile defense.

———

A month and a half later, President Reagan stunned the world, much of his cabinet, and a large part of the Pentagon when he called for a crash program to design a shield to protect the United States from incoming ballistic missiles. It came at the end of a speech on his national security program. Reagan had to find a way to reset the debate in Congress about the defense budget. The nuclear freeze movement had become so potent and Reagan's response to date had encompassed little more than Cold War chest pounding. The speech started defensively: "When I took office in January 1981, I was appalled by what I found. American planes that couldn't fly and American ships that couldn't sail for lack of spare parts and trained personnel and insufficient fuel and ammunition for essential training," he said. Now, though, the country was building a new generation of bombers, and was on track to field a new ballistic missile submarine each year. The army was fielding its Bradley Armored Fighting Vehicles, its first new tanks in two decades, and the navy was growing, too. Reagan said that while he knew that "all of you want peace . . . so do I. I know too that many of you seriously believe that a nuclear freeze would further the cause of peace. But a freeze now would make us less, not more, secure and would raise, not reduce, the risks of war . . . It would reward the Soviets for their massive military buildup while preventing us from modernizing our aging and increasingly vulnerable forces," he said.

Reagan urged his audience to tell their senators and congressmen "that you know we must continue to restore our military strength. If we stop in midstream, we will send a signal of decline, of lessened will, to friends and adversaries alike."

All this was conventional Reagan. What came at the very end of the speech was a Reagan whose voice wasn't often heard: "My predecessors in the Oval Office have appeared before you on other occasions to describe the threat posed by Soviet power and have proposed steps to address that threat. But since the advent of nuclear weapons, those steps have been increasingly directed toward deterrence of aggression through the promise of retaliation." Reagan said he knew of a different way.

"I am directing a comprehensive and intensive effort to define a long-term research and development program to begin to achieve our ultimate goal of eliminating the threat posed by strategic nuclear missiles. This could pave the way for arms control measures to eliminate the weapons themselves. We seek neither military superiority nor political advantage. Our only purpose—one all people share—is to search for ways to reduce the danger of nuclear war."[3]

The ominously named Strategic Defense Initiative was, for Reagan, the way he would untwist the Mobius strip of nuclear deterrence and give himself leverage to negotiate with the Soviet Union. He meant what he said about sharing the technology with the Soviet Union.

He had told the Vatican's Secretary of State, Cardinal Casaroli, in late 1981 that because "there was no miracle weapon available to with which to deal with the Soviets . . . we could threaten the Soviets with our ability to out build them, which the Soviets knew we could do if we chose." Once this dominance was established, "we could invite the Soviets to join us in lowering the level of weapons on both sides."[4] Reagan knew that the SDI would upset the balance of deterrence. That was part of the reason he went forward with the speech.

Americans understood what Reagan intended to do. Their reaction was initially positive, according to public opinion polls conducted by the Republican Party for the White House. The response from hardliners in his own government was negative. Secretary of Defense Caspar Weinberger thought it impractical and a waste of money. Secretary of State George Shultz thought Reagan had been sold a bill of goods on its technological feasibility, and he chafed at having barely been given a heads up. "I didn't think it had been thought through," he said later.[5] Deputy Chief of Staff Mike Deaver thought the SDI would backfire and reinforce the image that Reagan was a warmonger.[6] The high priesthood of nuclear theorists blamed Reagan for gutting the understandings that had kept the peace between the two superpowers.

On a practical level, the SDI announcement temporarily extricated Reagan from the mess the MX missile fight had made in Congress and gave the administration a policy that countered favorably with the nuclear freeze movement. Its chief proponent in the armed services was Admiral James Watkins, the chief of Naval Operations, a Roman Catholic who shared Reagan's visceral mistrust of the mutually assured destruction doctrine.

Watkins became the unofficial apologist for strategic defense, corralling support service by service, starting with his own. To the air force, he noted that SDI would require advancements in launch technology. To the army, he emphasized the power and applicability of so-called third generation weapons using directed energy. To other Reagan advisors, he could be blunt about the politics: the freeze movement required a direct answer. In February, Watkins had given a short briefing to the president; Reagan was so impressed that he asked McFarlane to start writing a speech immediately. Weinberger was present at the meeting, so his protestations at having not been privy to the speech beforehand struck Admiral John Poindexter, then a deputy national security advisor, as a little rich. "Nobody at that meeting said, 'Mr. President, this is a crazy idea.'" The chiefs did not endorse it outright, though, and in retrospect must have assumed that the idea would be fleshed out considerably before it was announced as policy. Poindexter and McFarlane kept the drafts of the speech to themselves and a few others. "We didn't want a lot of second-guessing from that side. It was simply starting an R&D program, so we didn't feel obliged to share drafts of the speech."[7]

The public conversation turned to SDI's practicality, which significantly hurt Reagan's efforts to sell the idea. The near-universal consensus among engineers was that a full shield could not be built, so some missiles would get through. Since that was the case, the shield wasn't really a shield; that it would take tens of billions of dollars and many decades to fabricate the technology to build a partial one was adduced to even by the program's scattered supporters. SDI, one critic said later, was an "instance of exceedingly expensive technology sold privately to an uninformed leadership by a tiny group of especially privileged outsiders."[8]

That group included the physicist and hydrogen bomb designer Edward Teller, who had visited Reagan four times during the past two years and who had given an interview the summer before criticizing the White House for delaying its announcement. Teller had his mind set on one type of defense, one that Reagan would never agree to, but which confused the debate quickly: a nuclear explosion, initiated in space, could be tampered to a laser beam that would destroy a volley of missiles. "Reagan would never, ever agree to a system that used nuclear missiles to shoot down nuclear missiles," Reed said. "But that was the first possibility that everyone saw, so suddenly, people were accusing Reagan of endorsing this new nuclear weapon."[9]

Daniel O. Graham, the former director of the Defense Intelligence Agency, had been a missile defense apostle for years, and had briefed Reagan on the technology in 1980. He became the public face of the SDI campaign, which further discredited the notion that Reagan's intent was peaceful. Graham was also a charter member of the school that regularly inflated the size of the Soviet threat.[10]

Reagan expected initial hostility from the Soviet Union. He hoped that he would convince its leaders over time that he meant what he said about sharing the technology. He believed that the world could not escape the nuclear Damocles sword with some sort of treaty. At least, he thought, a treaty had to be preceded by a technology that would change the calculus.

The American president did not understand how hollow his words sounded to the Soviets. The Americans had leapt ahead of the Soviets in one key way: they had applied technology to warfighting and managed to make the world much smaller. American missiles were significantly more precise than the Soviets'. The Pentagon had, according to Soviet spies, a sophisticated electronic warfare program that, for all the Soviets knew, might be deceiving them. After a period of stasis, the army, air force, and navy were building—just as Reagan bragged—new boats, new planes, and new tanks. Their economy was turning around, too. And then, the Evil Empire...

From his sickbed in Moscow, Yuri Andropov thundered about Reagan's insincerity. He saw the SDI speech as a parlor trick. The decision to go ahead with it had been so closely held in America that none of the Soviet spies, or friendly American journalists, had an inkling of it. Certainly, he had never been briefed about Reagan's long-standing interest in a missile defense shield. It must be a ploy, he told his arms control negotiator, Oleg Grinevsky. Reagan's own criteria betrayed his real intentions: Any system of defense had to be cost effective for both countries to use, and this wasn't. It had to be workable, and no one thought it was. And it had to be physically fortified enough to survive an enemy sabotage effort, and no one knew what it looked like, so that question was unanswerable.

Andropov joked bitterly that Reagan was a dumb actor. Who was the scriptwriter who had invented the SDI theme?

Grinevsky and Andropov's top aide wrote the Soviet's formal reply to Reagan, which ran in Pravda on March 27. "When the Americans build their missile defense system, the Soviet nuclear weapons will prove outdated. But the American nuclear power will still be up to date and efficient. This means that the US is getting an opportunity to get away with the first nuclear strike."[11]

The Soviet response promised "adequate response measures," which Pravda did not outline. If the Americans managed to get a real missile defense operational, Andropov told Grinevsky, then missiles would have to be launched from elsewhere. Andropov's kidneys were failing, but he was animated enough to pantomime the strategy. According to Grinevsky, he raised his right hand and left it hanging in the air. It represented Reagan's American SDI satellites. The Americans would be waiting for the Soviets to launch an ICBM, the Soviet leader said, which they'd interdict from space. He jabbed, mimicking an anti-satellite laser weapon.

"But we'll deliver a strike from here" he said, as his left hand shot up, mimicking a submarine missile arc.[12]

CHAPTER 14

Provocations

ON APRIL 3, V. K. BONDARENKO, THE CAPTAIN OF THE Soviet Victor II attack submarine, K-305, was celebrating his thirty-eighth birthday, somewhere below the surface of the Okhotsk Sea in the western Pacific. Bondarenko and his crew of about eighty had been patrolling the waters off the Kamchatka Peninsula for several months. It had been an ordinary cruise, except for a period of 42 minutes on a month earlier, when they had tracked a US Navy submarine that was using the cover of fishing vessels to avoid detection.[1]

A few weeks after that, Bondarenko received orders from the commander of the Soviet Pacific Fleet. The K-305 was to track the USS *Enterprise*, the nuclear-powered US Navy aircraft carrier, as it crossed the western Pacific on its way to San Francisco. Soviet Navy intelligence expected the *Enterprise* to maneuver along with the USS *Midway* to the 180th meridian, the International Date Line, when the *Midway* would break off and return to its home port.

Bondarenko's sub sailed through a narrow passage called Bussol Strait near Kurile Islands, and in open waters, decided to navigate to a position where he could monitor the rendezvous. The K-305's sophisticated electronic surveillance sensors picked up alarming sounds.[2] The crew opened up their guides to the US Navy and compared the pings and bleeps to the emitter characteristics on file. They matched those of a Spruance-class destroyer—a type of ship not supposed to be in the area. Bondarenko's electronic warfare officers guessed that the Spruance was headed toward the Kuriles.

He shifted course, moving the submarine from the path of the destroyer. Sticking to his orders, he would surface once every four hours to relay information back to the Soviet fleet and pick up new information. Slowly, the intelligence picture filled in. He thought he had picked up an entire carrier battle group supposed to be elsewhere in the world.

At 3:00 a.m. Moscow time, his sonar discovered clear signs of a constellation of US ships. Fusing sonar, radio, and radar returns, he searched for a place to hide so he could track them without being detected. He found a blind spot about 5.5 kilometers behind the *Enterprise* itself. The submarine ran silently from then on out. No radio messages came in or went out. Bondarenko told his crew to grab hold of what they could. There might be bumps and sudden depth changes ahead.

Bondarenko gave an order to ascend to periscope depth to take a picture of the ship. His first officer told him that the camera attached to the periscope had no film. The KGB officer on board was supposed to have the film ready, but he didn't know where it was. Embarrassed and indignant, Bondarenko ordered a ship wide search for simple film. How could they have forgotten something so critical? The Soviet Navy would insist on photographs, or else they might not believe Bondarenko saw what he saw. "A photograph is a document," Bondarenko later wrote. It was proof the job was done.[3]

Finally, a roll was located, and pictures were snapped. Every moment the periscope poked above the water was a moment of potential danger, but that was the job. When the K-305 ascended to periscope depth, Bondarenko saw that the *Enterprise* was being restocked with supplies by a ship to its starboard, cruising next to the USS *Bainbridge*. They were moving slowly, at about 12 knots.

Bondarenko didn't know whether he'd been detected. He got his answer as soon as the *Enterprise* had finished its resupply. The American ship doubled its speed and changed direction.

Bondarenko decided to dive under the *Enterprise* to a depth of 200 meters and watch the carrier from below. He tracked a number of surface ships, but no submarine—and yet—one had to be there, with a bead on the nose of *his* ship, still hidden somewhere in the Barents Sea.

This electronic dance continued for hours. The K-305 would peek up to see what was happening and then dive down and take evasive action.

The picture was jumbled. There were, at times, patterns that matched the sounds of a second aircraft carrier, but there was no way the aircraft carrier could maneuver to that position without its movement being detected.

Bondarenko decided to be bold. He was in open waters, and at periscope depth, he could not threaten the surface ships. He would use his visibility as a deterrent against hostile action. The US wouldn't dare fire at a Soviet ship they could see. That might precipitate war. So, the K-305 stayed at periscope depth for two hours and began to track the communications between the ships.

The ships seemed not to notice him, or care, if they did. He did not know if his ship was still being tracked until, after another period of submersion, he broke the water to find a Sea King anti-submarine helicopter right on top of him.

The helicopter was making tight circles. The Soviet sub was at bull's-eye position. This frightened Bondarenko, but he dared not overreact. "Peaceful times" did not require him to order evasive maneuvers. The Americans had caught him, just as he had caught them. Fair was fair. The sub went back underwater.

"Of course, this was the wrong decision," he wrote years later.

The next time the K-305 was preparing to surface, Bondarenko saw a shadow on the visual display. It looked like a fish, perhaps a dolphin. Bells rang, and lights flashed green and red. He ordered a dive and then silent running. He had nearly crashed right into the bottom of a destroyer.

Ten minutes later, the K-305 popped up for a cautious look. Bondarenko swung his periscope around to find a ship watching him. The K-305's acoustical array had picked up nothing. No sonar. No radar. Had the US developed a silent ship that submarines could not track? No. It turned out that one of his own operators forgot to turn on power after its last period of running silent, another elementary mistake.

For the next few days, Bondarenko monitored radio traffic indicating the imminent arrival of a third carrier, the USS *Coral Sea*, which was steaming toward them from the West Coast. He could see other ships of all types rendezvousing at a staging point—three aircraft carriers and two dozen other ships. They were headed toward the Kamchatka Peninsula. Bondarenko sent a flash message to the Soviet fleet.

He had stumbled into the biggest US Navy fleet exercise of the year,

FleetEx 83. The *Midway*, the *Enterprise*, and the *Coral Sea* were the anchors of a forty-odd conglomeration of ships conducting a massive show of force, involving tens of thousands of sailors and hundreds of aircraft. Although the scope of the exercise was classified, the US Navy had announced the war games beforehand. They knew the Soviets would be watching.

But Bondarenko had the fortune to pop up right in the middle of a highly secret component of the exercise: he had begun tracking the *Midway* as she maneuvered slightly off course, toward the Kuriles. The *Midway*'s mission during FleetEx 83 was to collect intelligence. When the ship reached a designated point off the Kamchatka Peninsula, navy warplanes took off from the deck and flew west, racing across the Zeleny Islands in the Lesser Kurile Ridge, overflying a Soviet naval training base and several of its most sophisticated anti-aircraft radars.[4] Those radars clicked on, and its anti-aircraft batteries warmed up, but it was too late: the navy had caught the Russians naked, and collected valuable intelligence about the radars.

From the Soviet perspective, the enemy managed to approach a crucial and sensitive port, violate airspace, collect intelligence, and fly back to open waters. The Americans had not been deterred from acting provocatively.

For years, the navy and the air force had been conducting similar probing missions in the Arctic.[5] Usually, the United States would send its aircraft to rendezvous points about 100 miles offshore. This type of provocation became habitual and therefore not particularly dangerous. But the Kurile incursion marked the first time the Americans seemed to overfly Soviet territory with warplanes, not reconnaissance planes.[6] Bondarenko did not know what was happening above the waters.[7] Sub captains during these encounters always operated under a veil of ignorance. Americans had, in fact, seen his ship several times. The first encounter was right after their own arrival on April 4, but the report was dismissed: the Americans thought their surveillance equipment had malfunctioned. A ghost sub, was what they called it. Two days later, a navy Intruder plane saw the K-305 raise its mast twice. The next day, after the Sea King helicopter surprised them upon rising, the navy had apparently dispatched a navy surveillance plane to track him, using sono-buoys dropped in the water.

Years later, Bondarenko would conclude that he twice had long windows where he could have attacked without warning: the first, from April 4 to April 6, lasted about 18 hours. The second, on April 6, was for eight hours.

———

The intelligence operation in the Pacific that day was inspired by plans of the architect of the US Navy's new cocksure strategy, the enigmatic and hard-charging secretary, John F. Lehman Jr. A practicing Catholic who liked to chase skirts and drink to excess, a political conservative who hated Communism with a zeal that few of his subordinates and superiors dared try to match, and a close friend to Reagan's National Security Advisor, Lehman came to his job proposing a new strategy to deal with the Soviet threat.[8]

In short, the navy would overwhelm whatever advantages the Soviets found elsewhere. Lehman would rebuild the US naval deterrent, upping its quotient of ships to 600, from a post-Vietnam fleet of 479.[9] The Soviets were vulnerable in the northern Pacific. Lehman and his team believed that navy prowess there would be the key to a new American nuclear strategy.

If Warsaw Pact nations ever invaded NATO, the Soviets should expect the US to decimate the USSR from its west, Lehman believed. He would establish this deterrent by projecting force. The US would own the territory. It would respect the rules when it was convenient and scare the Soviets into submission when warranted. Showing the flag would fuse the peacetime mission of force projection, forcing the Soviets to shift resources to defend the Pacific, with a threatening prewar specter of nuclear defeat.[10]

A protracted nuclear conflict meant more battle platforms; the navy could survive with eight or ten in peacetime, but during a nuclear war, it might need twice that many.[11] Lehman chose James "Ace" Lyons Jr., an aggressive, bluff-calling admiral who shared Lehman's penchant for action, to take command of the 2nd Fleet, based in Norfolk, which included 150 ships in the Atlantic Ocean and an expanse of territory from the Caribbean to Norway. Lehman and Lyons believed that the United States had been too timid for years in its fleet exercises. The last time the US had maneuvered its ships anywhere near the Soviet deep-water ports in the Arctic Circle was 1975—and they were 120 miles from Soviet territory at that time.[12] They stayed south of the North Cape on the tip of Norway; sailing above that point "would be an unacceptable provocation to the Soviets," and cross the informal "tripwire" that kept the two navies apart.[13]

Lyons wanted to send submarines into the Barents Sea through the icy waters between the UK, Greenland, and Iceland—the heavily monitored but precarious gap in the North Atlantic that the Soviets used to send their ships into international waters from the other side of the Kola Peninsula.[14] The Soviets had developed a supersonic precision bomber, the Backfire, for defense; any surface convoy that tried to transit this Greenland-to-UK-to-Iceland (GUIK) gap would face—potentially—a hail of cruise missiles.[15]

In August of 1981, under the cover of a ferocious hurricane in the North Atlantic, Lyons and two carrier battle groups had zoomed through the gap, using sophisticated electronic warfare techniques to confuse the Soviet intelligence systems set up to detect him.[16] Most of the ships had participated in an announced naval exercise called Ocean Safari. The exercise had a special ending. Lyons, blessed by Lehman, would use the occasion to demonstrate to Congress (and to the Soviets) what the new strategy was all about. The National Security Council did not know of the plans in advance, although Lehman would later insist that President Reagan had a general idea.[17]

When Lyons and the fleet reached a point off the Kola Peninsula, they waited. With precise intelligence—they knew when Soviet reconnaissance planes would be down for refueling because of near-real-time transmission of the take from an American KH-11 photo-reconnaissance satellite—they could decide when to twist the knife. Soviet radar beams swept the skies fruitlessly. The US knew the Soviets' precise vulnerabilities.[18] And then, at the right moment, F-14 Tomcats, operating a thousand miles away from the nearest carrier, buzzed the Soviet reconnaissance planes that were looking for them, sending the Soviet military into panic.

And then, in 1983, he did it again. Again, it was successful. Again, it provoked a storm of protests from the Soviets. Lehman found it absurd that his campaign would cause unnecessary brinksmanship. An overflight (or two) of Soviet territory would not pose a risk of war, he believed.

And the navy had done its homework beforehand, he insisted. "We had fairly reliable grasp on the level of risk and of what Soviet reactions to various initiatives we did would be," Lehman said years later. "All the naval exercises in the North . . . running practice strikes aimed at the Soviet Union, submarines operations, deployments of tactical nuclear weapons. This is not done on a blind gamble or a rolling of a dice." He did not deny that it made the Soviets jittery.

CHAPTER 15

Diamonds

SPRINGTIME FOR LEE TROLAN IN GERMANY WAS NOT peaceful. The American and his band of brothers were on their own in Killianstädten, West Germany, hours from a big American base, dealing with threats from leftists, spies, and saboteurs. Germany's antinuclear Green Party counted among its members young Germans who staffed the watchtowers of his base. His German counterpart, Major Frank Schrodter, could not transfer them away simply because of their political affiliation. The base was under siege, almost weekly, its perimeter ringed by students, Catholics, Greens, and occasionally more violent agitators. On one occasion, more than 25,000 protestors filled Killianstädten and marched to the gate of his base, demanding to be let in. The troops on the perimeter politely rebuffed them and gave the children among them candy.

Schrodter was under pressure, too. He announced to Trolan one day that no German troops would shoot protestors, even if they managed to break in to the compound. The Germans didn't want a Kent State. "Frank, I've got only fifteen infantry guys here," Trolan told him. He'd gotten an intelligence briefing that many of the protest groups had been infiltrated with spies—from the KGB, GRU, the Stasi—and would use the cover provided by the political demonstration to create incidents where the Americans might act rashly to protect themselves. Schrodter said he sympathized, but those were his instructions.

Mustering up his hoo-rah, he said: "I tell you what, Frank. That's okay. It'll be okay."

"*Ja?*"

"Ja, Ja. We've been killing Germans for the better part of a century, and we ain't going to stop now."

Schrodter laughed.

Trolan was accustomed to passive spying. It was impossible to cover lines of sight from hills surrounding the base, and the state of the fencing tarp was such that anyone could reach through the barbed wire and grab a handful as a souvenir. At least once a week, the nuclear warheads were taken from their vault, ventilated, and inspected. Trolan assumed that the spies had cottoned to the schedule and were watching, noting the time it took to move the warheads from their rails to the missiles, and preparing violent sabotage scenarios if war ever came.

Trolan took seriously the threat of peacetime sabotage, too. The left-wing, anti-imperialist Baader-Meinhoff gang, which terrorized Germany in the late 1970s, was on the decline, but offshoots remained in the area. When one of its leaders, Christian Klar, had been arrested in 1982, the West Germans found maps of targets, the Killianstädten custodial site among them.

Trolan's site was regularly bombarded with phoned-in bomb threats, too. One coincided with a large protest in April 1983, and Trolan found it scary. The phone in the security shack rang, and the caller had asked to speak to Trolan by name.

A German male's voice warned him that explosive devices had been placed in the nuclear barn. As Trolan transcribed the threat, the man on the other end of the line began to read off a series of digits. They sounded familiar to Trolan, but he didn't know why, until he hung up the call.

He pulled a binder out of a safe and paged through to a list of warheads he had most recently signed for. Parts of the serial numbers matched the mystery digits given by the caller. The caller somehow had access to detailed, highly classified information about nuclear weapons. This was no ordinary bomb threat.

Trolan alerted his security team, which was down-range, and locked down the site. He called headquarters, asking for an EOD team from Hanau. He asked for reinforcements from a Marine contingent based near Stuttgart. Then he punched a button that put him in touch with the major NATO and American military command posts in the world. "This is Captain Lee Trolan, 501st Air Artillery Brigade, Killianstädten. I'm reporting an OPREP 3 Pinnacle. There's been a bomb threat against my site, and the caller knew a partial serial number for one of my nukes."

In military parlance, an Operating Report, category 3—OPREP 3 with the flag word "Pinnacle"—meant that an event had taken place within the past fifteen minutes that could reasonably be expected to require the attention of the president or the secretary of defense if it got worse.

Within hours, the EOD team had cleared the site, but Trolan elected to keep the base on alert. He did not know whether the East Germans or the Soviets or whomever had anything else planned for him. He did not sleep much that year. He often pulled duty seven days of the week for sixteen hours each day.

"The pucker factor was high," he remembered.[1]

———

Five-hundred-and-fifty kilometers away from Killianstädten and its hornet's nest of protestors and spies, the East Germany foreign intelligence service, the Main Directorate for Reconnaissance, or HVA, was on the verge of a coup. A nineteen-year old American named Jeffrey Carney, an air force linguist who worked at an outpost of the National Security Agency's massive mountainous field station near Teufelsberg in West Berlin, stumbled across the border after a night of heavy drinking and a failed suicide attempt.[2] He was out of uniform, and the American and German soldiers manning the exit portal at Checkpoint Charlie didn't give him a second look.

In East Germany, Carney marveled how time had seemed to stop since 1945. At the customs office, he shoved his air force ID under the nose of a young East German conscript. "I want to speak to a representative of your government," he said. *Just like in the spy movies,* he told himself.

He waited for fifteen minutes in a small room. Two men entered. Carney told them he wanted to defect. He even used their preferred term for East Germany—the German Democratic Republic. The men did not seem impressed. Are you with the CIA, they asked him? "No. The NSA," he replied. The men, he recalls, "looked at each other uncertainly but without emotion. They then turned their heads back to me. This is what is commonly known as the Moment."

After "the Moment," he was in. The HVA officers secreted him out by bus to an apartment building. There, he met Ralph, an interrogator, and began to pour out his secrets.[3]

Concerned that he was dealing with a "dangle," a provocateur sent to mislead him, Ralph began to extricate Carney's intentions. *Did he really want to defect just because he disagreed with his government policies? In the West, you could disagree, in public. People disagreed all the time.*

"Well . . . We violate your airspace all the time," Carney said.

Hmm, said Ralph.

"Well, all of these Polish hijackers. We basically encourage them and treat them like heroes. We do all kinds of things, some illegal. And not just here." Carney said he had access to top-secret intelligence reports from the CIA and the NSA from around the world.[4]

Ralph was skeptical.

How did an airman, a linguist, have access to top-level intelligence reports from North Korea and elsewhere?

"Security sucks," Carney said.[5]

Carney told him that these reports showed how the US view of the Soviet Union, repeated *ad nauseum* by its political leaders, was distorted. These reports showed how weak the Communist bloc was, how little their economy was growing, how their defense spending didn't seem to be increasing, and how much difficulty they were having with precision weapons. But there was Ronald Reagan, on television, thundering about the enormous Soviet threat. Something about the whole world was off to Carney.

Ralph asked him if he had access to codes, codebooks, coding equipment the NSA used to decipher the signals from the East Germans and Soviets and also used to ensure that NATO communications were kept secure. Carney insisted he didn't have access to codes. Ralph did not believe him.

A week later, when Carney delivered the first documents to the HVA, Ralph rejected them. "We aren't interested," he said. Carney had provided clear-text decrypts from his own monitoring, which were valuable, he had assumed, because they would give the East Germans a window into their own communications vulnerabilities. But Ralph kept asking about the codes.

Carney concluded that the HVA "was truly ignorant of the mission and capabilities" of the NSA. That meant he was more valuable to them. He was, as he would say, their first agent in place there.[6]

Gradually, Carney and Ralph would come to understand each other's wants and needs. The Stasi gave Carney a Minox camera to take miniature photographs of documents they wanted. The top of their wish list included active war plans, to which Carney did not have access, but also maps showing where NSA had tapped into junction boxes in Berlin, and phone directories. And they gave him moral support. "Every time you cross, you have no idea how many people are out there supporting you, directly or indirectly," Ralph told him.[7]

Carney remembered a conversation he had with an experienced F-16 pilot. The US was always railing about the Warsaw Pact's numerical superiority in the European theater. A lot of aircraft. But it didn't matter a whit. "Because one F-16 can lock onto a whole group of their aircraft over the horizon, launch, and fly away before the Soviets can see us!" he had bragged. "Their pilots will die or be ejecting before they even see our guys on the screen!"[8]

NATO had a huge hidden advantage, it turned out. Using secret electronic warfare programs developed largely by the United States, it could control the air, and with control of the air, it could control the ground. Carney came to believe that American technological advancements were decades ahead of the Soviets'. An intelligence program called CREEK FLUSH had allowed the air force to obtain the electronic signatures of half the air defense radars in East Germany. Another classified program collected the unique emissions given out by Soviet and Warsaw Pact fighter jets. Every measurement and signal was meticulously catalogued and analyzed as part of a program called TROJAN.[9] Its electronic warfare capabilities were worth hundreds of old fighter jets. *A bigger picture was coming together*, Carney thought.

The West's secret advantage over the East lay in its plans to preemptively disrupt the warfighting machines of the Warsaw Pact and the Soviet Union at the first hint of conflict.

———

HVA had two other spies at Teufelsberg. Chief Warrant Officer James Hall, who his handlers nicknamed "Ronny," had volunteered to spy for the

Soviets in 1982, and, in a burst of verve, decided he could sell the same documents to the HVA.[10] Its analysts could put together a complete picture of this new secret world of electronic warfare by fusing Carney's and Hall's information together,[11] supplemented by the stolen documents supplied by a third operative, code named "Optik," who has never been identified.[12]

Wolf's deputy, Horst Männchen, was in charge of signals intelligence, and had his own empire: several thousand employees and twenty different departments. He had plenty of access to West German communications and West German SIGINT secrets—the West Germans were very sloppy about their own security—but strict compartmentalization meant that he knew little of what the Americans were doing. And the Americans ran the show.[13] A liaison to the KGB worked in his outer office.

The HVA often stole secrets they did not share with the Soviets. Among them, according to former CIA historian Ben Fischer, "were NATO assessments of the Warsaw Pact, which contained information the Soviets had withheld from their allies." In his book, published after the fall of the Berlin Wall, the HVA's legendary spymaster Markus Wolf complained that he "knew more about American nuclear strategy" than he did about the locations and configurations of Soviet nuclear weapons in Europe. "Soviet secrecy, he maintained irritated and alienated many otherwise loyal East Germans."[14]

Wolf's crown jewel was Rainer Rupp, code named TOPAZ, then the head of NATO's Current Intelligence Group. An HVA talent spotter had recruited Rupp when he was a student. Rupp found in socialism a path to prosperity for ordinary people. In 1977, he landed a job in the international economics section of NATO and was quickly promoted. By 1983, he had direct access to all ongoing NATO intelligence activities. He knew about the pact's nuclear weapons release procedures. He knew what NATO knew about the Warsaw Pact. Every six weeks, Rupp would service a dead drop with a film canister containing dozens of classified documents.[15]

Werner Grossman, Wolf's top deputy, first learned of Project RYAN in late 1982, from Vladimir Kryuchkov, the deputy KGB chairman and head of the its First Chief Directorate, who told him "he was very worried about an imminent attack of NATO against the Warsaw Pact. He even spoke about the 'imminent danger' that World War III was about to break out."

East Germany would have a leading role in developing the surprise nuclear attack indicators, the RYAN warnings, even though its leaders were skeptical of the premise. "We were asked to draw up a list of indicators that could point toward an atomic first strike," Grossman recalled. "We set up a situation room, where all Western military bases were pinpointed. We recorded all changes in these stations. We were connected to our military Intel-service and to the Moscow headquarters."[16]

Wolf knew that Rupp would contact him if war were imminent, because he had supplied the spy with a covert communication device for use in an emergency. Wolf was never convinced of the utility of RYAN. He thought it was make-work for the KGB. But he passed along RYAN's requirements to his branch chiefs, including Männchen. Männchen's network of eyes and ears paid close attention to the American nuclear weapons sites in West Germany. If NATO was preparing to attack, activity at those sites would be among the first indicators.

Männchen's spies could intercept tens of thousands of phone calls simultaneously and conduct near-simultaneous traffic analysis from the patterns they formed. He controlled more than seventy intercept stations along the border and had hundreds of operatives inside of West Germany, fortified by dozens of disguised mobile signals intelligence gathering vans. The vans could report back to the East using encrypted communications during emergencies. Männchen knew that the Soviet military intelligence had around five hundred covert agents in these denied territories, too, and the GRU Special Forces—the Spetsnaz—had their own signals gathering equipment.

From 1955, when the first nuclear weapons arrived in West Germany, the East Germans, the KGB, and the GRU had worked to decipher the complicated communications procedures involved in releasing nuclear weapons.

By 1983, they had worked out the format for the Emergency Action Messages. They had mastered all the exercise schedules, and the radio transmission formats, too.[17]

On Männchen's orders, they tuned their radios and intercept equipment to one unit that would be a critical link in the decision chain if NATO decided to attack: the 59th Ordinance Brigade—Lee Trolan's unit.

CHAPTER 16

Spy vs. Spy

BY 1983, KEN DEGRAFFENREID, THE DIRECTOR OF IN-
telligence programs at the National Security Council, was spending
almost all of his time on triage. "The US was suffering a hemorrhage of
secrets that, we at least in the intelligence community, judged to be of strategic importance," he said. "It wasn't just good spy versus bad spy. The loss
of American secrets was actually having a strategic effect, in those days,
aiding the Soviet Union and harming the United States."[1]

It would take a decade before the extent of the Soviet and Warsaw Pact
penetration of the United States intelligence apparatus was discovered,
but clues were everywhere. The Soviets had been particularly successful in
penetrating the closed-off world technical intelligence gathering by using
HUMINT—human spies.

Since the mid-1970s, the Hungarians ran a spy ring that operated
from the heart of the US Army in Europe. Its pearl was Sergeant First
Class Clyde Conrad, who had earned the nickname of "Mr. Plans" to his
colleagues, because he knew the various NATO war plans almost by rote.
He saw everything, and for more than a decade, he had passed almost
everything to the Hungarians, including one of the holiest documents:
the US Army Europe's full plan to transition from peace to war, entitled
OPLAN 4012. It included the regular, secret revisions to the NATO General Defense Plan, which gave specifics on everything from the procedure
for launching tactical nuclear weapons to the locations of the beachheads
and firewalls the NATO forces would establish during the first part of a
conflict.

In 1983, Conrad helped the Hungarians in other ways, too. He re-cruited sources from other units, serving as a spymaster to the spies. His most productive protégé was a twenty-year-old army sergeant from Florida, Roderick Ramsay. At that tender age, he was given a supreme responsibility: he was the custodian for top-secret documents for the Army's Eighth Infantry Division, which was deployed across Central Europe. Ramsay provided Conrad with all measures of secrets, for which he was well compensated. But the Hungarians had a fetish: anything nu-clear they'd pay a premium for. In his day job, Ramsay worked closely with the custodians of NATO's nuclear command and control secrets, and slowly ingratiated himself with the crypto techs who worked in the Emergency Action Centers.[2] "These guys—they were the guardians of the PALs, right, the nuclear cookies. . . . I got them to teach me all these different elements of cryptography," he bragged years later. "And then . . . eventually, I was trusted enough to be handed the keying material they stored for destruction because they didn't want to go out in the cold and do it themselves at the fire pit we used for document destruction."[3] All of the blue-chip cipher material went to the Hungarians, who resold it to the Soviets, who could, with a little bit of ingenuity, reverse-engineer the entire tactical nuclear command and control system NATO relied upon in Europe.[4] Once they knew how it worked, and what the format of the messages were, and on what frequencies they were carried, and how the crypto computers interpreted the photons that carried the information, they could inject spoof messages into the system, effectively bricking the entire nuclear enterprise. Whether Ramsay indeed left his base carry-ing items like Sealed Authenticator Systems—"the cookies"—or expired onetime decryption pads can only be conjectured. If he did what he says he did—and the government today believes that he did much of it—the nuclear posture of the United States and NATO and the secret proce-dures used to protect that posture—itself a bulwark of defense against the Soviet Union and their satellites—might have been irretrievably compromised.

Ramsay's identity was discovered years later; in 1983, the CIA and the army knew only that the war plans were compromised. (The CIA had moles in the Soviet military research establishment, who would describe to the CIA handlers the documents presented to them to interpret.[5])

As dangerous as Ramsay was, he wasn't the only—or even the most damaging—nuclear-secret pilferer.

Over the course of seven years, from 1967 to 1975, Chief Warrant Officer John A. Walker turned over some of the country's most significant military secrets to the Soviet Union. When he retired, his friend, Jerry Whitworth, continued where he left off. Walker's motive was money. He spent lots on prostitutes and lots more to try to keep his wife happy. When a woman looked at him crossways, a fellow sailor said, "he would unzip his breeches" in a heartbeat. He was unhappy and erratic, except on his binges. His friends knew this; the navy did not. Walker was nearing bankruptcy.[6] His most valuable asset was his security clearance: Top Secret, with access to cryptologic material. Officially, he volunteered himself to the Soviet Embassy in Washington, walking in under the nose of the FBI, which monitored every movement in and out of the Sixteenth Street complex. (His spying may actually have begun earlier.)[7] But when he did show up in Washington, he brought sample documents, including schematics of advanced submarine systems and diagrams of rotor wire settings for an encryption machine called the KL-47, which protected the US Navy's most sensitive traffic. The KGB resident at the time, Boris Solomatin, knew at once that he was a genuine walk-in. When Solomatin, against all protocol, introduced himself, Walker "didn't say anything about his love for communism or for the Soviet Union. And because of that, he showed himself to me to be a decent man because as a rule, the people who want only money always try to camouflage their real desire. They try to act as if they are ideologically close to us. But Walker did not," he said later.[8]

So important was Walker that Solomatin kept knowledge of his recruitment to only two other KGB officers in Washington. In short order, Walker would leave thousands of classified documents at a dead drop in Virginia, all of which Solomatin forwarded to the KGB's 16th directorate, responsible for stealing enemy communication. Walker handed over war plans, documents describing procedures to relocate politicians in the event of disasters, details about technology the US used to track ships. The Soviets digested all of this hungrily. But both Walker and his KGB handlers knew that his most valuable secrets were the code keys that he regularly stole from the vault he worked in, keys that would allow the KGB to decrypt intercepted traffic.

A few months later, hostile forces intercepted the USS *Pueblo*, an NSA spy ship, off the beaches of North Korea. Cryptologists on board tried to destroy documents and equipment before their imminent capture. But the North Koreans managed to recover something they had probably been tipped off by their Soviet friends to look for: a big, boxlike machine called the KW-7.[9]

To anyone who had never seen it before, the KW-7 looked like a toy telephone operator set. The decryption key, which was the starting point for that day's encryption scheme, was the combination of unique wire settings that operators had to engineer carefully each evening, usually around dusk. Key settings were distributed to cryptologic officers like Walker, who would then distribute them across the fleet. Since the NSA, which made the codes, had no way of delivering new keys daily, and since over-the-air encryption was not yet feasible, months' worth of keys had to be stored in advance.

The Soviets now had a functioning KW-7 machine in their possession. Walker had given them its working schematics. They also had old keys and occasionally new ones, too. Solomatin would later tell an interviewer that Walker "enabled your enemies to read your most sensitive military secrets. We knew everything! There has never been a security breach of this magnitude and length in the history of espionage. Seventeen years we were able to read your cables!" He was not exaggerating. (In 1985, when Walker was arrested, the Secretary of the Navy John Lehman said that Walker's espionage would have given the Soviets a decisive advantage during nuclear war. A former director of the NSA testified in court that Walker's work had "powerful war-winning implications for the Soviet side."[10])

Walker saw his handlers only twice a year. He could not provide daily keys. But if the Soviets had gotten a KW-7 to work on their own, and if they'd figured out the inner workings of the device's encryptor, they might not have needed them. The KW-7's wire arrangement code was replaced by punch cards. The cipher machine was by that time similar to another that the Soviets had in their possession: the KG-13, which was used inside the United States to protect messages from the National Command Authority to the strategic nuclear forces, and to send CRITIC messages—high-priority intelligence bulletins intended for the president—back to NSA headquarters.[11]

In 1982, James Atkinson was an air force cryptographic maintenance technician assigned to the Eighth Air Force and Second Bomb Wing at Barksdale Air Force Base in Louisiana. He was slight, withdrawn, and preternaturally curious. In junior high school, he had taken an apprenticeship with AT&T and learned three computer languages. By age nineteen, he had security clearances giving him access to high-grade Strategic Air Command cryptologic systems.

Atkinson was tooling around with a disassembled KG-13. Hundreds were scattered throughout Europe, linking nuclear weapons depositories with NATO headquarters in Belgium and the Strategic Air Command headquarters at Offutt Air Force Base. The Strategic Automated Command and Control System, or SACCS, was a two-way data communication system of record for America's nuclear missile forces. It handled everything from exercise traffic to nuclear authentication relays from the president. Emergency Action Messages from the National Military Command Center were routinely retransmitted over SACCS lines, as were targeting updates, intelligence indicators, troop disposition assessments, and command platform positions.

SACCS was not designed to withstand the effects of a nuclear war. It was designed to *initiate* one. The latest iteration, which was fielded in 1975 worldwide, ran its data over wires, hard lines, and many of its terminals were secured by KG-13s. SAC had no more secure form of means of communication. Maintaining absolute secrecy was essential. If there was one type of message you don't want the enemy reading, it's the message that gives direction to the nuclear forces.[12]

Each KG-13 weighed about 250 pounds. It had the dimensions and look of a file cabinet with dozens of diodes, switches, and fuses, and dials to modulate the power. A sheath of impenetrable rare-earth metals surrounded it, to prevent eavesdroppers from picking up on emanations from within that could allow spies to sniff up the unencrypted data before it reached the sensitive and classified encryption systems inside of it.

To turn on the encryption, the operator would insert a hard paper card with random square cuts into a built-in reader. That would trigger an electronic cascade of logic gates, and *that* sequence would combine with random electronic noise generated from a special black diode inside. An encrypted data stream would result. To protect the process from an outside source, like a laser, from somehow "reading" the encryption in progress, the NSA hardened the entire case with radio-frequency-deflecting shielding. To protect the inner modules, the NSA made them easy to break if the potted seal that surrounded them was tampered with.

One day in late 1982, Atkinson thought he had discovered a flaw with certain KG-13 variants. It involved the interface of the electronic bits with the material used to conduct power inside the machine. The system was accidentally leaking unencrypted data in the form of electronic noise into the power lines that supplied it. It would be easy for a spy, he wrote, to "place an inductive pick-up on the power lines or master station ground at some distance away" and read the product. Much of it would be garbled, but enough would be clear. And since the KG-13 did not change keys often, it would be easy for a cryptanalyst working for the enemy to read large amounts of in-the-clear text. It looked to him as if the flaw was engineered into the system, not deliberately, but as an artifact of its design.

"The hardware changes made over a twenty-year period had only increased the seriousness of the problem and had not mitigated it," he said.

Atkinson reported the problem to his superiors. They told him to stay quiet. He understood that replacing the machines would be an enormous endeavor and had to be done secretly, lest the Soviets discover that the mainstay of American encryption for twenty years had been compromised. While the NSA worked to fix the problem, the SAC wanted to know whether the Soviets had discovered the flaw and figured out how to beat it, particularly for radio systems that transmitted the ciphered text in the clear—that is, without scrambling, but encoded in different characters.

They sent so-called barium meals—faked or marked pieces of intelligence—through the main SAC communications system that used the KG-13. Sure enough, these "incendiary messages" provoked responses by the Soviet divisions that the US intelligence community regularly watched.

In 1979, Air Force Lieutenant Christopher Cooke sold the Soviets a bundle of top-secret information about the SIOP, ICBM targeting data, flag words, and message formats used to communicate nuclear release instructions. If the Soviets could not read the codes that protected this information, it mattered little whether they had it. But if they had working KG-13 and KW-7 machines, and they had placed taps at the right junctions, they might have been able to read some of the most sensitive secrets of the government before their intended recipients had the chance to decipher them.

The United States managed to recruit a number of spies, although none had access to the codes. Until the end of the Cold War, the US knew little about the massive signals intelligence operations run by the KGB and the GRU. Their longest-serving asset was Dmitri Polyakov, by 1983 a major general in the KGB. His CIA cryptonym was BOURBON. His contributions to US policy were immense during tranquil times, but they shaved billions of dollars off Pentagon research budgets when the American military began to rebuild. Since 1978, a Soviet radar analyst, Adolf Tolkachev had been giving Americans information about the vulnerability of Soviet air defense and interceptor systems.

His detailed knowledge of Soviet radars helped the US build jammers and decoys designed to defeat them. His window into the state of research into high-altitude radar systems allowed the US to develop a laser designed to confuse them. He passed documents about Soviet electronic warfare projects, about MiG-31 fighters and their weaknesses, helping the US "to enjoy almost total air superiority of Soviet-built fighters for decades," according to David E. Hoffman, who read CIA cables describing the spy's accomplishments.[13]

Despite all this information, the US lacked significant political sources inside the Soviet Union. HUMINT was hard, and as an open society, the US was disadvantaged. To compensate, the US had grown giant ears and giant eyes, hoping to solve the problem of nuclear war warning by collecting so much intelligence that a Soviet strategic surprise would be improbable.

By 1983, four Keyhole (KH-11) satellites in high orbit provided continuous near-real-time coverage of Europe and the Soviet Union. Their charged coupling device absorbed reflected photons from the illumination of the sun to provide crisp, detailed, daytime coverage of virtually any target. Codenamed CRYSTAL, each looked like the back edge of a pool cue, as long as a bus, with four broad solar energy panels reaching out to each side.[14] The KH-11 constellation was often used as a taskmaster. When imagery planners received an urgent request from the DIA—tell us, for example, how many missiles are being transported along this road—a cell in the Joint Chiefs of Staff would validate the requirement through the intelligence community, and the NRO would begin to move and focus the CRYSTAL's collection that day. Depending upon their location and on weather, the requirement could be satisfied within twenty-four hours. For Soviet missile launches, two could be programmed to focus on a specific spot, giving imagery analysts, like television directors, two live images to choose from. SIGINT satellite ears collected large volumes of military communications, often from deep inside the Soviet Union. In 1979, the first of several Chalet SIGINT satellites was launched to pick up UHF radio transmissions; they looked like flying soccer fields, and the Soviets had no idea what their intended targets were until years later.[15] The Navy Oceanic Surveillance satellite system called White Cloud would track ships based on emission patterns and even voice prints. The NSA had seventy ground stations across the globe. The navy had tapped two underseas cables that were vital links in the Soviet military communication system. The CIA snuck into East Germany and Poland and planted hundreds of bowling-ball-shaped devices that could detect acoustical signatures from large trucks; they could track the movements of material from Soviet nuclear storage sites. The joint CIA-NSA listening post at the embassy in Moscow kept track of the movements of Soviet dignitaries. The United States had the world wired.

———

If the Soviets went on alert for any reason, the US would know. At the headquarters of the US Strategic Air Command in Omaha, hair-trigger alerts were ordinary. Those manning the battle stations each day knew, to the exact number, what the disposition of the Soviet forces, including how many SS-20 Pioneers—mobile missiles—were out of garrison, what their bomber dispersal readiness pattern looked like, where their submarines were. But SAC, along with the National Military Command Center at the Pentagon, also knew, to the second, how much time they'd have to reach the president. They had his schedule faxed directly, and planners worked with the White House Communications Agency to fix dead spots, like if the president were going to travel in a long motorcade.

Al Buckles flew regularly on the Looking Glass, the 24-7 flying command post missions intended to be a visible deterrent to the Soviets.

Before each shift, he would get into a unique frame of mind. And they practiced, daily.[16] If the Soviets were holding an exercise, each move would be compared to what been done previously, and if US nuclear assets had to be adjusted on the fly, then so be it. Before he flew, he would be given a target package, letting him know which nuclear submarines would be in charge of that day's alert.

The Soviets developed mobile missiles and knew how to hide them from the US reconnaissance satellites. The US, in turn, borrowed satellites used by the Department of Agriculture to count bean fields and figured out how to determine whether earth had been moved recently. They could tell, from extensive computer analysis, where the Soviet mobile missile complexes could go and where they couldn't. That intelligence helped SAC nuclear targeters plan daily coverage patterns.[17]

Around 1980, the Defense Intelligence Agency formed a classified intelligence task force to look for vulnerabilities in the Soviet nuclear command, control, and intelligence system. The contraption the Soviets had built to reconstitute their government after a first nuclear strike was enormous, employing about one hundred thousand. The CIA believed that the main Soviet alternate government facilities were well maintained and kept open, though they detected "bureaucratic difficulties and apathy" among the leaders of the KGB's Fifteenth Directorate, which was broadly responsible for continuity of government and civil defense propaganda. But they knew next to nothing about them.[18] For years, the CIA and NSA had tried to map the architecture of the Soviet civil and military communication network in Moscow.[19] How would communications be re-rerouted? What were the wartime locations of the alternate mobile and airborne command posts? What were the technical vulnerabilities? Any bit of information helped: homing frequencies, gain levels, even message-processing times. In 1981, the Joint Chiefs of Staff asked for a full estimate on the effects of a nuclear attack against Soviet C3 systems. Would a knockout blow be possible?[20] Maybe—but so much of the hardened communications lines were buried underground where no Western intelligence agency could excavate without being observed.[21] CIA officers were sent to trace the suspected route of the line in Moscow using sonar-like carts that resembled lawnmowers, capable of finding tunnels deep within the ground. CIA scientists analyzed soil samples from across the city, and the agency added to its order of battle such formerly mundane but now crucial civil engineering documents as water-table estimates from Moscow's equivalent of a public utility.[22] The NRO orchestrated additional satellite passes of suspected entry points, and back in Langley, analysts recanvassed a cache of Soviet military engineering specs for civil defense bunkers in Moscow that had been given to the agency in the 1970s. They looked for seemingly empty and seemingly randomly placed fields near KGB, military, and political sites—with bushes or abandoned concrete blocks that could be used to hide ventilation shafts. For about fifteen years, the US had known about an enormous public works project that connected the Kremlin bunker with Vnukovo-2, the Central Committee's private airport located 15 kilometers southwest of the center of the city. The cover designation for this line was "D-6." Those who used it called it "Moscow 2." DIA analysts suspected that the underground network traversed the city's biggest college and a university known to train KGB agents (and, therefore, capable of hosting contingency facilities," as well as the graduate university that trained Soviets in generalship and warfare. It also seemed to connect to Stalin's alternate seat of government at Ramenki, an enormous underground cavern that could shelter Soviet leaders from nuclear attack in the 1950s but, like American bunkers, was rendered obsolete by ICBMs.

The D-6 line ran parallel to the first subway line built in Moscow. The CIA found evidence of a second system that bisected the line right near Moscow's Garden Ring Road. It would make sense to layer a secret project underneath a main artery because the continued presence of construction equipment would not be suspicious. This second line supposedly attached itself to the Soviet ABM launchpads that protected the city, as well as an alternate command post for the Soviet General Staff.

In 1982, the CIA estimated that the Ramenki complex alone could house as many as ten thousand civil servants. It was a live facility. And the underground subway seemed to be expanding, quickly, as if the Soviets were anticipating a conflict. The Russian underground continuity line had dozens of nodes, most of them unknown to American intelligence.

The CIA's 1982 estimate identified six confirmed secret subway entry points and, by analyzing patterns of construction, concluded that there were at least a dozen that remained hidden. So wherever important Soviet officials congregated, they could be evacuated underground and taken to command posts elsewhere, easily, and instantly rendering them invisible to American intelligence eyes and ears, which, in any warning of possible war, would focus on finding them.

Those working nuclear strategy worried that the Soviet leadership could, by the early 1980s, survive a decapitation attack while American leaders would be left unprotected. The Soviets, too, began to feel increasingly vulnerable about a decapitation attack. Their system of command and control was centralized. The political leaders would never delegate control of the nuclear apparatus to the military.[23]

When Soviet generals and defense officials were interviewed about nuclear policy after the Cold War, they insisted that a nuclear war plan as such did not exist. The policy—deter the US from attack—was as firm as it could be. The mechanisms were fluid. The war plans themselves could be infinitely flexible and adaptable, the missile easily retargeted by commanders in the field. And so they were. But the authority and ability to use nuclear weapons would never devolve from the grip of the small cadre of men who ran the country.

At the apex was the Soviet version of the National Command Authority—in wartime, the Supreme High Command—the VGK. The General Secretary of the Politburo and the Minister of Defense jointly possessed a set of warning, authorization, and launch codes. The commands would be transmitted through the chief of General Staff to the three nuclear commanders—the commander of the Strategic Rocket Forces, the commander of the Soviet Air Forces, and the commander of the Soviet Navy. The KGB created, distributed, and controlled the elaborate set of codes that fulfilled the ambit of the nuclear release procedures. Without a "permission" command, the General Staff could do nothing; the theater commanders could not launch weapons. The General Staff would then communicate with the nuclear CinCs, who would, in turn, relay commands to the medium-range ballistic missile regiments and the ICBM forces by an automated system called SIGNAL.

In essence, SIGNAL could "turn on" the entire missile system for a certain area, or, if the leadership so desired, it could brick it. In its first iteration, the missileers themselves would be responsible for turning the launch keys. But SIGNAL's computer logic was so advanced that, by the middle 1970s, actual rockets could be launched by pressing buttons in the main Soviet General Staff command post—something the Pentagon's National Military Command Center could never do.[24]

The US focused on creating redundant radio-frequency pathways to transmit emergency war orders that were then decoded by the nuclear-generated units. The Soviets worked on creating redundancies for SIGNAL, for WAVE, the control system used by the Soviet Navy, and WING, for the Soviet Air Force. With a valid permission command, only those weapons designated as viable by an early command—"a preliminary command"—could be launched. In the early 1980s, the Defense Minister possessed one half of the permission command code; the General Secretary possessed the other.

Obtaining information about the Soviet nuclear command and control system was among the highest priorities given to the US intelligence community. It was not lost on the Soviets that Western spies tried to monitor the location of the nuclear-enabled officials at all times. Diversions, with multiple motorcades and "accidental" in-the-clear transmissions, would not be sufficient for counterintelligence purposes. It was still easy for the Americans to figure out the location of at least a handful of these military and civilian officials at all times.

In 1979, the KGB began to supervise and test a new system, called Kazbek, that would allow encrypted voice and data conferencing, would interface with the existing cable system, and could also tap into a high-frequency system for redundancy. It would give the Soviet General Secretary the means to conduct business as normal and confer with his commanders whenever he wanted; it also preserved political control of the nuclear decision architecture. The Soviets were also testing their own version of the US nuclear football, but these would be different: the Chegets, as the Soviets called them, would allow the political leadership to conduct nuclear war wherever they happened to be. Their development was a natural response to fears of decapitation.[25]

The CIA's Moscow station learned from a KGB source about the massive communications upgrade. They studied it as best they could and fed data from observations back to Washington and Omaha, where a team from the NSA and the CIA's Office of Technical Services, supplemented by SAC experts, tried to figure out what it was and how it worked. At some point in 1982, a critical connection point—where the Kazbek system connected to the legacy nuclear direction system—was discovered. Another access—one that tapped into one of the several cables linking Soviet electronic warning system sites with Moscow command posts—was discovered a bit later. It took a few years, but the US was able to "track the Soviet leadership by homing into the signal," a former senior NSA official said.

This intelligence fed into special plans designed to deceive the Soviets into thinking that the world was about to end. Both sides had spent hundreds of millions of dollars on electronic warfare and deception programs by the 1970s. Most were directed at spoofing, or preventing the spoofing, of spy satellites and radar.[26] By 1980, the US had a distinct edge and the confidence that went with it.[27] The year Reagan was elected, the military publicly chartered its first Joint Electronic Warfare Center at Kelly Air Force Base in Texas. In 1981, the Air Force Electronic Security Command inaugurated an offensive electronic warfare unit, the 6910th Electronic Security Wing, and based its operatives alongside nuclear war planners in Germany.[28] The EW doctrine began to morph from tactical to strategic: the US, in secret, was targeting major Soviet command and control networks.[29]

A former intelligence official said that engineers for one project figured out how use a computer and a satellite to generate the radar returns from nuclear bomber flights that didn't exist and convince the Russian early-warning systems that fighter jets were on their way. "[W]e would launch them on the path that would cause the Russian alerting networks to light up and say that we were coming." For frontline forces that would actually make it into the air, the US had developed spoofing mechanisms designed to fool the Soviet radar systems into thinking they were looking at something different than what they were. "It would cause them to doubt whether they were looking at the right airplane or the right missiles or not," the official said. By 1982, electronic warfare specialists began to test them. These "Special Technical Operations" were coordinated by the Pentagon's blandly named Joint Special Studies Group.[30] The JSSG's classified charter: find ways to spoof and deceive the Soviet nuclear command and control system.

One of the most provocative US black programs, at least to the East Germans who received a full briefing on it a few years later, went by the cover term CANOPY WING. US spies uncovered a vulnerability that would render the many Soviet high-frequency communication systems, even ones that could be quickly reconstituted after a nuclear attack, susceptible to sophisticated jamming and spoofing. The army chartered the CANOPY WING in 1982 as a response.[31]

CANOPY WING's goal was to translate the NSA's all-encompassing mastery of Soviet electronic signatures into a weapon that could be used to blind and deafen the Soviet-Warsaw Pact command and control facilities at the outset of a war. One CANOPY WING project built an electronic mock-up of the Soviet C3 facility at Zossen, the command post for all Soviet forces in East Germany, and practiced injecting electronic darts into its tubes. (To ward off this kind of attack, the Soviets dug an underground tunnel from the massive compound to a field some seven miles away and also experimented with backup antennas that hid underground and would pop up if a sensor detected that the primary ones had been destroyed.)[32]

The base of CANOPY WING operations in Europe was the NSA's field station in Berlin. Jeffrey Carney did not have access to CANOPY WING's daily operations, but he would pick up snatches of information about the plans from indiscrete colleagues and then pass them along.

CANOPY WING and intelligence about other electronic warfare programs frightened the Soviets. It suggested that the US was years ahead of them in terms of strategic deception. It suggested, further, that the US was close to achieving actual capacity to fool the Soviets into seeing what the US wanted them to see, which would mean, in essence, that the US could attack first without the traditional signs of warning their intelligence apparatus might pick up.[33] "Viewed in this context, CANOPY WING cut the Gordian Knot of preemption," Ben Fischer, a former CIA chief historian concluded.[34]

The Soviet Union's then-secret Perimetr project, which would allow the high command to bypass human judgment and allow a computer to determine whether the country was under attack and then to retaliate by automatically launching nuclear weapons was designed as a failsafe back in the 1970s, when the US was just barely contemplating the feasibility of protracted nuclear war.[35]

But by 1983, advances in electronic warfare had given Perimetr a new reason to exist. The US had even begun to test some of these new capabilities in highly calibrated exercises overseas.

CHAPTER 17

Green Shoots

IN WEST GERMANY, CAPTAIN LEE TROLAN REMEMBERS the sweating. Temperatures often topped 100 degrees. The stress was acute. "If you asked me then whether I thought we were going to have a shooting war with the Warsaw Pact, that summer, I would have said, yes. There was just too much going on for me not to have that mentality. We had to prepare for war." Every weekend, he had to disperse protests around his sites. The number of nuisance threats seemed to be increasing. Trolan felt his men were not ready. The German recruits were too raw; his MPs, too tired.

He was guarding nuclear weapons with six men for every ten he should have had, working seven days a week. In the past, Trolan would beg his tactical evaluators to ding him on manpower, just to make sure the higher-ups at NATO headquarters or the army saw the reports. A major series of exercises called Autumn Forge, would test the 501st Artillery Brigade's durability. The final exercise in the series was in November. Able Archer. The basic scenario was the same: the Warsaw Pact would launch a massive land invasion. NATO would retaliate with air strikes and repel a thrust through Germany using nuclear artillery, including the warheads controlled by Trolan.

At the time, the Pentagon and NATO told the media that Able Archer was a tabletop nuclear procedures exercise. Germany's political situation dictated this delicacy. And this description was true for most NATO units, which would participate by telephone or ignore it altogether. But Trolan's brigade and the other custodial units would have to act as if they'd gone to war. They'd move their bases to full-alert status. They'd don their wartime gear. They'd practice transferring custody of the nuclear warhead to the West Germans. A Martian (or rival intelligence agency) watching their preparations from the outside would not know whether Able Archer was an exercise or the real thing.

Trolan was not convinced his unit would perform well. He decided to send a direct message to the army: as the commander of the nuclear weapons storage site, he could no longer guarantee its security. " 'Hey, army: our warheads aren't safe,' was basically what I said."[1]

His terse memo got the army's attention. Trolan was promised a fix within days. But reinforcements wouldn't arrive for months. NATO was overtaxed. Its member countries were preoccupied by the politics of the INF (intermediate-range nuclear forces) deployments and under pressure from the United States to display resolve against Soviet belligerence. Those political realities filtered down to Trolan's unit. His older nukes were just not that important; the newer Pershings and GLCMs on the way took priority. So did Reforger.

Reforger was an actual, annual invasion by the US of West Germany, albeit friendly and invited. Because the Warsaw Pact had a large advantage in terms of the sheer size of its ground armies, the United States had to figure out how to get tens of thousands of troops to Western Europe in an emergency. The Return of Forces to Germany—*ReForGer*—exercise, became a mainstay of civic life in West Germany, the most visible military deployments each year. Commanders held ceremonies near bases. Some villages held pageants and fairs for the visiting US soldiers.

With every subsequent Reforger, planners tried to compress the time it took to move troops. The Military Airlift Command, tasked with moving troops and equipment, complained every year about the greater demand on their resources. The Joint Chiefs of Staff burdened them on purpose. Reforger was an instrumental part of NATO's deterrence.

In September 1983, the revised war plan for the defense of Europe, CINCEUR OPLAN 4102, assumed that three-fourths of reinforcements, about one and a half full divisions, would arrive within three days of an immediate deployment order and would proceed to their designated marshaling areas and material sites, which held prepositioned tanks, guns, ammunition, and even MREs (meals ready to eat).[2] The goal would be to stock Europe with at least three full divisions within seven to nine days of the order. Until 1983, that had never been realistically tested before.

———

In May 1983, Hollywood producer John Badham was finishing his movie about a teenage computer hacker played by Matthew Broderick whose curiosity nearly annihilates the earth. *War Games* would premiere at Cannes, find success all over the world, and be nominated for three Academy Awards. Pop culture's auteurs were making money off the prospect of a confrontation between the Soviet Union and the United States.

ABC was preparing a major publicity blitz for a graphic made-for-TV movie about the aftermath of a conflict with the Soviet Union, and it had the attention of the White House. (NBC had done a miniseries, *World War III*, the year before.) The BBC was working on its own apocalyptic production, called *Threads*.[3] Director John Milius had tapped the actor Patrick Swayze to star as the hero of a movie called *Red Dawn*, about a Soviet invasion of the United States. Arnold Schwarzenegger was filming *Terminator*, a movie about a computer-generated apocalypse. A board game called Nuclear Escalation, about when "missiles start flying" after diplomacy fails, was among the highest-grossing of the year.[4] Not to be outdone, Milton Bradley released a sequel to its popular Apocalypse: The Game of Nuclear Devastation.[5] Also that year, the game Gulf Strike, about a war in the Middle East that went global, was seen as so realistic that the Pentagon would ask its author, Mark Herman, to become a consultant.[6] A German band, Nena, released "99 Luftballons," an ethereal song about floating balloons. Antiwar protestors appropriated it, suggesting that its lyrics poetically described false blips on radar screens that could herald a nuclear war. It topped the charts in Europe and was number 28 on *Billboard*'s Top 100 in the United States. On the bookshelves, nonfiction titles *Inside the Soviet Army*, *What About the Russians and Nuclear War*, *Dead Ends*, *Nuclear War in the 1980s*, and the Pentagon's own *Soviet Military Power* were popular. Simon & Schuster published a *War Atlas*. Marvel Comics had just reintroduced readers to GI Joe.

Had consumers of culture been privy to the real battleground at this particular moment, they might have felt as though they were being force-fed vegetables. Ronald Reagan's National Security Council had little direction, and his Soviet policy seemed adrift. Reagan seemed comfortable leaving his advisors with ambiguous instructions. More than once, Alexander Haig had told Reagan that diplomacy was the art of removing ambiguity. Reagan's "habitual cheery curiosity," he wrote, "made it at times difficult to know when he is agreeing or disagreeing, approving or disapproving."[7]

Charles Hill, the executive secretary at the State Department recalled that "Every meeting I ever heard about or saw was a flop. There was no meeting that ever reached any conclusion whatsoever, because every meeting—no matter what the subject was . . . would end in deadlock."[8] For several years, the president's intentions did not always match his words. His words often did not match America's actions. The vacuum empowered rival power centers to snipe at each other, bringing conflicts into the press. Purists on the NSC believed that the State Department, blanching from two and a half years of a more confrontational foreign policy, went out of its way to double-deal with the White House. Foggy Bottom's institutionalists believed, in the words of one Reagan advisor, that his firmness and realism "were merely intransigent and naïveté," and that his policies "were therefore not to be implemented but circumvented."[9]

So the principal job of the National Security Advisor, Judge William Clark, to manage policy had failed. But as a faithful reflection of Reagan's brain, Clark excelled, even though he was skeptical of the direction Reagan wanted to go in. If the boss wanted to negotiate with the Soviets, Clark would find the person who could best help Reagan figure out how to negotiate. Jack Matlock Jr. was the only logical choice.

Matlock, fifty-three, was the US Ambassador to Czechoslovakia. His genial face and wide forehead belied an almost ruthless commitment to his mission; his friends would note that his only anger "tell" was his eyebrows; they would arch when he was about to make a hard point. He spoke fluent Russian, having served as deputy chief of mission in Moscow during the Carter administration. Indeed, he had spent nearly seven years in the USSR, and had a knack for no-bullshit diplomacy that scared and impressed his rivals. He had been asked to take a demotion—he would be the senior National Security Council official in charge of Soviet policy— but Reagan's policy was adrift, Matlock thought, and an able American does not refuse the request of a president.[10]

"For better or worse," Judge Clark told Matlock in late April 1983, "The president has decided he wants to negotiate with the Soviets. No one on the staff knows how to do this. That's your job."[11]

There were green shoots. The Soviets were in the process of releasing the Pentecostal hostages that Reagan spent a lot of time thinking about. The foreign ministry had accepted talks to upgrade the Washington-to-Moscow hotline. They were making small moves on strategic arms reduction talks. The president and Andropov had exchanged workmanlike letters on Afghanistan. Matlock won an early battle by convincing the president to agree to reopen consulates in Kiev, and the Soviets and the US had just agreed to resume cultural exchanges.[12]

"Reagan's thinking was, 'We've recovered our strength, he got his tax cut passed, and now we're going to see if there's a willingness to talk,'" Matlock said. The SDI and "Evil Empire" speeches hadn't poisoned any of these small agreements.

Relative to the past, the substance of the relationship was looking more solid. But the environment could have been a lot better.

———

Averill Harriman, an observer would later write, was that rare human being "who had the support of Roosevelt and the respect of Stalin."[13] The American ambassador who tended to the Allied relationship during the final years before the end of the war in the Pacific and the start of the Cold War, he managed to earn the confidence of every Soviet premier from then on, and was a regular letter writer to Soviet Politburo members and leading culture figures. His identification with the Soviets led to persistent suspicion that he had turned spy, even if not wittingly. Conservatives mistrusted him. But Harriman, in his eighties, had no illusions about the Soviet regime. He clung to his eyewitness view, as he would frequently point out when challenged, that the Soviets used Marxist rhetoric the way that Americans used religious rhetoric, and that Soviet leaders wanted stability above all else.[14]

He had a standing invitation to visit the Soviet Union, and he intended to use it one last time to try to do some good.[15] But he was wary about the mission and worried that his Soviet friends would ask him to explain President Reagan's rhetoric, something he was not well equipped to do.

On May 5, Harriman paid a courtesy call to Shultz, and to a deputy, Larry Eagleburger. Harriman was solicitous, despite being in enormous pain. He had suffered from bone cancer for years, and had hid it from everyone except his doctor and his wife. What would President Reagan like to achieve from my visit? he asked.

"Estimate their desire for a better relationship with us," that's the president's first priority for your meeting, Shultz told him. *Try to figure out what their wants are, their needs are, what the basis is for whatever they request.*

"You know these guys better than anyone else," Eagleburger said.[16]

Reagan, Shultz insisted, wanted a better relationship, but the signals from the Kremlin were contradictory. He told Harriman about the president's secret meeting with Dobrynin brokered by Shultz months earlier: the two-hour visit and the proffer Reagan had made—release the evangelicals and we won't crow.

"Dobrynin has no authority," Harriman said.

Shultz agreed. "But he reports back" to Andropov directly, and doesn't use the Gromyko filter. He's an honest broker—the first honest broker that Reagan had dealt with face-to-face.

Should I tell anyone about Dobrynin? Who knows about it? Harriman asked.

"Take the view that the discussions are not secret. Acknowledge the meetings if asked," Shultz replied. But emphasize, if they ask, that you're there as a private citizen, going to Moscow to get your own sense of their thinking.

"I'll say I'm a private citizen," Harriman confirmed. He said he wanted to "help move the relationship forward."

But he would be asked to square Reagan's rhetoric with his own intercession, as a private emissary on behalf of the American government, he told the Secretary of State.

"I don't know they take all these rough statements," he said.

They take them "hard," Shultz acknowledged.

"I don't know how to explain it to them," Harriman said.

"The Soviets are *not* holding back," Eagleburger interjected. "They called Reagan a liar."

Soviet leaders, Harriman said, had never personally criticized Reagan—only their propaganda machines did.

Safer ground, Harriman suggested, would be Soviet violations of SALT II. Shultz cautioned him not to get into specifics.

Harriman murmured back. "I do wish the president would be more careful."[17]

On Thursday, June 2, Andropov welcomed Harriman and his wife back to Moscow. The ambassador brought a token he knew the General Secretary would appreciate: an autographed photo of Franklin D. Roosevelt, the American president who allied with the Soviets to defeat Germany in the Great War.

There would be no chit-chat that day. Andropov picked up a paper and started to read from a prepared statement.

He knew Harriman was concerned about the state of relations between the two countries. And "there are indeed grounds for alarm," Andropov said. "Forty years ago, Mr. Harriman, you came as ambassador to the United States to the Soviet Union. We were then allies. We succeeded in rising above the differences in our social systems and united in the face of fascists and defended the peace in the world."

"Today, "he continued, "the Soviet people and the American people have a common foe—the threat of war incomparable with that we went through previously. This way may not occur through evil intent but could happen through miscalculation. Then nothing would save mankind."

The current administration, he said, "is moving toward the dangerous red line," with its "military preponderance, speaking ill, and economic and other kinds of harm." The Soviets would not take the abuse Reagan "throws down our throats."

At the end, he asked Harriman for his views.

I cannot speak as a private citizen for the administration, Harriman began.

"That goes without saying," interrupted Andropov.

Harriman agreed that the US sometimes acted in ways that made it difficult for both sides to improve relations. But he insisted that the policy of the United States was not malevolent. He asked Andropov for a message to send back to Reagan—or to the American people. Andropov said he didn't want Harriman to interpret his criticism as a sign that he was unwilling to take steps himself, just that there would have to be reciprocity.

It was Reagan, he told Harriman, who was making one-sided demands and then refusing to act reciprocally. Harriman asked him for a suggestion to make the situation easier. Andropov said he would "think it over."

Harriman left the meeting with a sense that, despite the incredible degree of tension, Andropov was willing to talk.[18]

In early August, Reagan offered Andropov two olive branches. First, he relaxed the embargo on the Soviet oil pipeline, which was easy to do, because the Soviets had almost finished the pipeline despite the embargo. Then, the US signed a new, five-year agreement to sell surplus wheat and corn to the Soviets. ("Farmers were dying for it," Shultz said later.[19]) A week later, the US announced it would renew a long-delayed negotiation on cultural affairs exchanges.[20]

For Shultz, there were minor victories. Maybe they would add up. Maybe they wouldn't. Opposition to each had been implacable for years. Shultz was confounded by the prevailing logic used by many of his colleagues: if Reagan gave the Soviets anything at all, they would sense he was weak and take advantage, somehow, in some way. Nonetheless, he knew where Reagan wanted to go. Shultz had a meeting with Gromyko scheduled for September 8. They would work on a plan to resume aggressive INF negotiations. The superheated atmosphere between the two countries seemed to be cooling.

CHAPTER 18

The Phantom (Part I)

AT MIDNIGHT ON AUGUST 31, A US AIR FORCE BOEING RC-135 heavy jet, whose given mission name was Cobra Ball, made slow figure-eight loops in the international waters off the Kamchatka Peninsula.

A day earlier, a Norwegian signals intelligence unit whose antenna coverage included the Soviet missile test range of Plesetsk had tipped the NSA about a possible launch. From the chatter, it seemed like the Soviets were going to test-fire a SS-25 Sickle missile. It would land, as Soviet test missiles usually did, near Kamchatka.

From the side, the RC-135 Cobra Ball jet looks distinctive, almost like a thick pen with a snub-nose tip. From below, it resembles a Boeing 747. Cobra Ball's high-resolution cameras could photograph the discarded stages of the missile in detail; analysts could figure out, based on "speed, trajectory and rate of fuel consumption" useful information about "warhead weight, guidance systems and the accuracy of Soviet warheads."[1]

Gathering intelligence on SS-25 was critical. The US believed it would become the primary missile fielded by the Soviet road mobile ICBM fleet. It could be launched from anywhere; its three warheads were precise; it could be reloaded, and it gave the USSR a significant second-strike capability. The Soviets had begun research on the SS-25 in 1977, and the US had little information about it.

That night, no missile was launched. The Soviets had long known that their preparations for launches could be detected and often used legerdemain to keep the US off guard. The lumbering RC-135 jet turned back

toward its base in Alaska before midnight, Tokyo time. It landed just after
2:00 a.m.

Forty-five minutes later, a clandestine NSA unit based in Wakkanai,
Japan, noticed Soviet radars in the Kurile Islands "snap on" and report
an unknown intruder in their airspace. A National Security Agency field
SIGINT unit in Misawa, Japan, detected bursts of encrypted communication from regimental air defense posts.[2] The small team at Wakkanai, whose
purpose was to see whether a permanent American presence there could
help upgrade its collection capabilities in the Far East, worked uneasily
with their Japanese counterparts. "Suddenly, an American heard an Sukhoi
Su-15 pilot shout the word "Zapustkal"—"a Russian expression the past
tense for firing a missile," journalist Seymour Hersh would later report.[3]

The NSA team stopped what they were doing and re-racked the au-
diotape. They heard what appeared to be a chase through Soviet airspace
of a large airplane, warnings given, and then the missile fired, along with
the words: "the target is destroyed." So secret was their operation that they
had no way to report to the NSA station in Misawa what they had gathered over a secure line. They gave the information instead to their Japanese counterparts, which delayed its receipt by NSA headquarters in Fort
Meade, Maryland, for hours.[4]

Gennadi Osipovich, a deputy regiment commander for PVO Strany,
the Soviet Air Defense Force, had shot down what he took to be an American reconnaissance aircraft flying under civilian cover that had twice entered Soviet airspace and refused to respond to numerous warnings to leave.

He had taken to the air between the two incursions and raced to catch
up to the plane. He approached it from the front and above; he could not
see its profile. He ordered it to identify itself on the international aero-
nautical emergency frequency, but heard no response. He electronically
interrogated the plane to see if it pinged as "friendly"—no reply from the
computer. He flashed lights at it. The pilot seemed to turn inland. As he
got closer, he swung around behind the plane; at a distance of 250 meters,
he saw the portholes of a Boeing 747.

At night, though, he could not see its silhouette. Osipovich had standing orders to fire on a plane that ignored warnings during the day; he had
to get special permission to fire on one at night. He knew that the US regularly used passenger airplane shells for reconnaissance patrols in Europe,

and he could not fathom how a real Boeing 747, with all of its sophisticated communications and navigation equipment, could wander so far off of its route. Since January, he had scrambled almost daily in response to American reconnaissance planes approaching the territory.

Osipovich fired his guns off the aircraft's stern. Only then did the plane begin to turn away, toward neutral waters. Osipovich was ordered to try to force the plane to land. He radioed that the plane was trying to escape. He was given an order to fire on it. He did. He saw a flash under the keel of the plane and then an explosion near its tail. The porthole lights went out.

"The target is destroyed," he said over the radio.[5] He began to return to his base.

On the flight deck of Korean Air Lines Flight 007, the pilot and first officer did not see the flares. They were not listening to the emergency frequency. They heard an explosion.

"Retard throttles!" the captain yelled.

A computer voice: "Attention: Emergency Descent! Attention: Emergency Descent!"

"Altitude is going up!"

"This is not working. This is not working."

"Manually."

"Cannot do manually.

"Attention: Emergency Descent!"

"Engines are normal, sir!"

"Put our your cigarette. This is an emergency descent!"

"Is it power compression?"

"Put the mask over your nose and mouth and adjust the headband!"

"Tokyo Radio, Korean Air Zero, Zero Seven!"

"Tokyo Radio Korean Air Zero Zero Seven, ah, we, we are experiencing . . ."

Thirty seconds later, the cockpit audio ends.[6]

Ten minutes later, the plane crashed into the sea off Sakhalin Island. The pilots had regained control, somehow, but there is no record of them having made any attempt to communicate further.

To the NSA, it was apparent that the Soviets thought they were firing on an American spy plane. It might have been the Cobra Ball aircraft, or perhaps another, similar jet, on a Rivet Joint signals intelligence mission, the type that PVO Strany had often chased in international waters.

KAL 007's pilots had made a navigation error, which was compounded by a quirk in the way the flight computer calculated its location.[7] These were ultimately immaterial to the crisis that followed.

The crisis response function of the intelligence community snapped on after the first reports came in about the unusual Soviet activity and the missing Korean airliner. The CIA's first conclusions, tentative and appropriately hedged, were based on the intercepts from NSA Misawa. Raw intercepts from one site had to be correlated with raw intercepts with several others. That would take hours. The intercepts from the secret station in Wakkanai wouldn't be ready for at least another twenty-four hours.[8] But policymakers wanted to know what had happened. The CIA's quick take, based on the NSA's initial reporting, was that the Soviet pilot probably knew before firing his missiles he was about to bring down a civilian airliner.

The air force came to a different conclusion. The radar returns showed that the Soviets began to track KAL 007 as it crossed the flight path taken by the Cobra Ball plane. The intercepts did not reveal explicitly that the pilot or anyone else had identified the plane, or had even been asked to confirm the identity of the type of plane beforehand.[9] By 9:00 a.m. on September 1, the head of Air Force Intelligence, Major General Jim Pfautz, was ready to show the Joint Chiefs of Staff a persuasive guestimate on what had happened. His staff had spoken with tanker pilots who had themselves mistaken the fuselages of 747s for RC-135s before, especially if they were underneath them, especially at night. His presentation was not well received, and he did not, to his later regret, push it through the intelligence bureaucracy himself. He figured that its conclusions spoke for themselves, and that the responsible officials would see them and take them into account. Most likely, he figured, the Soviets had panicked and responded based on poor-quality intelligence and made all-too-human errors. The shoot-down had not been deliberate.

Secretary of State George Shultz had been on his Labor Day vacation for approximately twelve hours when he took a phone call telling him that the Soviet air defense force had likely downed a passenger plane. He took it as a gut punch. His press conference, at 10:45 a.m. on September 1, the first given by a US official about the matter, was described by a journalist as "controlled fury."[10] Whatever the Soviets thought they were shooting at, whether it was a passenger plane or even if they did think it was a spy plane, he was revolted that they had decided to fire on it. "Loss of life appears to be heavy. We can see no excuse for this appalling act," he said.

When he heard the news, Oleg Gordievsky knew what had happened. "I said, 'I'm absolutely sure it was shot down by the Russian, uh, the Soviet air force.' And my colleagues all agreed with me. And next day it became clear that it was true."[11]

Arkady Guk returned from Moscow a day later bragging that he had been in the center of all the action and bearing gossip, according to Gordievsky: "It turns out that, out of the six major control stations watching the space, the air and the water, the waters along the eastern coast of the Soviet Union. Out of six stations, four were not functioning. Just because of Russian laxness . . . only two were functioning."[12]

Inside the Reagan administration, policy lines hardened. Weinberger wanted to expel all suspected spies, freeze Soviet assets, and walk out of arms control negotiations. The State Department reflected the id of its boss. This issue was not a bilateral one, something to use to advance a negotiating position. This tragedy was an atrocity. "At State our position was that we should join the world in indignation at what the world was angry about which was the killing of peaceful air travelers," Tom Simons said.[13]

Reagan stayed in California for a day too long. He was lured back to Washington when his political advisors said his absence might become an election-year issue. They formed common cause with younger, ideological aides who wanted the president to return to make an aggressive, uncompromising broadside against the Soviet Union. But Shultz had gotten instructions from Reagan to keep negotiations on track. Reagan wanted the administration to be careful in what it said.

Reagan's relative serenity in the days after the shoot-down puzzled even his harshest critics, who could only conclude that crises somehow brought out his best instincts. Journalist Seymour Hersh would later note in his history of the shoot down that Reagan's decision to stay in California, literally away from the fray, "provided a bottom line for the inevitable bureaucratic infighting about what to do. The administrative apparatus of the presidency with its options, papers and analyses, would be limited to dealing with diplomatic or economic sanctions."[14]

History did not record Yuri Andropov's first response to the disaster. He was in the hospital when the Politburo held its first meeting to discuss the aftermath. Konstantin Chernenko summed up the conclusions of those present: "We should proceed firmly on the basis that this violation constitutes a deliberate provocation by imperialist forces aimed at distracting attention from the major peace initiatives put forth by the Soviet Union." That wasn't just the propaganda line. That was what Soviet leaders present, including Mikhail Gorbachev, and Dmitriy Ustinov, the Defense Minister, had come to believe, despite its improbability.[15] The KGB issued telegrams to its residency, urging them to spread this message. Gordievsky says those cables were ignored.

By September 2, 1983, the NSA's Wakkanai station intercepts had been analyzed. One of them caught the words of another pilot who had scrambled that night. The pilot spoke about his pursuit of an American spy plane, an RC-135. Major General Pfautz had been exactly right in his assessment that the Soviet had confused the aircraft.

"The point is that the National Command Authorities of the United States—before they take any action against the Soviets—have to go look at the forces," Pfautz said later. "What is the likelihood that the Soviets would deliberately shoot down a civilian airplane without any forces on alert, any forces keyed? The Soviets are just like we are, with junior officers on duty . . . were working on edge, scared to death."[16]

At 2:00 p.m. ET on September 1, CIA Director William Casey briefed a simmering White House on the available KAL 007 intelligence. The pilot had pulled next to the aircraft—he said so himself—and so there was no way he couldn't know what he was shooting at. An air force general made a cursory effort to suggest that maybe the Soviets had gotten the track confused with the American spy plane. Casey dismissed this idea, saying that the timing didn't match up. He did not seem to understand that the opposite was true. The timing matched exactly.[17]

On Friday, September 5, President Reagan called the shoot-down a "crime against humanity."

Like a news anchor, he introduced an excerpt from the NSA's Misawa intercepts. They played as the camera stayed on Reagan's grave face. Those watching heard grainy voices speaking in Russian. There was no translation given.

"Those were the voices of the Soviet pilots," Reagan continued. "In this tape, the pilot who fired the missile describes his search for what he calls the target. He reports he has it in sight; indeed, he pulls up to within about a mile of the Korean plane, mentions its flashing strobe light and that its navigation lights are on. He then reports he's reducing speed to get behind the airliner, gives his distance from the plane at various points in this maneuver, and finally announces what can only be called the Korean Airline Massacre. He says he has locked on the radar, which aims his missiles, has launched those missiles, the target has been destroyed, and he is breaking off the attack."[18]

American journalists have interviewed Gennadi Osipovich a number of times about the moments before he pulled the trigger. Two parts of his story are consistent. He says his ground commander never asked him whether he had visually identified the aircraft as a 747, and he insists that he was pretty sure, although not certain, that it was. What was in his mind, he said, was a pattern of previous provocations from Americans. And he had his orders.

The Soviet general staff knew two facts. One: the radars that tracked the Korean Airliner had also tracked the RC-135 from the same x in the sky earlier in the evening. Two: there was no evidence in the cockpit recordings they had that Osipovich knew he was shooting at a civilian airliner, and plenty of evidence that other pilots thought they were chasing a spy plane. They then observed two immediate American responses: the insistence, based on secret intelligence, that the spy plane had nothing to do with the passenger plane *and* the promise of indisputable evidence that the targeting of a passenger plane was deliberate.

From the Soviet perspective, it *was* hard to imagine a passenger airliner going so far off course. Another, more logical conclusion: the evidence put out by the Americans was faked. And if the Americans were presenting fake evidence to the world as fact—something the Americans rarely did (this, even the Soviet leadership admitted)—it became likely that the entire incident was a fabrication designed to torment the Soviet Union and put the Americans into a dominant position.[19]

Paul M. Cleveland, the deputy chief of mission at the US embassy in Seoul, spent the first few days trying to fill in the blanks. "In a few days, President Reagan took to the airwaves blasting the Soviet action in his characteristically 'Evil Empire' fashion," he said later. "He blasted them for purposefully shooting down a civilian flight and killing many innocent civilians. I was not at all happy with the Reagan speech because, by that time, we in Seoul had come to understand the error that the Soviets made. I thought Reagan's accusation did not altogether fit the facts—at least as we knew them."

It was an accident.

In exaggerating the Soviet perfidiousness, the president had unwittingly contributed to the sense of siege that Yuri Andropov felt during the final few months of his life.[20] "If anyone had the illusion about the possibility of an evolution for the better in the policy of the present administration, recent events [have] dispelled them completely," Andropov said, probably from his sickbed.

———

From September 10 to 13, 71 percent of the 16,000 US Reforger forces checked in on time, including elements of the III Corps, the 75th Ranger Regiment, and the 1st Cavalry Division. They flew or sailed to Europe from 26 US airports on 130 flights. The navy hauled 1,355 wheeled vehicles, 50 armored tanks, and 300 other pieces of heavy weaponry across the Atlantic. For the first time, a US National Guard unit deployed to Italy. The troops practiced maneuvers in Central Germany, observed the forward positions they would take if called upon to exercise the European war plan, tested interoperability with NATO aircraft, and practiced recovering downed pilots. The Rangers, experts at building airfields where none had existed, were driven through the country, there to provide extra security at the reserve war stock sites and to protect convoys to and from custodial nuclear caches. Soviets watching Reforger would have also noticed these other firsts: NATO staged additional troops in the Netherlands for the first time since World War II. And C-141 aircraft flying nonstop from Hunter Army Airfield in Georgia, dropped 280 Rangers into Northern Germany at night.[21]

CHAPTER 19

The Phantom (Part II)

THREE MONTHS AFTER HER REELECTION, MARGARET Thatcher was casting about for new ways to engage the Soviet Union and assert herself more confidently on the global stage. She convened a summit of Russian experts at Chequers and left in late September for a trip to the United States. Thatcher had identified a way forward. Based in part on intelligence that Gordievsky had provided, she sensed that a number of younger members of the Politburo, including Mikhail Gorbachev, were waiting out the older generation. They had instincts about reform, that if properly cultivated, could provide the foundation for a much less contentious, much less dangerous East-West interchange. Ronald Reagan's speeches—his first to the British Parliament and the later one that referenced the Evil Empire—reduced the superpower rivalry to a contest between two countries, which, to Thatcher, it most was not. "We're all in it. We're all a part of it, and it's quite wrong for the Americans to throw their weight around and to imply that we are just satellites," she said privately. "We all live on the same planet," she said publicly.[1]

When she met Reagan in private, she told him that she was encouraged to hear that he would not break off discussions with the Soviets after the Korean Air disaster. Thatcher began by saying, according to minutes of the meeting, "that we had to make the most accurate assessment of the Soviet system and the Soviet leadership, there was plenty of evidence available about both subjects so as to establish a realistic relationship: whatever we thought of them, we all had to live on the same planet."

Reagan said he agreed. According to Thatcher, he had two questions for her. "First, the Russians seemed paranoid about their own security: did they really feel threatened by the West or were they merely trying to keep the offensive edge? The second question related to the control of Soviet power itself. He had always assumed that in the Soviet Union the Politburo controlled the military. But did the fact that the first public comments on the Korean Airliner incident had come from the military indicate that the Politburo was now dominated by the generals?"[2]

She left Washington feeling as if she had made her point. Reagan's responses suggested he understood, perhaps not as viscerally as she did, but well enough, that European countries had real skin in the game.

———

When she had told them she would be traveling alone to Moscow, Suzanne Massie's friends thought she could be kidnapped, or worse. But there she was, a Swiss-born American scholar of Russian literature, traveling alone, in Moscow's Sheremetyevo Airport, just twenty-two days after a Soviet air defense pilot shot up a passenger plane. An early-morning flight had left her exhausted. She was not sure she would be granted entry. It had been eleven years since she was kicked out of Russia, ostensibly for fraternizing with ordinary Russians without the permission of the government. As she walked up to the customs booth, she shivered, remembering how she had been treated in 1972, when her visa was revoked, and her body was roughly searched by border guards.[3]

She had been trying for years to get her visa back, stymied by the Russian bureaucracy. In the intervening period, she wrote for *Life* and had finished a book about the thousand years of Russian culture before the 1917 revolution, and found herself in the regular company of journalist-travelers like Hedrick Smith, now the *New York Times*' White House correspondent, and Ty Cobb, an Army intelligence officer who had been granted a rare visa to study energy policy.

It was Cobb who asked her for seven autographed copies one day. She knew he had made friends in the Soviet Union but didn't know how high; she was astonished when one of the inscriptions she was to write was addressed to Yuri Danilevich—the patronym of the then-intelligence chief and soon-to-be General Secretary, Yuri Andropov. In the summer of 1983, she finally received a visa. The KAL shootdown postponed her trip, but the Russians did not cancel it. They were eager to meet her.

A guard eyed her passport suspiciously. He picked up a phone, talked to someone and then, she would later remember, "the welcome metallic clunk of a mechanical stamp. My passport was handed back to me, and with a wave of dismissal, and a click, the barrier opened."[4] Massie arrived on a Friday. She sensed that her Russian tour guides, a motley mix of officials whose connections to the intelligence services she would confirm only later, seemed to want to tell her something, but what it was, specifically, they would not say. That Monday, regular Muscovites returning to work had a voracious appetite for her views about the clash between East and West. Every Soviet official she met, she said later, had been "stung deeply" by Reagan's reference to the Evil Empire. "Over and over, they came back to it, seeming to take every word our president uttered as gospel, and although I tried to remind them to look at his deeds, I was brushed aside."

The next day, on September 26, she received an audience with Radomir Bogdanov, the deputy director of the powerful USA Institute think tank and a high-ranking intelligence officer who was one of the Kremlin's chief Americanologists. She was stunned when he conceded that the Soviets had been responsible for the shoot-down of the plane. None had conceded this to her—or anyone—at this point. "Then, suddenly, his eyes flashing, and punctuating his remarks by shaking his fist, he exploded: 'You! You don't know how close war is.'" Massie thought he was exaggerating. Soviets are conspiratorial, by nature, she had come to believe. A French journalist had warned her before she left that the Soviets seemed determined to create a crisis by insisting that a crisis was at hand. But something in Bogdanov's voice nagged at her. She was not allowed to resume her academic work during the rest of her two-week stay and wondered, if not for her connections to senior members of the US military establishment, why the Soviets would have even bothered to let her come.

That night, at a quarter past midnight Moscow time, Stanislav Petrov, the deputy director for combat algorithms at the Russian Ground Command and Control Center, was about to decide whether the five scintillations on his screen, which looked like specks of glitter against a tuxedo jacket to him, were intercontinental ballistic missiles, the first volley in a surprise American nuclear attack against the Soviet Union.[5] Officers in a half dozen other bunkers across the Soviet Union listened on the Soviet nuclear party line, waiting for his answer. For all he knew, Yuri Andropov, the General Secretary, had already been notified.

As the clocked ticked, as data came in, time slowed down.

Petrov was a rational man, a trained engineer, young enough to be skeptical of Kremlin propaganda about the United States. He understood the rhetorical games that both sides played.[6] Twenty-one days earlier, of course, a Soviet Army air defense fighter on patrol had destroyed a Korean passenger plane it mistook for an American spy plane. Two hundred and twenty-nine innocents had died. The Soviets recovered only their shoes. Ties between Moscow and Washington froze. The Americans had just finished a NATO exercise, Reforger, where they deployed 15,000 troops to Western Europe in record time, the biggest rehearsal of that type the Soviets had ever seen. NATO was on the verge of salting Western Europe with new nuclear missiles that could reach the Russian border within minutes of first detection. The KGB was warning the Politburo that Americans were itching to invade the island of Grenada and oust the Soviet-friendly occupation government there. Reagan had postponed a summit with Andropov until next year.

And then there were Reagan's words. He had urged Christian supporters to "beware of the temptation of pride—the temptation of blithely declaring yourselves above it all and label both sides equally at fault, to ignore the facts of history and the aggressive impulses of an evil empire." That empire was, for better or worse, the country where Petrov and his wife were raising their two young children.

The way he told it, Petrov never wanted to join the Soviet military. He did not have the bearing of a soldier. He was slight and nerdy. While other kids played with toys, he tinkered with them. He wanted to be an engineer. However, his parents forced him to enlist at age seventeen.[7] His father had served Russia, and they insisted, so should he.

Petrov was smart, but also lucky. The Soviet military was starved for talented scientists in the 1970s, desperate to catch up to the United States and the West on military, economic, and agricultural fronts, and Petrov found his career fast-tracked. At age twenty-nine, he was assigned to one of the Soviet military's highest priority projects—an early warning system for nuclear missiles that would replace an aging version built during Nikita Khrushchev's tenure as General Secretary.[8]

Petrov designed the algorithms that would allow massive, ground-based mainframes to determine whether a flash of energy was merely a random burst of photons or an intercontinental ballistic missile launch. The satellites were given the formal designation of US UR, but they were known in the military as the Oko constellation. *Oko* meant "eye." The Soviets knew the West was watching each successive Oko launch, calibrating their war plans for its eventual completion, and that Americans were in the process of upgrading their entire strategic deterrent. That was one reason that the USSR openly proclaimed Oko's full operational status in 1982.

Petrov knew better. Oko's eyes were occluded. The hardware was raw, and the system was glitchy.[9] Oko had occasionally failed to detect missile launches that the Americans announced in advance. Hard lines linking the half dozen or so ground stations with Petrov's early-warning bunker at Serpukhov-15 in Kurilovo, about 70 miles southwest of Moscow, would blink out.

Now a lieutenant colonel, he occasionally served as battle staff commander for the staff of engineers, emergency action specialists, political and military intelligence analysts, and communicators who manned the Soviet's equivalent of NORAD. If an Oko satellite registered a hit, he would decide who to call and what to say to them.

Petrov did not like pulling the nuclear watch at Serpukhov. He felt unlucky when he was recalled from home, often on twenty minutes' notice. His twelve-hour shift would begin around 8:00 p.m. In an imposing chamber outside the watch room, he would inspect each of the 120 or so officers and enlisted men who would serve as the Soviet's eyes and ears that night.

If he found a uniform too crumply, he could yank the offender out of line and replace him.[10] The starch discipline reflected the seriousness of the mission, and Petrov, despite his desire to be elsewhere, followed protocol. Shift changes took an hour. The outgoing watch commander briefed him on the day. He would then page through the latest intelligence on American and NATO exercises, troop movements, and even political news. By 9:00 p.m., a subordinate would call the Kremlin's command center, reporting that Petrov was now in charge.

Petrov knew the mechanics of the early-warning system as well as anyone. He also knew that, in the event of an actual emergency, the rules, rehearsals, and run-throughs might give way to chaos. In a glass-enclosed office several meters away, KGB political officers had their own line to the Kremlin. They could, in theory, disagree with his call. They had access to real-time intelligence that he did not. The officers were friendly, but he did not know what they said behind closed doors.

The watch room was two stories tall. The battle staff sat at their consoles, their eyes moving from displays on their desks to the large projection screens that wallpapered one end of the room. One, fed from a reconnaissance satellite, showed a nearly live view of Earth, from high polar orbit. Petrov could tell the time by watching the slow progress of the boundary between shadow and sunlight over the European, Asian, and American continents.

The more important of the two was the Oko display. It had an electronic map of the globe with the USSR and the US outlined and American nuclear missile bases marked with crosses.[11]

About fifteen minutes past midnight, Petrov was troubleshooting. One of the satellites was fluctuating in its orbit, and engineers were trying to send signals from the ground to correct it. Soviet satellites harnessed gravity in elliptical Molniya orbits, which gave them wide coverage of the North American continent and its oceans. But the movements had to be calibrated or the Russians would be blind to large swaths of the world. The satellites also had to dance in unison. Radar hits had to be triangulated so that the computers could quickly project the trajectories of ICBMs.

Petrov sat behind a console in the back of the room, sipping tea with an assistant. He had just finished his supper, a cheese and sausage sandwich.[12] His satellites had good coverage of the United States, where it was early evening. Half the continent was bathed in sunlight; half was dark.

Then came the siren: an insistent, repeating *blaang*, "almost too loud," Petrov later remembered, and not at all like the siren used in exercises. He stood up. Underneath the monitors, a huge electronic banner began to flash in red and white. Oko's prisms were bombarded by the energy signature of what its computers interpreted as an intercontinental ballistic missile launch from somewhere inside the United States.

He first felt something resembling shock. Heads turned to him. What should they do? His instinct told him this alarm was a mistake. He didn't know why it was a mistake, but he knew. It had to be.

Check your systems, Petrov ordered. Please report the functioning of your systems. But as he ran through scenarios, the claxons stopped. The warning banners disappeared. The satellite was no longer registering a missile event.

He picked up a phone on his desk and told the Kremlin to stand down. False alarm.

At that exact moment, he remembered later, the siren blared again. The officer on the other end of the phone could hear it, too. Another potential event, from a similar area, somewhere in the western United States.

One by one, Petrov's team reported in. The main computer was functioning. Its backup was functioning. The communication links were functioning. Other sensors were online.

A backup command center that monitored a less sensitive early-warning system picked up nothing, although Petrov knew that those sensors were not designed to detect launches so quickly.[13]

A third underground command center, this one operated by a special section of the Soviet Army, opened a line to Petrov.

Then: a third event. At that point, the computers were programmed to presume that, with three detections in a short period of time, an attack was under way. The banner in the front of the room changed, too. "Missile attack," it flashed. Then came a fourth. Then a fifth.

The satellites were seeing *something*. The information they received flowed into two independent processing systems. The warnings could not be triggered if only *one* of them was working. A computer dedicated to assessing the probability of a launch based on all available data had just reported in: it was high.

At that point, Petrov's training should have ended the debate. He was responsible for the sensors in his own small box, and they were going off. The Americans had decided to start a nuclear war.

As inconceivable as it is to us today, Petrov was inclined to think that Americans would. In one sense, he could not do his job without being able to assume the worst. He *had* to; every missileer in their silos had to *assume* that the enemy would strike, because if they harbored any doubts, they'd never be able to blast through a well-fortified wall of cognitive resistance to nuclear war.

To answer the question of whether the United States had launched a missile, Petrov knew it had to be informed by even the less answerable question of whether they ever would.

And if they would, how? His rule of thumb, taken from military intelligence guesstimates, is that the US would try to decimate the Soviet Union with a first strike. Hundreds of missiles would be launched at once. This, of course, was exactly what the Soviet Union would do if they, God forbid, decided on a similar course.

If, on the other hand, only one missile was detected, it could be an accident. Petrov, reasonably enough, assumed that his American equivalents could make the same type of mistakes, maliciously or innocently, and bypass the official chains of command. He would make the call, but the real question at that point would be whether the US used the MOLINK (Moscow link) hotline between the Pentagon and the Kremlin to beg the Soviets not to retaliate. Out of his hands, entirely.[14]

Only three Soviet leaders had the authority order a retaliatory strike. Two of them would have to concur to do it. Since it would take about 20 minutes for an ICBM from the US to reach Moscow, Soviet leaders had, at most, about 16 minutes to make their own decision, or else their missiles would fizzle in their silos and their fighter bombers would be incinerated before they got off the ground.

Petrov knew that ICBMs should have been visible to the Russian reconnaissance satellites for at least 180 seconds after launch—that was when the final stage of their rockets burned out. But there was nothing. No flashes, no fire, no contrails. The satellites picked up American test launches all the time. The analysts knew what to look for. This time, they just didn't see it.

So, he made the call *again*. He wasn't totally sure, but he was pretty sure. This was a false alarm. He didn't know what it was, but it was not a missile launch.

When he hung up the phone, his stomach was tight.[15]

He waited until a backup set of ground-based sensors that would register missiles as they dove over the meridian reported in, as they did, a few minutes later. There was nothing.

He had been right. A hurried investigation by the Soviet general staff would later determine that the Okos picked up reflections from high clouds passing over F. E. Warren Air Force Base in Wyoming.

The failure of the Okos that night panicked Soviet war planners. For years, all their war games had come to the same conclusion: in a nuclear conflict, the side that struck first would be the only side with anything left at the end.[16] While the public discussion of nuclear war focused on the missiles themselves, on their quality, their fail-safe mechanisms, their numbers, and locations, military strategists knew that nuclear doctrine depended on much deeper parities.

————

Erich Mielke, the head of the Stasi, had a few choice words for KGB deputy chairman Vladimir Kryuchkov when the latter made a visit to Berlin in late September. The Soviet response to the KAL 007 downing was not aggressive.

"This event had exceptional elements of surprise," Mielke thundered. "What could have come out of this? We have to be extraordinarily vigilant. Nobody can say in advance what is going to happen; whether this plane incident could lead to a provocation transforming into a war. I note the problem of surprise over and over again. This surprise can lead to a war."

The prevailing (yet private) Soviet theory, as articulated by Kryuchkov: The Americans had fiddled with the electronic flight computer of the Korean Air plane and had forced it to go off course. That, or the Americans knew the flight was off course and failed to warn the Koreans, smelling a chance to score a coup against the Soviets.

"We did not know that the downed plane was a civilian airliner. Our pilots were not aware of that. We were convinced that it was a military aircraft. When the regional ground command issued its orders, it did not know it was a civilian airliner. We are not going to make this public, but this was just how it was. We were convinced that this was a special aircraft on a specific reconnaissance mission," he said, according to a secret East German cable.

"Our radar detected the plane prior to its violation of our airspace, about 600 to 800 kilometers before Kamchatka. The dot on the radar approached Kamchatka—the area where we have military bases. Some of them are nuclear bases. Our services were to a certain extent shocked that the plane headed directly towards Kamchatka. Such a brazen incident had never happened before. Thousands of planes fly through the air corridors there. Previous violations were just about between 1 and 5 kilometers. Yet until 1 September 1983, there had been no single incident involving a direct flight over Kamchatka."[17]

Proof?

Kryuchkov said that a US reconnaissance satellite had made three passes over the area that night. Clearly, the US was watching it intently, waiting for the launch of the Soviet missile. Kryuchkov implied that the detection of the satellite passes was the reason why the SS-25 missile that day was canceled.

Mielke's immediate concern was the Pershing II deployments. From his vantage, they threaten the defense of the state he was charged to protect. He asked Kryuchkov for assurance that Andropov was still intent on negotiating. It might be propaganda to say that the US was holding everyone else in Europe hostage for its own agenda, but that applied to the East Germans, too.

"You have to talk with everybody and argue against the missile deployment. Everybody, even the biggest enemy, has to be addressed in order to make it clear that a nuclear inferno will leave nothing behind of him," the Stasi chief said.[18]

———

When she arrived back in the US, in early October, Suzanne Massie believed she had been chosen by the Soviet leadership to deliver a message to President Reagan. Using her connections, she arranged a short meeting with Bud McFarlane. She had just twenty minutes to make her case.

In Washington, CIA deputy director John McMahon asked his deputy Robert Gates to follow up on a tip: the Soviet military intelligence high command had sent out a secret instruction urging its field offices to establish networks of "stay behind" illegals (civilian spies) to reconstitute its intelligence-gathering capability of the USSR after a war.

———

Meanwhile, the new, official, and highly secret plan to save the American presidency in the event of a decapitation attack from the

Soviets—Pegasus—was floundering. Its main architect, Thomas Reed, had left government. Vice President Bush and a few aides now oversaw the program, which was metastasizing throughout the corridors of the government's secret national security bureaucracy.

Pegasus's basic concept—its opponents called it a conceit—was that the White House could be anywhere.

During an emergency, or upon the receipt of warning of an imminent attack, the president, or the secretary of defense, would authorize the execution of Pegasus.

Then:

A presidential successor would be chosen at random.

A presidential emergency facility would be chosen at random.

A backup facility would be chosen at random.

A government on wheels would roll out from five secret locations across the United States. Lead-lined trucks with hidden satellite dishes, command posts, medical supplies, food, and secure phones would rendezvous the randomly chosen presidential successor. The convoys would have everything a president needed to perform three critical functions: to exercise command and control of the military and the nuclear forces; to communicate with other governments as head of state; and to communicate with the American people as head of the executive branch. FEMA revised a circular that spelled out how agencies would cooperate with the "new" president. Its title, "Succession to the Presidency Under Emergency Conditions," was classified secret.[19] The convoys could be self-sustaining for six months.[20]

The powers available to the American president during an emergency are wide-ranging. Most are not secret: the president can quarantine areas, use federal troops to put down insurrections, seize infrastructure deemed to be critical, like power plants, federalize certain industries, and even require food rationing. But Eisenhower recognized that a president surviving the start of a nuclear war would require, in essence, a series of super-extraordinary powers to reconstitute the basic functions of government.

In 1954, the first series of standby executive orders, known formally as Presidential Emergency Action Documents (PEADS), were written. Collectively, they formed Annex A to the "Federal Emergency Plan D," described as "a plan for nuclear attack on the United States with little or no warning."[21] Plan D allowed the president to seize assets at will, declare martial law, freeze wages and prices, cancel debts, print emergency money, spend money at will, decide the value of currency, indemnify whomever he wanted, and suspend habeas corpus in cases.[22]

When Plan D was declared—and just how the president would declare this had never been clear—it meant that he was deliberately bypassing Congress and claiming for himself emergency authorities and powers that Congress otherwise would have to give to him. If Congress was still around, and emergency measures were required, the president would submit to them a binder of standby legislation giving him all but unlimited power. These documents, called "Documents for Contingencies (Other Than a Plan D Situation) Which Justify Application of Emergency Measures on a National Scale," were so highly classified that members of Congress were not able to see them in advance.[23]

In order for a president to use these extraordinary powers, a president had to be found.

Under the aegis of Project Pegasus, if and when the disaster struck, the president would himself be flown to the primary random site; if the president died, and if there was no immediate word on a surviving successor, the randomly chosen successor would be, for all intents and purposes, the acting president.

"We kept a scoreboard at the [National Military Command Center] to see where every constitutional successor was. During peacetime, we tried to keep at least one away from Washington at all times," Reed said.

The author asked Reed to give a scenario where Pegasus would be activated.

"Let's say that you're in the NMCC, and if all these sensors go off, and you've got fifteen ICBMs incoming, the operations director would say, okay, who do we got? The Secretary of Agriculture is in Kansas City, so make him the designated successor. A randomizing computer would roll the dice and say, 'Go to the Armory in Colorado Springs,' or wherever. And the project would connect the successor with the team, and there it was."

During peacetime, a small group of forces would guard the convoys and vaults with Plan D PEADS and Other-Than-D documents and numerous emergency action checklists. These units were given cover names, too. They were called CONUS, Communications Support Units. One was based in Ogden, Utah; another was in West Virginia.

"As opposed to the Soviet concept of building underground facilities, we chose to put more emphasis on mobile facilities that would be much more difficult to target and thus would survive. That doesn't mean that we didn't have any underground facilities, because during this time period another facility was built under the East Wing of the White House, but mobile is what we focused on," former National Security Advisor John Poindexter said.

CHAPTER 20

The Day Before the Day After

ON OCTOBER 10, 1983, REAGAN AND SEVERAL ADVISORS watched a private screening of an ABC television drama about the struggle to survive in post-nuclear-war Kansas City. *The Day After* cost $7 million to make, even after many of its stars decided not to take a salary. Highly graphic in its depiction of both the physical and emotional suffering experienced by a group of families, it left Reagan depressed. Conservatives thought the movie was inflammatory, and the White House was bracing for backlash after the movie's air date in November, but Reagan wrote in his diary that night that "My own reaction: we have to do all we can . . . to see that there is never a nuclear war."[1] Death weighed on the president's mind for the rest of the month.

Congress had grown skeptical of the Marine peacekeeping mission in Beirut, which had lasted for more than a year and had a very nebulous mission.[2] Two Marines had been killed in August after taking a direct hit from a Lebanese army mortar round. On October 17, Reagan had tearful conversations with the parents, and then the young widow of one of them.[3] On October 18, he called Thomas Dine, the executive director of the American Israel Public Affairs Committee, to thank him for pressuring Congress to give the president flexibility to keep the troops in the country.

"You know, I turn back to your ancient prophets in the Old Testament and the signs foretelling Armageddon, and I find myself wondering if—if we're the generation that is going to see that come about," Reagan told Dine. "I don't know if you've noted any of those prophecies lately, but, believe me, they certainly describe the times we're going through."[4]

That day, Reagan held a National Security Council meeting where intelligence about a potential terrorist attack against the Marines in Lebanon was high on the agenda. In late September, the NSA had intercepted a call from the Iranian ambassador in Damascus confirming that he had passed along permission to attack the US Marines barracks. The US didn't know when and where.

All the while, Reagan was wrestling with his personnel problems. His best friend, Judge Clark, was on his way out as National Security Advisor. Chief of Staff James Baker wanted the job. Conservatives on his team, including Edwin Meese, resisted. The White House settled on Bud McFarlane as a compromise, and Reagan had to tell Jeane Kirkpatrick, the firebrand conservative who was his emissary to the United Nations, that she would not be getting the job she coveted. He offered her a counselor position in the White House. She declined. Reagan told her he would not accept her no.[5]

And then, on October 23, a massive truck bomb destroyed the Marine mission, killing 249 American soldiers. Reagan was awakened with the news. The death toll rose throughout the day. US bases around the world upgraded their readiness condition.

The next day, the US sent an invasion force into Grenada, a tiny pearl-shaped island in the southern Caribbean. For years, conservatives had watched warily as Marxist dissidents on the island began a slow creep toward militancy. The Soviet and Cuban military had established beachheads there already. In mid-October they drove the island's prime minister, Maurice Bishop, from office. Reagan had promised to keep the Western Hemisphere free from Soviet influence. Kirkpatrick, at the United Nations, had taken charge of this promise, and urged Reagan to intervene if Grenada's government appeared in jeopardy.

There was a technicality: Grenada was a British colony. Queen Elizabeth was the head of state. The Marxist coup had not upset Thatcher; she barely knew where Grenada was. And its leaders had reassured the British foreign office that they would do no harm to British citizens there. Thatcher's Foreign Secretary said as much in Parliament, insisting that the situation was under control.[6]

What about the large US Navy presence in the region? Was this a prelude to an invasion? No—the US reassured the British through formal channels that the fleet was there to rescue American citizens, just in case.

Reagan intended to keep the mission a secret from Thatcher to protect the lives of the forces who would secure the island. He sent a last-minute missive to the prime minister suggesting that he was considering an invasion and asked for her thoughts. A few hours later, before she could reply, he gave the execute order. When Thatcher found out, she called Reagan and chewed him out. One Reagan advisor recalls hearing Reagan's baleful attempts to mollify her. But only "Margaret . . . but Margaret . . ." was able to come out of his mouth.[7]

Reagan chose to invade Grenada, although the coup's timing was not his. The consequences of his failure to consult with Thatcher proved costly. On the eve of the deployment of cruise missiles, he had undercut her authority, teaching her the lesson, as one critic told her, "that no undertakings that may be offered by the United States—either as to the use that it might make of missiles stationed in this country or as to the consultations that would precede such use—ought to be relied upon."[8]

Relations between the British and the United States, and between Reagan and Thatcher, had reached a new low. The number of antinuclear protestors at a later march in London reached a new high: 400,000. Public opinion was turning against deployment.

———

In Europe General John R. Calvin had taken command of the Army's VII Corps in July of 1983. If the Soviets attacked, his 73,000-man infantry, supported by a 100,000-strong logistics army, would be NATO's first line of defense along West Germany's border with East Germany and Czechoslovakia. Calvin had served in the infamous Fulda Gap, too, and had a fuller understanding of NATO's strengths and weaknesses than just about any commander in the field at the time. "We had not done much thinking beyond the first battle of a campaign, believing that we would be reinforced, or we could go nuclear," he observed. He pushed for more exercise time; the turnover in his unit was so rapid that he had no way to know whether his units understood their wartime responsibilities. He had 5,000 tactical nuclear weapons under his "janitorial" umbrella, as he liked to say, including the custodial units of the 59th Ordinance Brigade. If those warheads were needed in battle, he'd be on the phone to request them.

He would often think about the dilemma he would face if there were ever pressure to "go nuclear." Here is how he put it later: "Such a decision would have to be political, and in my opinion, would be an impossible choice: if nuclear weapons were not to be used but only threatened, we would be faced with the question of how to survive a massive conventional attack that we believed the Warsaw Pact was capable of mounting. Without timeline political guidance to conduct one form of defense or another, we would not stand a good chance."

He worried that NATO political leaders did not know enough to know whether they would ever want to use nuclear weapons. He was convinced that the Soviets seemed "distant and enigmatic," which made them seen more dangerous than they were up close. He resolved to try and meet his counterparts more often. [9]

———

Two weeks before Able Archer, Captain Lee Trolan was summoned to NATO school in Oberramergau, a pastoral village near Munich. SHAPE had revised its nuclear weapons release procedures, and all the custodial commanders had to be taught the new system. Over four days, in between pleasant breakfasts and cocktail hours, he took a refresher course on the NATO nuclear operations policy, learned about the new procedures, and participated in a tabletop exercise. Even decades later, Trolan would not discuss the content of what he learned; he had no reason to believe that the nuclear weapons employment procedures were still classified, but he had sworn an oath to protect this information for life, regardless.

An unclassified syllabus given to Trolan shows that the class was important enough for SACEUR Rogers to have spent time recording a filmed greeting to them. Representatives from all the NATO nuclear commands were there, and the exercise time was quite extensive. [10]

Two other participants provided a bit more information. One, who asked for anonymity even decades later, said: "The message formats changed from about 30 characters to around 60 or 70. That was for security reasons, because we knew the Soviets had figured out the old format, and because the Pershing deployments meant that we had to be able to convey more information in the message body about targets, especially because they were going to be used for selective strikes."

The new procedures would be exercised for the first time during the nuclear release phase of Able Archer 83.

CHAPTER 21

Able Archer 83

FOR ITS FIRST FEW DAYS, ABLE ARCHER WOULD BE A paper exercise, a table read. It would proceed according to a script. Then, field units like Trolan would begin to "play," but in real time, using real communications procedures. The Able Archer Directing Staff at each command post held complete copies of the script as well as a list of what the military calls "effects"—inputs that had to be practiced and objectives that NATO war planners wanted to achieve. The Directing Staff was responsible for ensuring that all of these boxes were checked. The task was complicated, because once they gave the players—the Blue side and the Orange side—their instructions, the players could act as they wished, and the Di-Staff would have to figure out how to inject new events into the script without losing the veneer of reality that made Able Archer exercises valuable.[1]

As the Able Archer Directing Staff moved into place, the Soviet and East Germans were putting the finishing touches on their plans to monitor the exercise.[2]

The deputy chairman of the KGB, Vladimir Kryuchkov, digested a report about the upcoming NATO war games from the Stasi. "I received information . . . saying the enemy were preparing for the possible military conflict . . . they were making moves, showing that it might have happened. We never thought that the situation brought us to the edge; nevertheless, it was a really tense moment. It was a matter of what conclusions were to be made. One couldn't exclude the possibility of a war with the use of nuclear weapons."

Kryuchkov briefed members of the Soviet Central Committee on the intelligence and then, following their wishes, sent warning telegrams to the KGB *rezidenturas* in Europe.

The point was not to panic anyone, he said, but to be extra cautious.[3]

Gordievsky recalls the first message: "There was a cable in the beginning warning the station that the Americans had a very important exercise, which could develop into something sinister."[4]

Gordievsky's boss, Arkady Guk, had asked Moscow for specifics: what signs should the London residency look for that might indicate NATO was within the seven- to ten-day window before a surprise attack? Kryuchkov ordered the First Chief Directorate to send him a rather obvious list that included these instructions: "Check for unusual activity at the Prime Minister's residence; observe whether large numbers of cars are parked around the Ministry of Defense in the evening; note the appearance in the streets of military detachments, or the announcements of a military alert, at bases; check for signs that the government has changed communication procedures—"indirect signs" may be the only indicators given."[5] Nothing of this sort was happening in London.

The KGB still struggled to make sense of its surprise nuclear attack (RYAN) indicators, and the East German intelligence agency, the HVA, still worried about their incompleteness. Strategic nuclear weapons could be launched immediately; the war checklists the KGB had prepared assessed whether war would start in half a year or a year. And there were thousands of them. Again, Erich Mielke and Markus Wolf complained to Kryuchkov. There had to be a better system "that denies the adversary the option of a surprise." They learned that the KGB research center responsible for RYAN had compiled seven binders' worth of ideas. The KGB's Institute for the Research of Operative Problems had yet to establish an assessment center.[6] Kryuchkov's briefing landed with a clunk. East Germany was at ground zero. The KGB's sluggishness in crisply defining the RYAN scenario was maddening. (Margaret Thatcher might have appreciated the irony of a Warsaw Pact country feeling hamstrung by the policies of the main center of power.)

The Soviet military ratcheted up its global readiness beginning in the middle of October. Its immediate concern was the now inevitable deployment of the Pershings, which for all the Soviets knew, had already been

secreted into NATO. Ustinov convened the Warsaw Pact defense committee in Berlin. "This extraordinary session of our committee is convened
due to the grave escalation of the international situation and, in consequence, of the growing danger of war against the socialist community. It is
due to the need to apply effective countermeasures to preserve the security of our states. The source for the growing danger of war is evident," he
said at the outset. "Dangerous tendencies, both in aggressive intention and
practical actions by Washington and NATO, get confirmed by an entire
range of circumstances.[7] The Soviets intended to send a signal to the West
that if they engaged in provocative "dangerous tendencies" during the deployment, Moscow would be ready.

HVA agents, meanwhile, had obtained a number of details about the
Able Archer exercise scenario, one of which was striking. They learned
that B-52s would participate for the first time, guided by an echelon of
observers from the Strategic Air Command. The B-52 presence meant one
thing to the Soviets: nuclear strikes.

So, the Able Archer 83 scenario *as imagined by the Soviets* thus began
with a Warsaw Pact invasion using conventional forces. It would be met by
a conventional response from NATO. That "play" would last several days.
Then, NATO would "discover" that the Soviets had captured or otherwise
rendered safe a cache of American tactical nuclear weapons. This discov-
ery would trigger a nuclear response from NATO—and then, the B-52s
would deliver a "strategic" response—sending its missiles all the way into
Soviet territory. According to Admiral Vladlen Smirnoff, the commander
of the Soviet Northern Fleet at the time, none of the Able Archer exercise
scenarios had ever *before* progressed from tactical to strategic use of nuclear weapons.[8]

Peter Harden, a tanker planner for the Eighth Air Force, supervised
the refueling operations for the B-52s during Able Archer from SHAPE
headquarters. "That was the first time they played with that bomber," he recalled. "That was significant for a number of reasons. People assumed that
if the B-52s were there, they'd have a strategic nuclear purpose, and not a
conventional purpose. It was really sensitive—a big concern at all levels."

He did not know at the time what the Soviets knew, but he made sure
to note in an after-action report that the word *strike*—associated with B-52s
and nuclear operations—was used far too frequently over the radios and

had to be quickly corrected. But the B-52's armaments were not nuclear. "They were all conventional. In fact, after the exercise, in the after-action report, we said that we weren't sure we should participate unless the exercises had more of a nuclear component to them. It just wasn't worth our time."[9]

November 4: STARTEX

Early in the morning of the start of the paper phase of Able Archer 83, the Soviets launched a rocket from the Plesetsk Cosmodrome, about 800 kilometers north of Moscow. Neither NATO nor the United States had been warned in advance. The path of the rocket was unusual. Instead of proceeding eastward, toward Soviet waters; its azimuth took it westward, toward the Arctic Circle and the array of American nuclear sensors and satellites. The rocket did not appear to boost anything into space, so the purpose of the launch confounded the American intelligence community.[10] Only once before had they monitored a Soviet launch like that—it was years earlier, and it had been announced. This was the first major Soviet missile launch since the KAL shoot-down.[11]

Camp Lejeune, North Carolina

President Reagan was in a reflective mood. The decision to invade Grenada, which had angered allies but was deemed a success, had been a small comfort to him at a raw moment. His thoughts turned toward God. "He has really held us in the hollow of his hand," the president confided in his diary. Today, Reagan was attending the first funeral for the Marines killed in Beirut. He greeted the widows and family members of the dead individually. They "would just put their arms around me, their head on my chest and quietly cry. One little boy, 8 or 9, handed me a manila folder saying it was something he'd written about his father. Later when I read it I found it was a poem entitled 'Loneliness.'"[12]

As he prepared for his trip to Japan and Korea, Reagan spent many hours thinking about the dead in Beirut and the wounded from Grenada. One afternoon, he tried to console the parents of one young soldier, an Army Ranger, who was mangled by shrapnel, both legs torn off, barely surviving.

November 6—SHAPE Headquarters, Mons, Casteau, Belgium

From SHAPE headquarters in Belgium and at five sites across Europe, twelve-hour shifts began on the evening of November 6. In the bland language of exercise planners, the first three days would feature "low spectrum conventional play," followed by "two days of high spectrum nuclear warfare."[13]

At the start, NATO engaged in conventional warfare, with Blue (NATO) forces pounding the attacking Orange (Warsaw Pact) forces along the entire German airfields. The Orange forces opened a new front in Britain, by attacking airfields and destroying Blue B-52s. To keep Orange tanks from protecting the Fulda Gap, the Blue side used chemical weapons. Blue was able to maintain positions until Orange follow-on forces reached the battle areas. On the morning of November 8, the commander of Blue forces asked for permission to use tactical nuclear weapons to repel the Orange invasion.

The nuclear operations cell in the bunker at SHAPE headquarters simulated what one NATO official calls "the big ask." The NATO political committee's proxies had to vote—or the exercise version of them had to pretend to vote—and then, the American president and the British prime minister had to give their assents. Figuring out how and when to use the weapons took time—the script called for a delay of about twelve hours between the first request and the follow-on permission for their use.[14] From that point on, the cells at the NATO command post codenamed ERWIN, in Rheinland-Pfalz, Germany, and CREST-HIGH, the wartime headquarters at Heinrich Hertz Airfield in Birkenfeld, played more prominent roles. Notably, participants at the site had to don their MOPP-3 gear—helmets, gas masks, and chemical suits. From the outside, a Warsaw Pact spy would see that the base had increased its security posture, in real life. By November 7, it would be clear to an observer that Able Archer 83 was not just a paper exercise.

———

A number of Warsaw Pact and Soviet regiments were on alert. Near Moscow, Captain Viktor Tkachenko waited anxiously in a small ICBM bunker buried in the ground. He had heard rumors that the Americans would wait until the eve of a major Soviet holiday, when ordinary Soviets were relaxed and happy, to launch World War III. The night before he reported for duty, he had a final dinner with his wife and two his young sons. He would miss their holiday party, so he had an extra glass of wine. He kissed them all, not knowing if he would ever see them again.

The briefing from the KGB commissars had been specific: the American exercise, Able Archer, would test strategic nuclear weapons procedures in Europe for the first time. This was proof that the Pershings, which were weeks away from hitting the ground, had strategic purposes. Some of them might already have been hidden in Europe. The Strategic Rocket Forces (SRF) had to be ready to launch a retaliatory attack.[15] That meant that Tkachenko, a junior officer, and a third man, whose job was to maintain communications, would spend their shifts in the bunker. A preliminary command had been issued to keep the line of communication between the SRF command center and the bunkers open and secure.

Throughout the holiday period, Tkachenko stayed on base, spending six hours at a time in the bunker. He waited for the last order—the one that would cause his hands to shake when he practiced it—the order to cut open an envelope containing combat orders, remove a key from a small red box inside a safe, punch in the codes, and turn the key to launch the SS-20 and SS-19 missiles in his arsenal. Each missile carried ten warheads. Each warhead could destroy a city many times over.[16]

"If we had received the order from the minister of defense, we would have known that that order was given not just out of the blue. We would have known that it meant that American missiles had already been launched and our wives and our children were targets of American attack and we had to retaliate," he told an interviewer years later.

On the evening of November 7, he was ready to turn the key.

Killianstädten, West Germany

Trolan's troop reinforcements had finally arrived days earlier, fresh off the plane from Grenada, ready for their new assignment as nuclear custodial site guards. He could smell the gunpowder on some of them. They weren't ready for the experience, and he would have to train them for long guard-duty shifts. But that would have to wait. First, he had to get through Able Archer.

During large exercises, multiple radio sites would broadcast the encrypted nuclear procedure instructions across the spectrum of frequencies. Trolan was taught to assume that his communications would be compromised during the first phases of a war. In practice, though, that meant that the East Germans and the GRU could listen to the high-frequency radios used by the army for back-up communications. Without a code book, they couldn't tell what the messages meant, but if the intelligence teams managed to correlate lengths of messages with actions their spies in the field had observed, they'd be able to guess, just based on the composition of the message, what it contained.

Trolan knew that the Killianstädten base would be under heavy observation by the enemy. His military intelligence briefers told him that the Soviets kept about 500 special forces troops in West Germany, with standing orders to sabotage communication towers and nuclear sites when NATO altered its readiness. He was sure that some of them were standing on deer traps in the woods somewhere watching him.

On November 7, the exercise began for Trolan with an unannounced recall of all of his troops and an order to turn up their readiness.

Alarms sounded, and the Americans, Belgians, and Germans broke into their ammo lockers and loaded up their wartime gear, and waited. The Luftwaffe unit attached to Trolan swarmed the launcher area and prepared to load weapons.

When the Orange team began to use chemical weapons during the exercise simulation, Trolan received an order to prepare his chem-bio kits.

NATO adopted "Minimize" procedures on many of its tactical radio networks early in the day on November 8, after the exercise corps commanders had requested permission to use a package of nuclear effects against the Orange invasion.

Later that day, a number of special signal battalions deployed from bases in West Germany. Gerald King led one of them: a team of soldiers detached from every company in his battalion to establish links between the classified 4th Allied Tactical Air Force wartime location back to headquarters at ERWIN.

"We used an unorthodox equipment configuration to provide tactical telephone and data communications to a fixed facility," he recalled later. "I was from A company, and had mechanics and drivers from [higher headquarters], a semiautomatic switchboard from B company and a microwave radio team from C company. Although we were successful, it was the only time that particular task was performed."[17]

At about the same time, the commander of all US forces in Central Germany transferred his headquarters from his wartime alert location, in the mountains near Eifel, Germany, to another mobile convoy.[18]

CHAPTER 22

FLASH Telegram

ƚ

KGB Rezidentura, London, England

OLEG GORDIEVSKY KNEW THAT SOMETHING UNUSUAL was happening. Fourteen of his colleagues in the GRU station in the embassy basement were scurrying around like mice. Couriers bearing top-secret cables from a communications station in an annex next to the Soviet embassy came in and out all day. Their work was so segregated that even Guk did not know what was happening. Gordievsky knew well enough not to ask.

The cipher clerk rushed out of his locked room with a Flash Telegram. He had never seen one before. It had the highest precedence over all other communication traffic. A Flash Telegram meant "pay immediate attention." He remembers the gist of the text:

The American exercise may be a cover for a supreme nuclear attack. Watch the signs and report immediately to use anything unusual—any special signs of preparation, including the evacuation of the ambassador or families from the American embassy.

The cable also noted that American bases around the world had beefed up their security.

Gordievsky kept calm. "What can we do? We know some panicky people in Moscow as critical, but we here regard the situation, in London, sitting in a major Western capital, we don't see anything critical." Still, he said, "I knew it was a dramatic moment, I knew Moscow was nervous."[1]

A separate version of the cable went to the Soviet's allied intelligence agencies.

Markus Wolf passed a query to his best source, the NATO intelligence officer Rainer Rupp, codenamed TOPAZ. Wolf waited for an answer.[2]

November 8 and 9—Moscow

General Colonel Ivan Yesin, the commander of the SS-20 Pioneer regiments for the Soviet Strategic Rocket Forces, spent the night in a special bunker. Just months into his first assignment as a general officer, and here he was, at ground zero of the global nuclear conflict. The Pershings and GLCMs were deployed specifically to counter the missiles he supervised. Large-scale NATO exercises were fraught with danger because he believed the Soviet intelligence assessments that the Pershing II warheads could reach Moscow within six minutes and decapitate the leadership. "It was under the pretenses of those exercises that a sudden nuclear strike could be delivered," he recalled.

Since November 2, his mobile regiments had been on alert—secretly. During peacetime, 10 percent of the SS-20 Pioneers were forward-deployed. During Able Archer 83, fully half—about 75—had been moved to their wartime positions, hidden by camouflage, near mountains 100 kilometers from their bases.[3] Some poked out of swamps. Special radar-absorbing paint covered all of them. Each missile had three warheads with 200 kilotons of nuclear explosives on board—"fifteen Hiroshimas, to the public," Yesin said.

If the order came, Yesin's men could have launched the missiles in 2 minutes and 30 seconds. Every six or eight hours, Yesin would receive a briefing from the GRU, and the frequency of the briefings increased as the exercise reached its climax. The commanders of his rocket regiments were in their command centers, kept in contact by radio link.

And he kept in contact with his boss, the chief of the general staff, Marshal Nikolai Ogarkov. Yesin recalls that Ogarkov spent at least one night in a command bunker during Able Archer. "During the climax of the NATO exercise, when the strategic missile forces were on the heightened . . . combat alert, I can say with a high degree of confidence that

Marshal Ogarkov was in the protected central command point of the armed forces of the USSR," he said.[4] The SS-20 Pioneer regiments would stay on secret combat alert until November 14, as would a dozen fighters capable of using nuclear ordinance.[5]

———

Mikhail Gorbachev insists he celebrated the October Revolution that week as planned and said he knew nothing of a war alert. But several of his colleagues betrayed a different understanding of the world. "Comrades, the international situation at present is hot, thoroughly white hot," Politburo member Grigory Romanov, told a large plenum of Soviet officials that day. Romanov's speech was officially sanctioned by the Politburo.[6] The Soviet Union would respond to American provocations by "the very highest vigilance."

Yuri Andropov was battling an infection and did not attend the speech. In its Top Secret National Intelligence Daily, the CIA noted that he had last been seen in public in August and had taken steps in the interim to keep rivals like Chernenko from taking anything more than a ceremonial role. "Andropov's absence in the current ceremonies many represent prudent medical caution rather than evidence of a totally incapacitating illness," the CIA concluded.[7]

Sergei Tarasenko, a top foreign ministry official responsible for relations with the United States, was taken aside by his boss, the First Deputy Foreign Minister Georgi Kornienko, and shown "a top-secret KGB paper . . . In the paper, the KGB reported that they had information that the United States had prepared for a first strike; that they might resort to a surgical strike against command centers in the Soviet Union; and that they had the capability to destroy the system by incapacitating the command center."[8]

At around the same time, Colonel Vitaly Tsygichko was asked to come up with new political approaches to deal with what he was told was the threat of imminent nuclear war from the United States and NATO. Tsygichko was a longtime Soviet defense analyst who, in retirement, had spent time in the United States and remained an informal advisor to the General Staff and spoke regularly with Andropov. "We had a perception that our enemies . . . surrounded us, and this mentality of a possible attack resulted in the bloated defense industry," he said.[9] He thought the war scare rhetoric was self-reinforcing—a way for the Soviets to scare themselves into uniting, a way of avoiding the serious difficulties that were breaking the country apart.

———

Andre Babian was a first-year cadet in the Military Institute of Foreign Languages in Moscow. He looked forward to the long November weekend. It coincided with the anniversary of the October Revolution, when the Soviets would celebrate the advance of the Bolshevik seizure of power in 1917. For Babian, it meant three days' liberty. For the first time since he left for Moscow, he was going to see his parents. They'd come all the way from the Republic of Georgia. On Friday, November 4, the school shut down—all the gates closed, suddenly.

All weekend passes were canceled. Married cadets could take a twenty-four-hour leave; the rest had to stay in their barracks. "No one would give us an explanation about what was going on, but they seemed really nervous." On Sunday, he was allowed to leave barracks, but he had to remain on the grounds of the Institute. A military geography professor later clued him in: NATO was conducting scale military exercises that might be a cover for a first nuclear strike.[10]

CHAPTER 23

Validate and Authenticate

Near the West German–East German Border

E. R. CAMPBELL, A CANADIAN ARMY OFFICER, DEPLOYED
from Frankfurt during Able Archer with a secret mobile alternative war
headquarters team. His job was to make sure that the deputy commander
in chief of NATO forces in Germany could communicate with the commander over long distances, specifically about the need to use tactical
nuclear weapons.[1] It was the first time the unit had been deployed from
headquarters during an exercise.

On the other side of the border, infantry battalion commanders from
the Soviet Group of Forces in East Germany had been driven to their wartime staging area and set up camp around trenches a few kilometers from
the border. The units were given a complete set of live ammunition—120
bullets for their AK-47s, three grenades, and two weeks' worth of food.[2]
They had never experienced this type of deployment before.

Killianstädten

On day two of the live Able Archer exercise, Lee Trolan's 501st's radar and
launch site buzzed with activity. Its command post, near the valley closer
to the town, was locked down. From somewhere nearby, Soviet spies
watched and listened. From mobile signals intelligence-gathering trucks
disguised as common transport vans, they could intercept the 501st's
security team's tactical voice communications. From 1,000 meters away,

special transceivers could suck up all the electromagnetic energy coming from antennas on the base. Mated warheads gave off special energy signatures. These, too, could be picked up by the Soviets.

The Soviets had tapped into junction boxes for the German public telephone system, allowing them to listen to the encrypted hum of secure voice traffic from Heidelberg and other major command centers. To foil eavesdroppers, the National Security Agency had upgraded the cryptographic machines on either side of the telephone. To prevent the adversary from determining patterns of communication, noise—electronic gibberish—was pumped into the system, indistinguishable from actual scrambled voice conversations.[3] But the Soviets had somehow managed to defeat this feature; they could tell the signal from the noise. If communications patterns changed, they'd know something was off.

They had also managed to determine which circuits were dedicated for the Emergency Message Authentication System (EMAS), over which NATO nuclear release orders were transmitted. Every hour, on the hour, the circuit would test itself by sending tiny encrypted bits to machine terminals located at the custodial sites, which would reciprocate, letting the system know that the line, in essence, was open. "We listened to the hourly circuit verification signal and believed we would recognize a release order," a senior Soviet general said later.[4]

But the format for those release orders had just changed. Trolan had gone to school to learn the new one.

During the nuclear release portion of the exercise, on November 8 and 9, for the first time, the custodial units would receive Emergency Action Messages with that new format. The messages would be about twice as long as the old release orders.

The Soviets did not know that the message formats had been changed before the exercise.

And a newly formatted message, most likely, is what they heard after the command to "minimize" nonessential traffic was given over all the nets on November 8, the prelude to the nuclear release phase of the exercise.

A sudden change in communication patterns.

A period of silence.

Unusual activity involving mated warheads.

Three RYAN signs—all explicable within the context of Able Archer, but each one reading to the Soviet eavesdroppers as an indicator of high alert for headquarters.

———

Jeffrey Carney's NSA station in Teufelsberg had a robust counter-for-eign-intelligence function. Their antennas and dishes were often pointed in the direction of their own side to detect the enemy's hidden transmissions. The NSA had also tapped into a cable line that fed into the KGB's 16th Directorate SIGINT (signals intelligence) station near Karlshorst, East Berlin. From space, satellites could pick up encrypted messages, too. As with the Soviets and their targets in the 501st, the content of the message mattered less than the pattern of the transmissions. Whenever the Soviets had to smuggle a lot of information out of East Germany, the NSA could figure it out.[5]

In the early evening of November 9, as Trolan waited to practice the release procedures, there was a spike in burst communication from the mobile Soviet and East German signals intelligence units hidden in East Germany. And the British SIGINT agency detected an unusual amount of activity between KGB's base in Karlshorst and Moscow.[6]

———

A nuclear release order might have four segments: an alphabetic flag word, which told the recipient what type of message it was; a coded series of digits corresponding to a specific action; a series of numbers that translated into the time the warheads had to be ready to be launched, and an authorization sequence, which, when decoded, would produce a series of digits that would unlock the weapons. A short one might look like this: X-STRIKE RED BRUSH 32F 2015 493823.

STRIKE RED BRUSH might mean "Open the safe for war." X-STRIKE RED BRUSH would mean "Open the safe for an exercise." (All exercise messages were prefaced with an X.)

Trolan and his NCO—an officer and an enlisted man, two different people—would use their own keys to open double-padlocked safes. Once the safes were open, Trolan and his NCO would grab its contents, called "cookies."

They'd compare the code they'd received from the EAM—say

32F—with the code printed on the outside of a pack of cards sealed by tinfoil in plastic shells. They'd crack open the shell of the cookie and remove a thin laminated card. It had a six-digit number on it. That number, when merged with the authorization code, would give them the PAL, or Permissive Action Link, code.

The PAL code, when dialed in to the top of a can-like mechanism on the outside of the warhead, would unlock an electromagnetic plug that sealed the C4 explosives inside the W-31 off from the plutonium core. The Americans would then insert—or fuse—a firing pin into the warhead, completing the arming circuit.

The release of the PAL code always came with a window-of-use timeline—2015 in our message. (If the team missed that time-on-target window, it had to resecure the warhead by reinserting the PAL and then had to call HQ and tell them that it failed.[7])

———

It was this type of Emergency Action Message—a "prepare for nuclear release" message—that "broke" but didn't validate. Three hours after this first invalid message came in, after Trolan had processed a dozen or more messages with the right format, his lieutenant handed him another enciphered communication.

The two took out theirs grease pencils and code books and worked it through.

It, too, broke. It, too, used the old format, the format the Soviets were used to hearing.

Once again, Trolan called the duty officer. Once again, he was told that the incorrectly formatted EAM had not been sent by anyone there—that it was impossible for him to be reporting what he was reporting.

Trolan had been exercising nonstop for thirty-six hours at this point. The lids of his eyes were pouchy, his pupils bloodshot. But now he felt a jolt of energy

The mysterious messages had to come from somewhere. Whoever sent them had to have the current codebook. Whoever sent them had to know the old message format. He knew the Soviets knew the old format... so maybe...

He rang his own headquarters on a regular telephone line and tried to explain the problem without revealing classified information. He knew the Soviets and East Germans were listening. He didn't want to alert them that the NATO Top Secret code might have been compromised.

But this time, the duty officer on the other end of the line cut him off. A unit in Northern West Germany had reported the same—they were getting messages that broke the code but wouldn't validate because they used the old format. The messages might be spoofs—deliberately fake messages that an enemy might use to disable the communications system during war.

"Before the exercise had started, I would have responded to them," Trolan said. "These messages didn't go out to any other units. It was explicit—they were sent to my unit. I know they had the codes. That's the only way to do it."

The codes, from the NSA codebooks, classified TOP SECRET CRYPTO, with rows of numbers for offline decryption—were swapped out every month.

If the Soviets had the codebooks that month, they might have had them for other months, too. If they managed to obtain the codebooks, which, for all Trolan knew, were kept in vaults and transported by armed couriers, could they obtain the Permissive Action Link unlock codes, too?

"It made the hair on the back of my neck stand up," he said.

As scary as that was to the twenty-six-year-old in charge of a dozen or so nuclear weapons with the firepower to incinerate a country, his next thought might have induced panic if he said it aloud. The microwave tower that shot its radio waves to Trolan's crypto shack was two kilometers outside the outer perimeter of the base, in forestlands, near a hill. He could see it from the steps of the hut, its red-air obstacle light flashing.

No one could physically access *his* message system without interjecting themselves between that tower and the antenna that fed into his crypto shack. That meant that the Soviet spies trying to sabotage the American nukes were right there with him, within maybe a mile of his nuclear warheads, watching them, as he scanned the dark German night for them.

The next day, a military intelligence team arrived at the Killianstädten site and took custody of the suspect messages.

"You going to explain to me what just happened?" Trolan asked.

"Probably not," he was told.

Trolan believes that the East German spies who were listening to his communications were confused, or maybe even panicked, when they tried to decrypt messages that used the new format.

"So, they began to inject the messages themselves to try and figure out if we had just done something like transferred from exercise to war."

"We looked pretty warlike, right at that moment."

"And if they were clamoring for information about a preemptive attack so that *they* could make a preemptive attack, they would throw everything they had at us," he said.

CHAPTER 24

Open Hatches

Brussels, Belgium

RAINER RUPP LEFT WORK AT NATO HEADQUARTERS
and drove to the outskirts of the city. He found a telephone booth and dialed a number. When he heard a "hello," he held a device up to the handset
that looked like an electronic calculator. The calculator emitted a crackle.
Then he heard a beep. He hung up.

In a few seconds, he had transmitted a coded response. It was decoded
at HVA headquarters. TOPAZ had confirmed to Wolf a key bit of information that Moscow needed to know. Nothing was happening. NATO was
not preparing for war. But the Soviets kept up their alert status.

November 10—Tokyo, Japan

On the day before he left for Korea, Ronald Reagan told the Japanese Diet
that the United States was frustrated by "the other side's unwillingness to
negotiate in good faith. We wanted to cut deep into nuclear arsenals, and
still do. But they're blocking the dramatic reductions the world wants."
Japan had lived horrors of nuclear annihilation.

"Despite this bleak picture," he said, "I will not be deterred in my
search for a breakthrough. The United States will never walk away from
the negotiating table. Peace is too important. Common sense demands
that we persevere, and we will persevere."

"We are people of peace," he continued. "We understand the terrible trauma of human suffering. I have lived through four wars in my lifetime. So, I speak not just as president of the United States, but also as a husband, a father, and as a grandfather. I believe there can be only one policy for preserving our precious civilization in this modern age. A nuclear war can never be won and must never be fought."[1]

Once upon a time, Reagan mused, "[W]e had rules of warfare. War is an ugly thing, but we had rules in which we made sure that soldiers fought soldiers, but they did not victimize civilians. That was civilized. Today we've lost something of civilization in that the very weapons we're talking about are designed to destroy civilians by the millions. And let us at least get back to where we once were—that if we talk war at all, we talk it in a way in which there could be victory or defeat and in which civilians have some measure of protection." He pledged he would not stop trying to negotiate with the Soviets until the world began to travel down the road to the total elimination of nuclear weapons.[2]

November 11—In the North Atlantic

Gary Donato, an assistant weapons officer on the ballistic missile submarine USS *Kamehameha*, assumed that Able Archer would be like every other exercise he had endured since he got to sea just a year earlier: a simulated simulation. The *Kamehameha* had sixteen nuclear missiles onboard, each of them bearing a couple of independently targeted warheads. The firepower Donato helped tend was the most lethal, most stealthy, and most survivable deterrent in the United States arsenal. The *Kamehameha* was twenty years old. Its home port was Charleston, South Carolina, its name an homage to the first king of Hawaii. Its crew called it "Kamfish." They called themselves King Kam's crew.[3]

Depending on the plan being exercised, several of those missiles were released to NATO targeteers for use in their general defense plan. While they cruised the North Atlantic in November, more than half of them were. Released. Donato thought the arrangement was weird. He had been taught in weapons school that only the National Command Authority—the president—could send a nuclear control order. On the boat, NATO—the Supreme Allied Commander in Europe, General Bernard Rogers—had the same authority. Donato assumed that the

US president would know well in advance if NATO ever decided to use the missiles and knew from unclassified literature that NATO's political committee had a lot of permutations to debate before it would formally request permission from the US to authorize the SACEUR to use missiles—but still—it was just a bit eerie to be taking nuclear release orders from a commander whose face he had seen in a black-and-white photo. The *Kamehameha* could spin up (bring the missiles online, in naval parlance) and launch nuclear missiles with just that NATO code.[4]

Every day, on every shift, the *Kamehameha* and its crew practiced. Sometimes, the captain, L. M. Jacobi, would make the practice more realistic by not telling the crew that the message received from the Joint Chiefs of Staff or from NATO wasn't real. For the first several days of Able Archer, the *Kamehameha* practiced diving and surfacing, diving and surfacing, moving here and there, practicing evasion techniques. The crew was operating at DEFCON 4.

Then, on November 11, it was cruising near Iceland, when an Emergency Action Message from NATO squawked on several radios at once. The first message directed its crew to load the NATO-committed nuclear missiles with their targeting package, bringing them to DEFCON 3. General quarters sounded.

Lieutenant Donato pushed the buttons to spin the missiles up. This was normal for an exercise. And usually the exercises ended there—a message ordering the submarine to spin down its missiles would arrive within fifteen minutes.

But then came another decoded order: "Release Authority Pending."

For the first time on his tour, the Kamfish was simulating DEFCON 2.

Donato did not know it was a simulation. The Captain and XO knew, but the weapons technicians like him did not. He was a few minutes away from releasing four of the nuclear missiles.

The release trigger was contained in a safe-within-a-safe. Donato opened the outer safe. He compared an enabling code he found on a laminated card with the one that had been sent over the radio from NATO. The codes matched. The order was authentic. One by one, the missiles registered in green on his console. They were spun up and ready. His junior officers were jittery at this point.

"I'm just hoping that we're going to get the spin down code," Donato told them. He was trying to reassure his men, because he was pretty sure this was all part of the exercise, but he really just didn't know. Donato went over the final firing with the procedure in his mind. The second safe was open, and the release trigger—a key—was ready.

If the final order came in, he would take the key, insert it into the launch-enable panel, punch in another code that came over the radio, and, with the captain simultaneously performing an identical procedure at a different console outside of his reach, twist the key.[5]

The *Kamehameha*'s missile hatches were open, as they were during any test, and Donato presumed that the Soviets were listening, probably from a sub hidden somewhere close by.

The longer the hatches stayed open, the more noise the sub produced. Usually, the Soviet submarine following it would send an active sonar ping, like a warning message, telling the Americans: *We're here, we know what's going on, so don't try anything cute.*

The pings were almost comforting. But the longer the hatches stayed open, the more alarmed the Soviets would be.[6] The *Kamehameha* was highly vulnerable to attack at launch depth with its hatches open. And there were no Soviet pings.

———

The exercise finally ended late in the day on November 11. Able Archer had involved no actual combat sorties, no actual movements of aircraft, no elephant trails, as the tanker planners would say. In later years, NATO's chief historian would insist that Able Archer involved no field units. SHAPE officers, members of the Able Archer Directing Staff, the nuclear operations cell at NATO, evaluators from SACEUR—all would express astonishment that the Soviets found anything unusual about this particular exercise.[7] But even they didn't see the whole picture.

A second, much smaller exercise was taking place in Europe at the same time. But it involved real troops and real flights. The US Air Force wanted to make sure that B-52s in Europe could be refueled efficiently during war. Under the new SIOP, these units had been given added responsibility to protect sea lanes of communication—inelegantly called SLOCs in naval terminology—from the Atlantic to the Mediterranean.

In early September, the air force approved a concept of operations for a joint air training exercise they called CRISEX 83. In late October and early November, five KC-135 Boeing Stratotankers would practice refueling B-52s in the air above Europe. And the B-52s would practice "high-altitude air target changes against a contingency target area"—meaning they'd move around quickly and change direction suddenly.

Beginning on October 28, the B-52s and KC-135 flying gas stations practiced their missions, at least two full sorties per day. These continued through November 7, when King Carlos of Spain witnessed a refueling near the coast after a B-52 marine beach assault practice. Other B-52s practiced postattack reconnaissance missions using a special intelligence platform called BUSY OBSERVER.[8] The tactical communications between the fighter jets and their command posts were not secured. None had the right type of encryption device.[9]

The Soviets listened. They had no way of knowing whether CRISEX and Able Archer were linked.

———

A few days later, an air force colleague told Jeffrey Carney, who had now been spying for the Stasi for six months, about a highly sensitive intelligence operation. A specially equipped C-130, normally used for the reconnaissance flights, would travel to West Berlin, sending out electronic signatures resembling the radar returns given off by a B-52 bomber. The Soviet Air Defense radars would light up.

Carney's team was asked to intercept the panicked communications from the Soviet operators that would result. "Believing that the event on their radar screens was a viable threat, they would inform superiors using actual emergency procedures." The test was designed to see how the Soviets reacted in conditions resembling the first stages of an invasion.[10]

Carney's face felt wet. He had to notify the East Germans. As he described it, he slipped away from work, went home, changed clothes, grabbed a train, and ran to the house of a contact whose job it was to talk to the Stasi on his behalf. The man greeted Carney in his bathroom. "Listen, get a pen and paper. You have to go to the East," Carney said. The man protested; he had a class to teach that morning.

Carney was insistent. The Soviets would think they were under attack in just five hours' time.[11]

PART III

ENDGAME(S)

CHAPTER 25

Sacrifice

RONALD REAGAN RETURNED TO THE UNITED STATES on November 14 knowing next to nothing about the war alert. The President's Daily Brief did not include a single item that entire week on Soviet or East German troop readiness. The US Army Europe daily intelligence reports did not flag anything out of the ordinary during this period, either.[1]

His trip had been a whirlwind of diplomatic events, fancy dinners, and resolute speeches. The highlight, for Reagan, was his trip to the Korean DMZ. He could hear North Korean propaganda from loudspeakers across the border. He spoke to troops, the men he considered "the closest to an enemy of Americans' forces, but their morale, their esprit de corps, is unbelievable."[2]

His mind on the troops who made regular sacrifices on behalf of the country, Reagan again expressed impatience with the pace of his policy toward the Soviet Union. He asked George Shultz to establish a pipeline outside the bureaucracy for direct communication with Russian leaders.[3] "I feel the Soviets are so defense minded, so paranoid about being attacked, that without being in any way soft on them, we ought to tell them no one here has any intention of doing anything like that. What the h—l have they got that anyone would want?" He told Shultz he wanted to give a major speech before the end of the year, or at the very least, before the restart of any negotiations.

In October 1983, Reagan had been poised to name Judge Clark to the post of ambassador to the Soviet Union. Matlock wasn't sold on the idea, because the Soviets seemed brittle from the KAL shootdown, but he understood that Reagan wouldn't have even entertained the notion of sending his best friend to Moscow unless he was committed to understanding the Soviets—to "penetrate an alien mode of thought."[4] Matlock began to cast about for Soviet experts to brief Reagan personally. Reagan's intent on moving forward impressed Matlock, but the president was too easily distracted, and staff squabbles, along with the Middle East crises, had preoccupied his time.

Bud McFarlane found the time to meet with the American scholar of Russia, Suzanne Massie, who had been holding on to her ominous message for nearly a month a half. They spent twenty minutes together in his office. She had rehearsed the message: the circumstances of her trip, the suspicion among ordinary Russians, the Bogdanov warning, the yearning for direct communication. McFarlane listened and then asked her to come back soon—for a two-hour meeting. When she did, she found herself volunteering to serve as an emissary. "I so much want for them to know we are not hostile," McFarlane told Massie. "Well, if you send me, they'll know you're not hostile," she replied.

Matlock found Massie sincere, if too eager. He could see that she charmed McFarlane—not in any unusual or inappropriate way, but with a voluble, intelligent charm that convinced men—especially military men—to be solicitous. Massie's reporting was interesting, but McFarlane was not ready to anoint her as an emissary, especially since the Soviets she spoke with regularly were Soviets to whom the US already had access. Massie had asked that she be given an official designation. She picked up Matlock's not-very-subtle hints that he was not as keen on her abilities as McFarlane was. She assumed that Matlock and others in the administration, having not worked regularly with strong women, just didn't trust her. Her point about "widespread anxiety" among Soviet intellectuals about US intentions was well taken, though,[5] and it jibed with two reports that Matlock had gotten in October. Sergei Vishnevsky, a Pravda columnist and probable KGB agent based in Washington, told him over lunch that the Soviet leadership "[was] convinced that the Reagan administration is out to bring their system down and will give no quarter; therefore, they have no choice but to hunker down and fight back."[6] And the ambassador to the Soviet Union, Arthur Hartman, sent word of an unusual conversation he'd had with Gromyko, who told him that his colleagues—the Soviet leaders—believed that Reagan did not even accept their legitimacy.[7]

Shultz and McFarlane asked Matlock to organize a weekly conclave with the sole intent of advancing US policy. Matlock set an agenda based on a common principle: nobody in the group was trying to bring the Soviets down. "All recognized that the Soviet leaders faced mounting problems, but understood that US attempts to exploit them would strengthen Soviet resistance to change, rather than diminish it."[8] Matlock's recollection is probably too crisp. It would be at least two years until Reagan's advisors stopped suggesting ways to inject instability into Soviet policies abroad; the CIA and navy did not cease their adventuring. But with the baseline set, Reagan could focus on ways to use the powers of the presidency for the good. The first meeting codified Matlock's approach: realism about the world as it existed, strength—there would be no unilateral disarmament—and negotiation; real progress toward a real reduction of threats would be ideal. An outline of notes Matlock prepared for the meeting also spells out the goals to which the United States would not aspire. It would not challenge the legitimacy of the Soviet system; it would not strive for military superiority; it would not try to force the collapse of the Soviet system.

Substantively, Reagan would articulate this approach in an interview with *Time* magazine, and he would extrapolate on it in a major speech originally planned just before Christmas. Matlock wrote a draft. Reagan didn't like it. He found it too pedestrian; too full of ideas that Reagan had already talked about. Nothing new. Matlock understood the criticism in a different way: "What he didn't understand was the degree to which his intentions had been misinterpreted and misunderstood by much of the public."[9] On November 18, Weinberger and Vessey briefed Reagan on the update to the nuclear SIOP. Reagan found the experience "most sobering." The plan now had 4,000 missiles directed at mobile Soviet targets. It increased the emphasis on targeting the Soviet leadership for decapitation. It called for an increase in the availability of national technical means— satellites and spy planes—for dynamic retargeting.[10]

In the days after the briefing, Reagan would compare the scenarios presented to him with the ABC movie *The Day After*. He complained about "crazy" generals who thought a war with the Soviet Union could be won, and would again pronounce the possibility of an actual nuclear war "unthinkable."[11]

As Reagan contemplated his next move, the US intelligence community was beginning to realize that something was askew in Europe and Asia.

Item: the US noticed that all Soviet combat aircraft had been grounded from November 4 through November 10. The CIA initially attributed this action as a decision by Soviet commanders to give the crews a few days off around the October Revolution anniversary. Before this instance, the Soviets had only grounded aircraft when they had felt threatened militarily, and wanted to prepare all crews for the possibility of a sudden attack.

Item: A weekly analytical document from the CIA's National Photographic Interpretation Center noted a large number of Soviet aircraft in East Germany were outside their hangers. MiG-23 fighters were moved to their alert positions near the runways.[12] And third, a report from the army's 766 Military Intelligence Detachment reported a large number of spot reports involving possible surveillance of US bases inside of West Germany.

Item: Analysis of that week's CREEK MISTY and CREEK FLUSH flights noted that Warsaw Pact air defense radars were kept turned on throughout the period. They ordinarily were turned on sporadically.

There were even more indicators:

- Reconnaissance flights out of the UK, code-named CREEK SCEPTRE, had reported unusual activity at Warsaw Pact air bases in Czechoslovakia.
- The air force reported that Soviet military weather broadcasts had been curtailed and then suspended for a period that coincided with the duration of the exercise.[13]
- The CIA reported that Marshal Nikolai Ogarkov had told a meeting of Warsaw Pact defense ministers that the Soviets would use more weapons deployed in the "oceans and seas" to counter the Pershings, which he insisted were unequivocally "first-strike" weapons because of their ability to avoid radar and reach targets near Moscow. He noted that

the Soviets would respond in the near term by stationing more SS-20s and target them on NATO bases.[14]

Finally, NATO intelligence reported that an unusually large number of Soviet "Bear" reconnaissance planes were crisscrossing the skies in Eastern Europe during the period of the exercise.[15]

CHAPTER 26

Warning of War

TAKEN TOGETHER, THE SIGNS WERE OMINOUS ENOUGH for Brigadier General Leonard Perroots, the deputy chief of staff for intelligence at SHAPE, to catalog them in a memo. He forwarded it to interested parties, including David McManis, the CIA's new National Intelligence Officer for Warning.[1]

McManis was one of the few agency senior officials who had been burned by nuclear brinksmanship before. On October 10, 1969, as a watch officer in the White House he had monitored the Soviet counterreaction to a bizarre gambit by President Richard M. Nixon to try to convince the Soviets to pressure the North Vietnamese into major concessions. Nixon decided to assume the mind-set of a madman. He ordered the strategic nuclear forces to ratchet up its alertness across the world, in response to nothing. Nixon hoped the Soviets would see the signs of increased readiness and, with deft hints by American diplomats, get the impression that Nixon might have gone mad. The Soviets would then capitulate to the Americans for fear of provoking the madman into doing something serious. McManis did not know at the time that Nixon and Henry Kissinger harbored such dangerous delusions; like his contemporaries, he had been told only that the Joint Chiefs of Staff was testing readiness. He learned the truth years later.[2]

By this point in late November 1983, the intelligence community and the State Department had reported a few anecdotes about Soviet fears of an armed confrontation with the United States. McManis's job was to collect them all and see if they meant something significant.

The CIA circulated a report from a foreign intelligence service about Viktor Grishin, the First Secretary of Moscow and an influential advisor to Andropov. A visitor to his dacha outside Moscow found him in disarray, walking around in his bathrobe and bedroom slippers, saying, over and over again, "Americans want war. There is going to be war."[3] Reagan read this in the President's Daily Brief.

Another report noted that Andropov's illness was a source of instability for the entire Soviet political leadership. The CIA followed his motorcade movements, noting that he spent eight hours a day at his office before returning to a special hospital at night for dialysis.[4] Though he had not attended Politburo meetings, he continued to see visitors regularly. One source reported to the State Department that his absence from official functions was causing a dangerous vacuum. There was considerable agitation at the middle levels of the Communist Party that the change Andropov had promised was not happening. If Andropov died, the Politburo would select a placeholder. The military would again have free reign to make foreign policy. This uncertainty contributed to the unease.[5]

On November 19, Defense Minister Ustinov snarled about "recent military exercises" conducted by the US and NATO. "These exercises are enormous in scope, and they are increasingly difficult to distinguish from real deployment of armed forces for aggression."[6]

The White House mailroom could not keep up with all the postcards it had been getting from the Soviet Union. Apparently, Pravda had asked its readers to send them to President Reagan urging peace. That was propaganda, of course. But thousands of ordinary Soviets had written extra messages on the cards. With a deputy, the State Department's Tom Simons spent one morning reading through many of them. "A lot of people who sent these things in were children, and organizations of veterans and grandmothers. They wrote statements such as, 'Please, Mr. President. We know war and we've been through war, and we don't want another war,'" he recalled. "I said to myself: these people are really scared."[7]

In late November, Herb Meyer, a top assistant to CIA Director Casey, circulated a memo with a blunt conclusion: a global outbreak of violence signaled the beginning of a new phase in the "global struggle between the

Free World and the Soviet Union." The Soviets had no doubt concluded by mid-1983 that US policy had fundamentally changed course; the president had deployed a truth weapon, calling them "Evil," a charge against which there was no real defense. Missiles had indeed been deployed to Europe, and on time, meaning that the Soviet propaganda effort had failed. The US economy was growing, while the Soviet economy was stagnating; its demographics were calamitous. By invading Grenada, the US rolled back Soviet efforts to spread its influence in the Third World. Where there was Soviet intrusion, insurgencies had broken out. The US defense budget was robust; Soviet projects to reconnect to Europe were floundering. Meyer predicted that the Soviets would respond by seeding violence throughout the world, blaming it as the "inevitable result of US policies," and then hope that the world forces the US to moderate.[8]

In Europe, the Pershings and GLCMs began to arrive on massive US Air Starliner planes, triggering massive protests. Subterfuge was needed to sneak the 160 Tomahawk cruise missiles through a ring of protestors at the RAF's Greenham Common, in Berkshire. West Germany accepted the first of about 90 GLCMs and 108 Pershings; the Netherlands and Belgium took in about 50 each. The Italian mafia helped the air force contain demonstrations in Italy, which took receipt of 112 missiles.[9] The decapitation missiles that wouldn't even give the Soviets time to go to the bathroom had been fielded. The SS-20 advantage was neutralized.[10] A few weeks later, the Soviets announced they would deploy more missiles.[11]

As Reagan often did when he thought of the existential realities of being president, he turned his mind to God. He told two reporters visiting from *People* magazine on December 6, "There were times in the past when we thought the end of the world was coming, but never anything like this."[12]

On December 8, the Soviets formally suspended Intermediate-Range Nuclear Forces (INF) Treaty negotiations. But Shultz gave clear instructions to his entire staff. Those who dealt with the Soviet Union and their allies across the world should take a lighter touch in the coming weeks and assure them that they had nothing to fear from the United States.[13] About progress, Shultz told staff: "I cannot get it through your heads that this man is serious." If there was anything they had to know about Reagan, it was that "he said what he thought."[14] Shultz worked to get a meeting with Gromyko at a security conference in Stockholm scheduled for mid-January. Matlock proposed a series of meetings between Weinberger and Ustinov, and JCS Chairman John Vessey and his Soviet counterpart, Nikolai Ogarkov.[15]

On December 12, Oliver North sent Jack Matlock a memo with the game plan for the next major global military exercise, called Night Train '84, which would include the annual "live fly" exercise run by the Strategic Air Command to test the new Single Integrated Operation Procedure, SIOP 6. Because the exercise would be visible to the Soviets, there were unambiguous political implications, as a briefing prepared by the Department of Defense acknowledged. Matlock was asked to approve. He read through the scenario. It called for the US to use tactical nuclear weapons in response to a nonnuclear Soviet attack.

Matlock and his deputy Ty Cobb urged that the exercise be altered.

"Anything involving the full generation of its nuclear forces and live firing of missiles—might not be such a good idea," they wrote back to North. "In particular, the scenario itself—if it should leak (it will)—would be used by critics of the administration both here and elsewhere as evidence that we are planning a nuclear war. This could seriously undercut the president as peacemaker and increase apprehension in Europe, where we still face a rocky road to keep the INF deployment schedule on track."[16] Could not the scenario end peacefully, instead of with a nuclear exchange, they asked?

(The answer, given months later, was "Nope.")

On December 13, Matlock forwarded McFarlane a letter from an American academic who had spent ten days conferring with senior Soviet officials. "The fear of war seemed to affect the elite as well as the man on the street," the letter writer had said.[17] McFarlane asked the CIA to prepare a memo for the president on the signs and signals the Soviets seemed to be sending about war.

The CIA knew nothing about Oleg Gordievsky's reporting at this point, but they found plenty of other intelligence indicators to catalog. On December 22, DCI Casey told Reagan that the CIA learned that the Soviet military had sent a message in November to its field agencies, warning them to be alert to signals of surprise enemy attack. This one order, Casey told the president was part of a large vein of reporting that suggested the Soviets perceived a higher likelihood that war would suddenly break out.

Before Christmas, the socialist Canadian Prime Minister Pierre Trudeau visited Reagan and warned him to watch his words: "I found myself telling him that he should communicate better, and that he's the expert communicator." Reagan did not like the lecture from a man whose insouciant demeanor brought a "naughty schoolboy" to mind.[18]

On December 30, the report McFarlane asked for was complete.

The CIA's conclusion was that the Soviet *agita* was a sign that US policies were working *well*. "Contrary to the impression conveyed by Soviet propaganda, Moscow does not appear to anticipate a near-term military confrontation with the United States. With the major *exception of* the Middle East, there appears to be no region in which [the] Soviets are now apprehensive that action in support of clients could lead to Soviet-American armed collision. By playing up the war danger, Moscow hopes to encourage resistance to INF deployment in Western Europe, deepen cleavages within the Atlantic alliance, and increase public pressure in the United States for a more conciliatory posture toward the USSR," the agency reported.[19]

CHAPTER 27

Ivan and Anya

Washington, DC

ON JANUARY 2, 1983, THE DEPUTY DIRECTOR OF INTEL-
ligence, Robert Gates tasked Fritz Ermarth, the new National Intelligence
Officer for the Soviet Union, to prepare a major intelligence estimate that
would focus primarily on the threat of war.[1]

Ermarth was a sharp student of the Soviet Union, having served as a
top CIA analyst for more than a decade. He had retired to the private sec-
tor in 1980. Three years later, Casey appointed him to fortify the agency's
understanding of the threat from the USSR. Ermarth believed that Soviet
strategic culture was inherently militaristic and aggressive, a direct consequence of its history since early modernity.[2]

As Ermarth read himself in to the intelligence, he learned that the US
knew quite a bit about Soviet war plans. "In effect, we had many of their
military cookbooks. This permitted us to judge confidently the difference
between when they might be brewing up for a real military confrontation
or, as one wag put it, just rattling their pots and pans. It allowed us to distinguish between isolated if purposeful military moves, mere anomalies,
and real military preparations for large-scale warfare."[3]

The SNIE would take him five months and encompass the range of
the intelligence that the air force, Defense Intelligence Agency, the army,
the navy, and foreign countries had collected. He would also solicit the
opinions of his colleagues through the community. He was confident he
could deliver a solid verdict.

———

On the eve of the first conference of the world powers since the November walkout of the Soviets from INF missile talks in Geneva, President Reagan delivered his long-awaited address. The State Department had prepared allies in advance; excerpts were even delivered to the Soviets with the direct intent of convincing them that this speech was going to be different; this speech reflected Reagan's true intentions and would provide a roadmap for his approach.

"I believe that 1984 finds the United States in the strongest position in years to establish a constructive and realistic working relationship with the Soviet Union," Reagan said in the East Room of the White House. "We've come a long way since the decade of the seventies, years when the United States seemed filled with self-doubt and neglected its defenses, while the Soviet Union increased its military might and sought to expand its influence by armed forces and threat.

"Three years ago, we embraced a mandate from the American people to change course, and we have. With the support of the American people and the Congress, we halted America's decline. Our economy is now in the midst of the best recovery since the sixties. Our defenses are being rebuilt, our alliances are solid, and our commitment to defend our values has never been more clear. America's recovery may have taken Soviet leaders by surprise. They may have counted on us to keep weakening ourselves. They've been saying for years that our demise was inevitable. They said it so often they probably started believing it. Well, if so, I think they can see now they were wrong. This may be the reason that we've been hearing such strident rhetoric from the Kremlin recently. These harsh words have led some to speak of heightened uncertainty and an increased danger of conflict. This is understandable but profoundly mistaken."

Reagan proposed that both governments begin to negotiate along three parallel tracks. First, "we need to find ways to reduce, and eventually to eliminate, the threat and use of force in solving international disputes." Second, the countries would work together to reduce the "vast stockpiles of armaments in the world."

"As I've said before, my dream is to see the day when nuclear weapons will be banished from the face of the Earth. Last month the Soviet Defense Minister stated that his country would do everything to avert the threat of war. Well, these are encouraging words, but now is the time to move from words to deed. The opportunity for progress in arms control exists. The Soviet leaders should take advantage of it."

Reagan wrote the final part of the speech himself.

"Just suppose with me for a moment that an Ivan and an Anya could find themselves, oh, say, in a waiting room, or sharing a shelter from the rain or a storm with a Jim and Sally, and there was no language barrier to keep them from getting acquainted. Would they then debate the differences between their respective governments? Or would they find themselves comparing notes about their children and what each other did for a living? Before they parted company, they would probably have touched on ambitions and hobbies and what they wanted for their children and problems of making ends meet. And as they went their separate ways, maybe Anya would be saying to Ivan, "Wasn't she nice? She also teaches music." Or Jim would be telling Sally what Ivan did or didn't like about his boss. They might even have decided they were all going to get together for dinner some evening soon. Above all, they would have proven that people don't make wars."[4]

The formal reaction was disheartening. "Propaganda," sniffed Tass. "A hackneyed ploy," grumbled Gromyko.[5] A week later, Pravda parodied Ivan and Anya: "Jim is unemployed, and he and Sally are fearful of FBI surveillance and amazed that Ivan and Anya fail to fit the common image of hounded, suppressed Russians. The stereotypes are reversed: Jim and Sally marvel at the freedoms of their Soviet acquaintances and hide from them the flaws of American society. Sally is a dishwasher," the *New York Times* reported.

———

Shultz met Gromyko in Stockholm a few days after the speech. Instead of lecturing at the foreign minister, Shultz brought no real agenda. He let Gromyko ventilate. And he asked Gromyko what it would take to restart negotiations.

Reagan pressed on. On January 17, he met Suzanne Massie for the first time. McFarlane would note that she seemed to understand instinctively how to communicate with the president. Indeed, she had studied him. One friend counseled her about Reagan's Christianity. Reagan considered himself a defender of Christian beliefs. Sometimes, he would move toward peace; when he felt himself under threat, he might take up a sword to defend them. Her charge: "bring out the pacifier, rather than the crusader."[6] She expected a small meeting with the president, McFarlane, and maybe Matlock. But McFarlane had convened the senior staff of the White House, including the president's chief political counselors and aides. "In my state of shock, they all seemed unnaturally tall, oozing with masculine power and importance." The president sensed her discomfort, took her by the arm, and led her to one of the two white armchairs in front of the fireplace in the Oval Office.

Reagan's first question: "How much do they believe in communism?"

"I can't tell you how all the Russians think," she replied cautiously, "[B]ut I can tell you what many of them say. They call them—[the communist leaders]—'the big bottoms,' and say, 'they only love their chairs.'" The true ideology was gone, she said; only its form remained.[7] For twenty-five minutes they talked, and Massie got through all of her talking points. Before she left, she had a question for Reagan. "When I go to the Soviet Union, I want to be able to say that I asked you this question and give them your answer. If you are elected to another term, will the policy you spoke of, small steps to improve relations, be a continuing policy of your administration?"

"Yes," Reagan said. "If they want peace, they can have it."[8]

———

The president of Yugoslavia, a former diplomat who had served in the Soviet Union, told Reagan a week later that the Soviet people were genuinely fearful, but if "we opened them up a bit, their leading citizens would get braver about proposing changes to their system."[9]

Anatoly Dobrynin, the Soviet ambassador to the United States, noticed after an informal poll of all countries allied with the Soviet system that the ice seemed to be cracking. All reported that the US had begun to talk more quietly.[10] US diplomats picked up signs from the Soviets, too.

But the CIA's Ermarth found the White House's optimism about an imminent reversal in Soviet behavior naïve. He understood the argument that President Reagan was articulating: the US was strong enough to negotiate now. But his study of the Soviet mind had taught him that dialogue could be deceptive. He thought the Soviets were just cranking back their war-scare hype because they saw it had not served their ends well.[11]

Even if Reagan had been reluctant, Shultz saw it as his job as Secretary of State to "force him to make these decisions, if nothing else."[12]

––––––

On February 8, Yuri Andropov died of kidney failure.

John Lenczowski on the National Security Council was openly, almost rebelliously skeptical of suggestions that Reagan attend his funeral. If the president were to attend the funeral, "it would send a major signal that real strength is eroding." It's an illusion, he wrote, "That peace is achieved by better atmospherics and by such direct dialogue as is sufficient to clear up misunderstandings." Large chunks of the American people might believe that, but they need to be reminded that "destruction of American democracy is one of those objectives."[13]

Reagan had no intention of going. He didn't like Andropov and found him to be a frustrating obstacle to his agenda. Vice President Bush would go in his stead. "Let him honor that prick," the president said. (More gentle biographers insist Reagan had said "guy" or "man," but Matlock and McFarlane confirm that the president indeed called Andropov a "prick.")

Six days later, the Politburo confirmed Konstantin Chernenko as the next General Secretary. An old Brezhnev protégé, he was seen by the CIA as a tool of the status quo and is "unlikely to [have] much latitude or inclination for moving the Soviet Union in new directions on either the domestic or foreign fronts."[14]

His speech on that occasion had shocked the world; the new guy seemed to be just as sick as the old guy. He wheezed as he spoke.

Mindful that Chernenko had little grasp on foreign policy and even less actual power, Reagan was propelled by a sense of primal urgency. "I had a gut feeling that I'd like to talk to him about our problems man to man and see if I could convince him that there would be material benefit to the Soviets if they'd join the family of nations," he wrote in his diary.[15]

Fritz Ermarth read squawks in the press that Reagan might be open to a summit. He wrote again to the White House, hoping for a reality check:

Getting the Soviets "back to the bargaining table" for a successful restoration of the dialogue, "or even seeing a sharp [reduction] of hostile Soviet propaganda need not necessarily mean that we've made our point [or] conveyed the message we want them to get."[16]

By this point, though, Reagan did not see himself included in Ermarth's royal "we." When Reagan wrote Chernenko for the first time, he did not propose a meeting, but he indicated that the United States would be open to talk just about any time. Chernenko responded in kind, with a three-page letter that avoided most of the usual Soviet agitprop. He even held out the prospect that relations between the two countries might one day be "good."[17]

───────

As he gathered input for the Special National Intelligence Estimate, Ermarth found himself battling naïveté from the White House and a large number of analysts inside the CIA who seemed to him to be rebelling against reality, convinced they had an elite duty to speak truth to power.[18]

One enduring problem for the CIA was that it was not charged with "net assessments," meaning that in its official estimates, it did not take into account the way that the plans, operations, and status of the US military affected the subject of whatever they were trying to figure out. Often, the CIA knew little about American military exercises. In the late 1970s, when CIA Director Stansfield Turner was asked to guess what damage the Soviets might do to the US and the US to the Soviets under certain scenarios, the DIA objected. Turner was told that net assessment, the strategic comparison of military forces, was the province of the Pentagon, and that the CIA should butt out. If the Pentagon didn't get to make those judgments, they wouldn't give them at all. Turner thought that the Pentagon used "net assessment" as a way to justify whatever policy had already been decided.

That wasn't to say that the Pentagon's conclusions were always wrong; the DIA's analysis of war games and military behavior were often first rate and, in hindsight, accurate. But the CIA had a similar level of expertise and access to more sources. Had the CIA been allowed to participate or observe Pentagon war games on a more regular basis, it might have enhanced the quality of its own intelligence products.

To his regret, Turner left behind an intelligence community where analysts would bias their conclusions because they knew that rivals would bias them in the other direction. Somewhere in the middle would be the truth.[19]

The son of a garbage hauler, William F. Casey was an introverted adventurer. By thirty-two, he was a well-compensated New York City attorney, and a spy, for the CIA's predecessor, the Office of Strategic Services (OSS). Casey was a canny spy, and he impressed his superiors. He was placed in charge of running clandestine operations all across Europe.[20] Postwar, his career ascendant, he entered politics but lost a 1966 race for Congress in New York, running as a moderate the same year Reagan was elected governor of California as a conservative. And then Casey used his own money to finance outsider campaigns in support of new friends such as Richard Nixon. By 1972, he was chairman of the Securities and Exchange Commission, then an Undersecretary of State in the administration, then head of the Export-Import Bank, and one of Nixon's closest domestic policy advisors. By 1979, he was one of the largest Republican donors in the country.

Casey was an insider, but he did not meet the conservative insurgent Reagan until 1979. Reagan's clarity on communism impressed him, as did his insistence on supply-side tax cuts. From his perch on the fifty-third floor of the Pan-Am Building in Manhattan, Casey threw his considerable financial support to Reagan. Not six months after meeting the tall, brash New Yorker, Reagan fired his campaign manager and appointed Casey.[21] He was not the best manager, but he got the campaign out of debt, and

Reagan did the rest on his own. Casey wanted to be Secretary of State. Too uncouth for that, he was given the CIA post instead.

Casey thought that the culture within the Directorate of Intelligence of the CIA had developed a particular and deterministic view of the Soviets, the upshot of which was a tendency to downplay the significance of strategic advancements.[22] That had been the genesis for the "Team B" exercise in intelligence analysis in the late 1970s, which helped convince Reagan that the United States faced a window of vulnerability and the Soviets were hell-bent on developing first-strike weapons. The CIA he inherited was more aligned with the State Department and the arms control community, especially on its policy side. Its military analysts—the folks who counted the bombers and missiles—tended to be more hawkish, but the senior analysts who wrote the major intelligence estimates were academics who seemed to be more conscious that they were serving the nation's commander in chief. Casey was one of the smartest men ever to serve the agency, but he held a disdain for elitists that was as thick as the glasses he wore.

"Many DI analysts thought part of their job was to offset the worst-case-ism of the Pentagon," said Ken deGraffenreid, Reagan's senior coordinator for intelligence on the National Security Council. "Their thinking was, 'We tell the truth. Those guys always want to build more B-1s and Minutemen and missiles and, therefore, they're going to show you the worst aspects of what the Soviets are doing, and it's our job to correct all that.'" Inside the CIA, those analysts would refer to themselves as "threat busters" and "balloon poppers."

Casey brought in a number of outsiders who shared his harder view about Soviet intentions, and promoted those internally whose output had been consistent.[23] In the 1980s, the White House seemed to want confirmation that the Soviet threat was real. Ermarth knew that it was, and that wishful thinking would not make it go away.

Well into his presidency, Ronald Reagan would cite the book that most influenced his identity: a from–the–bootstraps tale of good triumphing over toil and evil by Harold Bell Wright called *That Printer of Udell's*. Reagan would have likely read the book in the form presented in this edition.

Despite a hawkish reputation and a heroic history of aggressive spymastering, Reagan's CIA director, William Casey, was seen by rivals inside the administration as a relatively honest broker of intelligence information during Reagan's first term. *Ronald Reagan Presidential Library*

General John Vessey, the chairman of the Joint Chiefs of Staff and one of the key architects of President Reagan's first SIOP. *Ronald Reagan Presidential Library*

As President Reagan recovered from an assassin's bullet, his senior staff tried to make sense of the world from the White House Situation Room. Somewhere under the desk pictured here is a duplicate nuclear football, brought to the room by National Security Adviser Richard V. Allen, just in case. *Ronald Reagan Presidential Library*

Thomas C. Reed trained as an engineer; developed an expertise in spy satellites, communication, and nuclear weapons; and was entrusted by President Reagan with the most secret program of his presidency, Project Pegasus, which would ensure the survival of the presidency even if Washington, DC, were obliterated. *Thomas C. Reed*

(*Left*) A military challenge coin shows the logo of the CONUS Communications Support Center, the cover designation for units involved with President Reagan's shadowy Pegasus project.

(*Right*) Most of the Reagan-era Pegasus effort to provide a fail-safe emergency government-in-waiting was dismantled by President Clinton in 1993, and some of its functions were transferred to FEMA. But its legacy endures: FEMA's Mobile Emergency Response Support convoys, of which there are at least six, would fall under the control of the White House Military Office during national emergencies, giving the president a mobile command post along the lines of the one Thomas Reed envisioned. *FEMA*

President Reagan did not think his speech to the National Association of Evangelicals would come to define his first term, but his speechwriting staff hoped otherwise: they saw it as pivotal in an effort to regain political momentum after the 1982 electoral success of the Nuclear Freeze movement. The world reacted to the term "Evil Empire" with a mix of surprise and disdain. Reagan would later insist that he owned the phrase and found no reason to apologize for it. *Ronald Reagan Presidential Library*

BY THE PRESIDENT OF THE UNITED STATES OF AMERICA

A PROCLAMATION

WHEREAS there have been substantial withdrawals of coin, bullion, and currency from banking institutions in the United States for the purpose of hoarding and acquiring goods for speculative activities; and

WHEREAS these conditions have created a national emergency; and

WHEREAS it is in the best interests of all bank depositors that limitations be imposed to prevent further hoarding of coin, bullion, and currency; and

WHEREAS it is provided in Section 4 of the Act of March 9, 1933, 48 Stat. 2 (12 U.S.C. § 95(a)), that

> during such emergency period as the President of the United States by proclamation may prescribe, no member bank of the Federal reserve system shall transact any banking business except to such extent and subject to such regulations, limitations, and restrictions as may be prescribed by the Secretary of the Treasury, with the approval of the President;

and

WHEREAS it is also provided in Section 4 of the Act that

> [a]ny individual, partnership, corporation, or association, or any director, officer, or employee thereof, violating any of the provisions of this section shall be deemed guilty of a misdemeanor and, upon conviction thereof, shall be fined not more than $10,000 or, if a natural period, may, in addition to such fine, be imprisoned for a term not exceeding ten years

and that

> [e]ach day that any such violation continues shall be deemed a separate offense;

The public has never been privy to the text of a Presidential Emergency Action Document (PEAD), a series of which endow the chief executive with extraordinary powers during existential emergencies. This draft PEAD, which was not put into effect, would have prevented Americans from hoarding currency during a nuclear war. *Ronald Reagan Presidential Library*

NATIONAL DEFENSE UNIVERSITY
FORT LESLEY J. McNAIR
WASHINGTON, D.C. 20319

DECLASSIFIED IN FULL
Authority: EO 13526
Chief, Records & Declass Div, WH
Date DEC 2 0 2012

PROUD PROPHET - 83

13-24 JUNE 1983

GLOBEX SERIES

MILITARY AND STRATEGIC ISSUES

WAR GAMING AND SIMULATION CENTER

218-92-0013
9

SECRET NOFORN

12 - M - 1487
Document # 1

In the summer of 1983, senior members of the Pentagon, including Defense Secretary Caspar Weinberger, participated in one of the largest tabletop war games organized to date. Almost every player left the exercise with a staggering sense of how inadequately prepared the military and civilian leadership was to ever prosecute a nuclear war against the USSR. *Department of Defense*

The Day After, a film about the aftermath of a nuclear exchange between the USSR and the United States, was broadcast on ABC in late November 1983. It remains the most watched television movie in the history of broadcasting. President Reagan screened it at the White House, finding it unsettling. His advisers debated how the White House should respond to public anxieties about the film. *Creative Commons license*

They told us it would be impossible for us to make this movie.
They told us it would be impossible for you to watch it.
We hope nothing is impossible.

The DAY AFTER
...beyond imagining.

ACE OFFICERS NUCLEAR WEAPONS RELEASE PROCEDURES COURSE I-34-39

17 - 21 OCT 83

No.	NAME	COUNTRY/SERVICE	COMMAND	BILLETS
1	COL MILLER, T.H.	US-A	LSEAST	Boeld
2	WGCDR BELAMY-KNIGHTS, P.G.	UK-AF	AFCENT	633
3	LTC BITTENBENDER, E.	US-A	AFNORTH	ABC-APT.
4	CDR BLYTHE, D.A.	UK-N	SHAPE	ABC-Hotel
5	WGCDR CLEGG, M.P.	UK-AF	CHAN	Kuschmierz
6	LTC HELMS, G.D.	GE-A	BALTAP	I.Bierling
7	CDR JONAS, M.	US-N	NAVSOUTH	ABC-APT.
8	LTC LOWENTHAL, P.	US-A	AIRSOUTH	633
9	LTC METSDORF, K.	GE-A	MOD-UK	BOQ
10	CDR MOSSE, V.	UK-N	MOD-UK	BOC/ABC
11	LTC MULDOON, P.W.	US-A	AIRSOUTH	633
12	LTC SACHON, U.	GE-AF	AFCENT	BOQ
13	WGCDR SEYMOUR, C.C.	UK-AF	AFNORTH	633
14	LTC STRUCK, S.H.	US-AF	AFSOUTH	633
15	CDR WICKS, G.W.	US-N	IBERLANT	K.Bierling
16	MAJ ANDONIS, J.	GR-AF	SHAPE	Magdalena
17	MAJ ANKE, G.	NO-A	MOD-NO	Schilcherhof
18	MAJ BURGESS, J.F.	UK-A	MOD-UK	Maderspacher
19	SQNLDR DALLISON, P.M.	US-AF	SHAPE	Kuschmierz
20	MAJ GILLENWATER, P.J.	US-A	AFCENT	Wenger
21	MAJ HOLSKEY, S.	US-AF	AAFCE	633
22	MAJ JENSEN, H.	GE-AF	MOD-GE	BOQ
23	MAJ LEWIS, G.A.	US-AF	USAFE	ABC-Hotel
24	MAJ MASERDONI, L.	IT-AF	SHAPE	Magdalena
25	MAJ PICCO, D.J.	US-A	EUCOM	BOQ
26	MAJ POTTSCHMIDT, J.	GE-AF	SHAPE	Boeld
27	MAJ RADER, J.	GE-A	MOD-GE	BOQ
28	MAJ REIF, G.P.	US-AF	SHAPE	Zur Rose
29	MAJ SCHLESER, L.C.	US-AF	USAFE	Zur Rose
30	MAJ SIRMANS, R.	US-MC	AFNORTH	633
31	MAJ STOKOE, J.H.	US-A	EUCOM	BOQ
32	CPT ANTON	US-A	EUCOM	633
33	CPT APONTE, B.L.	US-A	EUCOM	Schilcherhof
34	CPT CLAUSEN, M.	US-A	EUCOM	BOQ
35	CPT DODSON, D.	US-A	AFCENT	Zur Rose
36	CPT GUITEAR, B.L.	US-A	EUCOM	Schilcherhof
37	CPT V. HEERDE,	NL-AF	AAFCE	I.Bierling
38	CPT PANELLA, J.B.	US-AF	USAFE	Zur Rose
39	CPT REEVERS, T.C.	US-A	EUCOM	BOQ
40	CPT TAYLOR, R.N.	US-A	AFCENT	633
41	CPT WILLIAMS, W.G.	US-A	EUCOM	Boeld
42	CPT GAMBRELL, A.D.	US-A	EUCOM	Schilcherhof
43	CPT TROLAN, W.L.	US-A	EUCOM	Wenger
44	CPT ALLARD, J.W.	US-A	EUCOM	Wenger
45	1LT BEERY, M.D.	US-A	EUCOM	Wenger/Lang
46	1LT BOETJER, M.C.	US-A	EUCOM	D.Kuschmierz
47	1LT DONELLY, R.S.	US-A	EUCOM	BOQ
48	1LT HOSTIAL, H.	GE-AF	MOD-GE	K.Bierling
49	1LT PATT, K.	GE-AF	MOD-GE	K.Bierling
50	1LT RAY, T.P.	US-A	EUCOM	K.Bierling

Even relatively low-ranking American officers had to be trained in the complex procedures designed to authenticate nuclear orders. Many were less than twenty-five years old and were given responsibility for warheads that could kill millions. *Lee Trolan Collection*

The syllabus that Captain Lee Trolan and others followed at NATO nuclear weapons release procedures school. The new procedures were first used in the Able Archer '83 exercise two weeks later, confusing and probably scaring the Soviet and East German intelligence agencies, neither of which had managed to get their own spies to tell them about the change. *Lee Trolan Collection*

NATO UNCLASSIFIED

MONDAY, 17 OCT 1983

TIME	SUBJECT	INSTRUCTOR
0745	REPORT TO ACADEMIC BUILDING	
0800-0815	OPENING REMARKS	COL FEDERICI (CMDT)
0815-0820	WELCOME BY SACEUR (FILM)	
0820-0845	ADMINISTRATION	LT GREIFELT/ LCDR BALLARD
0845-0855	COURSE INTRODUCTION	WGCDR O'DWYER-RUSSELL
0855-0930	NATO ORGANIZATION AND FUNCTION	LCDR BALLARD/ LTC MOHR
0930-0950	COFFEE BREAK	
0950-1045	SACEUR'S NOP	WGCDR O'DWYER-RUSSELL
1050-1145	NWRP MESSAGE FLOW	LTC BARKER
1145-1200	CLASS PHOTO	VIS AIDS
1200-1330	LUNCH	
1300-1345	LOCAL AREA BRIEFING (OPTIONAL)	CPT HAYE
1345-1415	COFFEE BREAK/NWRP PACKET CHECKOUT	
1415-1500	INTRODUCTION TO NWRP MANUAL	LCDR BALLARD
1505-1550	SELECTIVE EMPLOYMENT PLANS	LCDR BALLARD
1555-1645	CWRP	COL DUREL
1800-1900	COURSE COCKTAIL PARTY AT NATO COMMUNITY CLUB. YOU ARE REQUESTED TO CONTRIBUTE $2.50 PER PERSON IN SUPPORT OF THIS FUNCTION. PAYABLE IN THE STUDENT ADMIN OFFICE.	

TUESDAY, 18 OCT 1983

TIME	SUBJECT	INSTRUCTOR
0800-1100	NWRP MESSAGES (IN DETAIL) (UNSCHEDULED COFFEE BREAKS)	LTC BARKER/LCDR BALLARD
1105-1200	INTRODUCTION TO THE PRACTICAL EXERCISE	LCDR BALLARD
1200-1330	LUNCH	
1330-1600	PRACTICAL EXERCISE (PROB #1) (ASSIGNED SYNDICATE ROOMS)	STAFF
1600-1630	REVIEW PROBLEM #1 (CLASSROOM #2)	STAFF/GROUP 1
	NOTE: CIVILIAN CLOTHING (COAT & TIE) MAY BE WORN TOMORROW.	

WEDNESDAY, 19 OCT 1983

TIME	SUBJECT	INSTRUCTOR
0800-1100	PRACTICAL EXERCISE (PROB #2 & #3) (ASSIGNED SYNDICATE ROOMS)	STAFF
1100-1130	REVIEW PROBLEMS #2 & #3 (CLASSROOM #1)	STAFF/GROUP 2
1130-1200	QUIZ (CLASSROOM #2)	STAFF
1200-1330	LUNCH	
1330-1630	OPTIONAL STUDY	

3.

NATO UNCLASSIFIED

The border between the Germanys served as the locus for World War III planning. Here, a German Federal Border Guard unit conducts a joint patrol with the 2d Armored Cavalry Regiment in March 1983. *US Army*

NATO's headquarters in Casteau, Belgium, the command post for Able Archer '83 exercise. *NATO*

The Soviet SS-20 Intercontinental Ballistic Missile menaced NATO countries until 1988.

The official unit patch of 59th Ordinance Brigade's 501st Army Artillery Detachment, which controlled nuclear weapons in the Fulda Gap. *U.S. Army*

Trolan worked with his German counterpart, Major Schrodter, commander of the 23rd Flugabwehrrak (FLARAK) Battalion, at the Killianstädten base. If he ever received an authentic nuclear release order, he would transfer custody of the warhead to Schrodter, whose unit controlled the weapons that would launch them. *Lee Trolan Collection.*

A small muster of men patrolled the grounds of the Killianstädten air artillery base in the Fulda Gap. The US controlled the warheads; the Germans controlled the Nike-Hercules missiles, seen here. *Lee Trolan Collection.*

The USS *Kamehameha*, with several dozen nuclear warheads on board, was on a deterrent patrol during Able Archer '83 and encountered a Soviet submarine in the North Atlantic. *Greg Pancerev*

Captain Lee Trolan and Major Frank Schrodter stand in front of a vessel containing a W31 nuclear warhead. *Lee Trolan Collection*

In the fall of 1984, W31 nuclear warheads were removed from the Killianstädten site. Here, a tractor prepares to load a vessel containing the last warhead Trolan ever protected into a US Army helicopter. *Lee Trolan Collection*

As Soviet SS–25 missile regiments waited for the call to Armageddon, President Reagan was visiting Asia. On November 11, during one of the final phases of Able Archer '83, Reagan had lunch with US troops along the Demilitarized Zone between South and North Korea. *Ronald Reagan Presidential Library*

0288
DECLASSIFIED
NLS *M02-002* #2
BY ___CVJ___ NARA DATE 11/13/03

КЕ: ... C: 17

CONFIDENTIAL

THE WHITE HOUSE

WASHINGTON

January 16, 1984

MEETING WITH MRS. SUZANNE MASSIE

DATE: January 17, 1984
LOCATION: Oval Office
TIME: 9:35 - 9:40 A.M.

FROM: ROBERT C. McFARLANE

I.   PURPOSE: To introduce Mrs. Massie to you before her trip to
Moscow, where she will be discussing unofficially and privately
the possibilities for expanding cultural and information exchanges.

II. BACKGROUND: Mrs. Massie is a noted author of books about
Russia. She and her husband co-authored Nicolas and Alexandra,
about the last Tsar and his family, and she has written several
others on her own. She was in Moscow in September and October
(just after the KAL shoot-down) and found her Russian friends in
the cultural and intellectual world fearful of the U.S. and eager
to see an improvement of cultural ties and better communication.
She offered to return to Moscow, if we wished, to convey our
interest in improving contacts and to solicit private and unofficial suggestions as to how this can be done best. If the Soviets
issue a visa for her, she will leave Thursday.

III. PARTICIPANTS:

    The President
    The Vice President
    Robert C. McFarlane
    Meese, Baker and Deaver at their discretion

IV. PRESS PLAN:

    None

V.   SEQUENCE OF EVENTS:

    Introduction
    Conversation for five minutes

Attachments:

    Tab A   Talking Points/card

cc: Vice President
    Edwin Meese   Prepared by:
    James Baker   Jack Matlock
    Mike Deaver

It took just five minutes for President Reagan to recognize that Suzanne Massie, a
specialist in Russian culture, shared his sensibility. Massie had been in the Soviet Union
after the KAL 007 shoot down and had been urgently seeking the White House's attention. She would become an important adviser before Reagan began his discussions
with Mikhail Gorbachev. *Ronald Reagan Presidential Library*

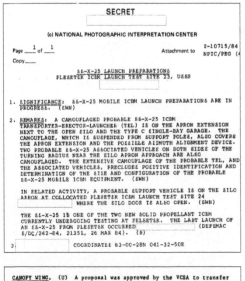

(*Top*) The Soviet Union engaged in unpretendingly provocative behavior by launching SS-X-25 missiles during a US military exercise in March 1984. This CIA document dated April 20, 1984, includes the following sentence: "The last launch of an SS-X-25 from Pelsetsk [SIC] occurred …" and there is a redaction. But the DEFSMAC citation shows the exact date: DEFSMAC S/DQ/242–84, 2152z, 26 MAR 84. *CIA*

(*Bottom*) Canopy Wing was a classified US Army electronic warfare program that was compromised in 1983 by an air force linguist, Jeffrey Carney, who worked at a National Security Agency outpost at Teufelsberg in West Berlin. Its existence has never been confirmed by the US government, but the author found an unredacted reference to the program in Army intelligence budget documents. *US Army INSCOM history, obtained via FOIA by www.governmentattic.com*

MEMORANDUM

NATIONAL SECURITY COUNCIL

<u>SECRET</u>   December 12, 1983

MEMORANDUM FOR OLLIE NORTH

FROM: JACK MATLOCK
                 TYRUS COBB

SUBJECT: Exercise Night Train 84

We are concerned with the political implications of this
exercize, and believe that they should be carefully weighed
before approval is given.

In particular, the scenario itself -- if it should leak (and we
must assume that it will) -- will be used by critics of the
Administration both here and elsewhere in the world as evidence
that we are planning for a nuclear war. This could serioulsy
undercut the President's image as a peacemaker and increase
apprehension in Europe, where we still face a rocky road to keep
to the INF deployment schedule on track.

If the exercise is essential, could the purposes be served with a
scenario which culminates, not in a nuclear exchange, but in a
peaceful solution following an alert?

By December 1983, the Reagan White House was receiving a stream of unsettling intelligence about the brittleness of Soviet leaders, and its top Russia hands, Jack Matlock and Ty Cobb, worked to reduce the possibility of misunderstandings. The two asked Oliver North, then an adjutant who liaised with the Pentagon, to change the ending for the planned Night Train '84 war games. The two men believed that the apocalyptic scenario would leak and might further exacerbate tensions. It did, they were, and the exercise went ahead as planned. *Ronald Reagan Presidential Library*

An air force linguist, Jeffrey Carney, provided the East German Stasi with thousands of valuable secrets about US war preparations against the Soviet Union and Warsaw Pact. He was arrested in 1992. *US Department of Justice*

In October 1983 (*left*), the Joint Chiefs of Staff briefed President Reagan on the first SIOP to incorporate the principles for "counterforce" targeting and "escalation control," which would allow, in theory, the president to respond with more agility to different warfighting scenarios around the world. The SIOP was revised two years later (*right*). *US Strategic Command video/National Security Archive*

Flaming Arrow was the code for one of the two supposedly secure communications paths linking the commander of US forces in Europe with nuclear artillery brigades. The East German Stasi, through its spies and ingenuity, had the entire system wired and, as seen here in this Top Secret report from 1984, had identified the 59th Ordinance Brigade's call signs (see the second bullet point—Stab der 59 Felzeugbrigade) as being of particular importance in the generation of nuclear alerts. (These documents were recovered after the war.) *Woodrow Wilson Institute Center Cold War International History Project*

A brigadier general in charge of Air Force intelligence in Europe, Leonard Perroots, was one of the first to recognize signals that the Soviet Union and Warsaw Pact forces reacted unusually to Able Archer '83, and he spent the better part of 1984 urging the CIA and others in the US government to pay attention. Perroots died in 2017. *Defense Intelligence Agency*

President Reagan met with Oleg Gordievsky, the ex-KGB spy, at the White House on January 21, 1987. *Ronald Reagan Presidential Library via the National Security Archive at George Washington University*

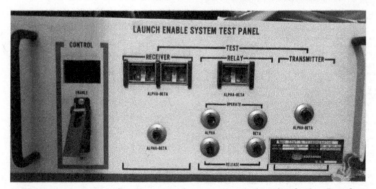

So dramatic were the reductions in nuclear weapons and warheads that President Reagan later negotiated with Mikhail Gorbachev that entire missile silos were gutted, and parts were sold to the public. The author purchased this authentic 1980s-era ICBM launch test panel from a seller on eBay.

CHAPTER 28

What Did We Miss?

Washington, DC

ARMY CAPTAIN STEPHEN SCHWALBE'S FIRST ASSIGNMENT out of school—he was just twenty-three—took him into the heart of the dispute within the intelligence community. He monitored the Soviet general staff for the Defense Intelligence Agency. His specialty was Soviet military exercises.[1]

When he first reported to the agency, his division chief dumped a thick folder of reports on his desk. Figure out if there's anything to see here, Schwalbe was told. He began to sift through the reports. There were lots of dots. A missile launch, out of character, in November.[2] Curious. The trajectory was retrograde—toward the United States. That was weird. But there was no follow-up on behalf of the intelligence community. Another report from the navy reported an increase in Soviet submarine readiness. There were NSA reports about anomalous patterns of Soviet air defense traffic. A dense packet of reporting, most of it from open sources, filled him in on what Soviet military officials were saying.

He pulled out a report from March 26, a few weeks earlier. His eyes jumped to two words: "polar route." It was describing the path taken by a Soviet ICBM, an SS-X-25, launched from the Baikonur Cosmodrome in Kazakhstan. Polar meant, obviously, over the North Pole. The missile had landed somewhere in the Arctic.

But the Soviets *never* launched missiles over the North Pole during tests or exercises—in fact, so far as he could tell, they had never before used that trajectory, period. *Not once.* A polar route offered the shortest trajectory to the United States from the Soviet ICBM fields; US early-warning systems were sensitive to the mere quiver of a leaf in those areas, and because it would take at least a few minutes after launch before NORAD could determine where the missile came from and where it would land, no Soviet commander in his right mind, Schwalbe thought, would test a missile that way. Analysts called it the "strategic corridor," because that route was saved for war. But here it was—the Soviet Strategic Rocket Forces had launched a missile toward the US with the deliberate intent to scare the US early-warning system for several minutes, without any advance warning.

The missile launch had been detected by NORAD, a missile threat conference was initiated, an alarm at SAC on Offutt had sounded, and for a few moments, the global nuclear enterprise had prepared for war. And then—nothing. No follow-up reports to ask why the Soviets had launched the missile, at that time.

A fragment from a NATO intelligence summary caught his eye. The British held their first nonpublic dispersal exercise with their new ground-launched cruise missiles on at night on March 10. Sixty-odd vehicles, part of the convoy, received an order to move to a forward position somewhere in the British countryside and set up for launch. It came as a surprise to some in the Pentagon. Even Richard Perle assumed that the UK would never actually move missiles around once they got them. The GLCMs were mobile in the way an elephant is mobile; it could move, but not without everyone knowing it. They had a massive logistics tail: "Dozens of vehicles, actually hundreds if you deployed them," Perle said later. "The idea that in a moment of tension we should start moving missiles off their bases was crazy. There's no way to hide them. They were highly vulnerable once they moved. The idea was that if they moved, they would diminish their vulnerability to a missile strike, but once they moved, a rifle, a hunting rifle would go right through the fuel tank."[3]

Schwalbe saw reports that the Soviets had detected the dispersal exercise. Then, a few days later, that anomalous missile launch.[4] Another sign: nearly a million residents of the Western Siberian city of Omsk were marched to the edge of their city, and one thousand were asked to march another 50 kilometers. Neither the US nor the Soviet Union had conducted exercises of this magnitude since the 1950s.[5]

The test from Baikonur was significant enough to make the President's Daily Brief on March 27. Reagan's reaction was not recorded. An aide told Reagan that he would ask Weinberger to look into whether the Soviets had failed to notify the US in advance, or whether the Pentagon had made some clerical error.[6]

———

Later that day, Reagan convened his senior national security staff to draw up a response to Chernenko. The president wanted to move toward a coherent and workable position on arms control even if the Soviets had nothing to offer in return at the moment. Time was too precious. His next letter to Chernenko would propose a turning point, of sorts.

Once again, Weinberger and the Joint Chiefs were not on the president's wavelength. They saw the exchange of views as exercises in mutual grandstanding. The Soviets had proposals. Chernenko's March 19 letter had four bullet points, but these were, in reality, just framing devices, ways to spin future negotiations to the benefit of the Soviet Union.

Weinberger had prepared a position paper urging Reagan not to move forward on any of this, including intermediate nuclear forces talks, until the Soviets had made significant concessions or had admitted their treaty violations. He had a valid point. When Reagan had agreed that the Soviets had made enough movement toward the Western position in January, he had someone to negotiate with: Andropov hadn't died yet. But General Secretary Chernenko didn't even seem there; he was even sicker than Andropov had been. Sure, Weinberger said, "we can negotiate notification of ballistic missile launches and hotline improvements," but "if we become too eager, the Soviet Union will sense weakness."[7]

Having heard Weinberger make that same argument before, Shultz came prepared. He spoke from notes, presenting a list of ten do's and don'ts. Don't make concessions for the sake of concessions, but don't let that mean that you do nothing; it would be a mistake to move away from a positive position on arms control, and if you do so, he told Reagan, you'll risk losing the support of Congress, the public, and American allies. Move forward, he urged Reagan, on confidence-building measures, like notification of launches, and the hotline improvements, and above all, don't stop working the issue because the Soviets have stopped. It was a rah-rah message aimed at Reagan's better angels, who nodded appreciatively, according to a witness in the room. Ken Adelman, Reagan's chief arms control negotiator, ticked off a list of concrete steps Reagan could work on.

General Jack Vessey, the Joint Chiefs chairman, urged caution. He wanted Reagan to focus his election-year capital on the defense buildup. The Soviets "can't or won't" negotiate until after the election, he said, and the allies "aren't carrying their load."

"There is no question," Reagan replied, "that the Soviet Union is trying to make us look noncooperative. I believe the Soviets want to avoid the onus for having walked out of Geneva." But his letter to Chernenko should be "substantive and positive." The US wouldn't make "unilateral concessions to get them back to the table, but I believe we must have a full credible agenda on arms control. Maybe we could build a record."

Maybe, for instance, having a limit on launchers isn't so bad, "so long as it is matched by warhead and throw-weight limits. In short, we need a position that takes part of their approach and melds it with ours so that they have a fig leaf for coming off their positions."[8]

Weinberger warned Reagan that his announcements might be misunderstood as new proposals, which would undercut the basic idea of not conceding to get the Soviets back into negotiations. Reagan was interested in something else: "My letter to Chernenko is an opportunity to get their attention. Have we given enough attention to the fact that they have a climate of insecurity?" It was time, Reagan thought, for a true turning point.[9]

————

The British noticed it first: Soviet ships were crawling out of their bases around the horn of the Kola Peninsula. It was only when they pushed past the North Cape, at Norway's tip, that the size of the fleet was detected. NATO first got a read on a passel of antisubmarine frigates on March 28; a day later, spotters observed the mammoth Kirov-class battle cruiser, the Soviet Navy's biggest surface warship, along with a protective cordon of a dozen others.[10]

On April 4, the US began the military exercise that Matlock and Cobb had been asked to approve in December; it was so large that it had three names: Night Train, Global Shield, and Rex '84. Night Train was run by the Joint Chiefs of Staff and tested communications between ground, mobile, and aerial nuclear and presidential command posts, as well as the logistics involved in handling mass US casualties associated with war. Global Shield tested the nuclear forces themselves. Rex '84 stressed FE-MA's continuity of government preparations and involved hundreds of US officials secretly moving to their various agencies' emergency relocation sites.

The Soviets were officially notified in advance by the Pentagon, and the military's public affairs officers worked overtime. The media was invited to watch and cover certain parts of the exercise, to broadcast to the world the might of the Strategic Air Command as it assumed its war footing. Much of the exercise would be conducted in the open ocean, where only foreign governments with reconnaissance and intelligence capabilities could watch.[11]

The exercise began when the US responded to a Soviet conventional invasion of Central Europe by using "non-SIOP" nuclear weapons—that is, intermediate-range missiles like the Pershing IIs. The world collapses into chaos. The Soviets then try to blind the US command and control system, first with a few select nuclear weapons, and then by destroying, via electronic warfare, the main Strategic Automated Command and Control System (SACCS) connections, which linked headquarters to missile control centers. Lines from March AFB in California went dead, and a second later the links from Otis AFB, MA went down. A gamma-radiation sensor network broadcast an alarm, and all hardened nuclear control sites across the US went into emergency shutdown. Before the gamma sensors could be cleared, another wave of sensors in Florida and Northern California lit up, and the four primary communication systems used to transmit emergency war orders sustained crippling volumes of traffic.

The president (or National Command Authority) authorized the employment of the SIOP, and the live-fly portion of the exercise began.

DEFCON 1: all of the primary strike bombers and refueling aircraft nationwide took to the air in full-blast combat climbs. B-52s launched cruise missiles.

The standby (post-retaliation) crews mobilized and were transported by bus to alternate locations (in a real war, the primary and secondary command and control facilities would be glowing craters).

Aircraft loaded with pallets of communications gear stayed near alert pads at a dozen US bases. "All of us already had gear on the aircraft, so all we had to do is jump into the alert trucks and fly to the aircraft (these trucks were to stop for nothing), and get the aircraft rolling into position to get off the ground and away|from the base," according to one Global Shield participant.

For days, the Strategic Air Command alert panels were in an almost constant state of alarm.

"We went on full lockdown, full generator power, and prepped evacuation vehicles to evacuate the post-detonation crews to the flight line," a crypto technician recalls. "We also power-upped the giant bulldozers and got them idling at the command post to be able to open a path to the flight line, and the crews on the flight line brought their bulldozers [normally used for open-pit mining] and got them idling for near-term use."

In the Atlantic Ocean, a Trident submarine surfaced at Guam, surprising even the stationmaster there. Its task was to serve as the ship of last resort for nuclear retaliation, so its secret pre-exercise disappearance was all part of the plan. For the first time, the navy was exercising its SCOOP plan. The acronym was classified at the time of Global Shield; it stood for Submarine Continuity of Operations.[12] At about the same time, a sub in the Pacific live-launched a Poseidon C3 missile with multiple warheads capable of reaching targets 2,500 miles away. Two carrier battle ships tracked north from the Sea of Japan, clearing routes ahead of an imagined attack into Siberia.[13] On April 5, two Minuteman missiles launched from Vandenberg Air Force Base in California.[14] In the skies of over Western Massachusetts, enormous K-135 Stratotankers tested their limits at altitudes of 40,000 feet and practiced refueling the nuclear bombers at speeds of more than 600 miles per hour.[15] The crews at Ellsworth Air Force Base in South Dakota practiced loading nuclear air-to-ground missiles called AGM-69s, several of which could fit into a B-52 Stratofortress alongside with three MK-28 nuclear missiles, carrying 350 kilotons of explosive force in a shell not much larger or thicker than a human.[16]

In the past, when either side exercised its strategic forces, the other side watched. That had been a Cold War rule, informal, surely, but just one of the norms that both sides happened to agree on. The bigger exercises, the ones well publicized and inflected with the purpose of real-world deterrents, were excellent opportunities to gather intelligence. Whenever one side would exercise its strategic forces openly, to be sure, the other would hedge—a few forces mobilized, extra sensors turned on, intelligence notices distributed—but there was one thing that had never been done, because to do it in the middle of an exercise would break the logic chain that both kept the superpowers in perpetual cold conflict and prevented it from turning hot. They never counter-exercised to the same degree, ever; they never shot missiles at the same time; they never rehearsed their nuclear procedures concurrently. It was plainly, nakedly dangerous, and both sides had understood this for thirty years.

But on the morning of April 4, just as Global Shield began, the Soviet Union again broke with convention. Without warning, the Soviet ship movements that NATO had been monitoring suddenly turned into an armada. The Northern and Baltic fleets launched 200 ships, 20 nuclear submarines, and 25 major surface warships on a path that set them streaming out of home ports; several began to cross the Atlantic.

———

Analyzing a war game in progress creates new grooves even in experienced brains. Schwalbe and his colleagues at the DIA had to figure out who was attacking whom, and who "whom" actually was. It was doubly difficult because NATO had not prepared for this exercise and had few reconnaissance assets in the region. Intelligence officers had to resort to an emergency mobilization plan they had assumed would never be used until a war began. Spy planes began to report back: there were Backfire bombers practicing antisubmarine warfare off the coast of Norway. Naval activity was reported in the Mediterranean, in the Baltic Sea, and even in the Indian Ocean. The British sent armed fighters and established a combat air patrol in the sea lane between the exercise area and its coast. NATO launched an airborne electronic warning plane. A NATO official told the *New York Times* that day that the exercise "had been mounted with surprising speed."[17] According to one source, Soviet bombers orbited continuously, practicing bombing raids on surface ships.[18]

The exercise included live-fire games in the North Atlantic and Norwegian Sea, with ships visible off the coast of Scotland and Norway. It surpassed any previous show of naval strength by the Soviets. Several hundred warplanes supported the fleet.[19] At the same time, another Soviet

surface squadron departed the Baltic Sea and headed toward the Norwegian Sea. Backfires deployed to the Kola Peninsula and began flying simulated strikes against this force.

At the same time, Soviet ground exercises "appeared" in several of the
Baltic states. Advanced Soviet electronic warfare planes strafed the Berlin
corridor, causing West Germany to lodge a formal complaint with East
Germany. Soviet alternate command centers were activated. Strategic
bombers flew to reinforcement airfields in East Germany. American and
NATO reconnaissance asserts monitored integrated strategic strike operations, including multiple launches of SS-20s and SLBMs.[20]

The British and NATO were worried. This behavior was unusual, and
provocative. They fed stories about the surprise Soviet exercise to American journalists. An article by R. W. Apple Jr. in the *New York Times* suggested as much. To the Associated Press, though, US officials "denied the
Soviet maneuvers caught Western allies napping. Sources said the ships
were under surveillance almost from the moment they left port."[21]

Schwalbe saw it differently. What if the Soviet Union, anticipating the
West's biggest annual nuclear and general war exercise, suddenly and without warning, held their own massive worldwide war games? What did it
mean that both superpowers rehearsed their nuclear release procedures in
real time, in the middle of the biggest exercises they'd ever held, a month
after Andropov dies? "This was just insane," he remembered years later. "It
had never happened before. All that you needed for war at that moment
was someone to drop a match down in a dry forest."[22]

CHAPTER 29

Arguing on Behalf of Soviet Fears

ON MARCH 28, *THE RED STAR*, THE SOVIET DEFENSE ministry's weekly newspaper, published an article by General A. S. Milovidov, a leading strategist of nuclear deterrence. Milovidov was famous for having once rejected "the assertions of certain bourgeois theoreticians who consider nuclear war unjust from any point of view." He spoke for a segment of the military that was trying to find ways to justify a push for more money. His words should have been a bolt from the blue. "The leaders of our party and state have warned quite specifically that the Soviet state's strategic forces are in a supreme state of readiness," he wrote. "[T]ough demands regarding combat-readiness are dictated by the virtually unlimited range of strategic nuclear missile weapons. That is why not only the troops in the immediate vicinity of the border (as was the case in the recent past) but also the entire armed forces and all military control systems must be in a state of high combat-readiness today."[1]

As if anticipating the question, Milovidov suggested that the distinction between exercise readiness and real-world readiness was no longer recognized by the USSR. The readiness encompasses preparation, he said, "[n]ot as a potential in a hypothetical sense but as real dynamic forces which manifest themselves in practice during sea cruises. Flights. Tours of combat duty, and military exercises and maneuvers."[2] This meant: the Soviets would treat all American exercises as real.

"Imagine if General Odom or Richard Perle had published a front-page article in the *Washington Post* saying that the US was going to be at the equivalent of DEFCON 2 for the next whatever amount of time," a

US intelligence official said later. "That's basically what Milovidov was announcing."

In Schwalbe's mind, there was little difference between the Soviet exercises and an advanced preparation for war. The Soviets had just said as much. He wrote a report, flagged it with enough code-word caveats to make sure it received the attention of higher-ups. The DIA director, Lieutenant General James A. Williams, found Schwalbe's analysis so compelling that he recommended it be briefed to Vessey, the chairman of the Joint Chiefs, and to Weinberger, the Secretary of Defense. One of Schwalbe's more sobering conclusions, based on an analysis of Soviet war games in 1983: The Soviets feared a surprise attack from the West. All of their major war games began with some sort of bolt-from-the-blue strike.[3]

From Europe, General Leonard Perroots attached his own observations about what he called "months and months of unusual behavior" by the Soviets, beginning after the KAL 007 shootdown and continuing through the end of the NATO exercise program in the fall, and the deployments of the Pershing IIs and GLCMs.[4] Soviet behavior during its March exercises, Perroots wrote, constituted a major shift in its thinking on the possibility of armed confrontation with the United States. The instability in the Soviet political leadership might also be emboldening the Soviet military to be extra aggressive, out of sheer fear. The Perroots memo suggested that it might be time to look at how US intelligence and military programs were influencing Soviet behavior in real time, a sly reference to the compartmented electronic warfare programs that the NSA and the air force had established.

———

Back in Britain, the Government Communications Headquarters (GCHQ) knew nothing of Perroots's memo. But Harry Burke, a seasoned GCHQ Soviet analyst who was assigned to the Joint Intelligence Committee's assessment staff, had just discovered Able Archer. He had assigned a small team to reanalyze Oleg Gordievsky's reporting with the signals and electronic intelligence that GCHQ had collected during the Able Archer exercise. His conclusions would be key to determining whether the JIC brought the report to the United States. They didn't play chicken with their American cousins, and a speculative single source report of a war scare would not benefit the relationship.[5] Burke faced skepticism. But he was the perfect messenger. He was known as a Soviet hawk, and his views about the nature of Soviet threat were uncompromising. Here he was, arguing on *behalf of Soviet fears*. According to an official who read his report, it included a list of indicators:

- the stand-down of the Soviet military during all or part of the exercise;
- an unusually large number of intelligence-gathering sorties by Soviet aircraft; and
- a change in the traffic patterns of the Soviet high-frequency command and control net, which GCHQ at the time had marked as a nuclear exercise.

"There was always a risk of sweeping innocent activities into the picture," said Michael Herman, a former GCHQ Soviet Desk chief who read the report. "On the other hand, the patterns of valid Soviet indicators could have a patchiness to them." He remembered a total Soviet military stand-down in 1969, part of its (real) preparations for a possible war against China. That was the only sign something unusual was going on.[6]

In late March, the US CIA representative embedded with the UK Joint Intelligence Committee, which met weekly, was given a version of the assessment based on Gordievsky's reporting through the SIS (Secret Intelligence Service), NATO intelligence, and the GCHQ analysis.[7] Its title: "Soviet Union: Concern About a Surprise NATO Attack."[8] There was a dispute about what Soviet leaders really believed—the JIC could reach no firm conclusion—but even the slightest hint of a misunderstanding could be catastrophic.[9] The analysis posed two questions. One: should NATO be more proactive to convince the Soviets that their exercise intentions are benign? Two, and more importantly: if they feared an attack, what does that mean about their read on Western intentions?[10] The British moved toward a stunning conclusion: the Soviet behavior "may reflect a concern . . . that the West might initiate a nuclear war and that this might be done as a surprise attack under the cover of an exercise."[11]

Sir Robert Armstrong, the highest civil servant in Britain, advised Margaret Thatcher that she should brief President Reagan directly.[12] In a memo marked with the highest classification the British had, he noted that the Soviet activity "took place over a holiday, it had the form of actual military activity and alerts, not just war-gaming, and it was limited geographically to the area, Central Europe, covered by the NATO exercise which the Soviet Union was monitoring."[13]

It would be near impossible not to reference the content of Gordievsky's reporting, which concerned the SIS chief, Sir Colin Figures. If the British provided any more information to the CIA about their source, they might accidentally reveal Gordievsky's identity. They had promised him that they would never share his name with anyone, not even with the Americans.

On April 10, Thatcher held a meeting to discuss the next steps. "We should consider what could be done to remove the danger that, by miscalculating Western intentions, the Soviet Union would overreact," she said.[14] Thatcher wanted to invite a senior member of the Politburo—perhaps Mr. Gorbachev"—to visit the UK later in the year.

———

The tear-line British reporting didn't throw a wrench into the mechanics of Ermarth's mammoth intelligence estimate. Neither the CIA nor the DIA had enough information to evaluate the reporting by the SIS source who made a direct link between the increased military exercises in November and a NATO exercise called Able Archer. Indeed, most of those who worked on the CIA estimate had never before heard of Able Archer.[15]

"If you believed in the RYAN scenario that the Soviets had, where the war had gone nuclear from the outset, you're spending an awful lot of money on forces that are just going to be destroyed at the outset of the war, so from a budgetary standpoint the reality didn't fit in with what the DIA had to justify," a former CIA official who helped prepare the SNIE said later. "There was just little support for the idea of a surprise nuclear attack. It fit into no one's institutional needs, and I think that people also sincerely believed that it could never be something the Soviets would actually fear."

On 18 May, Ermarth's SNIE was ready. "Implications of Recent Soviet Military-Political Activities" concluded that "Soviet actions are not inspired by, and Soviet leaders do not perceive, a genuine danger of imminent conflict or confrontation with the United States. This judgment is

based on the absence of force-wide combat readiness or other war preparation moves in the USSR, and the absence of a tone of fear or belligerence
in Soviet diplomatic communications, although the latter remain uncompromising on many issues." Though Soviet actions . . . are influenced to
some extent by Soviet perceptions of a mounting challenge from US foreign and defense policy . . . these activities do not all fit into an integrated
pattern of current Soviet foreign policy tactics." Further, the estimate
found that each provocative or unusual Soviet action had "its own military
or political purpose sufficient to explain it."

The report's conclusions were based on the absence of other indicators. Moscow didn't put all of its units on combat alert, so it clearly didn't
intend to go to war. But what would the indicators of an all-out war be?
Why would Moscow go out of its way to try to secretly heighten combat
readiness of some units unless the Soviets were genuinely afraid that the
US might misinterpret *their* moves as a step toward war? Indeed, to meet
the criteria implied by Ermarth's estimate, the Soviet Union would have
had to ramp its war machine deliberately and visibly—something that
they might not want to do if they intended to control the escalation. Of
Gordievsky's reporting and other reporting the US had about the RYAN
indicators, the CIA confidently insisted that none of it reflected a real
concern. Instead, the directives ordering the search for signals of nuclear
attack were designed to stiffen the spine of the Soviet worldwide intelligence-gathering apparatus, the CIA believed. All of this was just pos-
turing, despite the CIA's acknowledgment that it knew little about the
political intentions of the Soviet Union.

David McManis, the National Intelligence Officer for Warning, had
seen the first reporting that General Leonard Perroots circulated in December 1983. He had read the report that the DIA later prepared—to
which Perroots had *again* appended his own notes. And he thought the
SNIE oversold its case.

McManis wrote a short personal memo to Casey, citing Perroots, suggesting that the US might want to be concerned that the Soviets might be
misreading their intentions. Even if that possibility was slight, it had to be
taken seriously. He reminded Casey that Casey had recruited him to bulk
up the CIA's warning capability, and in his considered judgment, the SNIE
had gotten it wrong.

On June 15, he followed up with a memo to the entire National Intelligence Council, including Ermarth: "Our concern stems from the number of discreet and individually trivial events that our rather superficial review has uncovered. In fact, we believe that several incidents summarized would be just the tip of the iceberg if a systematic review were accomplished," he wrote. Diplomatically, he insisted that he did not disagree with the "basic conclusions" of the SNIE, which he characterized, generously, as suggesting that each action could be explained individually. (The SNIE, of course, had reasoned that because each could be explained individually, they could all be explained collectively. McManis strongly disagreed.) He proposed a "new and continuing review."

Casey added a cover note, under the heading: "US-Soviet Tension," and briefed Reagan directly on June 20. It began: "I attach here a rather stunning array of indicators of increasing aggressiveness in Soviet policies and activities." That got the White House's attention. President Reagan read it. One paragraph stood out:

> The behavior of the armed forces is perhaps the most disturbing. From the operational deployment of submarines to the termination of harvest support to the delayed troop rotation, there is a central theme of not being strategically vulnerable, even if it means taking some risks. It is important to distinguish in this category those acts which are political blustering and those which may be, but also carry large costs. The point of blustering is to do something that makes the opponent pay high costs while the blusterer pays none or little. The military behaviors we have observed involve high military costs . . . adding thereby a dimension of genuineness to the Soviet expressions of concern that is often not reflected in intelligence issuances.

The memo further warned, "The Soviets have concluded that the danger of war is greater and will grow with additional INF emplacements and that reduced warning time inherent in Pershing II has lowered the Soviet confidence in their ability to warn of a sudden attack."

McFarlane was suspicious of McManis's follow-up memo. He thought the official intelligence estimate had gotten it about right—that the Soviets were trying to drive a wedge between the US and Europe on Strategic Defense, and had just overplayed their hand. And the National Security Council questioned the motives behind the British warnings of war. "It seemed to us more probable than not that the British were using Gordievsky as a way to attempt to get Reagan to tone things down a bit," another Reagan national security aide who attended the meetings and read all of the intelligence said years later."[16]

But McFarlane could see that the president found it really scary. He asked Casey to take a fresh look at the intelligence.[17] On June 24, the Joint Chiefs of Staff wrote to the National Intelligence Council asking for a full intelligence community estimate on recent Soviet military exercises.[18] Beginning in July, McManis's warning staff began to publish on its own a monthly assessment dealing directly with the threat and perceptions of war from the USSR.

———

During a briefing with Casey, Reagan asked about the British's apparently awesome source.

"Why don't we have someone like that on our team?" he wondered.[19]

At the CIA, Casey mentioned Reagan's aside to a subordinate.

That began a quiet effort inside the agency's Directorate of Operations to try and identify who the SIS had been talking to. Professional jealousy was not the reason: in order to evaluate the bona fides of the source, they had to know more.

CHAPTER 30

How Can This Be?

AS SHULTZ TRIED TO FIGURE OUT HOW TO ESTABLISH a foundation of trust that preserved the American bargaining position without unduly frightening the Soviets, and as the president considered the words that escaped the barriers of his own teeth, the nuclear SIOP's demands continued to shape military procurement and policy.

Outside of the confines of the Strategic Defense Initiative, the air force had created a top-secret program to develop a road-mobile ICBM, one that would "ensure a reliable means of retaliatory attacks against some, non-time urgent counter-value targets." The ICBM convoys would look no different than a row of trucks—the US had 11.5 million commercial vehicles on its highways every day—and could be easily hidden.[1] The Strategic Air Command was thinking ahead, to a day when it would have the intelligence to ride out a first strike and respond with Strategic Launch Under Confirmed Attack, SLUCA, another acronym that, when used in polite conversation, conferred the assumption of secret knowledge. In 1984, the air force asked companies to submit bids to build the weapon. It would become known, to the chagrin of the Pentagon, as the "Midgetman."[2]

Reagan reined in his administration's rhetoric. Weinberger wanted to give a provocative speech to the American Legion, but on the president's instructions, the White House toned it down. It could too easily be used to paint Reagan as a warmonger.[3]

The president had been feeling out his staff about the possibility of asking for a meeting with Chernenko, an objective that acquired urgency after Reagan had read the reports from Gordievsky and the SNIE, and the McManis memo. In his gut, Reagan wanted to move on it. "It lends support to my idea that while we go on believing and with some good reason, that the Soviets are plotting against us and mean us harm, maybe they are scared of us & think we are a threat," he wrote in his diary.[4]

To McFarlane, Reagan would often ask: "How can this be? How could they be so misguided about the impossibility of our entertaining the notion of a first strike?" McFarlane was still cautious and told Reagan that the Soviets probably wanted to create the illusion that they were more afraid than they really were. "[But] the Gordievsky debriefs were quite shocking to me in the sense that this extremely reliable source, an insider, was reporting genuine alarm in the Soviet leadership," he said later.[5]

In August, Shultz and the State Department began to get "mysterious signals" from Soviet contacts that Gromyko might, just might, want to be invited to the United States and to have a chat with Reagan.

Shultz told Reagan that he was sure the president would want some time to think it over.

"No, I don't want to have to think it over. I think we should definitely do it," Reagan said.[6]

He had a feeling that "we'll get nowhere with arms reduction while they are suspicious of our motives as we are of theirs. I believe we need a meeting to see if we can't make them understand we have no designs on them but think they have designs on us. If we could once clear the air, maybe reducing arms wouldn't look so impossible to them."[7]

———

In West Germany, Lee Trolan presided over a departure ceremony in Killianstädten. The base would stay open, but his nukes were leaving. NATO had decided to move them out. At 6:00 one morning, he briefed a team of security officers from all across Germany on the complicated operation. On a chalkboard, he sketched out the scenario. Chinooks would land; the barn doors would open; the nuclear warheads, secure in large barrel-like canisters, would be wheeled into the helicopters. The soldiers had orders to shoot on sight anyone who tried to interfere. He said a final good-bye to Major Frank Schrodter of the Luftwaffe.

As the warheads left Killianstädten, Trolan left West Germany and left the army for a more stable career as a civilian consultant. Within two weeks, his old site had a new commander, and it had new nuclear missiles: the Pershing IIs.

CHAPTER 31

Roll the Dice

THE KGB'S FIRST CHIEF DIRECTORATE DROVE ITS LONDON *rezidentura* up the wall with piles of new RYAN requests in 1984. These directives distracted the officers from other duties. Morale plummeted. A number of Gordievsky's friends returned to Moscow in frustration. Arkady Guk's alcoholic rages made life there miserable. And because "it was the deliberate policy of the Center and the Party to make Soviet communities abroad feel as isolated as possible," it seemed like every small incident—even a flat tire—would be interpreted as a dangerous provocation by the enemy.

Gordievsky's double life complicated his comings and goings from the embassy. One day, he could have sworn he saw Arkady Guk race by his own car in a Mercedes quite close to the Bayswater flat where he would be debriefed by the SIS. He saw Guk later in the day; Guk had indeed been in the area but had not seen him.[1]

Even routine medical care could produce a scare. The SIS recommended to him a good dentist to fix a crown, and while the procedure was being performed, the British Security Service, MI-5, happened to notice Gordievsky's car—a Soviet diplomat's car—was parked near a doctor's office frequented by the British establishment. Not knowing about Gordievsky's work for SIS, MI-5 launched an investigation. The SIS managed to quash it.[2]

In June 1984, Gordievsky got wind of the type of operation that made every double agent cringe. Someone had slipped highly secret documents in the mail slot on the door of Guk's house. He had to be very careful; he had to tell the British, and the British had to find the traitor, but they had to figure out how to find him—or her—without betraying the connection to Gordievsky. One of the documents that Guk had received particularly frightened him. It was a list, created by MI-5 of known and suspected KGB officers in London. His name was there—that was fine. But the list ranked the officers on the basis of how certain their true identities had been established. It might have been suspicious to Guk if the British had positively identified Gordievsky's true position. Luckily, the MI-5 roster graded Gordievsky's KGB status as uncertain. He was safe, for the moment.

Maybe the documents were a test—maybe the "agent" was a dangle—designed to force the KGB into giving secrets of its tradecraft. This occurred in residencies around the world often enough, although rarely in Britain.

As soon as he could, Gordievsky convened a meeting with SIS. John Scarlett was out of town, so Joan, his translator, met Gordievsky alone. "I'm sure this is some sort of operational game that the security services are playing with the KGB, but we'd better make sure." Joan's response "was classically calm." "As far as I know," she said, "there is no operational game in progress."

Gordievsky left the next day on holiday to Moscow. In the meantime, the British hunted for its mole. They found him—an MI-5 officer named Michael Bettanney. Gordievsky worried that his bosses would connect him to Bettaney's arrest, but Guk still thought the documents were a provocation and paid it no attention.[3]

It would be for Guk a career-threatening mistake. The British used the occasion to kick him out of the country. Back in Moscow, he was reprimanded for letting a real spy slip through his grasp. Gordievsky found himself in good standing with the Center. A friend had put his name into contention to succeed Guk as resident in London, but the knock against him was his relative lack of experience in the city—just three years at that point. Gordievsky's patrons suggested a way to seal the deal politically. Mikhail Gorbachev, now the Ideological Secretary of the Party, had just decided to make a trip to Britain, to see Margaret Thatcher, later in the year.[4] If the trip went well, fate might smile on Gordievsky.

———

In Moscow, Rainer Rupp's comprehensive reports on NATO intelligence had finally broken through the pervasive sense of fear and paranoia that separated the line officers from their elder leaders.

"In order to allay the concerns of the Soviets, I scanned all the documents—whether important or not—and sent them to the [Stasi]. Since all documents were officially numbered, the comrades in the Stasi and Moscow could clearly see that nothing was missing and nothing important had been overlooked. At the height of the crisis, this was supplemented by daily messages to East Berlin. And since they had a corresponding confidence in the sources, Moscow finally dropped the option of a preemptive counter-attack," he said.[5]

Not entirely, though. The Perimetr system, which would give the Soviets a decapitation-proof method of launching its weapons, was tested in secret in November 1984. Two missiles were launched; one of the missiles successfully transferred the launch-enabling codes to the other. By 1985, the system would be partially operational, although its mechanics, fail-safes and connections to other command and control nodes remains, to this day, opaque.[6]

But Perimetr's secrecy all but obviated its use as a deterrent. If the Americans didn't know the Soviets had such a system, it would not technically exist, given the doctrines laid down by the nuclear priesthood. If the Soviets knew nothing about Project Pegasus, it, too, would not factor into the calculations made by the General Staff.

In one sense, both sides were hedging rationally. In another sense, though, these two secret projects provisioned the leaders of both countries with intestinal fortitude. They could negotiate more freely if they had more confidence that their side would survive an attack under any circumstances—and if they as presidents were enabled to serve more effectively as safety catches on the nuclear trigger.

If Perimetr served as a central control switch for the entire Soviet nuclear system, and if the On button was physically tied to the Soviet presidential football—the Cheget—then the politicians in charge had finally achieved full, positive control over the launch of Soviet nuclear weapons.

If the United States's Project Pegasus provided a presidential successor with the means to control nuclear releases after a first strike by either side, it would reduce the chance that a brigadier general in an airplane would instigate World War III.

But Pegasus was in trouble. Its ambit cut across at least twenty classified programs,[7] and there were immediate hassles over security clearances and oversight. The cover agency, DMSPA (Defense Mobilization Systems Planning Activity), needed a strong manager, someone well versed in the world of clandestine projects who had no patience for bullshit. Jim Wink, a veteran CIA case officer with a knack for problem solving, was officially tapped to be DMSPA's deputy director. His task: "get the damned thing to work," he said. "People didn't know what other people were doing. They didn't know how to tie it all together, and they weren't sure they could even work together."

Wink divvied up responsibilities. The FBI would identify the proposed relocation sites based on a statement of requirements from the Pentagon. The sites had to be out of the way, not near any major military target or civilian center, and be large enough to support the team of about two hundred that would occupy it for six months. The US Marshals Service would work with the presidential successor support teams and provide transportation for them to the sites. The Joint Special Operations Command would supply an *in-extremis* force to guard the relocated president. NIESO, the emergency intelligence cadre, would ensure that the president was informed about vital foreign activities. The WHMO (White House Military Office) would upgrade the president's ability to receive information from NORAD. Presidential successors were given new identification cards that allowed the government to use the public telephone system to somehow ping them. FEMA would manage the president's execution of the post- or inter-war government, Wink said. The Defense Communications Agency would link the sites to a classified Interagency Communications System (ICS), which interfaced with a new White House crisis center (project code name: MEDUSA) and other command centers. "For the first time, everyone was thinking reconstitution and not just prevention, assuming a president survived," Wink said.

DMSPA brought them all together through exercises. They took over continuity planning from FEMA for the "Readiness Exercise" series—Rex, as it was called. They modeled attacks under "Condition Alpha"—bolt-from-the-blue decapitation strikes that would take out the notional Pentagon and its backup sites as well as "Condition Bravo" scenarios, which presumed that "sufficient warning" would be provided for a whole range of plans and transportation scenarios—JEEP, JATS, Constant Blue—to be rehearsed.

"We exercised everything, or as much as possible. We even tried to see if we could reconstitute the government from overseas. We picked two embassies that would probably be clean given a nuclear war with the Soviet Union, and sure enough we found out that we could."

They tried to model the bizarre what-if scenarios: If an elected official came back, what would happen if he tried to take the government back? Whose war orders would the Pentagon follow? No one knew; the question was never really answered. "One of the theories we never tested was that if the FBI brought back the Congress after a nuclear war, and there was a new Senate [president] pro tempore or a new Speaker, would he have become president?"

Would he have? the author asked Wink.

"I don't know," he said. "It never came to that."

At FEMA, and at the Department of Defense, skepticism about DMSPA and its intentions were met by an iron wall of secrecy. "No one was read in to these continuity of the president programs, at that level, except for accountants, so all we could do is go by rumor," a former senior FEMA lawyer said. "There is no legal basis whatsoever for a temporary transfer of power."

A successor—say, the Secretary of State—could technically refuse to become president; the chain of succession would bypass that successor, moving to the Secretary of the Treasury. But then, the Secretary of State, so long as he held that title, could decide at any subsequent point to reclaim the powers of the president at will, bumping aside the Treasury Secretary in a legally sanctioned coup.

"Who knows what would have happened? Our goal was to get someone who people recognized out front in front of the people and the world, in communication with everyone else, someone who could stop a war, if necessary," Thomas Reed said later.

The project's secrecy allowed these questions to fester, but they also allowed bureaucratic opponents to throw up obstacles. And costs and problems began to mount. The Army's 7th Signal Command was given the task of testing and operating the mobile communications equipment. Its colonels were read in to parts of the program, but they were often in the dark about the endgame. In addition, the DMSPA team had trouble securing space for emergency communications tests on existing satellites.

And they'd have to wait (years) for the multibillion-dollar Milstar satellite configuration to be functional, because the convoys were supposed to be linked through secret "add-on" pods that would be used only in emergencies. (Engineers designing these pods had no real idea whether they'd work on the new satellites.) The trucks purchased for the convoys were too heavy for the roads they were supposed to travel, and many had to be discarded.[8] Contractors hired to work on the hidden contingency equipment caches began to fight each other, and the program managers could not sort out who was responsible for what.

More troubling: Congress largely ignored DMSPA, because DMSPA largely kept Congress out of the loop. Even though part of NSDD-55's mandate called for each branch to work cooperatively during national emergencies, the legislative branch refused to share with the executive branch sufficient information about its own continuity programs. That meant it was hard for DMSPA to create real-world exercises that simulated what might happen during nuclear war.

CHAPTER 32

A New Hope: But Still, Star Wars?

THE PHOTO OP WAS CAREFULLY STAGED, THE PHOTOG-raphers and correspondents waiting behind a rope line for hours, but the musical accompaniment could not be helped. As Reagan shook hands with Andrei Gromyko for the first time, on September 24, 1984, a pianist was trolling "It Never Crossed My Mind." When Gromyko once again crossed Reagan, this time on his way out of a cocktail party for world leaders at the Waldorf Astoria, the song "Take the 'A' Train" masked a particularly vigorous spasm of a conversation. The White House really wanted the picture. Here was Reagan, about a month from the election, eager to meet with the Soviets, desirous of a long-term relationship, so he said, and expansive. Lips couldn't be read, and the contents did not leak. What did was from the Soviet side: Gromyko asked Nancy Reagan if her husband believed in peace, and when she answered yes, he urged the First Lady to whisper "peace" in his ear every night.[1]

The president's first meeting with a member of the Soviet Politburo answered a campaign charge from Walter Mondale, who regularly noted that Reagan had promised to talk to the Soviets from the start of his presidency and had failed to do so. It was a victory, too, for Shultz, who had to move mountains to make it happen. Gromyko would do it, he told Shultz earlier in the year, it if were accompanied by a concrete willingness to address Soviet interests. Shultz was desperate to make this happen. Not oblivious of the political advantage it would confer domestically, Shultz believed that a face-to-face meeting would nourish Reagan's instincts about negotiations. The only way forward was to talk, directly, president to president (or, in this case, long-serving foreign minister). The details of what he would say mattered, but they mattered less than getting a meeting. The president's confidence in his ability to persuade, Shultz believed, could create its own momentum. The table of options for arms control would expand by sheer force of will.[2]

To get the meeting, Shultz had to herd cattle and would even agree to yield to a little bureaucratic blackmail. A secret US review of Soviet compliance with arms-control agreements had circulated through the precincts of conservative Washington for months, and hawkish senators openly suggested that the president's refusal to declassify it was evidence that he had become a hostage to the hidden pro-negotiation dovish cabal that Shultz led.[3] Shultz had no illusions about the Soviets. He just did not think their violations were more important than the urgent need for presidential diplomacy.[4]

Weinberger had come to see SDI in much the same way as the Soviets did. It was to him a de facto weapons system, albeit defensive in nature; its construction was destabilizing, and because it conferred an advantage to the United States, the Soviets could easily use it as a bargaining chip to perpetuate their first-strike advantage with ICBMs if Reagan opened any sort of negotiations about it. The Soviets should *never* learn they had *nothing* to fear from it.[5]

But Reagan was two steps ahead. He wanted the Soviets to see the world as he did, to recognize the link between the portentous and circular arms race and the need to pursue a technology that would give both sides, simultaneously, the freedom to act as though they did not fear a first strike. Weinberger and others were stuck on a reading of the Soviets that would predispose them to press the advantage immediately; Reagan, on the other hand, believed that absent the fear of decapitation, the Soviets would be much more amenable to significant arms reductions.

This was why Weinberger opposed any sort of meeting between Reagan and a Soviet leader. He played to Reagan's own fears about Soviet might. Appearing too eager, the Secretary of Defense would say, over and over, would show weakness.[6] Six days before the president went to New York to see Gromyko, Weinberger told Reagan that "now is a very inappropriate time for any proposals."[7]

This was an old argument to Shultz, and he wasn't having any of it.

The idea of a general palaver now and specifics later was absurd. "We have been around for four years. What have we been *doing*?" he all but shouted to Weinberger in the meeting.

Reagan had been studying the Soviet Union and its history, corresponding with Suzanne Massie a half-dozen times. He had developed a capacity to see the Soviets as they saw themselves. Their concerns, he said, were two: "a fear of invasion, a fear of being surrounded." The Soviets approached *everyone* with suspicion. Something stuck in his mind from a recent conversation he had with Hans-Dietrich Genscher, the vice chancellor of West Germany. The Soviets still had barbed wire up to mark how close to Moscow Hitler had advanced in what they called the Great Patriotic War, Genscher had said. Do not underestimate how much the Soviets fear the US–West Germany alliance. "The US is allied with [West Germany]," Reagan said to Weinberger. "The Soviets have great fear of [NATO's] capacity. *How do you argue with this fear?*"[8]

"Maybe," Reagan said, "we need a general discussion to clear the air, telling them here are the reasons we fear your actions. We are not going to seek advantage, but we will keep our defenses up." To Weinberger, Reagan insisted that the US had to "show an understanding" of Soviet concerns in order to get beyond the stalemate.

This caught Weinberger off guard. Okay, he told Reagan, "make them understand that we understand their fear, yet we still can't let them possess enough force to dominate the world."

Shultz jumped in. "But suppose that Gromyko says, 'Okay, let's talk.' Why not set a date before the end of the year? Could we say yes?"

"No," Weinberger said, "we have not figured out a full approach."

We don't need a full approach, Shultz said. Just an agreement on where we want to end up.

Weinberger urged Reagan to scale back his ambitions. "Viewing this meeting as a theater for progress is wrong," he told the president.[9]

It was not lost on Matlock that, in theory at least, Reagan easily could have replaced Weinberger or somehow ordered his troops to align themselves more publicly with his stated goals. It was almost as if the president would deliberately equivocate in order to make Shultz work for the victories that the president knew were in his best interests. But the truth was probably more prosaic: Reagan would not fire his close friend, whose counsel he valued on most issues, and he did not want to alienate the military, whose cooperation he needed to make SDI— his SDI—work.

On a windy Friday afternoon, three days after their orchestrated cocktail party tête-à-tête, Reagan and Gromyko met for six hours in the Oval Office. Reagan was prepared to do a lot of listening.[10] Gromyko's speech to the United Nations earlier that week had more saber rattling than substance, although it ended with a call to negotiations that Reagan appreciated.[11] "It is extremely important not to miss the chance," he had said. The newspapers Reagan read that morning noted how much friendlier Gromyko appeared to be after meeting with Walter Mondale than he had ever been after a meeting with Shultz. But he also scanned reports of a suddenly scheduled speech by Chernenko himself, a sign that when Reagan was speaking to Gromyko, he was speaking to a unified Soviet leadership.[12]

Gromyko and Reagan sat together on a couch. A participant described it later as a great ventilation of their views. Each man had the chance to give his full, historical account of the hostilities and then air his complaints about the other's intransience, and then huff and haw about capitalism or communism. Then they talked about things they had in common. They were both grandfathers. After it ended, both men knew they had not agreed to anything, although Reagan managed to slide in a few proffers about space weapons that Gromyko undoubtedly noticed. The substance was less important than the impression the meeting gave. Both the Soviets and the United States benefited from it. Gromyko took home a large chit; the US president was directly addressing the Soviet Union as a country capable of determining its own future, and had accorded him the respect of a near-summit to back that up. Reagan got a great talking point for his reelection, but most critically, he had entered the arena of negotiation after far too long an absence. Weinberger need not have feared what his boss might say to a wily Soviet; Reagan, of course, stuck to his guns. Both men left the meeting with confidence that something better, more substantial, could happen down the line. Direct presidential intervention had produced a non-zero-sum result.[13]

Shultz would come to believe that Gromyko had been dispatched to Washington in order to size up Reagan for a future meeting with Chernenko—or whomever was in charge of the Soviet Union at the time.[14]

Mikhail Gorbachev arrived at the Soviet embassy in London to a grand ceremony and a rope line on December 15. He intended to shake the hands of everyone in the embassy.

"I had a curious feeling that I should conceal myself behind someone else and not appear in the picture, for fear that one of my colleagues might later be branded with having had a traitor at his shoulder," Oleg Gordievsky would later write.

His colleagues' first impressions of Gorbachev were tinged by racial animus. His face seemed Mongoloid. His accent was South Russian, "regarded in Moscow and St. Petersburg as unpleasant and ugly." Gorbachev, they concluded, was a provincial pretender. They ignored the speech he made—in which he explained to the embassy his view that American policy was not constructed by a cabal but instead as the result of three competing branches of power—and focused on the optics.[15] He was just an apparatchik.

Margaret Thatcher disagreed. Gorbachev seemed to be quite authentic. And he didn't speak in the worn communist parables. The British enthusiastically described their five-hour discussion as "very friendly." The Soviet readout said that it had been "businesslike."[16]

At one point, Thatcher recalled in her diaries, Gorbachev had

pulled out a full-page diagram from the *New York Times*, illustrating the explosive power of the weapons of the two superpowers compared with the explosive power available in the Second World War. He was well versed in the fashionable arguments then raging about the prospect of a "nuclear winter" resulting from a nuclear exchange. I was not much moved by all this. I said that what interested me more than the concept of the nuclear winter was avoiding the incineration, death and destruction which would precede it. But the purpose of nuclear weapons was, in any case, to deter war not to wage it. They had given us a greater degree of protection from war than we had ever known before. Yet this could—and must—now be achieved at a lower level of weaponry. Mr. Gorbachev argued that if both sides continued to pile up weapons this could lead to accidents or unforeseen circumstances and with the present generation of weapons the time for decision-making could be counted in minutes. As he put it, in one of the more obscure Russian proverbs, "once a year even an unloaded gun can go off."

Toward the end of the discussion, Thatcher noted that the Soviets wanted SDI stopped at almost any price.

I knew that to some degree I was being used as a stalking horse for President Reagan. I was also aware that I was dealing with a wily opponent who would ruthlessly exploit any divisions between me and the Americans. So, I bluntly stated—and then repeated at the end of the meeting—that he should understand that there was no question of dividing us: we would remain staunch allies of the United States. My frankness on this was particularly important because of my equal frankness about what I saw as the president's unrealistic dream of a nuclear-free world.

As she watched his motorcade depart, Thatcher hoped that she had just spent five hours talking with the next Soviet leader. "For, as I subsequently told the press, this was a man with whom I could do business."[17]

———

For Gordievsky, the visit was successful, too. Of course, Gordievsky had received inside information from the SIS about Thatcher's agenda, and Thatcher received Gordievsky's latest gossip about Gorbachev. Though a rival claimed as his own the memos that Gordievsky wrote, the success of the visit reflected well on the head of the PR line. Gordievsky was promoted to acting *rezident* on April 28, 1985. The West now had an asset at the highest levels of the KGB at the very moment the world was yearning to know everything possible about the bona fides of Gorbachev.

Fourteen days earlier, Aldrich Ames, the chief of Soviet counterintelligence for the CIA, walked into the Soviet embassy in Washington and asked to speak with the resident. Ames would later say he wanted money and planned to give the KGB the names of double agents that Moscow already knew about. But the light treason had whet his appetite. Ames had not personally participated in the close-hold investigation into the great intelligence source the SIS claimed to have, but he was familiar with the CIA's conclusion: a political officer in the embassy named Oleg Gordievsky was the likeliest candidate.

On Thursday, May 16, 1985, Gordievsky received a summons. He was to return to Moscow at once for consultations with the chairman of the KGB himself. That sent shivers up his spine. The next day, he received a second telegram, which made him feel slightly less nervous: be sure to have prepared a briefing on British politics, it instructed. So maybe that was all Moscow wanted from him. Gordievsky's SIS handlers did not believe the telegrams were a sign of impending capture. They were excited about the prospect of hearing almost directly from the chairman of the KGB himself. Normally, his case officers would be the ones to urge him to go to ground at the slightest hint of trouble, and Gordievsky would shake off their concerns. Here, though, it was Gordievsky who desperately wanted them to urge him to stay in London, to defect, with his family. They did not.

Before he left, Gordievsky reviewed and re-memorized the complicated escape plan that the SIS had cooked up for him if he ever found himself in a tight spot in Moscow.[18]

CHAPTER 33

Not to Miss the Chance

THE DAY AFTER HE WAS SWORN IN AS GENERAL SECRETARY, Mikhail Gorbachev was told that Ronald Reagan "is trying persistently to capture the initiative in international affairs, to create an image of America as a country that is purposefully striving to improve relations with the Soviet Union and to improve the global political climate," in the words of his propaganda chief and close advisor, Alexander Yakovlev. Gorbachev was ambitious to meet Reagan as an equal; it would be "in the national interest of the Soviet Union. We should agree to it, but without haste. We should not help create an impression that it is Reagan solely who pushes the buttons of world development."[1]

Reagan himself inched forward. A Soviet defector confirmed to him that his country's leaders nursed an odd feeling that the US might actually be a threat to their existence.[2] The president was willing to confide in his diary that Weinberger and Casey were increasingly at odds with his policy on just about every subject, and even resolved to tell both men to defer in their pronouncements to Shultz (who was very, very frustrated by the pushback he was getting for all of his efforts). As the historian James Graham Wilson has noted, Reagan's aversion to confrontation and his familial loyalty to Weinberger and Casey was too strong, probably to the president's own detriment.[3] He would continue to equivocate at critical moments, but in one sense his silence spoke louder than his actions: he allowed Shultz to make a lasting imprint on his policy, and in doing so, he convinced the Soviets that the Secretary of State spoke for him, and not the legacy interests of the Pentagon or the CIA or the nuclear priesthood.

"I wanted them to know that we were looking at them realistically, and wanted them to know that the only way we were going to have agreement was on the basis of deeds, not words," Reagan said.[4]

———

Oleg Gordievsky arrived in Moscow with a shadow. He could tell by the subtle differences in body language that came with each interaction. At the border, the guard inspecting his passport had to make a phone call. That was never a good sign. He found that his apartment had been burgled, probably to sneak in surveillance bugs. He could not sleep his night back. He all but knew he was caught; he kind of wanted the KGB to just get on with it and confirm it to him. And he wondered, of course, who had betrayed him.[5]

Still, when he showed up at KGB headquarters the next day, he was asked to organize his mind around a briefing about Britain once again, and he allowed himself a tiny hope that he was being paranoid. A few days went by. Then he got a call from a superior: "Two people want to speak with you about high-level agent penetration of Britain," he was told. It was too sensitive to discuss at headquarters, so they would go somewhere else. The day was hot and sticky, as Gordievsky remembers it, when he showed up at a cottage in the suburbs of Moscow. He was served a sandwich and a spot of brandy.

Then he woke up, in his underwear and a vest, barely able to remember what had happened. He was under interrogation. His chief inquisitor was the head of the KGB's Fifth Chief Directorate, its internal counterspy arm. Strangely, he was driven back to his home. The next day, he showed up at work—as if nothing had happened. But now he was led into an office there, and told that while they knew he had been deceiving them—"if you only knew what an unusual source we heard about you from!"—he could keep his job in the KGB, albeit not in an operational role.

At this point, Gordievsky had no idea what to think. If they had the goods on him, they would not have let him go. If they knew he was a traitor, he would have been beaten—and not clumsily drugged at a cottage somewhere. He assumed that he would be under heavy surveillance—perhaps the KGB needed to catch him in the act before it could justify the arrest of the London resident—but had no one to bounce ideas off of. He was alone on an island in the middle of Moscow.[6]

A few days later, his wife, Leila, returned with his children. "I'm afraid I'm in big trouble. We can't go back," he told her.

Leila: "What do you mean?"

Oleg: "We can't ever go back to London."

Leila: "Why on earth not?"

He lied to her. It was stupid KGB intriguing, he said.

His children, knowing very little of Moscow, began to pine for England. He found this heartbreaking.

Gordievsky began to realize that he had a choice to make. If he stayed with his family, he would certainly be killed, and they might be imprisoned. If he escaped, he'd live, and he might never see them again, but he could probably use his life as a bargaining chip to keep them alive, too.

For the past seven years, SIS case officers in Moscow risked their lives to check a signaling point that had been dedicated solely to help Gordievsky begin his escape. Even when he was in London, the spot was watched, because the KGB officers who were watching the SIS officers could not associate a "deviation from the pattern with the absence of Gordievsky," the historian Gordon Corera later wrote.[7]

To signal the British, Gordievsky would have to stand near a lamppost with a Safeway shopping bag at precisely 7:00 p.m. on a Tuesday. For days, he worked on a plan to get to the spot without surveillance. When Tuesday came, he found himself there—and no one seemed to see him. What he gotten wrong? Had the British abandoned him? He tried again a week later, and waited twenty-four agonizing minutes before he saw the countersignal—a very obviously British man carrying a shopping bag. The two men looked at each other, and Gordievsky begged for help, only with his eyes.

He would have to trust that the signal had been passed correctly. Either way, he was going to execute its next steps. Within a week, he would be dead, or he would be free. The plan involved a maze of what Gordievsky called "dry cleaning"—shaking surveillance in the heart of Moscow—and using fake identity cards to take train trips to different locations.[8]

He ended up near "a large stone in the forest" somewhere south of Finland.

He waited there for hours.

And then the funny-looking man with the Harrods bag drove up in a car, accompanied by two women. Gordievsky packed himself into the trunk and found bottles of water, an empty bottle in case he had to pee, and sedatives.

The British had been tracked by the KGB, too, and the team had to move quickly.

At a checkpoint near the border, a guard maneuvered a canine around the car. It had sniffed out Gordievsky.

But one of the women—the wife of an SIS officer—thought quickly and fed the dog some chips while the guard wasn't looking. The dog's concentration was now elsewhere.

Hours later, the car stopped, and the trunk popped open.

"Awkwardly I scrambled to my feet, my trousers hanging down. All round stood the glorious, soaring, clean pines of a Finnish forest."

He saw his SIS case officers.

He was free.[9]

For the first time ever—or since—a Western spy had been smuggled out of Moscow.

CHAPTER 34

To Geneva

ELEVEN DAYS BEFORE REAGAN WAS TO MEET GORBACHEV, Matlock finally had the chance to put together a Soviet seminar for the president.

He sensed that if Reagan figured out how to appeal to Gorbachev's interests, the Soviet leader would respond in a way that could creatively disrupt the old arms-control paradigm, just as Reagan was attempting to do with the Strategic Defense Initiative. When Reagan spoke of complete disarmament, as he often did, many of his military advisors worried about how to ground his point of view. Matlock believed the opposite: Reagan's passion and sincerity in these moments was the strongest weapon in the American arsenal.

The presentations would have to be short and concise. To elevate the meeting's importance, Matlock had to ensure that the National Security Council would attend. This proved hard; Weinberger, for one, thought it was a colossal waste of time.[1]

R. Mark Palmer, the forty-four-year-old Deputy Assistant Secretary of State for Eastern Europe, tried to stack the deck with participants who would bring Reagan down to earth. Arnold Hoelick of the RAND Corporation did not believe that the Soviet system would allow Gorbachev to reform it even if he wanted to. Sovietologist Richard Pipes, brought back from exile, was still pressing Reagan to tighten economic sanctions against the Soviets. Reagan had consulted with Jim Billington, the head of the Woodrow Wilson International Center for Scholars before. Adam Ulam, a

Polish-born intellectual historian, had strong views of how Marxism continued to influence Soviet policy making.[2]

The outsider, and the one Matlock was counting on, was Nina Tumarkin. She was one of two women who would be in the room (Roz Ridgway, a senior State Department official, as the other); Tumarkin was the only guest who had not been to the White House before. And ideologically, although not a doctrinaire Massachusetts liberal, she did not subscribe to the president's domestic agenda.

Matlock's deputy, Ty Cobb, had given Tumarkin her main charge: tell Reagan about how the Soviet people see their leadership. Explain the pressures on Gorbachev from below. Give the president a feel for how the Soviets understand the United States. All this, she was told, would have to be squeezed into three minutes, or the president would lose interest.

The day of the seminar, Tumarkin arrived early. Like any first-time visitor to the White House, she was nervous and worried she'd be out of her depth. She paid close attention to every detail, reading these powerful men whose names and faces she knew mostly from the news.

She was ushered into the cabinet room, a few steps away from the Oval Office. Its door was closed, and she marveled at its enormous lock plate and keyhole. "Reminds me of Alice in Wonderland," she said to Cobb. He smiled and replied, "The resemblance to Wonderland around here is more than just a keyhole."[3]

Bud McFarlane, the National Security Advisor, wandered in, along with Matlock. McFarlane gripped Tumarkin's hands and looked into her eyes. "I really thank you for coming. I really thank you." His charisma and bedroom eyes were slightly creepy, but when she later told her friend, the lobbyist Anne Wexler, about the encounter, she understood his gaze to be an artifact of his Marine training. That was just how McFarlane greeted everyone.

Then the president bounded in. Tumarkin froze.

"Move," Matlock whispered to her.

She stepped to the side.

He introduced her to the president, who nodded and said "hello," and walked around the room to greet the other guests.

"We're here today to do something useful to help the president understand the Soviet Union," McFarlane said by way of introduction.

As they settled into their chairs, Reagan had two things on his mind.

"You know, I was asked by someone whether I would give the Soviets veto power over SDI, and I gave them a two-word answer: 'Hell no!' And then, I'm sometimes asked if I'm fed up with Gorbachev, and I tell them, 'Not yet!'"

Tumarkin got the impression that Reagan had been fed the lines in order to ease any tension. As her fellow guests began to present their ideas, she looked around the room. Weinberger sat to the president's left. He looked gaunt, "the kind of man who makes dreadful things in his basement at night," she wrote in her diary. He did not seem happy to be there and did not say a word during the session.

First, Billington gave an overview of the Soviet mood, peppering his remarks with allusions to "new visions," cultural revolutions, and esoteric comparisons to other eras. Bill Hyland, a former aide to Henry Kissinger and strong proponent of ballistic missile defense, urged Reagan to stick with SDI. "It gives you great leverage," he said.

When it was Tumarkin's turn, she remembered that she had been told to look directly into the president's eyes and to speak slowly. She turned her body to face him. George Shultz, the Secretary of State, moved his chair back so there was only a few feet of distance between the scholar and the president.

Mikhail Gorbachev, she began, "sees himself as certainly, and portrays himself, as a peacemaker. This image is received positively by the Soviet people." She noted that that very morning marked the sixty-eighth anniversary of the Russian Revolution. They'd celebrate with a parade in Red Square, and to Americans, that read as militaristic. But the Soviets, she said, associated with it strength. "They see themselves as peacemakers. When I was in the Soviet Union last year, I talked with a lot of veterans, including a little old lady in Red Square. I told her I was an American. She smiled and said, 'Ah, you've seen our military parade, so now you see that we want peace?'" It might seem like a paradox, she said, but the Soviets feared war in their marrow. Strong leadership keeps the Soviets out of war, and Gorbachev was seen as a strong leader.

Reagan interrupted: "You speak of the Russian people expecting and respecting a strong leader. Is Gorbachev anything like Peter the Great?"

There was a moment of silence. "I'm reading about Peter the Great, and boy, was he tough," the president said.

Tumarkin said that Gorbachev seemed vigorous in comparison to other Soviet leaders as of late—and she chose her words carefully, because Reagan was not exactly a young man—but implied that the Soviet people had lost confidence in their leadership until Gorbachev came along.

Whether Gorbachev was that leader—she couldn't yet say.

Her time running short, she moved to her advice.

Don't be confused by the Soviets' constant references to Communist ideologies. They aren't guidelines for policy, she said, as much as they are a ritual, a way of connecting with the past. "Look at them the way an anthropologist would look at the incantations of a tribe," she told Reagan. He did not seem to understand what she meant.

The US and USSR have wholly different systems but need common ground to begin a discussion. "You can support Gorbachev's love for his country. You can tell him that you respect and appreciate the Soviets' bravery in the great World War. That you understand why the Soviets would be so patriotic." Doing so, she said, "would move him and cost you nothing and be generous of spirit."

Matlock made a private note here. Reagan had mentioned the Soviets and World War II before, but it might have a greater effect if he said something in person, or to the Russian people directly. Tumarkin handed Reagan a framed photograph. He studied it for a while. It showed three men and a woman, their faces crinkly from age, all with medals around their necks. They stood in Red Square on Victory Day in 1984. The Soviets, she noted, lost 20 million people in that war.

"I could tell them what I did during the war, because Gorbachev was just a youngster during the time," the president said.

Tumarkin had finished her presentation. She did not know what to think of Reagan's reactions. From reading his face, she could see that he had listened. She noted that he was reading her lips and that he had a hearing aid. But she did not know whether he had learned anything.

Ulam went next, describing the Soviet capacity for mischief making in the third world. "Professor Tumarkin, by the way, is right about human rights. The Soviets are really defensive about human rights."

She had suggested that Reagan not dwell on the topic in public—they get very defensive and discussions tend to bog down.

Pipes spoke up. "Mr. President, you are the first president to question the Soviet system, and that is quite right. The problem is not weapons, it's relations. Britain and France have nuclear weapons, but we don't worry about them. I think pressing them on human rights is a good thing."

"When I was president of the Screen Actors Guild," Reagan replied, "I learned that real negotiations take place in the men's room."

But the president moved back to the point: the conversations should be private, as they had been with Nixon working with Brezhnev on Jewish immigration—and more recently, "when our private discussions got the Pentecostalists out of the embassy."

After a few more quips, the meeting was over, and the president was ushered out. The guests lingered and gave their own postmortem. Vice President Bush told them that it was the most fun meeting on the Soviets he could remember in a while.

Tumarkin was thrilled by the moment and confused by the president's reactions. She believed she had acquitted herself well, but she did not know whether the president would find her ideas valuable. She did not know what to make of his mind or his comprehension.

————

That same day, newspapers and pundits were scoring the president's prospects. Their background sources in the White House were not unanimous; some were optimistic that the summit would accomplish something meaningful. Others were not.

Right before Reagan left for Switzerland, the *Washington Post* and the *New York Times* obtained a private memo from Weinberger urging Reagan to stick to his guns on the Strategic Defense Initiative and stress to Gorbachev that the US would negotiate nothing until the Soviets complied with the letter of existing arms-control agreements.[4]

The leak sent McFarlane and Shultz into fits of apoplexy. Its goal was transparent, because Reagan had heard Weinberger argue strongly for SDI as the sine qua non for months—the Defense Secretary was "more Catholic than the Pope" on SDI—and had become more optimistic than Reagan about the program's technological feasibility. Weinberger wanted to use the allegations of Soviet chicanery on ABM treaty violations to persuade Reagan to rethink a decision the president had made a month before: to comply with the spirit of the 1972 treaty, Reagan would not allow new SDI-related programs to be tested in the field.[5] This was intended as a gesture to Gorbachev. The CIA and Margaret Thatcher suggested that Gorbachev intended to use the Geneva meeting as a venue to try to convince Reagan to return to the core of the framework of the ABM Treaty—which would mean the effective abolition of SDI—and perhaps persuade Reagan to sign the SALT II treaty that Jimmy Carter had abandoned after the Soviet invasion of Afghanistan.[6]

This was significant for the Pentagon, because most of its ballistic missile programs had been folded into SDI, and everything related to SDI was considered to be on the outer bounds of that treaty. If the Pentagon could not test SDI, it would stand to lose billions of dollars; existing ballistic missile projects that were permitted by the treaty would lose momentum; the Soviets could continue to research and test their anti-satellite weapons with impunity, and moreover, the Soviet perception of its national security interests would supplant the United States's as the departure point for arms-control talks.[7]

The leak was designed to replant the argument in Reagan's head on the eve of his departure. Knowing that Gorbachev would make his opposition to SDI the centerpiece of the summit, Reagan wanted to say, in essence, "We're moving forward with it, but we won't do anything threatening, because we'll stick with the treaty," McFarlane said later.[8]

He believed that the Pentagon leak undercut Reagan because the Soviets could use it as a straw man as often as they wished during the first round of negotiations. For Matlock, it was vital that the president get to know Gorbachev on his own terms. The SDI trap laid by the Pentagon was as close as he'd ever seen to a Pentagon sabotaging a president.[9] (Reagan wasn't too perturbed; didn't everyone already know what Weinberger thought anyway?)

Oleg Gordievsky, in a memo from his hideaway in London, advised Reagan that "bureaucratic devices"—small gestures that gave the Soviet governing apparatus real work to do—would be the easiest way to reduce the tension and paranoia between the two countries.

He understood that Reagan would attempt to sell Gorbachev on the idea of sharing the fruits of SDI research—a "trick," was the way Soviets would see it, unless it were offset by significant reductions in offensive weapons.

Gorbachev's priorities "are arms control and Soviet/United States relations. Everything else is secondary," Gordievsky wrote. "It is psychologically important for the Russians to feel that they are the equal of the United States."[10]

Eleven days later, Reagan took Gorbachev's measure for the first time, at the Château Fleur d'Eau, an eighteenth-century retreat with a view of Lake Geneva.[11]

After the photographers left them alone, Reagan began with a rehearsed preamble. Yes, the two men would talk about arms control, but wouldn't it be better if the two men both agreed to reduce the suspicions each held about the other, first? If not, anything else they said would be "empty." "You and I were born in two small towns which nobody ever heard of and no one expected anything from either of us," he said.

For his part, Gorbachev thought Reagan was trying too hard. The point of the meeting, after all, was to get to know each other and build trust, so the president didn't have to draw attention to the subtext. The Soviet leader saw Reagan's opening words as a gambit, a sign that the American did not intend to make meaningful progress on arms reductions right then and there.

Gorbachev told Reagan that his starting point was reality: neither man could afford to ignore the other anymore. Moving forward would require sacrifices from both sides and enormous political will. So long as each country recognized the other as legitimate, and capable of pursuing its own interests without intending to harm the other, there was progress to be made.

Reagan spoke then of the "courage, the sacrifice" that the Soviets had made in World War II—the last time the Americans and the Soviets had been manifest allies—and said he understood that the Soviets had no desire for war.[12]

After both men aired their views of the world, Gorbachev took Reagan aside and informed him that Soviet scientists were predicting that a major earthquake would strike California or Nevada within the next three years, and while he assumed Reagan already knew such information, he felt duty-bound to share it. Reagan, confused by Gorbachev's abrupt change of subject, responded didactically; the Californian knew about his earthquakes and assured Gorbachev that American scientists were doing all they could to predict them.[13]

The next day, Reagan handed Gorbachev a letter with starting points for a way forward. The first was easy: a reduction in offensive weapons. Gorbachev was on board. In response to the second—"intermediate nuclear forces"—Gorbachev insisted that French and British weapons had to be included. And the third was strategic defense. There, Gorbachev would not yield, as Gordievsky had projected. Why should he trust the United States to share its research into space weapons? (He, too, had read the newspapers and knew what the Pentagon was up to.)[14] Well, why did Gorbachev keep referring to space weapons? Reagan wanted to know. SDI did not envision any such thing.

From there, the substance of the summit bogged down into a debate about the strategic and political feasibility of a space-based defense shield.[15] Gorbachev would not budge, and neither would Reagan.

But this was not a failure; the talks did not founder. They were a beginning.

Reagan decided to invite Gorbachev to the United States the next year; Gorbachev accepted immediately. The two men, having spent hours together, would keep working the problem, as only they could do. Negotiators at lower levels had also agreed on six new starting points for talks— exactly the type of "bureaucratic devices" that would give the Soviets firm evidence of progress, as Gordievsky had suggested.

"Maggie was right. We can do business with this man," Reagan told his cabinet when he returned to Washington.[16]

"And the world," Jack Matlock wrote, "breathed a sigh of relief."[17]

Epilogue

If the testimony of spies memorializing their accomplishments in retrospect can be accepted as somewhat reliable testimony, and if the subsequent counterintelligence investigations by US and West German officials did their due diligence, here is what we can say, for sure, that elements of the intelligence leviathan that the Soviet Union nominally controlled *should have been able to figure out* by 1983:

- They knew the locations of US tactical nuclear warheads in West Germany.
- They knew the call signs and code phrases associated with exercises and general war.
- They knew the frequencies and communication systems that carried nuclear execution messages.
- They were able to intercept a significant amount of top-secret naval communications traffic between the US and its deployed warships.
- They knew at least part of the exercise plan for NATO's Able Archer 83.
- They knew the war plans; they had stolen several iterations of NATO's general war plan for Europe.
- They knew how the US Army in Central Europe would prepare for a war, defensively or otherwise.
- They knew the top-secret formats of nuclear execution messages.
- They knew that the US had begun to experiment with sophisticated electronic warfare against the Warsaw Pact's command and control system.
- They knew the battle rhythm of the nuclear-armed 59th Ordinance Brigade and the 501st Army Artillery Detachment, and they could tell when something was amiss.

- They knew how to manipulate several code-making and code-breaking machines that NATO used to transmit emergency action messages.

When I reeled off this list to a former senior CIA official who was involved in weighing Soviet intentions at the time, he paused and then responded this way: "You know, there's a theory about all this. The more, the better, right? Let's say they did know all of this. Maybe even, they had access to nuclear cookies, or to codes. Let's say they could listen to our communications. They had a spy in the main battle staff of NATO. So, wouldn't it be logical that, if they knew all of this, they would know our intentions? They could figure out, because they knew our secrets, whether we were preparing for war. In a way, if they're going to know some of our secrets, they might as well know all of them."[1]

In a way. Perhaps the US and the Soviet Union were so good at spying that they could see well enough into each other's brains to determine intent; perhaps all the pieces of the three-dimensional chessboard were visible.

But there are strong reasons to doubt that the Soviets knew all that we think they knew. We don't know how much of the information that the Stasi obtained was processed up the chain in a way that was actually useful for KGB analysts at the highest levels in Moscow. Gordievsky and many others were certain that the analytical process was so broken that policy makers saw reliably poor intelligence that confirmed their biases. We don't know how intelligence was shared, or in what time frame; we don't know whether it was believed. Indeed, the evidence suggests that while the Stasi had obtained a good, but incomplete, version of the Able Archer playbook, the GRU, the Soviets' military intelligence arm, had (for some reason) less information about Able Archer; the KGB knew next to nothing about it. Internal rivalries cloud the picture.

Further, it's one thing to know a secret; it's quite another to believe that what's real is *true*; each side was convinced that the other side was executing a massive disinformation campaign, and planted secrets were par the course. The theory that knowing a lot of the enemy's secrets can help determine his intentions is attractive, but it founders on the shoals of one of the most persistent and pernicious of cognitive biases: that the adversary thinks the same way we do; that his assumptions, intentions, needs, wants, and endgames largely track with our own. The United States and the Soviet Union simultaneously disclaimed and pursued first-strike contingencies for different reasons. They did not share a basic definition of what strategic stability even meant.[2] The CIA now instructs analysts not to fall into the brain trap of assuming that their reality is a mirror image of their adversaries', or that they can know an adversary by trying to reason through their mental assumptions.[3]

The politicians, strategic thinkers, generals, and intelligence professionals who made hard choices in the early 1980s deserve to be ranked in the upper echelons of historic achievement. They helped win the Cold War. They deserve credit for that. But their distinguished careers should not be tarnished by a hubris that afflicts many of them today: *Everything the Russians did was* maskirovka— *strategic deception. American geniuses saw through it all.* The opposite bias—the mirror fallacy—a conviction that "the other side" thinks as you do—got them into this mess in the first place. In 1983, and in 1984, too, a number of Soviet leaders feared that the United States was on the verge of abandoning deterrence and on the precipice of attempting some sort of first nuclear strike. They were not "rational *cum* reasonable, and thus utterly predictable and controllable," as the historian Keith P. Payne has written.[4]

Facing sophisticated electronic warfare programs that could cut off their ability to retaliate, provocations in the air and at sea, menacing language from a president determined to rebuild an already strong military, the confidence possessed by an enemy that a nuclear war might be survivable after all, and, most of all, age, bloat, and the stagnation of their own system, the Soviet leaders can be forgiven if they did not fully subscribe to the tautologies and incantations offered up by America's nuclear priesthood at this moment in history.

Now we know. We know that, *at the same time* that the Politburo tried to turn NATO against the United States, the Soviet military quietly enhanced the alert status of its bomber crews, endorsed the diversion of trucks away from the harvest and toward military uses, prepared intelligence stay-behind networks in Europe, updated plans to kill Western leaders at the last moment before an attack, and even shot down a civilian airliner that had crossed into its airspace.[5] We know this because we now have the actual cable traffic that the First Chief Directorate of the KGB was telling its stations overseas at the time, equivalent to secret directives from the director of the CIA to his top ten lieutenants. We know this because we now know a lot more about the internal thinking of the Soviet military and political elite at the time, what they said at the time, in private, away from eavesdropping ears, away from American judgments. We know this because, after retrospective reconstruction of the intelligence, the Soviets had managed to secretly mobilize their nuclear forces during this period in direct response to NATO exercises; large movements of troops and personnel that were detected months afterward by American intelligence.[6] The CIA has now formally acknowledged that it got the intelligence wrong; that it underestimated the way that real fear shaped Soviet policy; several senior intelligence officials have acknowledged much greater flaws. One told me it was the greatest intelligence failure in the history of the United States. Another, Robert Gates, the deputy director of intelligence at the CIA during this period, has called it a "monumental" failure.

Ronald Reagan has been depicted by popular historians as a rebellious antinuclear war zealot, a crusader who overruled his hardline advisors and managed to secure agreements that dismantled more nuclear weapons than any president before or since.[7] Another school finds in this period the seeds of a major "reversal" in his approach, from confrontational to accommodating, because he became afraid of the dire risks of nuclear war. The "rebellious" Reagan has been embraced by his partisans because it shows him to be an active participant in world affairs, the opposite of the amiable dunce who allegedly took daily naps and talked often of Christian eschatology.[8]

In his diary, here is how Reagan himself describes what happened:

> Three years had taught me something surprising about the Russians: Many people at the top of the Soviet hierarchy were genuinely afraid of America and Americans. Perhaps this shouldn't have surprised me, but it did.
>
> During my first years in Washington, I think many of us in the administration took it for granted that the Russians, like ourselves, considered it unthinkable that the United States would launch a first strike against them. But the more experience I had with Soviet leaders and other heads of state who knew them, the more I began to realize that many Soviet officials feared us not only as adversaries but as potential aggressors who might hurl nuclear weapons at them in a first strike; because of this . . . they had aimed a huge arsenal of nuclear weapons at us.
>
> Well, if that was the case, I was even more anxious to get a top Soviet leader in a room alone and try and convince him we had no designs on the Soviet Union and Russians had nothing to fear from us.[9]

This makes sense to me. It is consistent with the evidence we have. Reagan's ruminations on the apocalypse, his near-death experience, and his sober accounting of nuclear warfare clashed with his optimism. His optimism won. It informed his view of Soviet leaders.

In a New Year's Day 2018 message, Kim Jong-un, the dynastic cult leader of a giant failed state, told the world that he now possessed a "nuclear button" on his desk. Since the button is the final image in our mental metaphor of what a nuclear decision chain looks like, Kim's signal was reasonably clear: he now has everything he believes he needs to actually launch some kind of nuclear weapon at a chosen target, and he can do so rapidly. The American intelligence community, in its classified estimates, has not found any evidence that Kim has shown much bluster in his nuclear pronouncements. From 2016 to the present, North Korea's demonstrated nuclear capacity has exceeded its projected/theoretical nuclear capacity so thoroughly that it would be folly not to assume that his statements are canon. Ostensibly, Kim pursued his nuclear weapons program to forever break free from the yoke of any other country—Korea has been subject to hundreds of territorial invasions over its 5,000-year history—and to gain leverage to pursue on its own terms reconciliation with South Korea, a new trade relationship with China, and legitimacy on the world stage thanks to an equalized bilateral relationship with the United States. He was ready to bargain, and he said so. The South Koreans immediately proposed talks.[10]

The US president, Donald Trump, rejected them.

Instead, he tweeted that his own nuclear button was "bigger" and "more powerful" than Kim's.

Three months later, Trump stunned the world, and much of his own staff, by agreeing to meet with Kim one-on-one. Less than a week later, he fired his Secretary of State and hinted that his entire national security cabinet would be replaced by the time such a meeting took place. Trump took a meeting that same week with a former Bush administration official who has openly made the case for preemptive attacks against North Korea. Then, he made that official, John Bolton, his national security advisor. A week later, his CIA director met in secret with Kim Jong-un. And North Korea vowed to give up its nuclear testing program. As this book goes to press, the Korean peninsula is thawing, for the first time in decades. But enmity with countries that have longstanding and deadly nuclear arsenals has only increased, even if the genuine progress on one front puts those conflicts in the background of our public mind.

Somewhere along the line, President Trump had read about Richard M. Nixon's "madman" stratagem to bully Hanoi (and China, and perhaps the Soviet Union) into concessions by hinting, through intermediaries, that he was crazy and would stop at nothing—including using nuclear weapons. That it did not work[11]—and indeed, almost backfired spectacularly[12]—is immaterial. The president believes rather straightforwardly that the less America's adversaries know about American intentions, the less likely they will be to threaten our interests. ("I don't want them to know what I'm thinking," he has said.[13]) It is not clear why Trumpian unpredictability, stated so openly, would do anything other than personalize a conflict in a way that narrows rather significantly the range of possible solutions. It is not clear how under-cutting the diplomatic efforts of your own Secretary of State and your allies does anything other than organize the conflict around the vicissitudes of personal pique and ego. It is not clear that the president understands this, or if he does, whether he cares.

In August 2017, *The New Yorker*'s Evan Osnos flew to Pyongyang and had dinner with Ri Yong Pil, an Americanist who worked for North Korea's foreign ministry. After a healthy serving of alcohol, Ri began to quiz Osnos on the inner workings of the United States's nuclear power centers. A few days before, Trump had promised a reign of "fire and fury" against North Korea if its nuclear menace ever threatened the national security of the United States.

"In your system, what is the power of the President to launch a war?" he asked. "Does the Congress have the power to decide?"

A President can do a lot without Congress, I said. Ri asked about the nuclear codes: "I've heard the black bag is controlled by McMaster. Is it true?" (He was referring to H. R. McMaster, the national-security adviser.)

No, the President can launch nukes largely on his own, I said. "What about in your country?"

His answer was similar. "Our Supreme Leader has absolute power to launch a war," he said.[14]

The US has no insight into these arrangements at all. In the event that the US truly believed that a war with North Korea was imminent, it would rely on South Korean commandos to try to decapitate Pyongyang's leadership, American cyberweapons to black out North Korea's command-and-control networks, untested laser drones to shoot down more deadly missiles, and a contingent of US special operations forces soldiers to try to find all of North Korea's nuclear warheads before they could be mated to missiles and launched. A US official with detailed knowledge of these plans told me that he has no confidence whatsoever that they would work. One major problem: the US does not know where North Korea keeps its completed nuclear bombs, and it does not know how easy it is for officers who aren't the Supreme Leader to launch them. "The US can't launch anything with an actual button. We have codes and systems and conference calls. Can Kim launch his arsenal with a button? Maybe. We have no idea," the official told me.

If President Trump, reacting to a North Korean missile launch toward Guam, were to decide to use a nuclear-armed submarine to retaliate, he could give an order and, within fifteen to twenty minutes, see it fully carried out.[15] As few as one—or perhaps as many as 100—warheads, conventional or nuclear-tipped or both, could be flying toward the Asian continent within minutes. There is no rule that requires the president to talk to anyone before authenticating his identity with the military and ordering a launch. A conference call would be convened over secure channels, but finding participants who might temper the president's instincts might take longer than the president is willing to wait.[16] Further, there is no formal mechanism for a nuclear release order to be declared illegal or invalid by anyone until after the fact. (A crossed-fingers assumption that no nuclear targeteer would transmit launch coordinates that sent a warhead over Austin, Texas, is the only real guardrail preventing a president from ordering a launch against Austin, Texas.) Commissioned officers are taught that they must challenge illegal orders, and the current steward of the US Strategic Command, General John Hyten, has in mind such a give-and-take with the commander in chief: "And if it's illegal, guess what's going to happen? I'm going to say, 'Mr. President, that's illegal.' And guess what he's going to do? He's going to say, 'What would be legal?' And we'll come up with options, with a mix of capabilities to respond to whatever the situation is, and that's the way it works. It's not that complicated."[17]

It is very, very complicated. If the original warhead that targeted Guam contained no ordinance but was meant to demonstrate that North Korea could easily target the territory and its military assets, the US might not necessarily be able to confirm this until after the system had prompted the president to retaliate. Even an empty warhead might detonate with a bang; in April 2017, a North Korean intermediate range test of a dummy warhead flew off course, and its propellants ignited close to the ground; damage was considerable.[18]

If General Hyten were to make this point on the conference call, Trump could ignore him. If Hyten were to show Trump chapter and verse that the law of warfare takes proportionality and restraint into account, Trump could turn to his own counsel or to someone else. If Hyten or perhaps the nuclear-strike advisor who bears the president's emergency satchel were to point out that, as good as satellite technology is, ghosts appear in the warning machine far more often than they should, and that the original North Korean missile might not even exist, Trump could, once again, turn his back. And who would blame him? By design, the system jams a president into making a decision before he can really know what he needs to know. It was thus during President Reagan's administration, and it remains so today. All of this is why pugnacious, contrived uncertainty is an expedient to war and why humility—a character trait that Ronald Reagan often used to the world's advantage—is its mortal enemy.

The philosopher Martha Nussbaum has written about the earth-moving emotional content of patriotism that can empower presidents and political leaders, often to the detriment of a tolerant nation that might suddenly find itself considering more narrow interests. But when that patriotic feeling becomes a universal; when the president wants everyone to have what we have, it can be a relentless reminder to keep pushing, to keep trying, to keep moving. That Reagan preferred sunny skies, smiles, optimism, and other happy things generated an impulse that allowed him to shape solutions to forces that would gray the bright world he saw. In some cases, like his refusal to acknowledge the AIDS epidemic, his emotional myopia was disastrous; in the case of the Cold War, it was essential.

He was amiable. He was no dunce. He remained a formidable Cold Warrior, ever mistrustful of the Soviet system, an ardent advocate for covert action, for the use of force when necessary, for a defense buildup that, when combined with a broad program of economic warfare, would try to squeeze the Soviet system into submission. But then, during this period, he began to try to understand the world through the minds of the Soviet leaders. He realized that he had to do so even if *they* could not extend their empathy to *him*. When he finally found a person who could—Mikhail Gorbachev—the two men seized on the chance to reduce the number of nuclear warheads aimed everywhere in the world.

Eric Schlosser, in his epic tale of how the then-most-powerful nuclear weapon in the US arsenal, a Titan II warhead, nearly destroyed half of Arkansas in 1979, enlivened the debate about nuclear weapons surety: what measures exist to make sure that accidents don't trip wires that can cause uncontrolled nuclear chain reactions? Why did the Pentagon choose for decades to treat accidents involving nuclear machinery with a mix of secret concern, cavalier public affairs, and official indifference? But the denouement to his story is a happy one: these problems have largely been fixed. Two scare scenarios: deliberate sabotage that leads to nuclear launches, on the one hand, and equipment foul-ups that cause a mated weapon to accidentally explode, on the other, are dramatically less likely to occur today than they were in the 1970s.[19] We are safer.

But as I write this epilogue, Russian president Vladimir Putin has 1,790 active nuclear warheads under his direct command. President Donald Trump has about 40 fewer. The two countries possess 14,000 more in reserve. While Trump promises to both upgrade the country's aging arsenal and (somehow, in contravention of treaties) add warheads to the alert force, Russia has fielded a mobile battalion that can threaten NATO capitals with cruise missiles, each with as many as six nuclear warheads. The Trump administration has asked Congress to fund development of a road mobile ballistic missile of its own. The INF Treaty, one of the world's most significant advances toward actual peace and nuclear de-alerting, is dying.

Putin does not believe that the American president will be a formidable adversary or a reliable adversary, perhaps one reason, aside from an animus toward former Secretary of State Hillary Clinton, why he chose to intervene in the US election on Trump's behalf. He sees Trump as pliable. He sees NATO as weak. His agents are able to murder ex-spies and Russian dissidents using banned chemical weapons—attacks that, had the wind blown slightly differently, might have killed hundreds of British citizens, thus thrusting the world into a scenario where Russia had attacked a NATO country using a weapon of mass destuction. What one sees is what one gets. The dimension of their relationship, and how it will evolve, is an almost existential unknown. Russia is aggressively asserting its prerogatives in the Middle East, the Arctic, Eastern Europe, and Asia, and NATO is once again conducting flashy exercises as a deterrent. China is, depending upon the president or the president's mood, a strategic adversary or a potential ally.

As the nation's attention turned to terrorism after 9/11, the nuclear enterprise of the US Strategic Command struggled through personnel cheating scandals, computer failures at nuclear launch sites, live weapons accidentally being substituted for dummy warheads, and bad morale and poor leadership.[20] After years of trying to reform and render reliable the basic command and control functions of the presidency, the Pentagon settled on a new construct: the Joint Systems Integration and Engineering Office. It would bring together all aspects of—here's another new acronym—NLCC (National Leadership Command Capabilities)—and be the single point of contact for their testing, fielding, and execution. The air force also designated the nuclear command and control system itself as a weapon, which makes it easier to fund needed repairs.

The SIOP remains a central buttress of defense policy. Under its modern incarnation, OPLAN 8010-12 (and currently being revised), the same linguistic conceits that bedeviled and delighted nuclear theorists are used as though the adversary should have a rational sense of their meaning. (There are no "major attack options" now—just "basic" ones.[21]) "Proportionality" in a limited nuclear strike—a concept that President Obama's nuclear posture endorsed—means what exactly? A published doctrine that promises that the US won't target civilians is possible . . . how?[22] In late January 2018, the Trump administration's Nuclear Posture Review, the first step in the chain of cateschisms that eventually find their way into war plans, proposes to modernize (i.e, build from scratch) two delivery systems, both cruise missiles that can bypass air defense systems and wind their way into enemy territory, and supposes that an arsenal with more lower-yield weapons—think tactical nukes—would enhance deterrence in various hot spots,[23] particularly against Russia, which plans for a conventional-to-nuclear escalation in NATO as a strategy, and North Korea, which rapidly and concretely established its nuclear deterrence in the final months of 2017. Will the restoration of a US capability to attack Russian military facilities and garrisons with lower-yield weapons convince Russia to become more compliant with existing treaties? Perhaps. The only way to escape the logic of nuclear deterrence is to unilaterally decide, probably on faith, that the world benefits from fewer weapons, *period,* and that the articles of nuclear doctrine are magical, just like the notion that, since nuclear weapons have not been used on the battlefield in seventy years, they never shall be again. Then again, Americans don't seem to believe in this sleight of hand. One of the reasons the errant "ballistic missile warning" message terrified Hawaiians who received it on their cell phones was that, in 2018, a North Korean nuclear attack on an American city was conceivable at the time. (If North Korea actually does "denuclearize"—a highly doubtful proposition—the scientists who built their arsenal won't have their brains wiped. And components for a nuclear warhead with the rough shape of a large bowling pin can easily be hidden and reconstructed within days.) As horrifying and clarifying as that low-grade information accident was, it is probably the tip of the iceberg. The depth of the iceberg is the instantiation of analog nuclear weapons in a digital world. The sabotage efforts the United States anticipates engaging in today are far more sophisticated than they were in Al Buckles's time. Cyberattacks against the nuclear command and control system might be preventable, but the idea that a nation-state or a terrorist can spoof the information ecosystem into thinking that an attack is underway—possibly precipitating a real-life counter-attack, has actually been war gamed at the highest, classified levels, and the hotwashes from these exercises scare the hell out of those who participate in them.

History largely syncopates and occasionally echoes. It does not repeat itself. But enough hasn't changed between 1983 and now to rule out a reality that we may face a day, soon, when our president might have to make a rapid decision about whether to authorize the launch of nuclear weapons. Intelligence has gotten better, but so has deception. The command and control system is more reliable, but the weapons are more accurate. We still envision the powers of the presidency through the metaphor of the nuclear trigger (although perhaps we might also see a drone strike), and yet we citizens are so skeptical of our political institutions that we elected a man who probably never wanted the job in the first place.

Today, President Trump can execute an emergency war order in less time than it takes to get a cheeseburger at a drive-through.

This fundamental proposition, a metaphor in extremis, generates the real power claimed by the executive of the American national security state and forms the basis for many of our political arguments. In our minds, we elect presidents whose fingers will hover over buttons, ready to unleash a series of commands to launch nuclear missiles.

But the US nuclear war–enabling machine does not work this way in practice, and it never has.[24] It attributes to the president a power he has only in law and in theory, taking it away from its real locus: the nuclear command, control, and communications system that the Pentagon manages and that thousands of men and women, most of them loyal to a fault, operate.

The nuclear historian Stephen Cimbala pictures a gun: "The function of the presidential center is *not* to act as a trigger to launch weapons, but as a safety catch preventing other triggers from firing."[25]

When the world seems peaceful, the safety is on. When the world is turbulent, the safety is slowly removed from its groove, and the system predisposes its users to act more quickly, with less time to deliberate.

But it turns out that this gun is so fragile that single points of failure could render it completely inoperable. The safety is a kluge. The enormously complicated physics of containing and then sustaining a nuclear explosion have proven far easier to understand and replicate than the technological and human-factor leviathans that arose in the United States and the Soviet Union to harness it. The soundness and reliability of nuclear command and control is largely a myth, a just-so story, designed to give everyone from American voters to their presidents a sense of comfort that the requirements on this side of the globe for mutually assured destruction to work in favor of peace—specifically, an elected president, with accurate knowledge of the world situation, good advice from subordinates, the technical means to transmit a launch order, the mechanisms to carry it out, and the ability to ride out a crisis—exist, prepackaged in a break-glass alcove somewhere in the White House Situation Room.

That means, in essence, that peace is a product of an ordinary human making the right decisions in extraordinary circumstances, trying to understand an adversary whose mind could well be fashioned by the elements of another planet, whose assumptions will never be his own.

Ronald Reagan realized that only presidents can truly understand the entire dimension of the nuclear problem, only presidents have the power to elevate global stewardship and sovereignty above patriotic partiality, and therefore only presidents can keep the world from the ash heap of Armageddon. It was, in his words, "the greatest responsibility of life—of any human being's life.[26]

Postscript

Jeffrey Carney, the air force intelligence analyst who spied for the Stasi, was arrested and charged with espionage in April 1991. He served twelve years in prison.

Rainer Rupp also spent twelve years in prison. He lives in Germany today.

Project Pegasus, a.k.a. Project 908, a.k.a. DMSPA, was terminated by President Clinton in 1992. FEMA took over many of its responsibilities and incorporated its communications technology into mobile command convoys that would be detailed to the White House Military Office in times of war. During Clinton's presidency, the WHMO and the Pentagon kept threadbare versions of these contingency programs alive. Their functions were scattered throughout the government. The September 11 terrorist attacks, and the potential threat of a suitcase-sized nuclear bomb detonation in Washington, brought the plans back into vogue.

Stanislav Petrov died in 2017.

Oleg Gordievsky met Ronald Reagan in July 1987, providing canny insight to the president on the eve of a summit. He was reunited with Leila and his family in September 1991. The separation had taken its toll, and Oleg and Leila separated shortly thereafter. He lives in London.

Acknowledgments

Nathan B. Jones, the FOIA guru at the National Security Archive, wrote the first essay I ever read about Able Archer. It was an unpublished master's thesis, and when, in 2009, he finished it, it challenged both the views of historians and the government's official version of Able Archer. He thought Soviet fears were real; almost everyone else assumed they were overstated. Nate has proven himself largely correct. He has done more than anyone to pry loose a number of previously classified documents and has brought together archivists across the world to find many others. Without him, our understanding of Able Archer would be impoverished. This book would look very different. Jones, David Hoffmann, and a number of other researchers used the government's own mandatory declassification review process to force the release of the 1991 President's Foreign Intelligence Advisory Board review of the "Soviet War Scare." For that alone Jones deserves plaudits. (His advocacy on behalf of FOIA is a subject worthy of numerous other positive adjectives). His colleague Thomas Burr pried loose a number of documents about the Ivy League '82 exercise and numerous other topics. Dr. Bruce Blair remains the essential civilian authority on nuclear command and control. He bravely revealed the system's inner workings and contradictions when doing so might have cost him his career. He read several chapters of this manuscript and spent hours patiently explaining difficult concepts to me.

Benjamin Fischer, who has served as the chief historian at the CIA, has done path-breaking, rigorous research on the war scare, on CANOPY WING, and on a number of other highly relevant subjects; he is responsible for helping to ensure that the public perception of these events matches the ones told in secret, by the secret keepers. His scholarship is a model.

Beth Fischer (no relation) was the first to link Reagan's "reversal" to the war scare. I don't agree with all of her conclusions, but her work is pioneering. Christian Ostermann, director of the History and Public Policy Program at the Cold War International History Project of the Woodrow Wilson Center, pointed me in the direction of declassified and translated HVA (Stasi) documents, which filled in numerous gaps in my knowledge and in our history. I am extraordinarily grateful to the men and women who spoke on the record for the first time, including Lee Trolan, Alfred Buckles, Thomas Reed, Nina Tumarkin, David McManis, Dr. Phil Karber, and Steven Schwalbe. Two historians deserve special thanks. Diego Ruiz Palmer untangled the complexities of NATO war plans for me, and James Graham Wilson, whose own excellent work I consulted regularly, helped me more fully appreciate Cold War historiography. Wilson also caught a number of embarrassing typos. Jason Saltoun-Ebin has probably spent more time at the Ronald Reagan Presidential Library and collected more documents than most historians combined. His annotations are as compelling as the transcripts of National Security Council meetings and critical correspondence he's obtained. I'm no shill, but if you're interested in diving into the history yourself, please visit his website: http://www .thereaganfiles.com/. Peter Burt is responsible for the declassification of critical Cabinet Office documents from the time of Margaret Thatcher.

I thank *The Week* and Ben Frumin for letting me crib my own work for the chapter on the John Walker spy ring.

Thanks to Flashback Television, producers of the 2008 documentary *1983: The Brink of Apocalypse*, who provided me with transcripts of their interviews, which allowed me to incorporate more fully the perspectives of Soviet military and intelligence officials. James Mann, David Hoffmann, and Eric Schlosser have written indispensable books on continuity of government, nuclear command and control, and nuclear weapons, respectively. Their work inspires me. There is no better resource on the history of Soviet strategic nuclear forces than Pavel Podvig: http://russianforces.org/podvig/. I check his website regularly.

The research librarians at the Ronald Reagan Presidential Library could not have been more gracious and helpful. Thanks, also, to the staff at the George H. W. Bush and Jimmy Carter libraries. The Central Intelligence Agency has acquired a poor reputation in scholarly circles for being stingy with information; they now deserve credit and praise for setting the standard for declassification and access by making available on their website tens of millions of pages of documents.

Emily, Penn, Moxie, and Zolten Jillette lent me part of their home to write in and made sure I was well-fed and well-watered. Thanks also to Kevin Truong, Christopher Lai, Stacey Scholder, Laura Davis, Ivan Leung, TinTin Vongphrachanh, Rebecca Haggerty, Gordon Stables, Vince Gonzales, Willa Seidenberg, Willow Bay, Noah Oppenheim, Josh Simon, Tara Brach, Sergio Garcia, Noon Salih, Jessica Perez, Gary He, and Patti, Roy, Jessie, Michael, and Eric Ambinder. My husband, Michael Park, is my rock and speaks my language of love. Now, I will have the time to speak his.

My agent, Eric Lupfer, gets triple kudos. He helped me find the topic to explore, helped me secure a contract to write about it, and, most importantly, could have not been more patient with me when my writerly anxieties popped up.

I thank Christian Grier and Paul Lewandowski for critical research assistance. Lewandowski helped me track down several hard-to-find sources. Amar Deol at Simon & Schuster was a helpful steward and guide. Patty Romanowski Bashe found numerous small errors that would otherwise have crushed my writer's soul.

Ben Loehnen at Simon & Schuster has been an exceptional editor and a great partner on this journey. Like the president at the center of this story, Ben has character, heart, and resilience.

All errors of fact and substance are my own.

Sources

ARCHIVES AND COMPILATIONS

Ronald Reagan Presidential Library and Archive (RRL)

George H. W. Bush Presidential Library (GBL)

Jimmy Carter Presidential Library (JCL)

The Reagan Files: a document compilation by Jason Saltoun-Ebin at www.thereaganfiles.com (TRF)

George W. Bush Presidential Library (GWBPL)

United States National Archives (NA)

Archives of the United Kingdom (AUK)

Prime Minister Margaret Thatcher's Archive (PMTA)

Library of Congress (LOC)

Forecasting Nuclear War: Stasi/KGB Intelligence Cooperation Under Project RYAN; A project of the Cold War International History Project at the Woodrow Wilson Center (WW), https://www.wilsoncenter.org/publication/forecasting-nuclear-war

National Security Archive at George Washington University (NSA), http://nsarchive.gwu.edu/

John Hines, Ellis M. Mishulovich, and John F. Shulle (BDM, Inc.), *Soviet Intentions 1965–1985, Volume I: An Analytical Comparison of US-Soviet Assessments During the Cold War*, declassified by the Department of Defense and hosted on the website of the National Security Archive at George Washington University (BDM)

War Scare interview transcripts, Interview conducted by producers for *1983: The Brink of Apocalypse*, Flashback Television, Ltd., Channel 4, 2008

Hoover Institute (HI)

Presidential Oral History Project, Miller Center, University of Virginia (OHP)

Harvard Information Technology Seminars (HITS)

Select Bibliography

www.betterworldbooks.com/077-AAF-584 [accessed June 16, 2015].

http://www.hoover.org/sites/default/files/uploads/documents/978-0-8179-4632-6_93
.pdf [accessed June 17, 2015].

http://www.thereaganfiles.com/19830316-shultz.pdf [accessed June 18, 2015].

http://www.thereaganfiles.com/shultz—gromyko-11884.pdf [accessed June 18, 2015].

Abrams, Herbert L. *The President Has Been Shot: Confusion, Disability, and the 25th Amendment.* Stanford, CA: Stanford University Press, 1994.

A Cardboard Castle? An Inside History of the Warsaw Pact, 1955–1991, National Security Archive Cold War Readers. Washington, DC: Central European University Press, 2006.

Aid, Matthew M. *The Secret Sentry: The Untold History of the National Security Agency.* New York: Bloomsbury Publishing, 2009.

Aldous, Richard. *Reagan and Thatcher: The Difficult Relationship.* New York: W. W. Norton & Company, 2012.

Allen, Richard. "Memorandum for the President," 1981, http://www.thereaganfiles
.com/19810722-nspg-20-2.pdf [accessed June 17, 2015].

Allen, Thomas. *War Games.* New York: Berkeley Books, 1987.

Anderson, Ross J. *Security Engineering.* New York: Wiley, 2010.

Andrew, Christopher, and Oleg Gordievsky. *KGB: The Inside Story of Its Foreign Operations from Lenin to Gorbachev.* New York: HarperCollins, 1990.

———. *Instructions from the Centre: Top Secret Files on KGB Foreign Operations, 1975–85.* London: Hodder & Stoughton, 1993.

Andrew, Christopher M., and Vasili Mitrokhin. *Mitrokhin Archive: The KGB in Europe and the West.* London: Penguin Books, 2000.

Anthony, Dolan. "Soviet-Americans Relations Speech," 1984, http://www.thereaganfiles
.com/document-collections/19840116-speech-ideas-from.pdf [accessed June 18, 2015].

Arkin, William, and Peter Pringle. *S.I.O.P.* New York: Sphere, 1983.

Arkin, William M. *American Coup: Martial Life and the Invisible Sabotage of the Constitution.* London: Little, Brown & Company, 2013.

———. "Our Risky Naval Strategy Could Get Us All Killed," *Washington Post,* July 3, 1988, http://www.washingtonpost.com/archive/opinions/1988/07/03/our-risky-naval

-strategy-could-get-us-all-killed/717d1b1a-9679-4ddb-8673-1cd2690672f0/ [accessed June 17, 2015].

Arnold, David Christopher. *Spying from Space: Constructing America's Satellite Command and Control Systems*, Centennial of Flight Series. Austin: Texas A&M University Press, 2005.

Association for Diplomatic Studies and Training. http://adst.org/wp-content/uploads /2012/09/US-NATO.pdf [accessed June 18, 2015].

———. *United Kingdom*, Foreign Affairs Oral History Collection, 2012, Country and Subject Reader Series, http://adst.org/wp-content/uploads/2012/09/United-Kingdom1.pdf.

Barnaby, Frank. *How to Build a Nuclear Bomb: And Other Weapons of Mass Destruction*. New York: Nation Books, 2004.

Barrass, Gordon S. *The Great Cold War: A Journey Through the Hall of Mirrors*. Stanford, CA: Stanford Security Studies/Stanford University Press, 2009.

Beschloss, Michael R. *At the Highest Levels: The Inside Story of the End of the Cold War*. Boston: Little, Brown, 1993.

Blair, Bruce G. *Strategic Command and Control: Redefining the Nuclear Threat*. Washington, DC: Brookings Institution, 1985.

Boldin, Valery, and Evelyn Rossiter. *Ten Years That Shook the World: The Gorbachev Era as Witnessed by His Chief of Staff*. New York: World Publications, 2015.

Boyne, Walter J. *Beyond the Wild Blue, 2nd Edition: A History of the US Air Force, 1947–2007*. New York: Thomas Dunne Books/St. Martin's Press, 2007.

Bracken, Paul. *Command and Control of Nuclear Forces*. London: Yale University Press, 1985.

Brook-Shepherd, Gordon. *The Storm Birds: Soviet Postwar Defectors*. New York: Holt, 1990.

Burrows, William E. *Deep Black*. London: Bantam, 1988.

Campbell, Kurt M. *Difficult Transitions: Foreign Policy Troubles at the Outset of Presidential Power*. Washington, DC: Brookings Institution Press, 2008.

Cannon, Lou. *President Reagan: The Role of a Lifetime*. New York: Public Affairs, 2000.

Casey Fearmongering http://www.thereaganfiles.com/19830524-budget.pdf [accessed June 18, 2015].

Cimbala, Stephen J. *Russia and Armed Persuasion*. Lanham, MD: Rowman & Littlefield Publishers, 2002.

Cirincione, Joseph, Miriam Rajkumar, and Jon B Wolfsthal. *Deadly Arsenals: Nuclear, Biological and Chemical Threats, Revised Edition*. Washington, DC: Carnegie Endowment for International Peace, 2005.

Clancy, Tom. *Hunt for Red October*. London: HarperCollins Publishers, 1993.

———. *The Sum of All Fears*. New York: Penguin USA, 2009.

Clark, William. "Analysis of Build-down Proposals," 1983, http://www.thereaganfiles .com/19830607-start-papers-for.pdf [accessed June 17, 2015].

Clark, William P. "Memorandum for the President, NSPG Meeting on the Airliner Shootdown," 1983, http://www.thereaganfiles.com/19830902-nspg-68a-briefing.pdf [accessed 18 June 2015].

Colodny, Len, and Tom Shachtman. *b030 B031: The Neocon Ascendancy, from Nixon's Fall to the Invasion of Iraq*. Sydney: HarperCollins Publishers Australia, 2009.

Dailey, Brian D. *Soviet Strategic Deception*. Lexington, MA: Hoover Institution Press, 1987.

David, Owen. *In Sickness and in Power: Illnesses in Heads of Government During the Last 100 Years*. Westport, CT: Praeger Publishers, 2008.

Davis, Tracy C. *Stages of Emergency: Cold War Nuclear Civil Defense*. Durham, NC: Duke University Press, 2007.

Deaver, Michael K. *Behind the Scenes: In Which the Author Talks About Ronald and Nancy Reagan ... and Himself*. New York: William Morrow & Company, 1987.

Derby, Ray. *The Shadow Government*. Washington, DC: Writers Advantage, 2002.

Dobrynin, Anatoly. *In Confidence: Moscow's Ambassador to America's Six Cold War Presidents*. New York: Three Rivers Press, 1997.

Draft Reagan Speech on Defense, Ronald Reagan Edit. "The Reagan Files," 1983, http://www.thereaganfiles.com/document-collections/19830323-draft-from-322-9am.pdf [accessed June 18, 2015].

Draft of Presidential Address: US Soviet Relations. "The Reagan Files," 1984, http://www.thereaganfiles.com/document-collections/19840116-sp-draft-0113-2pm.pdf [accessed June 18, 2015].

Draft of Presidential Address to the National Association of Evangelicals, RR Edit. "The Reagan Files," 1983, http://www.thereaganfiles.com/document-collections/19830308-evil-empire-sp.pdf [accessed 18 June 2015].

Evan, Thomas. *The Very Best Men: Four Who Dared: The Early Years of the CIA*. New York: Simon & Schuster, 1995.

Fischer, Beth A. *The Reagan Reversal: Foreign Policy and the End of the Cold War*. Columbia, MO: University of Missouri Press, 2000.

Ford, Daniel F. *The Button: The Pentagon's Strategic Command and Control System*. New York: Simon & Schuster, 1985.

Frei, Daniel. *Perceived Images: US and Soviet Assumptions and Perceptions in Disarmament*. Totowa, NJ: Rowman & Allanheld, 1986.

Gaddis, John Lewis. *Strategies of Containment*. New York: Oxford University Press, 2005.

———. *The Cold War*. London: Allen Lane, 2005.

———. *We Now Know: Rethinking Cold War History*. Oxford: Clarendon Press, 1997.

Gates, Robert M. *From the Shadows: The Ultimate Insider's Story of Five Presidents and How They Won the Cold War*. New York: Simon & Schuster, 1997.

Glain, Stephen. *State vs. Defense: The Battle to Define America's Empire*. New York: Crown Publishing Group, 2011.

Goodman, Melvin A. *Failure of Intelligence: The Decline and Fall of the CIA*. Lanham, MD: Rowman & Littlefield Publishers, 2008.

Goodman, Melvin A. *Gorbachev's Retreat: The Third World*. New York: Praeger, 1991.

Gordievsky, Oleg, *Next Stop Execution* London: Pan Macmillan, 1995.

Gordon, Barrass. "The Renaissance in American Strategy and the Ending of the Great Cold War," *Military Review*, 2010, 100–110.

Grachev, A. S. *Gorbachev's Gamble: Soviet Foreign Policy and the End of the Cold War*. Cambridge: Wiley, John & Sons, 2008.

Grand Strategies in War and Peace New Haven, CT: Yale University Press, 2015.

Gromyko, Andreï Andreevich. *Memoirs*. New York: Doubleday, 1989.

Hackett, *The Third World War*. London: Imperial College, 1979.

Haig, Alexander Meigs. *Caveat*. New York: Macmillan, 1984.

———. *Inner Circles: How America Changed the World: A Memoir*. New York: Warner Books, 1992.

Hamrick, S. J., and W. T. Tyler. *Deceiving the Deceivers: Kim Philby, Donald Maclean and Guy Burgess*. New Haven, CT: Yale University Press, 2004.

Hanhimaki, Jussi M., Odd Arne Westad, and Jussi Hanhimäki. *The Cold War: A History in Documents and Eyewitness Accounts*. New York: Oxford University Press, 2004.

Hannaford, Peter. *Reagan's Roots: The People and Placers That Shaped His Character*. United States: Images from the Past, 2012.

———. *Recollections of Reagan: A Portrait of Ronald Reagan*. New York: William Morrow & Company, 1997.

———. *Remembering Reagan*. Washington, DC: Distributed to the trade by National Book Network, 1994.

Hastings, Max. *Retribution: The Battle for Japan, 1944–45*. New York: Knopf, 2008.

Hennessy, Peter. *The Secret State: Whitehall and the Cold War*. London: Allen Lane, 2002.

Hersh, Seymour, M. *The Price of Power: Kissinger in the Nixon White House*. New York: Summit Books, 2015.

———. *Target Is Destroyed*. New York: Random House Trade, 1986.

Hoffman, David. *The Dead Hand: The Untold Story of the Cold War Arms Race and Its Dangerous Legacy*. New York: Knopf Doubleday Publishing Group, 2009.

James Mann. *The Rebellion of Ronald Reagan*. New York: Viking Books, 2009.

Johnson, Loch K., and James J. Wirtz. *Intelligence: The Secret World of Spies: An Anthology, 3rd Edition*. New York: Oxford University Press, 2011.

Kahn, David. *The Codebreakers*. London: Sphere, 1978.

Keegan, John. *Intelligence in War*. London: Random House Group, 2010.

Kengor, Paul, and Patricia Clark Doerner. *The Judge: William P. Clark, Ronald Reagan's Top Hand*. San Francisco: Ignatius Press, 2007.

Kengor, Paul. *God and Ronald Reagan: A Spiritual Life*. New York: ReganBooks, 2004.

Kerrigan, Michael. *Cold War Plans That Never Happened: 1945 to the Present*. London: Casemate Pub & Book Dist, 2012.

Kipp, Jacob W. "Russian Military Doctrine and Military Technical Policy: An American Military Historian's Perspective," *Comparative Strategy*, 13 (1994), 25–41, http://dx.doi.org/10.1080/01495939408402951.

Krugler, David F. *This Is Only a Test: How Washington, DC, Prepared for Nuclear War*. New York: Palgrave Macmillan, 2015.

Lang, Andrew. "CONVERGENCE: The Politics of Armageddon," http://www.prop1.org/inaugur/85reagan/85rrarm.htm [accessed June 17, 2015].

Larsen, Jeffrey, and Kerry Kartchner. *On Limited Nuclear War in the 21st Century, Google Books*. Stanford: Stanford University Press, 2014

Lawrence, Freedman. *US Intelligence and the Soviet Strategic Threat*. London: Macmillan, 1986.

———. *Evolution of Nuclear Strategy*. London: Macmillan in association with the International Institute for Strategic Studies, 1989.

Lehman, John F. *Command of the Seas*, 2nd ed. Annapolis: US Naval Institute Press, 2001.

Leitenberg, Milton. *The Soviet Biological Weapons Program: A History*. Cambridge, MA: Harvard University Press, 2012.

Lettow, Paul. *Ronald Reagan and His Quest to Abolish Nuclear Weapons.* New York: Random House Trade, 2006.

Managing Nuclear Operations. Washington, DC: Brookings Institution, 1987.

Massie, Suzanne. *Trust But Verify: Reagan, Russia and Me: A Personal Memoir.* Augusta: Maine Authors Publishing, 2013.

Mastny, Vojtech. *Russia's Road to the Cold War: Diplomacy, Warfare and Politics of Communism, 1941–1945.* New York: Columbia University Press, 1980.

Matlock, Jack. *Autopsy on an Empire.* New York: Random House Value Publishing, 1997.

Matlock, Jack F. *Reagan and Gorbachev: How the Cold War Ended.* New York: Random House, 2004.

McCaslin, Leland C. *Secrets of the Cold War: US Army Europe's Intelligence and Counterintelligence Activities Against the Soviets.* Solihull: Helion and Company Press, 2013.

McFarlane, Robert C., and Zofia Smardz. *Special Trust.* New York: African American Family Press, 1994.

———. *Special Trust.* New York: Cadell & Davies, 1994.

McManis, David. Telephone interview, 2015.

Medvedev, Zhores A. *Andropov.* New York: Penguin Books, 1984.

Meese, Edwin. *With Reagan: The Inside Story.* Washington, D.C.: Regnery Gateway, 1993.

Menges, Constantine Christopher. *Inside the National Security Council: The True Story of the Making and Unmaking of Reagan's Foreign Policy.* New York: Simon & Schuster, 1988.

Miller, Jerry. *Stockpile: The Story Behind 10,000 Strategic Nuclear Weapons.* Annapolis, MD: Naval Institute Press, 2010.

Mitrokhin, Vasil. *KGB Lexicon: The Soviet Intelligence Officer's Handbook.* London: Routledge, 2002.

Moore, Charles. *Margaret Thatcher: The Authorized Biography: From Grantham to the Falklands.* New York: Knopf Doubleday Publishing Group, 2013.

National Security Council, "Meeting on Strategic Forces Modernization," 1983, http://www.thereaganfiles.com/19830414-nsc-77.pdf [accessed June 17, 2015].

National Security Council. *Discussion on Defense Programs,* January 28, 1983, http://www.thereaganfiles.com/19830128-nsc-73.pdf.

National Security Council. "Meeting on The Strategic Defense Initiative," 1983, http://www.thereaganfiles.com/19831130-nsc-96-sdi.pdf [accessed June 18, 2015].

National Security Council. "Meeting on NSSD-181," 1982, http://www.thereaganfiles.com/19820416-nsc-45.pdf [accessed June 17, 2015].

National Security Council. "NSDD 102: US Response to Soviet Destruction of KAL Airliner," 1983, http://www.thereaganfiles.com/nsdd-102-kal.pdf [accessed June 17, 2015].

National Security Council. "NSDD 12: Strategic Forces Modernization," http://www.thereaganfiles.com/nsdd-12-strategic-forces.html [accessed June 18, 2015].

National Security Council. "National Security Council Meeting on TNG," 1981, http://www.thereaganfiles.com/19811013-nsc-22.pdf [accessed June 17, 2015].

National Security Council. "Preparations for Round III of START, Minutes of NSC Meeting," 1983, http://www.thereaganfiles.com/19830125-nsc-72.pdf [accessed June 17, 2015].

National Security Council. "Terms of Reference for High Level USG Mission to Europe on Soviet Sanctions," 1982, http://www.thereaganfiles.com/19820226-nsc-43.pdf [accessed June 17, 2015].

"National Security Decision Directive 32," 1983, http://fas.org/irp/offdocs/nsdd/nsdd-32 .pdf [accessed June 17, 2015].

National Security Planning Group. "Meeting on US Soviet Relations," 1983, http://www .thereaganfiles.com/19830110-nspg-49.pdf [accessed June 17, 2015].

National Security Planning Group. "Minutes from Meeting," 1983, http://www.thereaganfiles .com/19830113-nspg-50.pdf [accessed June 17, 2015].

National Security Planning Group. "Nuclear Arms Control Discussions S," 1984, http://www. thereaganfiles.com/19840327-nsc-104-arms-contr.pdf [accessed June 18, 2015].

National Security Planning Group. "Our Future Course in the Immediate Nuclear Forces Negotiations," 1983, http://www.thereaganfiles.com/19830110-nspg-49-discussion.pdf [accessed June 17, 2015].

National Defense University. *C3I: Issues of Command and Control*, ed. by Thomas Coakley, 1990, http://www.dtic.mil/get-tr-doc/pdf?AD=ADA264195 [accessed June 18, 2015].

Naval War College: Newport Papers. "Selected Naval Strategy Documents," http://fas.org/ irp/doddir/navy/strategy1980s.pdf [accessed June 17, 2015].

Neustadt, Richard E. *Thinking in Time: The Uses of History for Decision Makers*. New York: Free Press, 1988.

Newhouse, John. *War and Peace in the Nuclear Age*. New York: Random House, 1989.

North, Oliver. *Under Fire*. New York: HarperCollins Publishers, 1991.

Oberdorfer, Don, Pavel Palazchenko, and P. Palazhchenko. *My Years with Gorbachev and Shevardnadze: The Memoir of a Soviet Interpreter*. University Park, PA: Pennsylvania State University Press, 1997.

Oberdorfer, Don. *The Turn: From the Cold War to a New Era, with an Updated Introduction and Afterword*. New York: Touchstone Books, 1992.

Ouimet, Matthew J. *The Rise and Fall of the Brezhnev Doctrine in Soviet Foreign Policy*. Chapel Hill, NC: The University of North Carolina Press, 2003.

Payne, Keith B. *Nuclear Deterrence in US-Soviet Relations*. Boulder, CO: Westview Press, 1982.

Perle, Richard Norman. *Hard Line*. New York: Random House, 1992.

Persico, Joseph E. *Casey: The Lives and Secrets of William J. Casey: From the OSS to the CIA*. New York: Penguin, 1991.

Pierre, Andrew J., Desmond Ball, and Jeffrey Richelson. "Strategic Nuclear Targeting," *Foreign Affairs*, 65 (1986), http://dx.doi.org/10.2307/20042875.

Pillar, Paul R. *Intelligence and U.S. Foreign Policy*. New York: Columbia University Press, 2011.

Pipes, Richard. *Vixi: Memoirs of a Non-Belonger*. New Haven, CT: Yale University Press, 2005.

Polmar, Norman. *Naval Institute Guide to the Soviet Navy*. Annapolis, MD: Naval Institute Press, 1991.

Presidential Address: US Soviet Relations, Additional Draft. "The Reagan Files," 1984, http:// www.thereaganfiles.com/document-collections/19840116-sp-draft-0112-1pm.pdf [accessed June 18, 2015].

Presidential Address: US Soviet Relations, RR Edit. "The Reagan Files," 1984, http://www .thereaganfiles.com/document-collections/19840116-sp-draft-from-0106.pdf [accessed June 18, 2015].

Pry, Peter Vincent. *War Scare: Russia and America on the Nuclear Brink*. Westport, CT: Praeger, 1999.

Reagan, Ronald. *Reagan: A Life in Letters.* New York: Free Press, 2004.

———. *The Reagan Diaries.* New York: HarperCollins, 2007.

Reagan, Ronald. *Reagan, in His Own Hand.*, ed. by Kiron K Skinner and Annelise Anderson. Waterville, ME: Thorndike Press, 2001.

Rhodes, Richard. *The Making of the Atomic Bomb.* New York: Simon & Schuster, 1998.

Ricks, Thomas E. *The Generals: American Military Command from World War II to Today.* New York: Penguin Press, 2012.

Rostow, Eugene. *Minutes of a Discussion on Arms Control During a National Security Council Meeting.* Ed. by Ronald Reagan Presidential Library, August 17, 1981, http://www .thereaganfiles.com/19810817-nsc-20.pdf.

Sagan, Scott Douglas. *The Limits of Safety: Organizations, Accidents, and Nuclear Weapons.* Princeton, NJ: Princeton University Press, 1995.

Saltoun-Ebin, Jason. "The Strategic Defense Initiative," http://www.thereaganfiles.com /document-collections/sdi.html [accessed June 18, 2015].

Schwartz, David N. *NATO's Nuclear Dilemmas.* Washington, DC: Brookings Institution, 2015.

Shevchenko, Arkady N. *Breaking with Moscow.* London: Grafton, 1986.

Shirley, Craig. *Reagan's Revolution: The Untold Story of the Campaign That Started It All.* Nashville, TN: Nelson Current, 2005.

Singh, Rajvir. *War and Peace in the Nuclear Age.* New Delhi, India: Intellectual Book Corner, 1987.

Soldatov, Andreï. *The New Nobility: The Rebirth of the Russian Security State.* New York: Public Affairs, 2010.

"Solid Shield '79," http://www.dtic.mil/dtic/tr/fulltext/u2/a094217.pdf [accessed June 17, 2015].

Stevenson, Charles A. *SECDEF: The Nearly Impossible Job of Secretary of Defense.* Washington, DC: Potomac Books, 2006.

"The Day After Able Archer," http://www.thereaganfiles.com/19831112.pdf [accessed June 18, 2015].

Thomas, C. Reed. *At the Abyss: An Insider's History of the Cold War.* New York: Presidio Press/ Ballantine Books, 2004.

Thomas C. Reed and Danny B. Stillman. *The Nuclear Express: A Political History of the Bomb and Its Proliferation.* Minneapolis, MN: Zenith Press, 2009.

Turner, Stansfield. *Secrecy and Democracy: The CIA in Transition.* New York: Perennial Library, 1986.

Turning Points in Ending the Cold War. Stanford, CA: Hoover Institution Press, Stanford University, 2008.

Volkogonov, Dmitriï Antonovich. *Autopsy for an Empire: The Seven Leaders Who Built the Soviet Regime.* New York: Free Press, 1998.

Wallace, Robert, Keith H. Melton, and Henry R. Schlesinger. *Spycraft: The Secret History of the CIA's Spytechs, from Communism to Al-Qaeda.* New York, NY: Dutton, 2008.

Weinberger, Caspar W. *Fighting for Peace: Seven Critical Years in the Pentagon.* New York: Little, Brown & Company, 1990.

———. *The Next War.* Washington, DC: National Book Network, 1996.

Weiner, Tim. *Legacy of Ashes: The History of the CIA.* New York: Viking, 2007.

Weisman, Alan. *Prince of Darkness: Richard Perle: The Kingdom, the Power & the End of Empire in America.* New York: Union Square Press, 2007.

Wilson, James Graham. *The Triumph of Improvisation: Gorbachev's Adaptability, Reagan's Engagement, and the End of the Cold War.* Ithaca, NY: Cornell University Press, 2014.

Winik, Jay. *On the Brink: The Dramatic, Behind-the-Scenes Saga of the Reagan Era and the Men and Women Who Won the Cold War.* New York: Simon & Schuster, 1996.

Wise, David. *Nightmover: How Aldrich Ames Sold the CIA to the KGB FOR $4.6 Million.* New York: Harper Collins, 1995.

Wright, Peter. *Spycatcher.* New York: Viking, 1987.

Zubok, Vladislav M. *A Failed Empire: The Soviet Union in the Cold War from Stalin to Gorbachev.* Chapel Hill, NC: University of North Carolina Press, 2009.

Notes

EPIGRAPHS

1 John Herbers, "Religious Leaders Tell of Worry on Armageddon View Ascribed to Reagan," *New York Times*, October 21, 1984, http://www.nytimes.com/1984/10/21/us /religious-leaders-tell-of-worry-on-armageddon-view-ascribed-to-reagan.html. Reagan wrote to a friend in 1982 that relying solely on nuclear weapons as a deterrent "leaves only Armageddon as a response to all brushfires into existence." Reagan letter to Lawrence W. Beilenson, February 2, 1982, in *Reagan: A Life in Letters* (New York: Free Press, 2004), 47.

2 Quoted in Martin and Annelise Anderson, *Reagan: Decisions in Greatness*, accessed via Google Books with permission of the Hoover Institution Press.

3 Admiral William Crowe, Chairman, Joint Chiefs of Staff, interview with Don Oberdorfer, 1993, in the Don Oberdorfer Papers, Princeton University (DOP).

4 John Hines interview with General-Lieutenant Gelii Viktorovich Batenin, conducted for BDM Federal Inc.'s study on Soviet Intentions: 1965–1985, declassified by the Department of Defense and hosted on the website of the National Security Archive at George Washington University, http://nsarchive.gwu.edu/nukevault/ebb285/vol%20 II%20Batenin.pdf.

MAJOR ACRONYMS AND PROGRAMS

1 SIOP 5 (1976) was the result of a Nixon-era process designed to give the president a more flexible set of options and more technical ability to withhold specific targets from nuclear salvos. The Joint Strategic Target Planning Staff spent two years working on revisions to the SIOP beginning in 1981, and the new SIOP, SIOP 6, took effect in late 1983. Approximately 7,000 "generated" nuclear weapons could target as many as 50,000 specific "ground zeroes." As of this writing, the "SIOP" exists as a concept, but its name has been changed to reflect current Pentagon nomenclature. It is STRATCOM OPLAN 8010-12: Strategic Deterrence and Global Strike.

PROLOGUE

1 Quoted in Edward Zuckerman, *The Day After World War III* (New York: Viking, 1984), 49.

2 General Russell E. Dougherty, "The Psychological Climate of Nuclear Command," in *Managing Nuclear Operations* (Washington, DC: Brookings Institution Press, 1987), 41.

3 Able and other first words are discussed at length in William A. Arkin's encyclopedic compendium *Code Names: Deciphering US Military Plans, Programs, and Operations in the 9/11 World* (New York: Steelworth, 2005).

4. "Reagan in Japan Pledges Closer Ties," *New York Times*, November 11, 1983.

INTRODUCTION

1 Recounted in Scott Sagan, *The Limits of Safety: Organizations, Accidents, and Nuclear Weapons* (Princeton, NJ: Princeton University Press, 1993).

2 Victor Israelyan, "Nuclear Showdown as Nixon Slept," *Christian Science Monitor*, November 3, 1993, at http://www.csmonitor.com/1993/1103/03191.html; William Burr, "The Nixon Administration, the 'Horror Strategy,' and the Search for Limited Nuclear Options, 1969–72: Prelude to the Schlesinger Doctrine," in the summer 2005 issue of *The Journal of Cold War Studies*.

3 Bruce Blair, "Mad Fiction: Book Review of David H. Hoffman's *Dead Hand*" at http://www.globalzero.org/files/bb_mad_fiction_2014.pdf.

4 Ibid.

5 Blair, *The Logic of Accidental Nuclear War*, 30–37.

6 John Hines interview with Andre Danilevich conducted for BDM Federal Inc.'s study on Soviet Intentions: 1965–1985, declassified by the Department of Defense and hosted on the website of the National Security Archive at George Washington University, http://nsarchive.gwu.edu/NSAEBB/NSAEBB426/docs/7.Interview%20with%20Viktor%20M.%20Surikov%20by%20John%20G.%20Hines-September%2011,%201993.pdf.

7 Sharon Ghamari-Tabrizi, *The Worlds of Herman Kahn: The Intuitive Science of Thermonuclear War* (Cambridge, MA: Harvard University Press, 2005), 238.

1. DÉTENTE'S RISE AND FALL

1 "Nixon and Brezhnev Sign Historic Arms Treaty," *The Guardian*, May 27, 1972.

2 Tim Weiner, *One Man Against the World: The Tragedy of Richard Nixon* (New York: Henry Holt & Co., 2015), 287–291.

3 Tim Weiner, "That Time the Middle East Exploded—and Richard Nixon Was Drunk," *Politico*, June 2015. Accessed: http://www.politico.com/magazine/story/2015/06/richard-nixon-watergate-drunk-yom-kippur-war-119021.

4 One such missileer was Bruce B. Blair, who would go on to become a trenchant critic of the nuclear command and control system.

5 Interview with former NSA official who has reviewed classified histories of this event.

6 Viktor Israelyan "Nuclear Showdown as Nixon Slept," *Christian Science Monitor*, November 3, 1993, http://www.csmonitor.com/1993/1103/03191.html.

7 Ibid.

8 John Hines interview with Andre Danilevich, conducted for BDM Federal Inc.'s study on *Soviet Intentions: 1965–1985*, declassified by the Department of Defense and hosted on the website of the National Security Archive at George Washington University.

9   Ibid.

10 Dale Roy Herspring, *The Soviet High Command, 1967–1989: Personalities and Politics* (Princeton, NJ: Princeton University Press, 1990), 162–164.

11 Herspring, *Soviet High Command*, 161; the Backfire, actually, had more significant geographical limitations than the US intelligence community had insisted. See: Thomas Graham Jr., *Disarmament Sketches: Three Decades of Arms Control and International Law* (Seattle: University of Washington Press, 2002), 55.

12 Jan Hoffenaar and Christopher Findlay, eds., *Military Planning for European Theater Conflict During the Cold War: An Oral History Roundtable Stockholm, April 24–25, 2006* (Center for Security Studies, ETH Zurich, 2006), 109; http://e-collection.library.ethz.ch/eserv/eth:474/eth-474-01.pdf.

13 Ibid., 181–183, 186, 189. See also: John Hines, Ellis M. Mishulovich, and John F. Shulle, *Soviet Intentions 1965–1985, Volume I: An Analytical Comparison of US-Soviet Assessments During the Cold War* by BDM Federal, Inc., September 22, 1995, 22–47; Diego A. Ruiz Palmer, "The NATO-Warsaw Pact Competition in the 1970s and 1980s: A Revolution in Military Affairs in the Making or the End of a Strategic Age?," *Cold War History*, 14:4 (2014), 533–573.

14 Hines et. al., *Soviet Intentions*, 50–52.

15 Peter Vincent Pry, *War Scare: Russia and American on the Nuclear Brink* (New York: Praeger, 1999), 12.

16 Ibid.

17 Hines et al., *Soviet Intentions*, 40.

18 Bruce Blair, *The Accidental Logic of Nuclear War* (Washington, DC.: Brookings Institution Press, 1999), 173.

19 Robert Levgold, interviewed for Jan Hoffenaar and Christopher Findlay, eds., *Military Planning for European Theater Conflict During the Cold War: An Oral History Roundtable Stockholm, April 24–25, 2006* (Center for Security Studies, ETH Zurich, 2006), 186–187.

20 Cimbala, *Russia and Armed Persuasion*, 114.

21 David Yost, "Strategic Stability in the Cold War: Lessons for Continuing Challenges," IFRI, 35, at http://www.dtic.mil/dtic/tr/fulltext/u2/a557632.pdf.

22 The measure adopted, Circular Error Probable, is best understood (per Lawrence Freedman's example: a missile with a CEP of 1 would be 50 percent likely to deliver its many warheads to some point within a circle with a radius of 1 mile, where the center of that circle represented the desired aim point. See Lawrence Freedman, *US Intelligence and the Soviet Strategic Threat* (Princeton: Princeton University Press, 1986), 99. See also: Pavel Podvig, "The Window of Vulnerability That Wasn't: Soviet Military Buildup in the 1970s—A Research Note," *International Security*, vol. 33, no. 1 (Summer 2008): 118–138.

23 Podvig makes this point well.

24 R-36M/SS-18 SATAN information sheet, Federation of American Scientists, http://fas.org/nuke/guide/russia/icbm/r-36m.htm.

25 Bruce G. Blair, email to author.

26 "GE and Ronald Reagan: The Mutual Gift That Keeps On Giving," *Politics Daily*, March

17, 2010, http://www.politicsdaily.com/2010/03/17/ge-and-ronald-reagan-the -mutual-gift-that-keeps-on-giving/.

27 Thomas W. Evans, "The GE Years: What Made Reagan Reagan," History News Network, http://historynewsnetwork.org/article/32681.

28 Ronald Reagan. "A Time for Choosing," Ronald Reagan Presidential Library, http:// www.reagan.utexas.edu/archives/reference/timechoosing.html.

29 Ibid.

30 Paul Lettow, *Ronald Reagan and His Quest to Abolish Nuclear Weapons* (New York: Random House, 2005), 52.

31 Ronald Reagan's Acceptance Speech at the 1980 Republican Convention, http://www .presidency.ucsb.edu/ws/?pid=25970.

2. TOWARD PROTRACTED NUCLEAR WAR

1 Memorandum from Hugh Carter to the president, July 11, 1977, SECRET, declassified.

2 Information on the evolution of the SIOP can be found in the extensive analysis by William Burr and others at the National Security Archive at George Washington University. http:// nsarchive.gwu.edu/NSAEBB/NSAEBB173/SIOP-4.pdf; http://nsarchive.gwu .edu/NSAEBB/NSAEBB173/SIOP-3.pdf; http://nsarchive.gwu.edu/NSAEBB/NSA EBB173/SIOP-5.pdf; http://nsarchive.gwu.edu/NSAEBB/NSAEBB173/SIOP-6 .pdf.

3 Author's interview with Ray Derby, former deputy director, OEP/FEMA "Special Facility" (Mount Weather).

4 Alex Larzelere, *Witness to History: The White House Diary of a Military Aide to Richard Nixon* (Bloomington, IN: Author House, 2009), 24, 61, 97.

5 (In 1974, a TWA 707 crashed into Mount Weather and severed the circuit linking the EBS to the rest of the world; if Mount Weather's location had ever been a secret, by Carter's presidency, its location would almost certainly have been prominently featured on Soviet nuclear targeting menus.)

6 Seminar on Command, Control, Communications, and Intelligence at the Harvard University's Program on Information Resource Policy (PIRP), http://www.pirp .harvard.edu/pubs_pdf/seminar/seminar-i80-6.pdf. June 1980.

7 Odom quoted in ibid.

8 Quoted in Bruce Blair, *Strategic Command and Control* (Washington, DC: Brookings Institution Press), 264.

9 Blair, *Strategic Command and Control*, 109n.

10 Odom, PIRP seminar, 181.

11 Joint Chiefs of Staff, "An Historical Study of Strategic Connectivity, 1950–1981." Top Secret, declassified, 334–337.

12 William E. Odom, "The Origins and Designs of Presidential Decision-59, a Memoir," in *Getting Mad: Nuclear Mutual Assured Destruction, Its Origins and Practice*, Henry D. Sokolski, Ed,180.

13 Headquarters, Strategic Air Command, History & Research Division, "History of the Joint Strategic Target Planning Staff: Preparation of SIOP-63," January 1964, Top

Secret, Excised copy, 242–244. Accessed from the National Security Archive at George Washington University.

14 Ibid.

15 Ibid.

16 Government Accounting Office. "Attack Warning: ADP Replacement for Warning and Assessment System Still Years Away," June 1986, http://www.gao.gov/assets/210 /208699.pdf.

17 An event ably recounted by Eric Schlosser in his excellent book, *Command and Control: Nuclear Weapons, the Damascus Incident, and the Illusion of Safety* (New York: Penguin, 2013).

18 "NORAD's Missile Warning System: What Went Wrong? A Report to the Chairman," Committee on Government Oversight, May 15, 1981, http://www.gao.gov/assets /140/133240.pdf.

19 Here's the sequence of events:

0521: Missile tracks suddenly appear on the display at NORAD. Within a minute, they disappear.

0525: The battle staff at the Strategic Air Command see 200 missiles inbound from SLBMs. The SAC controller hits his fast alert klaxon.

0529: Four minutes later, SAC sends an Emergency Action Message to all forces declaring a higher alert posture. At the same time, NORAD reports an all-clear. There is mass confusion. Over the next ten minutes, the NMCC convened a missile display conference, and then a more serious air threat conference.

0551: The Airborne Command Post for the Commander of US Forces in the Pacific launches, per the SAC alert posture.

0553: The Commander of US Forces in the Atlantic now sees the SLBMS that are no longer appearing on NORAD's screen.

0557: The director of operations at the NMCC conveys an all-clear worldwide.

20 Scott Sagan, *The Limits of Safety: Organizations, Accidents, and Nuclear Weapons* (Princeton, NJ: Princeton University Press, 1993), 99–100, 126–131. Klaxons sounded, and bombers moved to their alert positions but did not launch.

21 State Department cable 295771 to US Embassy Moscow, "Brezhnev Message to President on Nuclear False Alarm," November 14, 1979, Secret: accessed: http://nsarchive .gwu.edu/nukevault/ebb371/docs/doc%203%2011-16-79%20DOD%20draft.pdf.

22 Memorandum to William Odom, April 12, 1978, Jimmy Carter Presidential Library, obtained by author.

23 Robert M. Gates, *From the Shadows: The Ultimate Insider's Story of Five Presidents* (New York: Simon & Schuster, 1993), 114.

24 Author's interview with a serving US Air Force officer.

25 JCS Strategic Connectivity Study 17; in 1978, Ellis and the Joint Chiefs of Staff issued a directive declaring it "mandatory" that the nuclear force commanders must possess the capability to transmit emergency war orders to strategic forces worldwide regardless of what else was happening. Filling this requirement would take billions of dollars and not be finished for more than a decade. The Joint Chiefs of Staff wanted a new satellite system to pinpoint the location of nuclear impact points, which would make retargeting

US missiles possible. They wanted to speed deployment of mobile computer terminals that could receive data from nuclear sensors in space. They wanted to field dozens more airborne refueling aircraft so that airborne command posts could stay in the air for longer than just a few days. Other must-haves included a suite of sensor upgrades to existing command post aircraft and ground terminals, the hardening of command centers and airplanes from electromagnetic pulses generated by high altitude nuclear blasts, a whole new fleet command post aircraft, and a reappraisal of the vice president's status during national emergencies. Most of these priorities would be funded by Congress. Others, including an idea to create a secret fleet of eighteen-wheeler trucks and stash them randomly at covert bases in the US, were tabled. By the time Reagan would be elected, SAC had established a special program office, Joint Strategic Connectivity Staff, dedicated solely to the communications element of the nuclear command and control enterprise.

26 "SOSUS," in *Proceedings of the US Naval Institute*, issue 25 (1987), accessed: http://www.navy.mil/navydata/cno/n87/usw/issue_25/sosus.htm.

27 Ibid.

28 There is more to the physics of sound cavitation than meets the eye.

29 Norman Polmar, *The Naval Institute Guide to the Soviet Navy* (Annapolis, MD: Naval Institute Press, 1991), 118–119.

30 David Owen, *Anti-Submarine Warfare: An Illustrated History* (Annapolis, MD: Naval Institute Press, 2007), 203–205.

31 James Schlesinger, "Nuclear Weapons Employment Review, 1974," April 10, 1972, Top Secret (http://nsarchive.gwu.edu/NSAEBB/NSAEBB173/SIOP-25.pdf), and Memorandum from National Security Advisor Zbigniew Brzezinski to President Carter, "Our Nuclear War Doctrine: Limited Options and Regional Nuclear War Options," March 31, 1977, Top Secret.

32 The LNOs had been developed by the military, for the military. Each involved a flight of between six and eight missiles launched at a single target. One LNO, for example, could take out the antiballistic system that ringed Moscow. Another could destroy the main early-warning radars and ground stations used by the Soviets in Siberia.

33 Why, he wondered, would a half dozen nuclear weapons launched at any of those targets in the Soviet Union be less likely to provoke a spasm of retaliation than if they were aimed to deter something like a Soviet invasion of Western Europe? From his memoir: "I tried to imagine President Carter sending Brezhnev a message over the Washington-Moscow hotline, telling him that an LNO would soon be coming, and not to panic because it consisted of only six weapons and was intended to underscore US credibility and lead to de-escalation. And suppose Brezhnev responded, 'I understand. I recognize your "credibility" problem, but now I have a credibility problem. So, I am launching only four nuclear weapons at Seattle. Do not panic. Additional strikes will not follow before we begin to negotiate.' What could the president do at this point? What guidance would he give his press secretary for explaining this nuclear exchange to the White House press corps? Would the press secretary ask the rest of the country to pray for those people in Seattle? How would he explain to the large surviving public that it had no civil defense capability? Polling at the time indicated that a large majority of Americans believed that as much as $6 billion was spent annually on civil defense. Was I in a MAD house?"

34 Odom, Memoir, 190.

35 President Carter's Secretary of Defense, Harold "Hap" Brown, had insisted early in the administration, when arms control and defense budget cuts were political priorities, that the US could provide the finite deterrence required with only two hundred nuclear weapons.

36 Zbigniew Brzezinski to Secretary of Defense and Secretary of State, "PD-59 Chronology," August 22, 1980, enclosing chronology, Secret. Obtained by the National Security Archive at George Washington University. Also: http://nsarchive.gwu.edu/nukevault/ebb285/vol%20ii%20Brzezinski.pdf.

37 Ibid. See also: http://nsarchive.gwu.edu/nukevault/ebb285/vol%20II%20Marshall.pdf.

38 Desmond Ball and Robert C. Toth, "Revising the SIOP: Taking War-Fighting to Dangerous Extremes," *International Security*, vol. 14, no. 4 (Spring, 1990), 65–92.

39 Ibid.

40 "Presidential Directive 59," TOP SECRET// CODEWORD, partially declassified. http://www.jimmycarterlibrary.gov/documents/pddirectives/pd59.pdf; Hines et al., *Soviet Intentions*, BDM http://nsarchive.gwu.edu/nukevault/ebb285/vol%20ii%20 Brzezinski.pdf.

41 Marshall Shulman to Secretary of State Muskie, "PD-59," September 2, 1980, Secret http://nsarchive.gwu.edu/nukevault/ebb390/docs/9-2-80%20Shulman%20critique.pdf.

42 Lee Carpenter. *Memoirs of a Cold Warrior: The Struggle for Nuclear Parity* (New York: Algora Publishing, 2009), 164.

43 A. Arbatov, "The Strategy of Nuclear Madness," *Kommunist* 4 (1981), Joint Publications Research Service, USSR Report: Translations from *Kommunist*, JPRS 786986, August 15, 1981, 117–127, quoted in Benjamin B. Fischer, "The Soviet–American War Scare of the 1980s," *International Journal of Intelligence and CounterIntelligence* (2006) 19:3, 480–518.

44 Jonathan Samuel Lockwood, *The Soviet View of US Strategic Doctrine: Implications for Decision Making* (New York: Transaction Publishers, 1993), 155–158; Stephen M. Millett, "Soviet Perceptions of Nuclear Strategy and Implications for US Deterrence," in *University Review*, March-April 1982.

45 Louis Rene Beres. "Presidential Directive 59: A Critical Assessment," US Army Strategic Studies Institute, 1981. Accessed: http://strategicstudiesinstitute.army.mil/pubs/parameters/Articles/1981/1981%20beres.pdf.

46 Michael McQwire, *Perestroika and Soviet National Security* (Washington, DC: Brookings Institute Press, 1991), 106.

47 Beres, "Presidential Directive 59."

48 Marshall Shulman to Secretary of State Muskie, "PD-59,"" September 2, 1980, Secret.

49 Ibid.

3. DECAPITATION

1 Author's interview with Robert McFarlane; author's interview with Thomas Reed.

2 Quoted in John Prados, "Team B: The Trillion Dollar Experiment," *Bulletin of the Atomic Scientists*, April 1993, 25.

3   General Richard Ellis interview with the Harvard PIRP, 1982; author's interview with Buckles.

4   Ibid.

5   Kati Marton, *The Great Escape* (New York: Simon & Schuster, 2007), 218.

6   Craig Nelson, *The Age of Radiance: The Epic Rise and Dramatic Fall of the Atomic Era* (New York: Scribner, 2010), 331. Teller also waxed eloquent about the third generation of nuclear weapons, but the image of a missile defense umbrella stuck in Reagan's mind. He would bring up missile defense anytime he was asked about American vulnerability to ICBMs. A defense shield became a cause célèbre for conservatives disenchanted with SALT and its limitations. Reagan would rip out articles on the science and stuff them in his coat pockets. Teller gave Reagan credibility, and to Reagan, if someone as brilliant and morally sound as Teller thought it could be done, well, then, it could be. Reagan never did embrace Teller's enthusiasm for nuclear weapons, and he never endorsed whatever particular method for strategic defense that Teller happened to be advocating. The future president had boiled it down: America was naked in the face of incoming ICBMs.

7   Recounted by Stuart Stevens, interview for University of Virginia's Presidential Oral History Program; author's interview with Richard V. Allen; others; Martin Anderson, interview for University of Virginia's Oral History Program; http://millercenter.org/president/reagan/oralhistory.

8   Author's interview with Buckles.

9   Ibid.

10 Herbert L. Adams, *The President Has Been Shot: Confusion, Disability, and the 25th Amendment* (Stanford, CA: Stanford University Press, 1994), 60–61.

11 Abrams, *The President Has Been Shot*, 45–53.

12 Del Quentin Wilber, *Rawhide Down* (New York: Henry Holt & Co., 2011), 98–99.

13 Wilber, *Rawhide Down*, 111–112.

14 Abrams, *The President Has Been Shot*, 85.

15 Abrams, *The President Has Been Shot*, 82–83, Author's interview with Allen.

16 Caspar Weinberger, Statement on Activities After the Assassination Attempt of President Reagan, RRPL.

17 Abrams, *The President Has Been Shot*, 90.

18 Alexander Haig, *Inner Circles: How America Changed the World: A Memoir* (New York: Warner Books, 1992), 346–347, 353–358, 372, 416–418; Alexander Haig, *Caveat* (New York: Macmillan, 1984), 151–154.

19 Haig, *Caveat*, 152.

20 Haig, *Caveat*, 153.

21 "Prudent to be prudent," see http://res.dallasnews.com/interactives/reagan-bush/.

22 Weinberger statement.

23 Richard V. Allen, "The Day Reagan Was Shot," *The Atlantic*, April 2001, http://www.theatlantic.com/magazine/archive/2001/04/the-day-reagan-was-shot/308396/.

24 Author's interview with Richard Allen.

25 Allen, "The Day Reagan Was Shot." In his memoir, Weinberger suggests that he did know that SAC forces were at DEFCON 4, because he reports his discussion with Jones

as being related to a move to DEFCON 3, but transcripts and audio from the Situation Room that day suggest that Weinberger had learned this after the fact.

26 Implicit in this argument, and one of the reasons it was so riveting, was that Haig and Weinberger were essentially arguing about who would be in charge of the decision to retaliate against the Soviet Union with nuclear weapons. As the senior cabinet member at the White House, Haig was within his rights to assume responsibility for decisions that the White House as an institution would make. But that authority was quite narrow. Had the Speaker of the House or president pro tempore arrived, by Haig's own reasoning, they—not he—would suddenly be in charge of the actions of the executive branch. And, of course, there was no formal power transfer mechanism at all. No one had actually given him power. There was no reason to think that he could simply assume power in the absence of other, more senior officials whom he knew to be alive and well, and yet out of reach or contact. And militarily, Haig had no authority at all. Very explicitly, command and control of the military passes from the president through the Secretary of Defense. Technically, the vice president has no formal role; he is not formally the "vice commander in chief of the military"; only if the president specifically delegates to him the power to act in his stead—something Reagan had not done—would the military have had any principled reason to accept the command authority of Vice President Bush over the explicitly delegated authority that the president shared with the Secretary of Defense. The term "national command authority" is perhaps the most powerful piece of ambiguous jargon on earth. It is defined by a Department of Defense instruction from 1971:

> The NCA consists only of the president and the Secretary of Defense or their duly deputized alternates or successors. The chain of command runs from the president to the Secretary of Defense and through the Joint Chiefs of Staff to the Commanders of the Unified and Specified Commands.

Both Haig and Weinberger had different ideas of what "national command authority" meant. And the White House staff generally believed that the power to order a nuclear attack or retaliation was in the hands of the vice president so long as he had the ability to authenticate an order, which, in practice, meant that he was able to communicate with the Pentagon or the Situation Room. After all, he had a football and a military aide. But legally, of course, the vice president has no formal role in the nuclear decision process until the power is given to him. But no such pre-delegation to Bush has ever been acknowledged, and Allen has said that one did not exist. Section IV of the Twenty-fifth Amendment, which permits the temporary transfer of all presidential powers, was never invoked.

Reagan and the Commander in Chief of the Strategic Air Command, General Richard Ellis, had discussed this during their first meeting. A year after the assassination, in a remarkable aside that few noticed at the time, Ellis would say about precisely this subject: "Let me just say that he's got the responsibility. It's established in law. Obviously, a man with that responsibility is going to make provisions for contingencies when he may not be available, or is incapacitated." He went on to acknowledge that the nuclear chain of command was not necessarily the chain of command that the law proscribed.

"As SAC commander, I was always satisfied that that was taken care of, and I think that's where we ought to leave the subject. Everyone likes to know exactly who is next in line, and who does what, but that's the president's decision, and he's not going to say much about it."

27 An Office of Emergency Preparedness circular, "Succession to the Presidency Under Emergency Conditions," was published in 1965 and was still in effect in 1981, but did not seem to factor into any of the deliberations of decisions that day. That circular, which is classified, directs the agencies of the executive branch to (a) identify the highest-ranking cabinet official in the line of succession and (b) assume temporarily that the directives of that person are valid, so long as they did not conflict with any existing law. The Emergency Action Procedures of the Joint Chiefs of Staff cite the circular as the authority for its intention to "poll" presidential successors during acute emergencies to find someone with a valid authenticator who can authorize a nuclear release. However, the commanders with pre-delegated nuclear authority weren't budding presidential successors. They were National Command Authority duly deputized alternates. So, what would happen if a presidential successor could not be found?

28 Ronald Reagan Diaries, Volume 1, entry for March 30, 1981. The entry was probably written on April 11 or April 12.

29 Paul Kengor's *God and Ronald Reagan: A Spiritual Life* (New York: Harper Collins, 2009), has a full discussion; author's interviews with Richard Cizik, Craig Shirley, Thomas Reed, and others.

30 The East-West metaphor I have borrowed from James Carroll, *House of War: The Pentagon and the Disastrous Rise of American Power* (New York: Mariner Books, 2007), 381.

31 Gastón Espinosa, *Religion and the American Presidency: George Washington to George W. Bush* (New York: Columbia University Press, 2009), 370–271.

32 Author Peter Hannaford (*Reagan's Roots*, Images from the Past Publishing, 2015), says Reagan was eleven when he first read the book; other historians say Reagan was twelve. Reagan himself says he was "ten or eleven." See: Edwards, 8–10; Letter from Ronald Reagan to Jean Wright, March 13, 1984, as preserved by the Harold B. Wright papers; http://gchudleigh.com/reaganletter.htm.

33 Reagan's letter to Jean Wright; Hannaford, *Reagan's Roots*, 55.

34 Just how near to the Eschaton American Christians were, and what precisely Christians ought to do about it, served as one of several major dividing lines in the larger church when Reagan was adopting his faith.

35 Kengor, *God and Ronald Reagan*, 130.

36 Edmund Morris, *Dutch: A Memoir of Ronald Reagan* (New York: Random House, 2011), 458.

37 Daniel Schorr, "Reagan Recants: His Path from Armageddon to Détente," *Los Angeles Times*, January 3, 1988, http://articles.latimes.com/1988-01-03/opinion/op-32475 _1_president-reagan.

38 Richard Cizik, the young evangelical who invited the president to speak to his group of unaffiliated churches in 1983, would explain Reagan's beliefs this way: "There is a

theological concept about the relationship between predestination and free will called antinomy. Free choice and predestination: they meet in the cloud, and where one begins and the other ends is a mystery."

39 Lettow, 50–54; Reagan's letter to Brezhnev; from Jason Saltoun-Ebin's collection: http://www.thereaganfiles.com/19810424-2.pdf.

4. MAN IN THE GAP

1 Associating a particular nuclear weapon with its yield is considered CONFIDENTIAL /Formerly Restricted Data by the Department of Defense, so I have elected to give a range for the W-31s. In our interviews, Trolan would not specify the yields or even the type of weapons associated with the Hercs, and he would not provide an estimate of the number of warheads he safeguarded in the vaults. My more specific information comes from sources with knowledge of the sites.

2 Author's interview with Trolan; See also: Bill Wilson. "The Fulda Gap," in Military History Online, http://www.militaryhistoryonline.com/20thcentury/articles/fuldagap .aspx; Associated Press, "Fulda Gap Is Key Point in NATO Defense Against Soviet Forces," March 1, 1987.

3 In 1982, a board game appeared for the first time in West Germany toy stores. American kids had been playing it for six years. Those who did knew more about the vulnerabilities of Germany than many Germans did.

The text on the cover of the game box was alarming enough: "If war ever again comes to Europe, the major Soviet thrust must be aimed at the powerful US forces guarding Southern Germany. In order to breach NATO defenses and break through to the heart of Europe, the armored columns of the Warsaw Pact must force their way through the . . . FULDA GAP."

4 Zuckerman, *The Day After World War II*, 51.1

5 Interview with Bruce Blair.

6 Kelleher, *NATO Nuclear Operations*, 452.

7 Interview with Captain William Bliss, interview conducted by producers for *1983: The Brink of Apocalypse*, Flashback Television Ltd., Channel 4, 2008.

8 Ibid.

9 "The Problem for Discovering Preparation for a Nuclear Missile Attack Against the USSR: February 1983," in Gordievsky, *Instructions from the Center*, 120.

10 Marco De Andreis, "Nuclear Command, Control and Communications," *Archivo Partito Radicale*, January 1, 1988.

11 Gordievsky, *Instructions from the Center*, 125.

12 Bruce Blair, "Alerting in Crisis and Conventional War," in *Managing Nuclear Operations*, 91.

13 Gope D. Hingorani and Rupert Brand, "Architectural Framework for the Evolution of NATO Integrated Communications System," *Signal*, October 1985.

14 Author's interview with Trolan.

15 Ibid.

16 Catherine McArdle Kelleher, NATO Nuclear Operations, in Managing Nuclear Operations, 449.

17 Blair, "Alerting in Crisis and Conventional War," in *Managing Nuclear Operations*, 113.

18 An air defenser who served in the 501st from 1985 to 1989 described a similar procedure.

5. PROJECT RYAN

1 Steven F. Hayward, *The Age of Reagan: The Conservative Counterrevolution, 1980–1989* (New York: Random House, 2009), 271.

2 Information about RYAN comes from translations by the Woodrow Wilson Center's Nuclear Proliferation International History Project, which obtained more than 200 pages of documents from the Federal Commissioner for the Records of the State Security Service of the Former German Democratic Republic (BStU) in Berlin, (https://www.wilsoncenter.org/publication/forecasting-nuclear-war), as well as the firsthand descriptions from Oleg Gordievsky, who was in Moscow at the time that RYAN was announced—especially his *Instructions from the Center: Top Secret Files on KGB Foreign Operations, 1975–1985*, coauthored with Christopher Andrew (London: Hodder and Stoughton, 1991), and Andrew's *The Sword and The Shield: The Mitrokhin Archive* and the Secret History of the KGB (Basic Books: New York, 1999), coauthored with KGB defector and archivist Vasili Mitrokhin.

3 Gordievsky, *Instructions from the Center*, 112.

4 "Deputy Minister Markus Wolf, Stasi Note on Meeting with KGB Experts on the RYAN Problem, 14 to 18 August 1984," August 24, 1984, History and Public Policy Program Digital Archive, Office of the Federal Commissioner for the Stasi Records (BStU), MfS, ZAIG 5384, pp. 1–16. Translated from German for CWIHP by Bernd Schaefer, http://digitalarchive.wilsoncenter.org/document/115721.

5 Quoted in Oleg Kalugin, *Spymaster: My 32 Years in Intelligence and Espionage* (New York: Basic Books, 2009), 353; for the sake of consistency, I'll refer to RYAN as RYAN, although other official sources have used variants, like VRYAN, with V standing for V, or "surprise." Historian Ben Fischer notes that the East German RYAN effort was codenamed Kernwaffenangriff (KWA), the German word for "nuclear missile attack." The infrastructure for KWA included a new situation room and the construction of new communications links back to Moscow. See Fischer, "The Soviet-American War Scare of the 1980s," 486.

6 Kalugin's word for Andropov, with whom he had a "father-son"-like relationship, was "paranoid."

7 Andrew and Mitrokhin, 213.

8 "Stasi Note on Meeting Between Minister Mielke and KGB Chairman Andropov," July 11, 1981, History and Public Policy Program Digital Archive, Office of the Federal Commissioner for the Stasi Records (BStU), MfS, ZAIG 5382, 1–19. Translated from German for CWIHP by Bernd Schaefer, http://digitalarchive.wilsoncenter.org/document/115717.

9 Diego Cordovez and Selig S. Harrison, eds. *Out of Afghanistan: The Inside Story of the Soviet Withdrawal* (London: Oxford University Press, 1995), 45–46.

10 For a discussion of these interests, see Andrei Grachev, *Gorbachev's Gamble: Soviet Foreign Policy and the End of the Cold War* (New York: Polity, 2008), accessed online.

11 Cordovez and Harrison, *Out of Afghanistan* 47.

12 Stephen J. Cimbala, *The New Nuclear Disorder: Challenges to Deterrence and Strategy* (New York: Routledge, 2016), 189.

13 Gordievsky, *Next Stop Execution*, 30–48.

14 Ibid., 64.

15 Ibid., 13.

16 Ibid., 172–173.

17 Gordon Brook-Shepherd, *The Storm Birds* (London: Grove Press, 1989), 206–217.

18 Gordievsky, *Next Stop Execution*, 215–229.

19 Ibid., 225.

20 Ibid., 225, 238–243.

6. WARNING

1 Bruce G. Blair, "Alerting in Crisis and Conventional War," in *Managing Nuclear Operations*, 79fn.

2 Andrzej Paczkowski, Malcolm Byrne, Gregory F. Domber, *From Solidarity to Martial Law: The Polish Crisis of 1980–1981*, reproduced by the National Security Archive (Budapest: Central European University Press, 2008), 17.

3 Author's interview with Gail Nelson.

4 National Security Council meeting, June 10, 1981, RRL, NSC Files/

5 John O'Sullivan, *The President, the Pope and the Prime Minister: Three Who Changed the World* (Washington, DC: Regnery, 2006), 126.

6 National Security Council meeting, September 15, 1981; from transcripts obtained from the Ronald Reagan Library and excerpted in Jason Saltoun-Ebin, *Reagan Files: Inside the National Security Council* (Santa Barbara, CA: Seabec Books, 2014)/

7 Ibid.

8 Ibid.

9 Author's interview with Gail Nelson.

10 Ibid.

11 But even Kukliński confused the intelligence picture—suggesting that the Polish defense establishment did not know how much rope they had left until the Soviets snapped. On December 4, 1981, he sent an urgent message to his CIA handlers warning of an imminent Soviet invasion. The DIA by that time had shifted its prediction from invasion to martial law, predicting an early December commencement. The dilemma for the agency was to be overly reliant on a single source for making their assessment of Soviet intentions.

12 Reprinted on a website that collected Kukliński's reports: http://www.kuklinski.us /page11.htm.

7. ZERO-ZERO

1 Author's interview with Richard Perle.

2 Perle gets credit for Zero-Zero as policy, but its genesis was West German: *null-losing*, or the zero solution, was first floated by Helmut Schmidt's own government to pacify domestic critics. As Strobe Talbott later wrote, "it was one of those distinctly European

euphemisms for avoiding unpleasant political realities." See: Strobe Talbott, *Deadly Gambits: The Reagan Administration and the Stalemate in Nuclear Arms Control* (London: Pan Books, 1985).

3   Richard Rhodes, *Arsenals of Folly: The Making of the Nuclear Arms Race.* (New York: Vintage Press, 155–157).

4   Author's interview with Peter Pry; author's interview with Tom Simons; author's interview with Jack Matlock.

5   Author's interviews with Perle, McFarlane, Lehman, and Matlock.

6   Author's interviews with McFarlane and Lehman.

7   Haig, *Caveat*, 203–205.

8   National Security Council meeting, April 30, 1981, published in Saltoun-Ebin's *The Reagan Files.*

9   Détente's proponents would find this glib: they saw agreements as currency between adversaries, and the more currency there was the more stable the world situation would be.

10 "Memorandum of Conversation, President's Working Lunch, Agostino Cardinal Casaroli, December 15, 1981," SECRET, at http://www.thereaganfiles.com/rr—cardinal-casaroli-12158.pdf; for an interpretation, see George Weigel, *The End of the Beginning: Pope John Paul, The Last Years, the Legacy* (New York: Random House, 2013), 140.

11 "Declaration Sur Les Consequences de L'Emploi des Armes Nucleaires" at http://www.casinapioiv.va/content/dam/accademia/pdf/documenta3.pdf.

12 Memorandum of Conversation with Casaroli.

13 "I've heard reports of the fervor of the underground Church in the Soviet Union itself, and stories of bibles being distributed page-by-page among the believers." Reagan had been corresponding regularly with John Koehler, an Associated Press editor who had traveled through Poland that summer. See Craig Shirley, "Another President, Another Pope," *US News and World Report*, September 24, 2015, https://www.usnews.com/opinion/articles/2015/09/24/ronald-reagan-pope-john-paul-ii-and-the-alliance-that-won-the-cold-war. Casaroli again pushed back. "Yes, there is a hunger for God in specific groups in Eastern Europe, but in general the youth are insensible to God. Also, despite strong religious beliefs among certain minorities, young people in general are apathetic." He emphasized to Reagan: "Time is not ripe for major change in Eastern Europe."

14 Quoted in Paul Kengor, and Patricia Clark Doerner, *The Judge: William P. Clark, Ronald Reagan's Top Hand* (San Francisco, CA: Ignatius Press, 2007), 164.

15 Robert G. Kaiser, "Haig Enthusiastic After Californian Gets Job at State; Old Friend of Reagan Appointed," *Washington Post*, January 24, 1981.

16 Quoted in Kengor and Doerner, *The Judge*, 117.

17 Kengor and Doerner, *The Judge*, 143.

18 *National Review* editorial on Judge Richard Clark, January 22, 1982.

19 Kengor and Doerner, *The Judge*, 150.

20 Ibid., 154–156.

21 Author's interview with Ken deGraffenreid.

22 Kengor and Doerner, *The Judge*, 166–167.

23 Ibid.

24 "Minutes of the National Security Council Meeting, October 13, 1981," TOP SECRET; a copy can be found here: http://www.thereaganfiles.com/19811013-nsc-22.pdf.

25 Judith Miller, "Rostow Predicts a Delay in Talks on Arms Limits," *New York Times,* June 23, 1981, http://www.nytimes.com/1981/06/23/world/rostow-predicts-a-delay-in -talks-on-arms-limits.html.

26 Rostow declassified, August 17, 1981, in *The Reagan Files.*

8. IVY LEAGUE '82

1 Ronald Reagan Diaries, Sunday, February 28, 1982.

2 "Memorandum from Robert Gates: CIA Participation in The IVY LEAGUE and NINE LIVES Exercise," April 14, 1982, formerly SECRET. Accessed via CIA CREST tool.

3 William Arkin and Peter Pringle, *SIOP, The Secret US Plan for Nuclear War* (New York: Norton, 1983), 27.

4 Arkin and Pringle, *SIOP*, 24–28.

5 Blair, *Strategic Command and Control*, 142.

6 Author's interview with Reed; Thomas E. Reed, *At the Abyss: An Insider's History of the Cold War* (New York: Random House, 2004), 240–243.

7 Author's interview with G. M. Houser; JCS, "Notice of Significant Military Exercise IVY LEAGUE '82," Ronald Reagan Presidential Library.

8 See, for example, Ron Rosenbaum, *How the End Begins: The Road to a Nuclear World War III* (New York: Simon & Schuster, 2011).

9 Author's interview with a Joint Chiefs of Staff nuclear planner who worked with North.

10 Desmond Ball, *Targeting for Strategic Deterrence* (Washington, DC: International Institute for Strategic Studies, 1983), 15–16.

11 Author's interview with a nuclear submarine commander serving in 1983.

12 "US-Atommanöver: Für Europa geheim," *Der Spiegel*, January 2, 1982, translated by Google.

13 On Crested Cap, see Source: History of the Headquarters, 7th Air Division 1 October 1983 – 31 March 1984, Secret, at the National Security Archive; Air Force Seventh Air Division, Ramstein Air Force Base, "Exercise Able Archer 83, SAC ADVON, After Action Report," December 1, 1983, Secret NOFORN. http://nsarchive.gwu .edu/NSAEBB/NSAEBB427/docs/7.%20Exercise%20Able%20Archer%2083%20 After%20Action%20Report%201%20December%201983.pdf.

14 Memo for William P. Clark, from Thomas C. Reed and Oliver North, February 3, 1982, Ronald Reagan Library.

15 "Ivy League After Action Report," March 15, 1982, Declassified, December 2014, obtained by author.

16 Ibid.

17 Interview with Reed; Stephen D. O'Leary, *Arguing the Apocalypse* (New York: Oxford University Press, 1994), 180. Reed wouldn't admit it at the time, but he wondered whether Reagan's religious fundamentalism—something his campaign staff went out

of their way to play down, because the establishment found it weird and menacing—would find a real-world application. Reagan had long been a student of Bible prophecy; he actively looked for correspondence between real-world events and passages from the apocalyptic canon: the Book of Daniel and, of course, the Book of Revelation. But if Reagan believed that history was foreordained, he also believed it could be changed. One belief did not logically flow from the other, but Reagan often held conflicting beliefs in his head. This one might be particularly useful.

18 "Memorandum for the President from Frank Carlucci, February 8, 1982," Ronald Reagan Presidential Library.

19 Author's interviews with Reed and Houser, and Memorandum from Thomas C. Reed to Michael Deaver, "President's Participation in March 1–5 Exercises," February 4, 1982, Top Secret, obtained by the National Security Archive.

20 Reagan's schedule for that day can be accessed at: http://nsarchive.gwu.edu/dc.html ?doc=3242129-Document-14.

21 Reed's account is backed up in parts by contemporaneous memoranda obtained by the National Security Archive at George Washington University, including http:// nsarchive.gwu.edu/dc.html?doc=3242124-Document-09, http://nsarchive.gwu.edu /dc.html?doc=3242125-Document-10 and others, located here: http://nsarchive.gwu .edu/nukevault/ebb575-Reagan-Nuclear-War-Briefing/.

22 Thomas Coakley, *C3I: Issues of Command and Control* (Washington, DC: National Defense University, 1990), 127, at http://www.dtic.mil/get-tr-doc/pdf?AD= ADA264195. Author's interview with Thomas Reed.

23 Jeffrey Richelson, "PD-59, NSDD-13, and the Reagan Strategic Modernization Program," *Journal of Strategic Studies*, vol. 6, no. 2 (1983).

24 Desmond Ball, "US Strategic Forces: How Would They Be Used?" *International Security*, The MIT Press, vol. 7, no. 3 (Winter 1982–1983), 31–60; William Arkin and Desmond Ball, *Strategic Nuclear Targeting* (Ithaca, NY: Cornell University Press, 1986), 57–58, 80.

25 Jeffrey Lewis, "Biscuits, Cookies and Nuclear Bombs," Arms Control Wonk blog, October 27, 2010, and comments. http://lewis.armscontrolwonk.com/archive/3066/ biscuits-cookies-and-nuclear-bombs.

26 See Blair, *Strategic Command and Control*, 257–264; Blair, *The Logic of Accidental Nuclear War*, 46; http://nsarchive.gwu.edu/NSAEBB/NSAEBB173/SIOP-4.pdf.

27 Michael P. Tkacik, *The Future of US Nuclear Operational Doctrine: Balancing Safety and Deterrence in an Anarchic World* (Lewiston, NY: Edwin Mellen Press, 2013), 233.

28 General Ellis interviews with the PIRP.

29 These would be the missile wings at Minot Air Force Base in Nebraska, F. E. Warren Air Force Base, Grand Forks, North Dakota; Wyoming, and probably, submarines at drydock in New London Connecticut, the air bases with SAC-generated bombers.

30 Blair, *Strategic Command and Control*, 285, 295.

31 Ibid., 147–148.

32 NATO commanders assumed that CINCEUR had pre-delegated authority during war. See: Marco Carnovale, *The Control of NATO Nuclear Forces in Europe* (Boulder, CO: Westview Press, 1993), 42.

33 Person with knowledge of the WHEP; Blair, "Alerting in Crisis and Conventional War," in *Managing Nuclear Operations*, 83–89.

34 Author's interview with Reed.

35 "Succession Team System Requirements," Undated Memo from Colonel Bill Odom, Jimmy Carter Presidential Library.

36 Lathan, quoted in Fred Hiatt, "Building a Force for World War IV," *Washington Post*, July 27, 1986.

37 North, *Under Fire: An American Story*, 35%, accessed via Kindle.

38 A comprehensive account can be found in Thomas B. Allen, *War Games: The Secret World of the Creators, Players and Policymakers Rehearsing for World War III Today* (New York: McGraw-Hill, 1987).

39 North, *Under Fire: An American Story*, 38%, accessed via Kindle.

40 Coakley, *C3I: Issues of Command and Control*, 126–128.

41 Thomas B. Allen, *War Games*, 205.

42 Reagan, *An American Life*, 550.

43 Author's interview with McFarlane.

44 North, *Under Fire: An American Story*, 38%, accessed via Kindle.

45 "Memorandum from Ronald Reagan to Caspar Weinberger, Creation of the National Program Office," September 15, 1982. TOP SECRET (National Archives).

9. BOGGING DOWN

1 *National Journal*, vol. 14 (1982), 1248.

2 Haig, *Caveat*, 145–152.

3 "National Security Council Minutes, May 24, 1982," in Jason Saltoun-Ebin, *The Reagan Files: Inside the National Security Council* (Santa Barbara, CA: Seabec Books: 2012, 2014), also at www.thereaganfiles.com.

4 John O'Sullivan, *The President, the Pope, and the Prime Minister: Three Who Changed the World* (New York: Regnery, 2006), 168.

5 Diary of Ronald Reagan. June 25, 1982.

6 Michael J. Hogan, *The Nuclear Freeze Campaign: Rhetoric and Foreign Policy in the Telepolitical Age* (East Lansing, MI: Michigan State University Press, 1994); Douglas C. Waller, *Congress and the Nuclear Freeze: An Inside Look at the Politics of a Mass Movement* (Amherst: University of Massachusetts Press, 1987); https://www.armscontrol.org/act/2010_12/Looking Back.

7 Ibid.

8 Roger Chapman and James Ciment, *Culture Wars: An Encyclopedia of Issues, Viewpoints, and Voices* (New York: Routledge: 2013), 708–709.

9 Mary McGrory, "Reagan Spokesmen Attack on California Nuclear Issue," *Washington Post*, November 2, 1982, cited in in https://www.armscontrol.org/act/2010_12/LookingBack#12.

10 John Isaacs, "The Freeze," *Bulletin of the Atomic Scientists*, October 1982, 9.

11 Stephen R. Weisman, "Reagan Calls Nuclear Freeze Dangerous," *New York Times*, April 1, 1983, http://www.nytimes.com/1983/04/01/world/reagan-calls-nuclear-freeze-dangerous.html.

12 Matthew Continetti, "Frozen in the Cold War," *The Weekly Standard*, August 4, 2014, http://www.weeklystandard.com/articles/frozen-cold-war_797360.html.

13 Richard Halloran, "Pentagon Draws Up Strategy for Fighting a Long Nuclear War," *New York Times*, May 30, 1982, http://www.nytimes.com/1982/05/30/world/pentagon-draws-up-first-strategy-for-fighting-a-long-nuclear-war.html?pagewanted=all.

14 Caspar Weinberger and Theodore Draper, "On Nuclear War: An Exchange with the Secretary of Defense," *New York Review of Books*, August 18, 1983, http://www.nybooks.com/articles/archives/1983/aug/18/on-nuclear-war-an-exchange-with-the-secretary-of-d/.

15 "National Security Decision Directive 33," accessed at http://fas.org/irp/offdocs/nsdd/nsdd-32.pdf.

16 Richard Halloran, "Weinberger Defends His Plan on a Protracted Nuclear War," *New York Times*, August 10, 1982, http://www.nytimes.com/1982/08/10/world/weinberger-defends-his-plan-on-a-protracted-nuclear-war.html.

17 Author's interview with Thomas Reed.

10. THE VIEW FROM LONDON

1 Author's interview with Secret Service agent on Reagan detail; former White House advance person.

2 Ronald Reagan, Speech to Members of the British Parliament, June 8, 1982, http://www.heritage.org/research/reports/2002/06/reagans-westminster-speech.

3 Aldous, *Reagan and Thatcher*, 117.

4 Gordievsky's description of the residencies in Copenhagen and the UK; *Next Stop Execution*, 151–154.

5 Gordievsky, *Next Stop Execution*, 248–249.

6 Andrew and Gordievsky, *KGB: The Inside Story*, 586.

7 Gordievsky, *Next Stop Execution*, 253.

8 Oleg Gordievsky, "But I Say He's the Best Man," *The Telegraph*, May 9, 1984, http://www.telegraph.co.uk/comment/personal-view/3605786/.-.-.-but-I-say-hes-the-best-man.html.

9 George P. Shultz, *Turmoil and Triumph: Diplomacy, Power and the Victory of the American Deal* (New York: Simon & Schuster, 1993).

10 Shultz, *Turmoil and Triumph*, accessed on Kindle without pagination.

11 quoted in Shultz, *Turmoil and Triumph*, accessed on Kindle without pagination.

12 Douglas C. Waller, *Congress and the Nuclear Freeze: An Inside Look at the Politics of a Mass Movement* (Amherst: University of Massachusetts Press, 1987), 156.

13 13: Nuclear Arms Control: Background and Issues, by Office of International Affairs, Policy and Global Affairs, National Academy of Sciences, Committee on International Security and Arms Control.

14 John Herbers, "Widespread Vote Urges Nuclear Freeze," *New York Times*, November 11, 1982, http://www.nytimes.com/1982/11/04/us/widespread-vote-urges-nuclear-freeze.html.

15 Nuclear Arms Control: Background and Issues policy paper by Office of International

Affairs, Policy and Global Affairs, National Academy of Sciences, Committee on International Security and Arms Control, 90–92; author's interviews with Matlock.

16 Author's interview with John Lehman and MacFarlane; Lou Cannon, *President Reagan: The Role of a Lifetime* (New York: Public Affairs, 1991), 260–263; Jay Winik, *On The Brink: The Dramatic, Behind-the-Scenes Saga of the Reagan Era and the Men and Women Who Won the Cold War* (New York: Simon & Schuster, 1996), 160–181.

17 Waller, *Congress and the Nuclear Freeze*, 163.

18 National Security Council meeting, April 21, 1982, TOP SECRET (TRF), http://thereaganfiles.com/19820421-nsc-46.pdf.

19 Author's interview with former DIA analyst.

11. 1983

1 Stuart Spencer, Oral History with the Miller Center at the University of Virginia, https://millercenter.org/the-presidency/interviews-with-the-administration/stuart-spencer-campaign-advisor.

2 See this advertisement: http://www.sunnylands.org/page/19/golf.

3 Center for Military History and Strategic Analysis Cold War Oral History Project Interview with Brigadier General Charles F. Brower, IV by Cadet William J. Keller, II, March 2, 2005.

4 The typical New Year's Eve scene described in *Vanity Fair* from 1998: http://www.vanityfair.com/magazine/archive/1998/08/ronnie-and-nancy199808.

5 Steven Weisman, "Reagan on New York's Holiday to Consult Foreign Policy Aides," *New York Times*, December 12, 1982, http://www.nytimes.com/1982/12/30/us/reagan-on-new-year-s-holiday-to-consult-foreign-policy-aides.

6 Richard Pipes, *Vixi: Memoirs of a Non-Belonger* (New Haven: Yale University Press, 2005), 302.

7 Philip Taubman, "CIA Seeks to Read Moscow Auguries," *New York Times*, February 2, 1984, http://www.nytimes.com/1984/02/13/world/cia-seeks-to-read-moscow-auguries.html.

8 George Crile, *Charlie Wilson's War* (New York: Grove Press, 2007), 103.

9 John Burns, "Pravda, Says Strategic Arms Talks Are Deadlocked and Blames US," *New York Times*, January 2, 1983, http://www.nytimes.com/1983/01/02/world/pravda-says-strategic-arms-talks-are-deadlocked-and-blames-us.html.

10 "National Security Decision Directive 75," Ronald Reagan Presidential Library; Pipes, *Vixi*, 188–207.

11 Don Oberdorfer interview with George Shultz, Don Oberdorfer Papers.

12 Michael Getler, "President Offers to Meet Andropov on Missile Ban," *Washington Post*, February 1, 1983, https://www.washingtonpost.com/archive/politics/1983/02/01/president-offers-to-meet-andropov-on-missiles-ban/564866cb-63ef-42b6-8962-e76a69051faa/.

13 Speech by Yuri Andropov to Political Consultative Committee in Prague. Translated by Svetlana Savranskaya from the National Security Archive, George Washington University. January 4, 1983.

14 Eugenia V. Osgood, "Euromissiles: Historical and Political Realities," *Bulletin of Atomic Scientists*, December 1983, 17.

15 Oleg Grivensky and Lynn M. Hansen, *Making Peace: Confidence and Security in a New Europe* (London: Eloquent Books, 2009); Oleg Grinevsky, *Stcenarii dlia tretei mirovoi voiny* (Moscow: Olma Press 2002), Google translation, 280.

16 Ibid.

17 Shultz, *Turmoil and Triumph*, accessed via Kindle.

18 Don Oberdorfer, *The Turn*, 19.

19 Lou Cannon, *President Reagan*, 269.

20 See Shultz, *Turmoil and Triumph*, accessed via Kindle.

21 Author's interview with Richard Perle; author's interview with Ronald Lehman.

22 Dobrynin, *In Confidence*, 508–512.

23 Kiron K. Skinner, *Turning Points in the End of the Cold War* (Stanford, CA: Hoover Institution Press, 2007), 69.

24 Quoted in Anderson and Anderson, 176.

25 Quoted in Shultz, *Turmoil and Triumph*, accessed via Kindle.

26 Author's interview with a former CIA official.

27 Author's interview with a former CIA official.

28 R. Judson Miller, *Getting to the Top in the USSR: Cyclical Patterns in the Leadership* (Stanford, CA: Hoover Institution Press, 1990), 96.

29 Margaret Thatcher, "Speech to Young Conservatives' Conference," February 12, 1982, http://www.margaretthatcher.org/document/105252.

30 Interview with a senior civil servant who was privy to the Gordievsky intelligence and to Thatcher's thinking; program for Young Conservatives lunch (832012 YC Lunch), The Margaret Thatcher Archives; Corera, 259.

31 Author's interview with senior UK civil servant.

32 Quoted in Dan Stone, ed., *The Oxford Handbook of Postwar European History* (Oxford: Oxford University Press, 2012), 457.

33 Ibid.

34 See Rebecca Johnson, "Pro Nuclear Propaganda in 1983: Lessons for 2012," published at https://www.opendemocracy.net/5050/rebecca-johnson/pro-nuclear-propaganda-in-1983-lessons-for-2013.

35 UPI, "Prime Minister Margaret Thatcher in a Strong Attack," February 12, 1983, http://www.upi.com/Archives/1983/02/12/Prime-Minister-Margaret-Thatcher-in-a-strong-attack-Saturday/4418413874000/.

36 Thatcher's Speech: http://www.margaretthatcher.org/document/105252.

37 Author's interview with McFarlane; author's interview with Ron Lehman; author's interview with former Reagan aide.

38 Gordievsky, *Instructions from the Center*, 112–123.

39 Ibid.

40 Gordievsky, *Instructions from the Center*, 49.

41 Author's interview with Robert Gates.

12. THE EVIL EMPIRE

1 His chief antagonist was not yet Walter Mondale, who was the leading Democratic presidential candidate. The two were tied in the polls; Reagan's standing had improved since December, when the *New York Times* noted a "stench" emanating from the White House and when Gallup's polls had Mondale leading Reagan in a hypothetical matchup by 12 points.

2 Frank Warner, "The Evil Empire Speech: The Full Story of Reagan's Historic Address," December 4, 2003: at: http://frankwarner.typepad.com/free_frank_warner/2003/12/story_of_reagan.html.

3 Ibid.; see "Drafts of NAE Speech," Ronald Reagan Presidential Library.

4 Aram Bakshian, "Oral History for the Miller Center at the University of Virginia," http://millercenter.org/president/bush/oralhistory/aram-bakshian.

5 Ibid.

6 Warner, "The Evil Empire Speech"; the author examined the documents Warner writes about.

7 Author's interview with Richard Cizik.

8 Reagan's draft speech can be found in the "Evil Empire" subject file at the Ronald Reagan Presidential Library.

9 Frank Warner, "In Nine Years, Soviet Empire Fell: Reagan's Evil Empire Speech Started Got It Started, and the Tide Turned in 1987 with Gorbachev," *The Morning Call*, March 5, 2003, http://articles.mcall.com/2000-03-05/news/3291248_1_soviet-press-agency-tass-nuclear-war-soviet-union.

10 Foreign Affairs Oral History Collection, USSR, Association of Diplomatic Studies and Training, http://adst.org/wp-content/uploads/2012/09/Russia.pdf.

11 Ibid.

12 Reed, *At the Abyss*, 143; author's interview with Reed.

13. SDI AND SABOTAGE

1 Andreas Parsch, SVC Lockheed HOE, at http://www.astronautix.com/lvs/hoe.htm.

2 A description of the HOE project can be found in a Government Accountability Office report completed in 1993, http://www2.gwu.edu/~nsarchiv/NSAEBB/NSAEBB456/docs/specialPlans_26.pdf.

3 Reagan speech on SDI, March 23, http://www.reagan.utexas.edu/archives/speeches/1983/32383d.htm; Cheryl Hudson and Gareth Davies, eds., *Ronald Reagan and the 1980s: Perceptions, Policies and Legacies* (New York: Palgrave Macmillan, 2008), 86–88.

4 See: http://www.thereaganfiles.com/rr--cardinal-casaroli-12158.pdf.

5 Oberdorfer interview with Shultz, section 1, p. 9.

6 Ibid.; a document can be found at the Thatcher Archives: http://www.margaretthatcher.org/document/110632.

7 Author's interview with John Poindexter; see also: Winik, *On the Brink*, 312–317; http://history.nasa.gov/sp4232-part3.pdf.

8 Quoted in ibid.

9 Author's interview with Reed.

10 Gregg Herken, "The Earthly Origins of Star Wars," *Bulletin of the Atomic Scientists*, October 1987, 20–28

11 Grivensky, in Skinner, 68–70.

12 Grivensky, in Skinner, 69–71; a second fallback, Andropov knew, was the Perimetr system, which was in beta testing mode when Reagan gave his SDI speech and would become at least partially operational shortly thereafter.

14. PROVOCATIONS

1   Bondarenko wrote this account: "Memories of Commander of PLAT K-305 Captain 1st Rank V. K. Bondarenko," PLAT K-305 Project671RTM; "Tracking the Multipurpose Carrier Battle Group *Enterprise* in April 1983," on a naval history website. It was reposted on a war games fan website: http://www.matrixgames.com/forums/printable.asp?m= 3807569. See also Seymour M. Hersh, *The Target is Destroyed: What Really Happened to Flight 007 and What America Knew About It* (New York: Random House, 1986), 18–20.

2   His ship was classed as an attack submarine, or Project 671RT. A description can be found in Polmar, 119.

3   Ibid.

4   Ibid.

5   Peter Schweitzer, *Reagan's War*, 132–133.

6   Author's interview with John Lehman, Secretary of the Navy.

7   Bondarenko oral history.

8   Gregory Vistica, *Fall from Glory: The Men Who Sank the US Navy* (New York: Touchtone, 1997), 18–22.

9   Vistica, *Fall from Glory*, 91. Lehman borrowed the number from a study conducted by Admiral Elmo Zumwalt, the chief of Naval Operations during Vietnam.

10 This description comes from an interview with Lehman and others. See also: Morris H. Morley, *Crisis and Confrontation: Ronald Reagan's Foreign Policy* (New York: Rowman & Littlefield, 1988), 86–89; US Naval Strategy in the 1980s, Selected Documents; http://fas.org/irp/doddir/navy/strategy1980s.pdf.

11 Vistica, *Fall from Glory*, 91.

12 Ibid., 104–105.

13 Ibid., 105.

14 Simon Duke, *United States Military Forces and Installations in Europe* (Solna, Sweden: Stockholm International Peace Research Institute), 181–194.

15 Andreas Fürst, Volker Heise, Steven E. Miller, *Europe and Naval Arms Control in the Gorbachev Era* (Oxford: Oxford University Press, 1992), 98–100.

16 Vistica, *Fall from Glory*, 135; by this point, the US Navy had begun to suspect that its fleet communications had been compromised, so Lyons conveyed his orders through separate channels that did not involve the use of previously generated National Security Agency coding keys. He was correct to do so; the Soviets, thanks to the efforts of Chief Warrant Officer John Walker, could intercept in real time—or re-create—almost every US Navy directive sent out after 1979.

17 Author's interview with Lehman.

18 Vistica, *Fall from Glory*, 132–133.

15. DIAMONDS

1 Author's interview with Trolan.

2 Carney, *Against All Enemies*, 144–147.

3 Ibid., 152–153.

4 Ibid.

5 Ibid., 154.

6 Ibid., 166–169. Carney's autobiography was censored by the NSA before publication, and almost all references to the agency are blacked out. Other sources on Carney's initial steps as a spy include http://www.spiegel.de/international/germany/interview-with -former-stasi-agent-about-the-nsa-a-975010.html; http://www.spiegel.de/international /germany/american-stasi-agent-describes-his-experiences-in-new-book-a-916374.html.

7 Carney, 189.

8 Ibid., 178.

9 Carney's book does not describe the details of the electronic warfare projects he knew about. This account comes from several sources, including a former NSA official who worked on these programs, and from accounts by Stasi officials of what Carney told the East Germans, and Benjamin Fischer, *CANOPY WING*.

10 *Traitors Among Us*, 320–322.

11 In 1985, Hall obtained a full concept of operations document for CANOPY WING.

12 Wolf saw the NSA sources as his prizes. He kept their identities so closely held that he did not inform his own SIGINT deputy, Horst Männchen, about the spies or their reporting until 1985.

13 Ben Fischer, "'One of the Biggest Ears in the World': East German SIGINT Operations," *Journal of Intelligence and Counterintelligence* (1998) 11:2.

14 Cited in Fischer, *CANOPY WING*.

15 Markus Wolf, *Man Without a Face: The Autobiography of Communism's Greatest Spymaster* (New York: Random House, 1997), 212–223; Wladek Flakin, "Cooling the Cold War," *ExBerliner*, January 3, 2013; http://www.exberliner.com/features/people/the -spy-who-saved-the-world/. See more at: http://www.exberliner.com/features/people /the-spy-who-saved-the-world/#sthash.gZQlKhkz.dpuf.

16 Werner Grossman, interview conducted by producers for *1983: The Brink of Apocalypse*, Flashback Television Ltd., Channel 4, 2008.

17 Author's interview with former NSA official who has spoken with Männchen.

16. SPY VS. SPY

1 Author's interview with deGraffenreid.

2 Navarro, 258; Neil. A Lewis, "Ex-Sergeant Charged with Role in Selling Secrets to the Warsaw Pact," *New York Times*, June 9, 1980.

3 Quoted in Navarro, 258.

4 An NSA official who spoke to Navarro revealed how easily the system could be reverse-engineered with the information. See Navarro, p. 278.

5 *Traitors Among Us*, 96–105; author's interviews with former US officials.

6 Major Laura Heath, "An Analysis of the Systematic Security Weaknesses of the US Navy

Fleet Broadcasting System, 1967–1974 as Exploited by CWO John Walker," unpublished master's thesis, Georgia Institute of Technology, 2001. Fort Leavenworth, Kansas (USA), 2005; http://fas.org/irp/eprint/heath.pdf.

7   A number of paragraphs in this chapter appear in an article I wrote for *The Week* on the occasion of Walker's death. See: Marc Ambinder, "The Quiet Death of America's Worst Spy," *The Week*, September 25, 2014, http://theweek.com/articles/443492/quiet -death-americas-worst-spy.

8   Details from a great overview of Solomatin life: http://www.crimelibrary.com/terror ists_spies/spies/solomatin/2.html.

9   John Prados, "The John Walker Spy Ring and the US Navy's Biggest Betrayal," *USNI News*, September 2, 2014, at http://news.usni.org/2014/09/02/john-walker-spy-ring -u-s-navys-biggest-betrayal.

10 See http://www.crimelibrary.com/terrorists_spies/spies/solomatin/5.html.

11 Author's interview with a former NSA official.

12 For SACCS info, see: http://fas.org/nuke/guide/usa/c3i/saccs.htm and http://www .telephonecollectors.info/index.php/browse/bsps/by-division-number/signaling -testing/doc_view/7980-314-411-504-i3.

13 David E. Hoffman, *Billion-Dollar Spy: A True Story of Cold War Espionage and Betrayal* (New York: Doubleday, 2015).

14 Described in an article at American Space: see http://www.americaspace.com/?p= 20825.

15 Charles P. Vick, CHALET-VORTEX – ZIRCON (2007), GlobalSecurity.Org, http:// www.globalsecurity.org/space/systems/chalet.htm.

16 Joint Chiefs of Staff, "WWMCCS Objectives and Management Plan," SECRET, January 1, 1976, SECRET, 7–11.

17 Author's interview with former SAC targeteer.

18 CIA, Soviet Civil Defense Alternative Headquarters/Command Facilities, November 1, 1979, TOP SECRET RUFF/CODEWORD, 1–17; James Carney, "Moscow's Secret Plans," *Time*, August 10, 1992; Department of Defense, "Military Forces in Transition," 1992 edition, Unclassified, 40–43.

19 See, for example: "CIA, Secret Institute for Guided Missile and Nuclear Energy Research Near the Serebryany RR, February 9, 1954," SECRET. Obtained via the CIA CREST tool.

20 "Memorandum for the Director, Defense Intelligence Agency, Soviet C3 Systems Data," December 17, 1981, SECRET. Obtained via CIA Crest tool, https://www.cia. gov/library/readingroom/docs/CIA-RDP83M00914R001200090035-6.pdf.

21 DIA, "Memorandum for the DDCI, Soviet Command, Control, Communications (C3)," March 8, 1982, SECRET. https://www.cia.gov/library/readingroom/docs/ CIA-RDP84-00933R000200030002-7.pdf.

22 Author's interview with former CIA official.

23 Benjamin B. Fischer, "The Soviet–American War Scare of the 1980s," *International Journal of Intelligence and Counterintelligence*, vol. 19, no. 3 (2006), 480–518.

24 This summary is informed by the following sources on the Soviet C3 network, primarily

Valery E. Yarynich, *C3: Nuclear Command, Control and Cooperation* (Washington, DC: Center for Defense Information, 2013). It can be accessed here: https://www.scribd .com/doc/282622838/C3-Nuclear-Command-Control-Cooperation; also, David E. Hoffmann, *The Dead Hand: The Untold Story of the Cold War Arms Race and Its Dangerous Legacy* (New York: Knopf Doubleday Publishing Group, 2009),147–148; Pavel Podvig, "History and Current Status of the Russian Early Warning System," *Science and Global Security* 10/1 (2002), 21–60. *Managing Nuclear Operations* (Washington, DC: Brookings Institution, 1987); and two works by Bruce Blair: *Strategic Command and Control: Redefining the Nuclear Threat* (Washington, DC: Brookings Institution, 1985), and *The Logic of Accidental Nuclear War* (Washington, DC: Brookings Institution, 1993).

25 Dmitry Adamsky, "The 1983 Nuclear Crisis—Lessons for Deterrence Theory and Practice," *Journal of Strategic Studies*, vol. 36, no. 1 (2013), 4–41.

26 One such account can be found in Warren Kerzon, *Throw a Nickel on the Grass, a Fighter Pilot's Life Narrative* (Lulu.com, 2016), 76–80.

27 For a Soviet view, see: Mary Fitzgerald, "Russian Views on IW, EW, and Command and Control: Implications for the 21st Century," Hudson Institute accessed at: http://www .dodccrp.org/events/1999_CCRTS/pdf_files/track_5/089fitzg.pdf.

28 25th Air Force, *Continuing Legacy*, web publication: http://www.25af.af.mil/Portals /100/25AF-Chronology%208.5X11-Dec2016.pdf?ver=2017-01-09-115552-620.

29 Beatrice de Graaf, Ben de Jong, Wies Platje, eds., *Battleground Western Europe: Intelligence Operations in Germany and the Netherlands in the Twentieth Century* (Amsterdam: Het Spinhuis, 2008), 148, 152.

30 Author's interview with former SAC general; Bruce D. Berkowitz, *The New Face of War: How War Will Be Fought in the 21st Century* (New York: Simon & Schuster, 2010), 45–84.

31 An unclassified reference to CANOPY WING can be found in an Army INSCOM historical document in 1988. It can be accessed here. http://www.governmentattic .org/17docs/USAINSCOMhistoryFY_1988.pdf. See Page 23. See Benjamin Fischer, "CANOPY WING: The US War Plan That Gave the East Germans Goose Bumps," *International Journal of Intelligence and Counterintelligence*, vol. 27, 431–464.

32 For information on Zossen's communications, see Blair, *The Logic of Accidental Nuclear War*, 140.

33 Fischer, *CANOPY WING*.

34 Fischer, *CANOPY WING*.

35 The US had begun to test ways to sabotage the Soviet nuclear command and control system. A system for nuclear command and control that bypassed the vulnerable electromagnetic links, and even, when switched on, could bypass easily-fooled human beings, suddenly seemed less crazy.

17. GREEN SHOOTS

1 Author's interview with Lee Trolan.

2 US Army, Reforger '83 et al., After-Action Report, Confidential, p. 7.

3 A history can be found here: http://tvtropes.org/pmwiki/pmwiki.php/Film/Threads ?from=Main.Threads.

4 Board Games: Apocalypse: The Game of Nuclear Devastation (1980), 2 Wars on Neptune, March 19, 2014, https://2warpstoneptune.wordpress.com/2014/03/19/board-games-apocalypse-the-game-of-nuclear-devastation-1980/.

5 "Nuclear Escalation," Board Games Geek blog, at: https://boardgamegeek.com/boardgame/1213/nuclear-escalation.

6 At the NSC, as the *New York Times* wrote, "European affairs on the national security staff in the hands of two junior specialists, John Lenczowski and Paula Dobriansky. Both have studied and written about those regions in universities without having served in diplomatic posts in Moscow or Eastern Europe. Mr. Lenczowski is 32 years old and Miss Dobriansky is 27."

7 Haig, *Inner Circle*, 546.

8 Ibid.

9 Constantine Christopher Menges, *Inside the National Security Council: The True Story of the Making and Unmaking of Reagan's Foreign Policy* (New York: Simon & Schuster, 1988), 198, 184.

10 Author's interview with Matlock.

11 Matlock, *Reagan and Gorbachev*, 9.

12 Author's interview with Matlock; author's interview with Simons.

13 David Mayers, *The Ambassadors and America's Soviet Policy* (New York: Oxford University Press, 2009), 139.

14 "wanted stability above all else," ibid., 163.

15 Walter Isaacson, Evan Thomas, *The Wise Men: Six Friends and the World They Made* (New York: Simon & Schuster, 2012), 728.

16 "Notes of Conversation with Secretary Shultz, Undersecretary Eagleburger, and Averell Harriman," May 1983, Ronald Reagan Presidential Library.

17 Ibid.

18 "Memorandum of Conversation: Meeting with CPSU General Secretary Andropov," June 2, 1983, Ronald Reagan Presidential Library.

19 Don Oberdorfer interview with George Shultz, section 1, p. 4, Don Oberdorfer Papers.

20 Marija Wakounig, *From Collective Memories to Intercultural Exchanges* (Hamburg: LIT Verlag, 2012), 241; Sonja Hillgren, "Reagan Ruled Out Another Grain Embargo to Retaliate," UPI September 30, 1983.

18. THE PHANTOM (PART I)

1 Hersh, *The Target Is Destroyed*, 53.

2 Ibid., 78–79.

3 Ibid., 90–91.

4 Ibid., 83–86.

5 Gennadi Osipovich, interview conducted by producers for *1983: The Brink of Apocalypse*, Flashback Television Ltd., Channel 4, 2008; Michael Gordon, "Ex-Soviet Pilot Still Insists KAL 007 Was Spying," *New York Times*, December 12, 1996, http://www.nytimes.com/1996/12/09/world/ex-soviet-pilot-still-insists-kal-007-was-spying.html?pagewanted=all.

6   Cockpit Voice Recorder Database, accessed at: http://www.tailstrike.com/010983. htm.

7   Murray Sayle, "Closing the File on Flight 007," *The New Yorker*, December 13, 1993, 90–101.

8   Hersh, *The Target Is Destroyed*, 118–119.

9   Ibid., 121.

10 Shultz, *Turmoil and Triumph*, accessed on Kindle.

11 Gordievsky, interview conducted by producers for *1983: The Brink of Apocalypse*, Flashback Television Ltd., Channel 4, 2008.

12 Ibid.

13 "Moments in Diplomatic History: The Downing of KAL Flight 007," Association for Diplomatic Studies and Training, at http://adst.org/2014/03/the-downing-of-kal -flight-007/.

14 Hersh, *The Target Is Destroyed*, 173. I believe Hersh errs in concluding that Shultz was facing a crisis of place in the administration before the shootdown, and that he used its aftermath to consolidate his power and regain his rightful place as the president's most trusted foreign policy advisor. For one thing, there was no rival; Clark was on his way out, James Baker had not made a serious play to be his replacement yet, and McFarlane and Shultz got along well. Weinberger's efforts to shut down negotiations had never succeeded, and there was no evidence from Reagan's diaries that he blamed the slow pace of engagement on anything other than the Soviet intransience.

15 Garthoff, 124.

16 Hersh, *The Target Is Destroyed*, 122–123.

17 Author's interview with McFarlane; author's interview with Matlock; see Hersh, *The Target Is Destroyed*, 154.

18 http://www.reagan.utexas.edu/archives/speeches/1983/90583a.htm.

19 See: "CPSU CC Politburo Session, Korean Air Flight 007," September 8, 1983, History and Public Policy Program Digital Archive, TsKhSD. F. 89, Op. 42, D. 54, pp. 4. Translated by Gary Goldberg. http://digitalarchive.wilsoncenter.org/document/115559.

20 "Statement by the General Secretary of the CC of the CSPU," Pravda, September 29, 1983.

21 Impressive, but not without serious problems. For one thing, the US troops had not been briefed on the war plan, or on its coastal cousin, OPLAN 4360, which dealt with defense of the continent and associated air-sea travel lanes. Accidents were common; troops were unfamiliar with the terrain and occasionally ran into one another. And the exercise, as massive as it was, accounted for only about 25 percent of the 60,000 troops that the classified war plan promised NATO ground commanders. They fretted that the exercises themselves depleted storage reserves too quickly, and asked the Pentagon to seriously consider rethinking reinforcing supply flows back to the United States.

19. THE PHANTOM (PART II)

1   Quoted in Aldous, *Reagan and Thatcher*, 146.

2   Quoted in Margaret Thatcher, *The Downing Street Years* (London: Harper Collins, 1993), 332; see also: http://www.margaretthatcher.org/document/109390.

3 Suzanne Massie, *Trust But Verify: Reagan, Russia and Me: A Personal Memoir* (Maine: Maine Authors Publishing, 2013), 60–65.

4 Ibid.

5 Interview with Stanislav Petrov, for *The Red Button*, a documentary produced in 2014, transcript obtained by author. See also: http://www.bbc.com/news/world-europe-24280831 and http://www.express.co.uk/news/history/579218/Nuclear-warRussia-Stanislav-Petrov.

6 Interview with Stanislav Petrov conducted by producers for *1983: The Brink of Apocalypse*, Flashback Television Ltd., Channel 4, 2008.

7 Petrov, *The Red Button* (2014).

8 Ibid.

9 Hoffman, *Dead Hand*, 6–11; Pry, *War Scare*, 37–38; Brian Harvey, *Russia in Space: The Failed Frontier*, 137; Anatoly Zak, "History of the Oko Early Warning System," on Russian Space Web, http://www.russianspaceweb.com/oko.html.

10 Petrov was interviewed extensively about that night for a documentary called *The Man Who Saved the World*, https://www.youtube.com/watch?v=VaPXVJWHji4; https://www.youtube.com/watch?v=oX83EzDofrc; http://themanwhosavedtheworldmovie.com/. This account and subsequent details come from his own words. See also: Petrov interview conducted by producers for *1983: The Brink of Apocalypse*, Flashback Television Ltd., Channel 4, 2008.

11 Ibid.

12 Petrov's interview for *The Man Who Saved the World*," describing the setup of the center.

13 Petrov interview conducted by producers for *1983: The Brink of Apocalypse*, Flashback Television Ltd., Channel 4, 2008.

14 Petrov described this process; also see interviews with General Rodionov and Igor Kondratiev conducted by producers for *1983: The Brink of Apocalypse*, Flashback Television Ltd., Channel 4, 2008.

15 Petrov interview conducted by producers for *1983: The Brink of Apocalypse*, Flashback Television Ltd., Channel 4, 2008.

16 General Rodionov interview conducted by producers for *1983: The Brink of Apocalypse*, Flashback Television Ltd., Channel 4, 2008.

17 "Stasi Note on Meeting Between Minister Mielke and KGB Deputy Chairman Kryuchkov," September 19, 1983, History and Public Policy Program Digital Archive, Office of the Federal Commissioner for the Stasi Records (BStU), MfS, ZAIG 5306, pp. 1–19. Translated by Bernd Schaefer. http://digitalarchive.wilsoncenter.org/document/115718.

18 Ibid.

19 Author's interview with a former FEMA official.

20 Tim Weiner, "Pentagon to Shelve Doomsday Project," *New York Times*, April 14, 1994.

21 See: "Appropriations for Independent Agencies (FEMA)," submitted to Congress, 1981.

22 The titles were (and are) classified. (E.G: PEAD 2: "Providing for the Reconstitution of Congress;" PEAD 5: "Providing for the Mobilization of the Nation's Resources").

23 Information from interviews with former senior officials who dealt with the Plan D

documents. For a good overview, see Edward Zuckerman, *The Day After World War III* (New York: Viking, 1984), 234–237.

20. THE DAY BEFORE THE DAY AFTER

1 Diary of Ronald Reagan, October 10, 1983.
2 "Blowup in Beirut: US Marines Peacekeeping Mission Turns Deadly," at http://www .historynet.com/blowup-in-beirut-us-marines-peacekeeping-mission-turns-deadly. htm.
3 Diary of Ronald Reagan, October 17, 1983.
4 From an Associated Press report, quoted by the *New York Review of Books*, January 1, 1984, http://www.nybooks.com/articles/archives/1984/jan/19/reagan-and-the -apocalypse/.
5 Diary of Ronald Reagan, Friday, October 16 to Wednesday, October 19, 1983.
6 Richard Aldous, *Reagan and Thatcher: A Difficult Relationship* (New York: W. W. Norton and Co., 2012), 150.
7 *Reagan and Thatcher*, 152–153.
8 Quoted in *Reagan and Thatcher*, 155-156.
9 John R. Galvin, *Fighting the Cold War: A Soldier's Memoir* (Louisville: University of Kentucky Press, 2015), 278–279.
10 "SHAPE ACE Officers Nuclear Weapons Release Procedures Course 17–21 October 1983," NATO Unclassified.

21. ABLE ARCHER 83

1 Interview with Joe Troxell, interview conducted by producers for *1983: The Brink of Apocalypse*, Flashback Television Ltd., Channel 4, 2008.
2 Ibid.
3 Vladimir Kryuchkov, interview conducted by producers for *1983: The Brink of Apocalypse*, Flashback Television Ltd., Channel 4, 2008.
4 Gordievsky, interview conducted by producers for *1983: The Brink of Apocalypse*, Flashback Television Ltd., Channel 4, 2008.
5 KGB Headquarters Moscow to the London KGB Residency, "Ref no. 1673/PR of 24.10.83," November 5, 1983, Top Secret, in Gordievsky, *Instructions from the Center*, 134–137.
6 "Ministry of State Security (Stasi), 'About the Talks with Comrade V. A. Kryuchkov,'" November 7, 1983, History and Public Policy Program Digital Archive, BStU, MfS, Abt. X, Nr. 2020, S. 1–7. Translated by Bernd Schaefer, http://digitalarchive.wilson center.org/document/119320.
7 October 20: "Statement by CPSU Central Committee and USSR Minister of Defense, Marshal of the Soviet Union D. F. Ustinov, at the extraordinary session of the Committee of Defense Ministers of Warsaw Treaty Member States on 20 October 1983 [in Berlin]," October 20, 1983, History and Public Policy Program Digital Archive, Federal Archives of Germany, Military Branch (BA-MA), Freiburg i. Br. Call Number: DVW 1 /71040. Translated for CWIHP by Bernd Schaefer. http://digitalarchive.wilsoncenter .org/document/111077.

8 Interview with Admiral Vladlen Smirnoff, interview conducted by producers for *1983: The Brink of Apocalypse*, Flashback Television Ltd., Channel 4, 2008.

9 Author's interview with Peter Harden.

10 Author's interview with a former SAC intelligence officer with direct knowledge of this launch and its aftermath. CIA Mobile Missile Launch Summaries reviewed by the author contain details about regular Soviet missile launches, and include their DEFSMAC catalogue numbers, which are useful for FOIA purposes. Unfortunately, the CIA redacted the date of each launch, probably to protect information about the orbits and capabilities of NRO imagery satellites. One summary, notes that an ICBM launched from Plesetsk represented the "first test of a missile to a broad ocean area." CIA, Monthly Index Photographic Exploitation Products, November 1983, TOP SECRET RUFF/CODEWORD, obtained through CIA CREST database. A CIA document dated April 20, 1984, includes the following sentence: "The last launch of an SS-X-25 from Plesetsk occurred . . ." and there is a redaction. But the DEFSMAC citation shows the exact date: DEFSMAC/DQ/242-84, 2152z, 26 MAR 84.) See: CIA, SS-X-25 Launch Preparations, TOP SECRET RUFF, April 20, 1984. Accessed via CIA CREST database: https://www.cia.gov/library/readingroom/docs/CIA-RDP84T00491R000101170001-7.pdf.

11 Author's interview with an American intelligence official; see also: Sven Grahn, http://www.svengrahn.pp.se/histind/strangeazim/strangeazim.html; see also President's Foreign Intelligence Advisory Board Report, "The Soviet War Scare," TOP SECRET CODEWORD, February 15, 1990, 70-75 (though redacted here, an SS-25 launch is mentioned elsewhere); and CIA, Mobile ICBM Activity: a straightforward account of "increased activity" can be found in CIA, Plesetsk Launch Test Site 5, USSR, TOP SECRET RUFF, December 1982 compilation, obtained through CIA CREST database; a discussion of heightened activity at one of the sites can be found in CIA, "Probable Long-Range Cruise Missile Launch Preparations, Lapustin Yar Missile Space Test Center SSM, USSR," September 28, 1983; TOP SECRET RUFF/CODEWORD redacted, obtained through CIA CREST database.

12 Diary of Ronald Reagan, November 4, 1984.

13 Strategic Air Command Participation in Able Archer, January 3, 1984, UNCLASSIFIED, collected by the National Security Archive.

14 See: NATO summary; interviews with Gene Gay and Captain William Bliss conducted by producers for *1983: The Brink of Apocalypse*, Flashback Television Ltd., Channel 4, 2008.

15 Interview with Thatchenko conducted by producers for *1983: The Brink of Apocalypse*, Flashback Television Ltd., Channel 4, 2008.

16 Ibid.

17 Author's email with Gerald King.

18 Author's interview with an Able Archer participant.

22. FLASH TELEGRAM

1 Gordievsky interview conducted by producers for *1983: The Brink of Apocalypse*, Flashback Television Ltd., Channel 4, 2008.

2 Exactly how Wolf contacted Rupp remains a mystery. Rupp was in contact with couriers every six to eight weeks.

3 Colonel General Ivan Yesin interview conducted by producers for *1983: The Brink of Apocalypse,* Flashback Television Ltd., Channel 4, 2008.

4 Ibid.

5 Stephen Glain, *State v. Defense: The Battle* to *Defense America's Empire* (New York: Random House, 2011), 429.

6 *The Great Transition: American-Soviet Relations and the End of the Cold War* (Washington, DC: Brookings, 1994), 135–137.

7 National Intelligence Daily, November 7, 1983, TOP SECRET, declassified. Obtained via the CIA's CREST tool.

8 William C Wohlforth, ed., *Witnesses to the End of the Cold War* (Baltimore: Johns Hopkins Press, 1996), 71.

9 Andreas Wenger and Victor Mauer, eds., *Military Planning for European Theatre Conflict During the Cold War: An Oral History Roundtable* (Zurich: Center for Security Studies, 2007), 113.

10 Author's interview with Andre Babian.

23. VALIDATE AND AUTHENTICATE

1 Author's interview with E. R. Campbell.

2 Author's interview with Andre Babian.

3 NSA Comsec history, declassified, 85.

4 "We listened to the hourly circuit verification signal and believed we could recognize a release order," Marshal Sergei F. Akhromeev said in 1995. Quoted in Tom Nichols, Douglas Stuart, Jeffrey F. McCausland, *Tactical Nuclear Weapons and NATO* (Department of Defense, 2012), 55.

5 Info about Karlshorst: https://www.cia.gov/library/center-for-the-study-of-intelli gence/csi-publications/books-and-monographs/on-the-front-lines-of-the-cold-war -documents-on-the-intelligence-war-in-berlin-1946-to-1961/4-2.pdf.

6 A former senior NSA official described the Soviet capabilities as well as the indication that the NSA had picked up a SIGINT surge; a former GCHQ official confirmed that, as part of a later review, the British had picked up an unusually large amount of encrypted SIGINT from Karlshorst that night.

7 Author's interview with Dan Nolan and Lee Trolan; this account also comes from the various recollections of officers who manned the EMAS system and can be found on the website run by Ed Thelen, about the Nike HERC sites in West Germany, http:// ed-thelen.org/index.html#ppl.

24. OPEN HATCHES

1 Ronald Reagan, "Address Before the Japanese Diet in Tokyo," http://www.reagan .utexas.edu/archives/speeches/1983/111183a.htm.

2 Ronald Reagan interviews with representatives of NHK Television, November 11, 1983; http://www.reagan.utexas.edu/archives/speeches/1983/111183c.htm.

3 From the ship's Facebook alumni page; http://www.public.navy.mil/subfor/under seawarfaremagazine/Issues/Archives/issue_12/kamehameha.html.

4 Author's interview with Gary Donato.

5 Ibid.

6 Ibid.

7 Interviews of Joe Troxell, William Bliss, etc., conducted by producers for *1983: The Brink of Apocalypse*, Flashback Television Ltd., Channel 4, 2008.

8 http://www.airpower.maxwell.af.mil/airchronicles/aureview/1986/jan-feb/chip man.html; KC-135 DEPLOYMENT TO MORON AB FOR EXERCISE CRISEX 83 (S), NSAR.

9 CRISEX 1-831 AFTER ACTION REPORT, (S), NSAR.

10 Carney, *Against All Enemies*, 228–233. He describes the event in his book; some details were redacted by the NSA. An intelligence official helped me fill in the blanks.

11 Ibid.

25. SACRIFICE

1 PIAB release; author's interview with Gail Nelson; see also: US Army Intelligence and Security Command Daily INTSUM, November 10, 1983, SECRET, obtained by the National Security Archive and published in Jones, *Able Archer: The Secret History of the NATO Exercise That Almost Led to Nuclear War* (New York: The New Press, 2016), 220.

2 Diary of Ronald Reagan, Sunday, November 13, 1983.

3 Diary of Ronald Reagan, Wednesday, November 16.

4 Matlock, *Reagan and Gorbachev*, Accessed on Kindle at 16 percent and 21 percent.

5 Memo from Jack Matlock to Robert McFarlane, December 16, 1983, Matlock Chron Files, RRPL.

6 Jack Matlock, "US-Soviet Relations," The White House Memorandum of Conversation, October 11, 1983, Matlock Chron Files, RRPL.

7 Author's interview with Matlock.

8 Matlock, *Reagan and Gorbachev*, 79–80.

9 Ibid., 81.

10 Desmond Ball and Robert C. Toth, "Revising the SIOP: Taking War-Fighting to Dangerous Extremes," *International Security*, vol. 14, no. 4 (Spring, 1990), 65–92.

11 Beth. A. Fischer, *The Reagan Reversal* (Columbia, MO: University of Missouri Press, 1997), 116–123.

12 "President's Foreign Intelligence Advisory Board Report, The Soviet War Scare," February 15, 1990, Top Secret Codeword, 8 see: http://nsarchive.gwu.edu/nukevault /ebb533-The-Able-Archer-War-Scare-Declassified-PRESIDENT'S FOREIGN IN-TELLIGENCE ADVISORY BOARD REPORT, THE SOVIET WAR SCARE, FEB-RUARY 15, 1990, TOP SECRET CODEWORD-Report-Released/2012-0238-MR .pdf.

13 From private sources; see also: "President's Foreign Intelligence Advisory Board Report, The Soviet War Scare," February 15, 1990, Top Secret Codeword.

14 "Minutes from White House Situation Room (06)," December 1983, Top Secret [RE-DACTED], Ronald Reagan Presidential Library.

15 Author's interview with a former US official who saw the intelligence.

26. WARNING OF WAR

1 Author's interview with former CIA official.
2 William Burr and Jeffrey B. Kimball, *Nixon's Nuclear Specter: The Secret Alert of 1969 and the Vietnam War* (Lawrence, KS: University of Kansas, 2015), 343.
3 Interview with former US official.
4 Interview with a former CIA official.
5 State Department Memo, "American Academic on Soviet Foreign and Domestic Policy," CONFIDENTIAL, December 20, 1983.
6 Marshal D. Ustinov, "Struggle for Peace, Strengthen Defense Capabilities," in Pravda, November 19, 1983.
7 Author's interview with Tom Simons.
8 Memo to the D/CIA and DD/CIA from Herb Meyer, November 30, 1983, accessed via the CIA Crest tool, http://www.foia.cia.gov/sites/default/files/document_conversions/89801/DOC_0000028820.pdf.
9 Reed, *At the Abyss*.
10 "Not even time for a trip to the bathroom'" see *At the Abyss*.
11 Rhodes, *Arsenals of Folly*, 180–183
12 See http://www.rumormillnews.com/ARMAGEDDON%20THEOLOGY.htm.
13 Author's interview with Ambassador Tom Simons.
14 Oberdorfer interview with Schultz, section 1, page 10 (DOP).
15 "Memorandum for Robert McFarlane from Ron Lehman and Jack Matlock," December 20, 1983, RRPL.
16 "Memorandum for Ollie North, Re: Exercise Night Train" (SECRET), RRPL.
17 "Memo from Jack Matlock to Robert McFarlane," December 13, 1983, RRPL.
18 Nicholas Wapshott, *Reagan and Thatcher: A Political Marriage* (New York: Sentinel, 2007), 148; Trudeau quoted himself in his memoirs. Pierre Trudeau, *Lifting the Shadow of War* (Toronto: Hurtig Publishers Limited, 1987), 92.
19 "Soviet Thinking on the Possibility of Armed Conflict with the United States," December 30, 1983, Secret.

27. IVAN AND ANYA

1 Fritz Ermarth, "Observations on the War Scare of 1983 from an Intelligence Perch," Parallel History Project on NATO and the Warsaw Pact (PHP), November 6, 2003, Stasi Intelligence on NATO, www.isn.ethz.ch/php, edited by Bernd Schaefer and Christian Nünlist
2 See http://fas.org/irp/agency/dod/dtra/russia.pdf; RUSSIA'S STRATEGIC CULTURE: PAST, PRESENT, AND FUTURE; Defense Threat Reduction Agency, Advanced Systems and Concepts Office, Comparative Strategic Cultures Curriculum, Contract No: DTRA01-03-D-0017, Technical Instruction 18-06-02.
3 Ermarth's recollections in an oral history roundtable, Jan Hoffenaar and Christopher Findlay, eds., *Military Planning for European Theater Conflict During the Cold War: An*

Oral History Roundtable Stockholm, 24–25 April 2006 (Zurich: Center for Security Studies, ETH Zurich, 2006).

4 Ronald Reagan, "Address to the Nation," January 16, 1984. http://www.reagan.utexas.edu/archives/speeches/1984/11684a.htm.

5 Quoted in Oberdorfer, *The Turn*, 73.

6 Massie, *Trust But Verify*, 94.

7 Ibid., 98.

8 Ibid., 100.

9 William E. Pemberto, *Exit with Honor: The Life and Presidency of Ronald Reagan* (New York: Routledge, 1968), 164.

10 Ibid.

11 "CIA Memorandum from Fritz Ermarth, US-Soviet Relations: Some Basics," January 12, 1984, CIA, Secret.

12 Oberdorfer interview with George Shultz, section 1, p. 8, DOP.

13 "John Lenczowski Memo to McFarlane," February 10, 1984, Ronald Reagan Presidential Library.

14 "Memo from the CIA," February 17, 1984, CONFIDENTIAL, Matlock CHRON Files, Ronald Reagan Presidential Library.

15 Diary of Ronald Reagan, February 22, 1984.

16 "Memorandum from Fritz Ermarth," February 27, 1984, SECRET, Obtained via the CIA CREST tool.

17 http://www.thereaganfiles.com/19840223.pdf; noted in Martin Anderson and Annelise Anderson, *Reagan's Secret War: The Untold Story of His Fight to Save the World from Nuclear Disaster* (New York: Crown, 2009), 155.

18 Inside the Soviet Analysis branch, known as SOVA, a number of career analysts remained bitter about how intra-intelligence wars helped scuttle ratification of the SALT II treaty in 1979 because of an intelligence mistake. Early that year, the National Security Agency issued a report declaring that a Soviet military garrison in Cuba was a "combat brigade." The designation was important; a combat brigade in Cuba would violate all sorts of international agreements reached after the Cuban Missile Crisis, it would scare the hell out of Americans, and it would nullify political support for treaty ratification. And the matter had been dealt with, successfully, by Richard Nixon the first time around, when the CIA did not believe the Russian presence in Cuba was combat oriented; there was not one iota of evidence that it was. The NSA having found a new "combat brigade" in Cuba, suddenly, created confusion within Congress and forced the CIA to clarify its analysis. After a series of leaks and public responses by the Carter administration attesting that the Soviet troops in Cuba were conducting only training exercises, the CIA and NSA decided to increase their technical collection just to be sure. The intelligence suggested that the Soviets were exercising in Cuba without Cubans participating. Trainers who don't train are practicing for war themselves—or so the intelligence community reasoned. And so, in a new special national intelligence estimate, the CIA reversed course and added to the National Intelligence Daily an item about the "new Soviet military brigade." Several politically vulnerable Democratic US senators who wanted to shake themselves loose from the Carter administration used this

information, which had quickly been leaked to the press, to delay the treaty ratification. By the time the Senate got around to voting on it, the Soviets had invaded Afghanistan, and Carter withdrew the treaty from consideration. The truth was that was *not* a new combat brigade in Cuba. The initial report on the "brigade" was ten years old; the NSA literally seemed not to have read the date of their original analysis. In 1979, the "combat brigade" had 2,000 troops, no tanks or missiles, and little ammunition. Its threat to the United States was minimal.

19 Turner, 246.

20 Smith, Richard Harris, *OSS: The Secret History of America's First Intelligence Agency*, 206–207.

21 King, Wayne, "Reagan Ousts Campaign Manager, Other Aides Quit," *New York Times*, February 26, 1980; Francis X. Clines, "About Politics: Reagan's Quiet Campaign Chief," *New York Times*, April 22, 1980.

22 Author's interview with Herb E. Meyer

23 His critics would accuse him regularly of shading the intelligence he brought to Reagan. Casey found this unfair; he was simply pushing back against an agency culture that had long since settled on an outdated view of the Soviets. The bias did not necessarily favor one policy or another. Melvin Goodman, the top analyst of third world countries, marveled at how the CIA "exaggerated the strength of the Soviet Union when there was a dearth of intelligence sources, and underestimated the Soviet threat when there was a plethora of sources. In the 1970s, the agency's political assessments tended to be measured and reflected a view that the Soviets had stopped believing their own rhetoric about the inevitable march of Marxist-Leninism, that the equilibrium between guns and butter in the USSR was shifting toward butter, and that the Soviet military sought parity, rather than an advantage. This meant, on average, that the agency undersold the expansion of Soviet strategic capabilities in the late 1970s. Interestingly, the White House had a stake in underselling them at the same time.

28. WHAT DID WE MISS?

1 Interview with Stephen Schwalbe; see also: David Y. McManis, "Monthly Warning Meetings for April 1984," CIA, SECRET, April 9, 1984. Accessed via CIA CREST database: https://www.cia.gov/library/readingroom/docs/CIA-RDP91B00776 R000100080009-4.pdf; https://www.cia.gov/library/readingroom/docs/CIA-RDP 84T00491R000101610001-8.pdf; https://www.cia.gov/library/readingroom/docs /CIA-RDP84T00491R000100460001-6.pdf; https://www.cia.gov/library/reading room/docs/CIA-RDP90T01298R000400060001-4.pdf.

2 A CIA document dated April 20, 1984, includes the following sentence: "The last launch of an SS-X-25 from Pel occurred . . ." and there is a redaction. But the DEFS-MAC citation shows the exact date: DEFSMAC/DQ/242-84, 2152z, 26 MAR 84.) See: CIA, SS-X-25 Launch Preparations, TOP SECRET RUFF, April 20, 1984. Accessed via CIA CREST database: https://www.cia.gov/library/readingroom/docs/ CIA-RDP84T00491R000101170001-7.pdf.

3 Author's interview with Perle.

4 Interview with Schwalbe; Sven Grahn, "Unusual Flight Paths of Missiles Launched

from Plesetsk and Baikonur," http://www.svengrahn.pp.se/histind/strangeazim/strangeazim.html; for indications of activity at the sites, see: Indications of Rail-Mobile SS-X-24 Launch, TOP SECRET RUFF, April 3, 1984, obtained through CIA CREST database.

5 Bruce Blair, *Accidental Logic*, 143; Soviet Civil Defense, "Medical Planning for Post Attack Recovery," CIA, SECRET, July, 1984, obtained by the National Security Archive, http://nsarchive.gwu.edu/NSAEBB/NSAEBB439/docs/UndergroundFacilities.pdf.

6 Author's interview with a Reagan national security aide who was privy to the briefing. The aide recalled the missile launch discussion after I showed him contemporaneous reports showing the Pentagon was concerned that the Soviets failed to notify them in advance.

7 "Nuclear Arms Control Discussion Minutes," March 27, 1984, quoted in TRF, 220–224.

8 Ibid.

9 Ibid.

10 Criton Zoakos, "Soviet War Games Are for Keeps," *Executive Intelligence Review*, April 17 1984: http://www.larouchepub.com/eiw/public/1984/eirv11n15-19840417/eirv11n15-19840417_018-soviet_war_games_are_for_keeps.pdf.

11 JCS, "Notice of Significant Military Exercise: Night Train, December 20, 1983," http://nsarchive.gwu.edu/NSAEBB/NSAEBB427/docs/17.Significant%20Military%20Exercise%20Night%20Train%2084,%208%20December%201983.pdf; Joint Chiefs of Staff, Exercise NIGHT TRAIN Final Report, July 12, 1984, http://www.dod.mil/pubs/foi/Reading_Room/Other/144.pdf.

12 A source with knowledge of the event; SCOOP operations are described by William Arkin, "The Beat Goes On," *Bulletin of the Atomic Scientists*, November 1997, 72.

13 Barry R. Posen, *Inadvertent Escalation: Conventional War and Nuclear Risks* (Ithaca, NY: Cornell University Press, 1991), fn 57, 149.

14 "Air Units Start Vast Exercise," *New York Times*, April 4, 1984, http://www.nytimes.com/1984/04/04/world/air-units-start-vast-exercise.html.

15 Bill Yenne, *B-52 Stratofortress: The Complete History of the World's Longest Serving and Best-Known Bomber* (San Francisco: Zenith Press, 2012), 110.

16 Ibid.

17 R. W. Apple Jr., "Soviet Is Holding Big Naval Games," *New York Times*, April 4, 1984, http://www.nytimes.com/1984/04/04/world/soviet-is-holding-big-naval-games.html.

18 Ibid.

19 "The Transformation of Soviet Maritime Air Operations—Air University," at www.au.af.mil/au/cadre/aspj/airchronicles/apj/apj90/sum90/5sum90.htm.

20 William Drozdiak, "Allies Protest Soviet Restrictions on Flights to Berlin," *Washington Post*, April 5, 1984, http://www.washingtonpost.com/archive/politics/1984/04/05/allies-protest-soviet-restrictions-on-flights-to-berlin/303dee89-1ea4-4f00-8fbb-50cf4ff1dd58/.

21 UPI, "The Pentagon Said Thursday . . . ," April 5, 1984: http://www.upi.com/Archives/1984/04/05/The-Pentagon-said-Thursday-the-size-of-the-Soviet/6656449989200/.

22 Author's interview with Schwalbe.

29. ARGUING ON BEHALF OF SOVIET FEARS

1 Quoted in Zoakos, "War Games Are for Keeps," *Executive Intelligence Review*.

2 Ibid.

3 Author's interview with Schwalbe; see also: Hoffenaar and Findlay, eds., *Military Planning for European Theater Conflict during the Cold War*, http://e-collection.library.ethz .ch/eserv/eth:474/eth-474-01.pdf.

4 The description comes from a senior CIA official who received the Perroots briefing.

5 Author's interview with Michael Herman; author's interview with former British intelligence official.

6 Ibid. See: Michael Herman, "Recollections Published for Berlin Conference on Able Archer," Cold War International Studies Project.

7 Author's interview with Rodric Braithwaite; author's interview with former senior advisor to Thatcher; author's interview with Robert Gates.

8 Document obtained by Peter Burt and published at the Nuclear Information Site: http://nuclearinfo.org/sites/default/files/E2%20200384%20note.pdf; https://nsar chive.files.wordpress.com/2013/11/document-1.pdf; https://nsarchive.files.wordpress .com/2013/11/document-3.pdf.

9 Memorandum from the DUS(P) to the JIC, "The Soviet Union and a Surprise NATO Attack," May 4, 1984, http://nuclearinfo.org/sites/default/files/E14%20Report%20 080584.pdf.

10 JIC (84)(N)45, "Soviet Union: Concern About a Surprise NATO Attack," at http://nuclear info.org/sites/default/files/E2%20200384%20note.pdf; see also: JIC paper on "Soviet Union and a Surprise Nuclear Attack," at https://nsarchive.files.wordpress.com/2013/11 /document-2.pdf; and https://nsarchive.files.wordpress.com/2013/11/document-3.pdf.

11 Ibid., JIC (84)(N)45 paper.

12 "Soviet Union: Concern About a Surprise Nuclear Attack," May 4, 1984, TOP SECRET UMBRA UK EYES ONLY, https://nsarchive.files.wordpress.com/2013/11/ document-10.pdf.

13 "Soviet Union: Concern About a Surprise Nuclear Attack," May 8, 1984; TOP SECRET UMBRA GAMMA US/UK EYES ONLY: https://nsarchive.files.wordpress .com/2013/11/document-9.pdf; http://nuclearinfo.org/sites/default/files/E10%20 Draft%20minute%20from%20Sir%20Robert%20Armstrong.pdf.

14 "Minutes from Sir Robert Armstrong," UK TOP SECRET, April 10, 1984; https:// nsarchive.files.wordpress.com/2013/11/document-7.pdf.

15 Author's interview with McFarlane; author's interview with Gates; author's interview with Matlock; author's interview with former senior US intelligence official; "President's Foreign Intelligence Advisory Board Report, The Soviet War Scare," February 15, 1990, TOP SECRET CODEWORD report, 11.

16 Author's interviews with several former Reagan administration officials.

17 "President's Foreign Intelligence Advisory Board Report, The Soviet War Scare," TOP SECRET CODEWORD, February 15, 1990, 18.

18 "Request for Interagency Intelligence Assessment from Director," Joint Staff OJCS, SECRET, June 26, 1984, obtained from CIA CREST tool.

19 Author's interview with a former senior NSC official; a former CIA official recalls Reagan asking about Gordievsky's identity at this point; a third CIA officer confirms that the agency began to do a quiet assessment of the source at this point.

30. HOW CAN THIS BE?

1 Carpenter, *Memoirs of a Cold Warrior: The Struggle for Nuclear Parity*, 148.
2 http://articles.latimes.com/1985-01-21/business/fi-14377_1_boeing-contract.
3 Diary of Ronald Reagan, Monday July 9, 1984.
4 Diary of Ronald Reagan, Thursday, June 14, 1984.
5 Bud McFarlane, interview conducted by producers for *1983: The Brink of Apocalypse*, Flashback Television Ltd., Channel 4, 2008.
6 Don Oberdorfer interview with George Shultz, section II, p. 16, DOP.
7 Diary of Ronald Reagan, July 10, 1984. This entry covers a period lasting longer than a month, so it is likely that Reagan wrote it around August 13, when Shultz visited him.

31. ROLL THE DICE

1 Gordievsky, *Next Stop Execution*, 264.
2 Ibid., 259–260.
3 Ibid., 253–259.
4 Ibid., 298–307.
5 Interview with Rainer Rupp, originally accessed at: http://www.workers.org/articles/2015/10/16/rainer-rupp-about-able-archer-his-work-in-nato-headquarters-the-syrian-war-and-the-conflict-with-russia/.
6 Nicholas Thompson, "Inside the Apocalyptic Doomsday Machine," *Wired*, September 21, 2009; http://www.wired.com/2009/09/mf-deadhand/?currentPage=all.
7 Tim Weiner, "Pentagon to Shelve Doomsday Project," *New York Times*, April 14, 1994.
8 Steve Emerson, "America's Doomsday Project," *US News and World Report*, August 7, 1987.

32. A NEW HOPE: BUT STILL, STAR WARS?

1 Francis X. Clines, "Reagan Meeting: Gromyko Asks for Closer Ties," *New York Times*, September 24, 1984, http://www.nytimes.com/1984/09/24/world/reagan-meeting-gromyko-asks-for-closer-ties.html.
2 See George Shultz, Miller Center Oral History Project interview; https://millercenter.org/the-presidency/interviews-with-the-administration; author's interview with Matlock.
3 Bernard Gwertzman, "Soviet Accepts Bid to Have Gromyko Meet with Reagan," *New York Times*, September 9, 1984, http://www.nytimes.com/1984/09/11/world/soviet-accepts-bid-to-have-gromyko-meet-with-reagan.html?pagewanted=all.
4 See, for example, his remarks in "Minutes from the National Security Council Meeting," September 9, 1984, TRF.
5 "The Soviets most fear SDI, and that is what they urge us to give up," he told Reagan; on Soviet views, see: Pavel Podvig, "Did Star Wars Help End the Cold War? Soviet Response to the SDI Program," at http://russianforces.org/podvig/2013/03/did_star_wars_help_end_the_col.shtml.

6 James Graham Wilson, *Triumph of Improvisation*, 85.

7 "Minutes from the National Security Council Meeting," September 9, 1984, TRF.

8 Ibid.

9 Ibid.

10 http://articles.latimes.com/1985-05-15/news/mn-8542_1_gromyko-meet.

11 Bernard Gwertzman, "Soviet Accepts Bid to Have Gromyko Meet with Reagan," *New York Times*, September 9, 1984; Raymond L. Garthoff, ed., *The Great Transition: American-Soviet Relations and the End of the Cold War*, 182.

12 Associated Press, "Arms Control Hope Voiced by Mondale After Gromyko Talk," September 29, 1984; Serge Schmemann, "Chernenko Talk Stresses Role of West," *New York Times*, September 9, 1984.

13 James Graham Wilson, *Triumph of Improvisation*, 85.

14 Don Oberdorfer interview with George Shultz, section III, p. 7, DOP.

15 Gordievsky, *Next Stop Execution*, 308–309.

16 Ibid.

17 Margaret Thatcher Diaries, http://www.margaretthatcher.org/speeches/displaydocument.asp?docid=109181.

18 Gordievsky, *Next Stop Execution*, 318–323.

33. NOT TO MISS THE CHANCE

1 "About Reagan," Alexander Yakovlev. Memorandum prepared on request from M. S. Gorbachev and handed to him on March 12, 1985. State Archive of the Russian Federation, Moscow. Yakovlev Collection. Translated by Svetlana Savranskaya, the National Security Archive.

2 Ronald Reagan Diaries, May 26, 1985.

3 James Graham Wilson, *The Triumph of Improvisation*, 86.

4 Don Oberdorfer interview with Ronald Reagan, DOP.

5 Gordievsky, *Next Step Execution*, 324–325.

6 Ibid., 333–335.

7 Gordon Corera, *The Art of Betrayal: The Secret History of MI6: Life and Death in the British Secret Service* (New York: Pegasus Books, 2013), 278.

8 Gordievsky, interview conducted by producers for *1983: The Brink of Apocalypse*, Flashback Television Ltd., Channel 4, 2008.

9 Gordievsky describes his rescue in detail in *Next Stop Execution*, 1–19.

34. TO GENEVA

1 Author's interview with Matlock.

2 "Six Experts on Soviet Give Reagan Briefing," *New York Times*, November 8, 1985, http://www.nytimes.com/1985/11/08/world/six-experts-on-soviet-give-reagan-briefing.html, and David Remnick, "The Day of the Soviet Watchers," *Washington Post*, November 8, 1985, https://www.washingtonpost.com/archive/lifestyle/1985/11/08/the-day-of-the-soviet-watchers/41b62dea-921e-48bb-b9a2-c58aefd983b0/.

3 Author's interview with Nina Tumarkin.

4 "Weinberger Letter to Reagan on Arms Control," *New York Times*, November 16, 1985,

http://www.nytimes.com/1985/11/16/world/weinberger-letter-to-reagan-on-arms
-control.html

5 Jack Nelson and Eleanor Clift, "Advisers' Discord Clouds Reagan's Arrival in Geneva: Confidential Weinberger Letter Urges No Compromise on Key Arms Issue," *Los Angeles Times*, November 11, 2017, http://articles.latimes.com/1985-11-17/news/mn-6918_1_arms-control/2; Weinberger interview with Don Oberdorfer, p. 11, DOP.

6 "Gorbachev Personal Agenda for November Meeting," CIA assessment, undated. http://nsarchive.gwu.edu/NSAEBB/NSAEBB172/Doc14.pdf.

7 Reagan did not agree with the Pentagon's use of SDI as an offensive weapon, and he only reluctantly agreed that it might prove useful as a bargaining chip later on. But his commitment to the idea allowed the Pentagon to force his hand. It was in his own interest for Gorbachev to see how much progress the United States had made, so Reagan allowed the Pentagon to stage a test of its new lasers; in September, the Pentagon destroyed an old US satellite with a missile, the first time the US had successfully deployed an antisatellite weapon. The Soviets saw this as a provocation.

8 Author's interview with McFarlane.

9 Author's interview with Matlock.

10 Memorandum to the president from Jack Matlock, "Gordievsky's Suggestions," October 30, 1985, TRF http://www.thereaganfiles.com/19851030-gordiyevsky.pdf.

11 During a walk-through, Nancy Reagan sat in the seat reserved for Gorbachev, leading her husband to remark upon how unexpectedly pretty the General Secretary seemed to be.

12 "Memoranda of Conversations Between Ronald Reagan and Mikhail Gorbachev," November 19, 1985, http://nsarchive.gwu.edu/NSAEBB/NSAEBB172/Doc15.pdf.

13 Ibid.

14 Oberdorfer, *The Turn*, 146.

15 "Memoranda of Conversations Between Ronald Reagan and Mikhail Gorbachev," November 19, 1985, http://nsarchive.gwu.edu/NSAEBB/NSAEBB172/Doc19.pdf.

16 Matlock, *Reagan and Gorbachev*, 164.

17 Ibid., 165.

EPILOGUE

1 Author's interview with a former CIA official.

2 David S. Yost, "Strategic Stability in the Cold War: Lessons for Continuing Challenges," *Proliferation Papers*, no. 36 (Winter 2011), 25.

3 See for example, this primer: https://www.cia.gov/library/center-for-the-study-of-intelligence/csi-publications/books-and-monographs/psychology-of-intelligence-analysis/art9.html.

4 Keith Payne, *The Fallacies of Cold War Deterrence and a New Direction* (Louisville, KY: University of Kentucky Press, 2001), 17.

5 President's Foreign Intelligence Advisory Board Report, "The Soviet War Scare, TOP SECRET CODEWORD," February 15, 1990, 55–73.3.

6 Ibid., 71.1.

7 See, for example, the excellent James Mann, *The Rebellion of Ronald Reagan* (New York: Viking Books, 2009).

8   Beth A. Fischer, *The Reagan Reversal: Foreign Policy and the End of the Cold War* (Columbia, MO: University of Missouri Press, 2000).

9   Ronald Reagan, *An American Life: The Autobiography* (New York: Simon & Schuster, 1990), 588–589.

10 Choe Sang-Hun, "South Korea Proposes Border Talks with North Korea After Kim's Overture," *New York Times*, January 2, 2018.

11 Tim Naftali, "The Problem with Trump's Madman Theory," *The Atlantic*, October 4, 2017, at https://www.theatlantic.com/international/archive/2017/10/madman-theory-trump-north-korea/542055/.

12 Ibid.

13 Michael H. Fuchs, "Donald Trump's Doctrine of Unpredictability Has the World on Edge," *The Guardian*, February 13, 2017.

14 Evan Osnos, "The Risk of Nuclear War with North Korea," *The New Yorker*, September 18, 2017, at https://www.newyorker.com/magazine/2017/09/18/the-risk-of-nuclear-war-with-north-korea.

15 Bruce Blair, "Strengthening Checks on Presidential Nuclear Launch Authority," draft for *Arms Control Today*, shared with the author.

16 Ibid.

17 Kathryn Watson, "Top General Says He Would Resist 'Illegal' Nuke Order from Trump," CBSNews.com, November 18, 2017.

18 Anik Panda and Dave Schermler, "When a North Korean Missile Accidentally Hit a North Korean City," *The Diplomat*, January 3, 2018.

19 This is a point Schlosser acknowledges.

20 "A Brief History of Alert Transformation," United States Strategic Command, Unclassified, 2012. Accessed at: https://www.scribd.com/document/238686392/A-Brief-History-of-Alert-Transformation; "Air Force Nuclear Mission Embraces Culture of Empowerment," US Air Force Public Affairs Command, 2015; Government Accountability Office, "DOD Has Established Processes for Implementing and Tracking Recommendations to Improve Leadership, Morale, and Operations," accessed at http://www.gao.gov/products/GAO-16-597R.

21 Hans M. Kristensen, "U.S. Nuclear Strategy after the 2010 Nuclear Posture Review," Federation of American Scientists, at http://fas.org/programs/ssp/nukes/publications1/Brief2012_Georgetown.pdf.

22 Joshua Trevithick, "Here's America's Plan for Nuking Its Enemies, Including North Korea," *The Drive*, April 7, 2017.

23 John R. Harvey, Franklin C. Miller, Keith P. Payne, Bradley H. Roberts, Continuity and Change in U.S. Nuclear Policy, RealClearDefense.com, February 7, 2018, at https://www.realcleardefense.com/articles/2018/02/07/continuity_and_change_in_us_nuclear_policy_113025.html.

24 See Bruce G. Blair, *Strategic Command and Control*, 15–18.

25 Stephen Cimbala, *Through a Glass Darkly: A Look at Conflict Prevention, Management and Termination* (New York: Praeger, 2001), 105.

26 Ronald Reagan, *An American Life: The Autobiography*, 257–258.

INDEX

Pages numbers beginning with 309 refer to endnotes.